American Higher Education in the Twenty-first Century

American Higher Education in the Twenty-first Century

Social, Political, and Economic Challenges

 EDITED BY

Philip G. Altbach, Robert O. Berdahl, and Patricia J. Gumport

The Johns Hopkins University Press ❧ *Baltimore and London*

© 1999 The Johns Hopkins University Press
All rights reserved. Published 1999
Printed in the United States of America on acid-free paper
9 8 7 6 5 4 3 2

The Johns Hopkins University Press
2715 North Charles Street
Baltimore, Maryland 21218-4363
www.press.jhu.edu

Library of Congress Cataloging-in-Publication Data
American higher education in the twenty-first century : social,
    political, and economic challenges / edited by Philip G. Altbach,
    Robert O. Berdahl, and Patricia J. Gumport.
        p.   cm.
Includes bibliographical references and index.
ISBN 0-8018-5888-7 (alk. paper). — ISBN 0-8018-5889-5
(pbk. : alk. paper)
    1. Education, Higher—Aims and objectives—United States.
2. Education, Higher—Social aspects—United States.   3. Education,
Higher—Political aspects—United States.   I. Altbach, Philip G.
II. Berdahl, Robert Oliver.   III. Gumport, Patricia J.
LA227.4.A45   1998
378.73—dc21   98-3331
                                                          CIP

❧ Contents

Part Two   External Forces

Part Three   The Academic Community

Part Four   Central Issues for the Twenty-first Century

~~~ Preface

Higher education faces unprecedented challenges as we approach the twenty-first century. This book provides an analysis of the central issues facing American colleges and universities. Our focus is on the complex relationship between higher education and the social and political forces that so significantly affect higher education. We have chosen the topics that we believe reflect the core issues. The contributors to this book provide an analysis of these issues; their perspectives, taken together, provide a multifaceted approach to the study of higher education.

We are indebted to the authors of the chapters in this volume. They are among the most prominent experts on their topics. This book is part of the research program of the Center for International Higher Education at Boston College. We thank Patricia Murphy for her editorial assistance and for her help in the preparation of the index.

American Higher
Education in the
Twenty-first Century

The Contexts of American Higher Education

Robert O. Berdahl, Philip G. Altbach, and
Patricia J. Gumport

This volume seeks to capture several critical dynamics in the higher-education/society nexus. Many aspects of the relationship between colleges and universities and their external environments have recently gained increased visibility in the media. Topics have included multiculturalism in the curriculum, racially based admissions procedures, violence and hate crimes on campus, grade strikes waged by graduate student teaching assistants, accountability to the state, assessment of student learning, monitoring of faculty productivity, scientific misconduct and fraud, university/industry partnerships, technology transfer, university mismanagement of indirect cost funds, and most recently, budget cuts and downsizing mandates from state legislatures.

In a system of higher education as large and decentralized as that in the United States, it is difficult to analyze the cumulative record of twentieth-century strains and transitions comprehensively, much less reassess priorities so that higher education will survive and prosper. However, there is analytical utility in examining the affairs of colleges and universities within their changing social, political, and economic contexts. Accordingly, the editors of this volume and its contributors share a common view of colleges and universities as social institutions embedded in the wider society and subject to society's constraining forces. This view, founded in what might be called the ecology of higher education, is broad, but it does not preclude using other conceptual frameworks, such as those based on theories of knowledge and development of the curriculum; those looking at career patterns and biographies of academic, administrative, and political personnel; and those using Marxist theories to examine relations between control of the economy and patterns of higher education.

We have divided the book into four parts. Part 1, "The Setting," opens with chapters by Philip Altbach and Roger Geiger, who analyze the dimensions of higher education over space and time, respectively. Altbach shows the ways in which universities and colleges around the world share common traits but, also, how they differ according to cultural, political, and economic conditions. Geiger uses American history to reveal both threads of continuity and dimensions of change, as colleges and universities in this country have evolved. The following two chapters establish the central conceptual framework for this book in analyzing autonomy (Robert Berdahl and T. R. McConnell) and academic freedom (Robert O'Neil) in the context of changing demands for accountability. Part 1 ends with an overview by Ami Zusman, who provides a brief analysis of key issues that will face American higher education as it enters the twenty-first century.

In part 2, "External Forces," our contributors grapple with the ways that various constituencies external to universities and colleges influence—and sometimes control—their past, present, and future development. Although in the U.S. federal system of government, states are given the primary constitutional jurisdiction over higher education, the chapter by Lawrence Gladieux and Jacqueline King shows how, at least in the domains of student aid, tax support for research, and tax policies, the federal government is now a major actor. Aims McGuinness's chapter illustrates the many issues that arise when the fifty states attempt to plan and coordinate higher education. The role of federal courts in interpreting higher education applications of affirmative action is analyzed in a chapter by Michael Olivas. Finally, the chapter by Fred Harcleroad shows that nongovernmental associations (foundations, higher education institution associations, accreditation agencies, consortia, and regional compacts in higher education) also impact higher education.

In part 3, "The Academic Community," our contributors examine how the previously examined interplay of issues, institutions, and external forces have affected the three internal constituencies: faculty, students, and administration. Philip Altbach's chapter on the academic profession shows the diversity that prevails, the changes and stresses that have been brought to bear, and its uncertain future. Eric Dey and Sylvia Hurtado's chapter urges us not to view students in a unidimensional manner but, rather, to see that students, colleges, and society interact in ways that change all three constituencies. Finally, Robert Birnbaum's chapter traces the evolution of the university presidency from its early days, when it was preoccupied with theology and student discipline, to current conditions, in which, more often than not, internal and external elements restrain presidential leadership.

In part 4, in-depth chapters analyze five of the important issues facing American higher education in the twenty-first century. D. Bruce Johnstone's chapter reflects on the difficulty in understanding the financing of enterprises as complex as universities and colleges, which are funded by such disparate sources as tuition, private endowments, and state and federal grants. Furthermore, student aid must be understood as a matrix that includes grants, loans, and work study at federal, state, and institutional levels. Patricia Gumport and Marc Chun, in their chapter on technology, point out how wrong earlier commentators have been in predicting the impact of innovation. They analyze the possible impact of technology on the nature of knowledge, on the process of teaching and learning, and on the social organization of teaching and learning.

Part 4 then turns to curricular matters, with Patricia Gumport's chapter dealing with graduate education and John Wilson's chapter with undergraduate issues. Gumport calls our attention to the particular ways that problems and policies relating to research have, since World War II, been joined to those of graduate studies, with severe consequences for both arenas. Wilson analyzes the political interplay between multiculturalism in the undergraduate curriculum and conservative concern regarding the canons of Western civilization and the alleged weakening of scholastic standards. Examining race in higher education, Philip Altbach, Kofi Lomotey, and Shariba Kyle analyze its impact on institutions, faculty, students, and curriculum. They cite conservative critics of affirmative action and demonstrate that this issue is still very much unresolved.

We have, in effect, posed macro questions like the following to ourselves and our contributors: Given our casting of universities and colleges as social institutions, what are they like today? What forces, either unique to our era or continuing from the past, are shaping higher education? What is the future of higher education, in the context of twenty-first-century America?

Universities as Social Institutions

Universities—and by extension many four-year and two-year postsecondary institutions—have generally had ambivalent relations with their surrounding societies—both involved and withdrawn, both servicing and criticizing, both needing and being needed. Eric Ashby identifies the central dilemma of this ambivalence: a university "must be sufficiently stable to sustain the ideal which gave it birth and sufficiently responsive to remain relevant to the society which supports it."[1]

The medieval universities of Europe developed as supranational institutions under the jurisdiction of a distant pope and operating in a uniform cultural milieu, which allowed them to combine practical learning for the "higher" vocations or professions with a search for universal truths. Later, when nation-states replaced the Catholic Church as the dominant authority over universities, the latter were often able to retain significant autonomy. Clark Kerr noted how remarkably stable many of these medieval universities have proven: "About eighty-five institutions in the Western World established by 1520 still exist in recognizable forms, with similar functions and with unbroken histories, including the Catholic Church, the Parliaments of the Isle of Man, of Iceland and of Great Britain, several Swiss Cantons and seventy universities."[2]

Of course, it was easier for a nation to grant its universities autonomy when only a small proportion of its youth were attending, when students were not going much beyond the trivium and the quadrivium in their curriculum, and when few, if any, state funds were involved. In the nineteenth century, however, three developments were to occur that would increase tension between autonomy and accountability. First, beginning in German universities and spreading to universities in other Western countries was the notion of the importance of science and research in higher education. Governments began to see the links among universities, economic growth, and military strength. Second, the Morrill Land-Grant Act of 1862 in the United States broadened the curriculum to include the agricultural and mechanical arts. This led to the diversification of higher education institutions, a larger and more heterogeneous student body, higher state costs, and the notion of university public service. The American pattern, like the German, eventually spread to other countries. Third, the public and governments grew reluctant to increase public spending, which led to increased accountability on the part of higher education institutions and to a constraint on their growth.

Martin Trow shows how the autonomy/accountability dichotomy has changed as higher education has moved from an "elite" system to a "mass" system—that is, from educating less than 15 percent of the college-age cohort to educating between 15 and 50 percent of it.[3] Trow also examines the probable consequences of another transition, to "universal access," which has been tried in only a few states.[4]

In the present era, questions have arisen about the usefulness of mass access and about whether higher education is a public good, which primarily benefits society and which, therefore, merits public expenditure, or whether it is a private good, which directly benefits the individual, who should therefore bear the cost.[5] Some have come to see higher education as a "mature industry," in which expansion will be slow; basic assumptions about the nature of the academic enterprise will focus on stability rather than on growth.[6]

A Matter of Definitions

The terms *autonomy* and *accountability* at first glance do not seem to present semantic problems. Taken most simply, *autonomy* means the power to govern without outside controls, and *accountability* means the requirement to demonstrate responsible actions to external constituencies. In theory, there is not necessarily incompatibility between being both highly autonomous and rigorously accountable. However, in practice, in cases in which more accountability is required, less autonomy remains. The ideal would seem to be a balance of both. Too much autonomy might render universities unresponsive to society, while too much accountability might destroy the academic ethos.

The dilemma, however, is more complicated. For example, given academic complaints about "intrusions" into institutional autonomy, one would like to know what the action in question is; academic freedom and institutional autonomy are not the same, and the academy's reactions should reflect this distinction. We need to distinguish among three concepts of autonomy:

—*Academic freedom* is the freedom of the individual scholar to pursue truth wherever it leads, without fear of punishment or of termination of employment for having offended some political, methodological, religious, or social orthodoxy.
—*Substantive autonomy* is the power of the university or college in its corporate form to determine its own goals and programs (the *what* of academe).
—*Procedural autonomy* is the power of the university or college in its corporate form to determine the means by which its goals and programs will be pursued (the *how* of academe).

These three concepts are obviously interrelated; for example, a college enjoying substantive and procedural autonomy would normally be better able to protect the academic freedom of its faculty (although autonomous Oxford and Cambridge in the early-nineteenth century denied academic freedom to their faculty, whereas nonautonomous Berlin University became known for its *Lehrfreiheit,* or academic freedom). Along another dimension, onerous procedural government controls would seriously hinder a college's ability to achieve its chosen goals. Notwithstanding such blurring of categories in real life, an examination of relations between higher education and government will be helped by distinguishing these three concepts.

Ashby envisions academic freedom as an "internationally recognized and unambiguous privilege of university teachers, which must be protected whenever and however challenged," even though "the question as to what constitutes autonomy in universities is anything but unambiguous, and the patterns of autonomy which satisfy academics in different countries are very diverse."[7] Therefore, in exploring autonomy issues it is helpful to clarify whether the intervention is in *procedural* or *substantive* matters. Intervention in procedural matters (preaudits and controls over purchasing, personnel, and some aspects of capital construction) can be an enormous bother to academe and often even counter to efficiency, but it does not usually prevent colleges or universities from achieving their goals. In contrast, governmental actions that affect substantive goals compromise the very essence of academe. What is needed in this sensitive area is negotiation of the roles of government and universities, leading to a division of powers and a decision on which one will make which decisions relating to academe. For Ashby, the real safeguard for autonomy lies in ensuring that the "essential ingredients" of autonomy "are widely understood among the public, politicians, and civil servants":[8]

— The freedom of universities to select staff and students and to determine the conditions under which they remain in the university.
— The freedom of universities to determine curriculum content and degree standards.
— The freedom of universities to allocate funds (within the amounts available) across different categories of expenditures.

The definition of *accountability* must also be examined. To speak of demonstrating "responsible actions" begs the following questions: What constitutes such actions? Who determines the form and content of the reporting process? What are the sanctions for inadequate performance? In addition to furnishing information on planning, programs, and budgets to justify public tax funds before the fact, colleges and universities are also held accountable after the fact. There are at least three ways in which postaudits can be conducted (for legality, for efficiency, and for effectiveness), with varying consequences. Traditionally, governmental postaudits have focused on legality and efficiency and, through such concerns, have exerted considerable pressure on colleges and universities to tighten their operational procedures. Normally, such pressures have not forced institutions to alter their substantive goals; however, a performance audit aspect of the accountability movement has arisen at the state level that focuses on the effectiveness of the policy area being examined. If extended more deeply into academe, this development could greatly affect its substantive dimensions.[9]

Three lessons arise from this discussion. First, governments ought to stay away from issues that threaten the academic freedom of persons undertaking teaching and research at colleges and universities. Second, governmental procedural controls are probably counterproductive and certainly irritating but do not justify the same academic outrage as legitimate threats to academic freedom. Third, in the crucial domain of substantive autonomy, government and universities must form a partnership wherein—while force majeure obviously lies with the former—sensitive mechanisms reconcile state concerns with accountability and academic concerns with autonomy. In the U.S.

federal system, the primary governmental interface for most public sector institutions—and some private sector ones as well—lies at the level of state government.

Cooperation, Coordination, and Consolidation

At least three major modes of resolution can be envisaged: bottom-up voluntary cooperation, top-down consolidated governance, or an intermediate form of statutory coordination that goes beyond cooperation but stops short of consolidated governance.

Comparative experience suggests that voluntary cooperation is normally unable to make tough decisions because the voluntary association usually operates on a principle of near unanimity, and objection from a threatened party usually halts the association's progress. Fred Harcleroad's chapter illustrates the many valuable ends that may be accomplished when universities and colleges cooperate, but such collaborative ventures have not usually included making difficult decisions. The consortium movement in the United States and the history of the British Committee of Vice-Chancellors and Principals bear witness to the limits of interinstitutional cooperation. Certain goals can be accomplished, but disagreements over serious issues cannot usually be overcome.

While authority to resolve differences between academic and governmental perspectives could be obtained through a political decision to merge all universities into one consolidated university, again, comparative perspectives suggest that this response could lead to too much accountability and too little autonomy. Those states in which such consolidation has occurred do exhibit top-down retrenchment, and this retrenchment often appeals to those who yearn for a simple method of accountability. But these states also often exhibit excessive centralization of power and a preoccupation with details of governance at the expense of careful planning and coordination.

Having revealed both voluntary cooperation and consolidated governance as ineffective in taking into account the legitimate perspectives of both academe and government in the area of substantive autonomy, we are left with coordination as the most desirable (or least undesirable) means of accomplishing this vital process.

Coordination: Political, Bureaucratic, Academic, and Market

A state that honors academic freedom and resists inappropriate procedural controls may nevertheless harm its system of higher education by intervening in substantive matters. The structure, function, membership, and staffing of the mediating agency thus become crucial. In discussing the role of such an agency as potentially a "suitably sensitive mechanism" in its responsibilities for coordination, we must heed Burton Clark's warning against treating the coordination process too narrowly, as only a function of a bilateral government/institutional relationship. In an insightful article entitled, "The Many Pathways of Academic Coordination," Burton Clark urges that, to the traditional political and bureaucratic modes of coordination, we add those modes emanating from the academic profession and the market. After being ignored by political analysts as major factors in the development of U.S. universities and colleges, the market and privatization are now being so aggressively pushed that excessive claims are being advanced on their behalf. What may be desirable for the economies of Central and Eastern European countries after decades of communist control may not be desirable for U.S. universities and colleges, which operate in a very different social, political, and economic context:

> The special function of political coordination is to articulate a variety of public interests . . . as these are defined by prevailing groups within and outside of government. The special function of bureaucratic coordination is to compose a formal system out of fragmented parts and to provide fair administration. The function of academic oligarchy is to protect professional self-rule, to lodge the control of academic work, including its standards, in the hands of those permanently involved and most intimately connected with it. And the special function of the market is to enhance and protect freedom of choice, for personnel, clientele, and institutions and thereby indirectly promote system flexibility and adaptability.[10]

The proportions of each mode of coordination vary markedly from one system to another. For example, earlier in Britain, British academics had a pervasive role in making the system function behind the formal facade of the secretary of state for the Department of Education and

Science, the civil servants in that department, and the University Grants Committee. Similarly, in the United States, a fundamental role was played by market forces based on student choice and fortified by institutional, state, and national student financial aid programs.

The simplified arguments connected with each of these modes of coordination run as follows:

— Political and bureaucratic coordination tends to overdo account-ability and to be insensitive to academe's needs for flexibility and creativity.
— Collegial or academic coordination may be preoccupied with the protection of autonomy and unresponsive to the public interest.
— Coordination by market forces may promote responsiveness to so-cial demand while relieving public authority of the burden and blame for deciding which programs and which institutions may survive during a period of retrenchment, but it may compromise the integrity of the university as the purveyor of truth and knowl-edge.

Thus, one is left with Clark's observation that most systems partake of varying degrees of the elements of coordination. What may be a correct balance for one system may not be appropriate for another system; and indeed, what may be correct for one system at one stage in its development may not be correct for that same system at another stage. There is no theoretical model for the correct balance at a given time, so we are left with making subjective judgments based upon common sense and upon both conscious and unconscious biases.

We are concerned in this book not only with how specific govern-mental actions affect the administration of postsecondary education but also with how broader societal forces impact the entire academic community. Unraveling the web of relationships between higher edu-cation and society is paramount to understanding the academic enter-prise and all that goes on within it. We hope that the following chap-ters will help readers make up their own minds about many of the pressing issues covered.

NOTES

1. Eric Ashby, *Universities: British, Indian, African* (Cambridge: Harvard University Press, 1966), 3.

2. Clark Kerr, *The Uses of the University* (Cambridge: Harvard University Press, 1982), 152.

3. Martin Trow, "Problems in the Transition from Elite to Mass Higher Education," in *Policies for Higher Education* (Paris: Organization for Economic Co-operation and Development, 1974).

4. Universal access means that no one is prevented from going to college for lack of resources or institutions; in some states, more than 50 percent of high school graduates go on to postsecondary institutions.

5. David W. Breneman, "The 'Privatization' of Public Universities: A Mistake or a Model for the Future?" *Chronicle of Higher Education,* Mar. 7, 1997.

6. Arthur Levine, "Higher Education's New Status as a Mature Industry," *Chronicle of Higher Education,* Jan. 31, 1997.

7. Ashby, *Universities,* 292.

8. Ibid., 296.

9. J. Folger and R. Berdahl, *Patterns in Evaluating Systems of Higher Education: Making a Virtue out of Necessity* (College Park, Md.: National Center for Postsecondary Governance and Finance, 1987).

10. Burton Clark, "The Many Pathways of Academic Coordination," *Higher Education* 8 (1979): 251–68.

Part One

The Setting

Chapter One

Patterns in Higher Education Development

Philip G. Altbach

Universities are singular institutions. They have common historical roots yet are deeply embedded in their societies. Established in the medieval period to transmit knowledge and provide training for a few key professions, in the nineteenth century universities became creators of new knowledge through basic research.[1] The contemporary university is the most important institution in the complex process of knowledge creation and distribution, serving as home not only to most of the basic sciences but also to the complex system of journals, books, and databases that communicate knowledge worldwide.[2] Universities are key providers of training in an ever growing number of specializations. Universities have also taken on a political function in society, serving as centers of political thought, political action, and political training. At the same time, academe is faced with unprecedented challenges, stemming in large part from a decline in resources. After almost a half century of dramatic expansion worldwide, universities in many countries are being forced to cut back on expenditures and, in some cases, to downsize. The unwritten pact between society and higher education that provided expanding resources in return for greater access for students as well as research and service to society has broken down, with significant implications for both higher education and society.

This chapter is concerned with the patterns of higher education development evident in the post–World War II period throughout the world, analyzing some of the reasons for these trends and pointing to likely directions for universities in the coming decades. Issues such as autonomy and accountability, research and teaching, reform and the curriculum, and the implications of the massive expansion of universities in most countries are of primary concern. Universities are international institutions with common historical roots but at the same time are embedded in national cultures and circumstances.

A Common Heritage

There is only one common academic model worldwide. The basic European university model, established first in Italy and France at the end of the twelfth century, has been significantly modified but remains the universal pattern of higher education. The Paris model placed the professor at the center of the institution and enshrined autonomy as an important part of the academic ethos. It is significant that the major competing idea of the period, the student-dominated University of Bologna, did not gain a major foothold in Europe, although it had some impact in Spain and later in Latin America.[3] The university rapidly expanded to other parts of Europe—Oxford and Cambridge in England, Salamanca in Spain, Prague and Krakow in Central Europe—and a variety of institutions in the German states were established in the following century.

Later, the European imperialist nations brought universities to their colonies, along with other accoutrements of colonialism. The British, for example, exported academic models first to the American colonies and later to India, Africa, and Southeast Asia.[4] The French in Vietnam and West Africa, the Spanish and the Portuguese throughout Latin America, the Dutch in Indonesia, the Americans in the Philippines, and other colonial powers also exported academic institutions.[5] Colonial universities were patterned directly on institutions in the metropole but often without the traditions of autonomy and academic freedom in the mother country.[6]

The university has by no means been a static institution but has changed and adapted to new circumstances. With the rise of nationalism and the Protestant Reformation in Europe, the universal language of higher education, Latin, was replaced by national languages. Academic institutions became less international and more local in their student bodies and orientations and were affected by their national circumstances, Protestant Amsterdam differing, for example, from Catholic Salamanca. Harvard University, although patterned on British models, slowly developed its own traditions and orientations, reflecting the realities of colonial North America. Academic institutions have not always flourished. Oxford and Cambridge, strongly linked to the Church of England and the aristocracy, played only a minor role in the industrial revolution and the tremendous scientific expansion of the late-eighteenth and nineteenth centuries.[7] In France, universities were abolished after the revolution, in 1793; gradually, they were reestablished, and the Napoleonic model became a powerful force not only in France but also in Spain and Latin America.[8] German universities, which were severely damaged during the Nazi period by the destruction of autonomy and the departure of many professors, lost their scientific preeminence.[9]

For the purposes of this chapter, two more recent modifications of the Western academic model are relevant. In the mid-nineteenth century, a newly united Germany harnessed the university for nation building. Under the leadership of Wilhelm von Humboldt, German higher education was given significant resources by the state, took on the responsibility for research aimed at national development and industrialization, and played a key role in defining the ideology of the new German nation.[10] German universities also established graduate education and the doctoral degree. For the first time, research became an integral function of the university, and the university was reorganized as a hierarchy based on the newly emerging scientific disciplines. American reformers further transformed higher education by stressing the relationship between the university and society through the concept of service and direct links with industry and agriculture. They also democratized the German chair system, through the establishment of academic departments, and developed the land-grant concept for both research and expanded access to higher education.[11] Thus, even institutions that seem deeply embedded in national soil have in fact been influenced by international ideas and models.

Virtually without exception, the institutional pattern followed by the world's universities derive from these Western models. Significantly, in one of the few remaining fully non-Western institutions, Al-Azhar University in Cairo, which focuses mainly on traditional Islamic law and theology, science faculties are now organized along European lines.[12] There are many variations of the Western model — open universities, two-year vocational institutions, teacher training colleges, polytechnics—but while the functions of these institutions differ from those of traditional universities, their basic organization, pattern of governance, and ethos remain remarkably close to the Western academic ideal.[13]

Networks of Knowledge and Higher Education

There are many explanations for the dominance of the Western academic model. The institutionalization of the study of science and, later, scientific research are central elements. The link between universities and the dominant world economic systems no doubt is an important reason for Western hegemony. In many parts of the world, academic institutions were imposed by colonizers, and there were few possibilities to develop independent alternatives. Indigenous institutional forms were destroyed, as in nineteenth-century India with the British imposition of European patterns.[14] None of the formerly colonized nations have shifted from their basically European academic model; the contemporary Indian university, for example, resembles its preindependence predecessor.

Japan, which was never colonized, recognized after 1868 that it had to develop scientific and industrial capacity and jettisoned its traditional academic institutions in favor of Western university traditions, importing ideas and models from Germany, the United States, and other countries. Other noncolonized nations, such as China and Thailand, also imported Western models and adapted them to local needs and conditions.[15]

The harnessing of higher education to the broader needs of national economic and social development was perhaps the most important innovation of this era. Western universities were seen as successful in providing advanced education, fostering research and scientific development, and assisting their societies in the increasingly complex task of development. Universities in both the United States and Germany fostered industrial and agricultural development. The idea that higher education should be supported by public funds, that the university should participate in the creation as well as the transmission of knowledge, and that academic institutions should at the same time be permitted a degree of autonomy was behind much of the growth of universities in the nineteenth century. Further, Western universities were at the center of a knowledge network that included research institutions, the means of knowledge dissemination such as journals and scientific publishers, and an "invisible college" of scientists. Most of the world's scientific literature now appears in one language, English. Even scholars in such industrialized nations as Sweden and the Netherlands often communicate their research findings in English. The large Dutch multinational publishers Elsevier and Kluwer publish virtually all of their scholarly and scientific books and journals in English.

The circulation of scholars and students worldwide—even the so-called brain drain—is an element of the international knowledge system, helping to circulate ideas and also maintaining the research hegemony of the major host countries. More than one million students study outside their home countries, the large majority of them from Third World nations and the newly industrializing countries of the Pacific Rim. They are studying in the industrialized nations, especially the United States, Britain, France, and Germany. Japan is both a major sending and major receiving country.[16]

As a result of their sojourns abroad, students gain expertise in their studies but also learn the norms and values of the Western academic system, often returning home with a zeal to reform their local universities. Frequently, foreign graduates have difficulty readjusting to their home countries, in part because the advanced training they acquire abroad may not be easily assimilated into less industrialized economies. Such frustrations, along with significantly better remuneration in industrialized countries, lead to the brain drain. However, in the contemporary world, brain drain is often not permanent. Members of the Third World scientific diaspora often maintain contact with their colleagues at home, contributing advanced knowledge and ideas.[17] They often return home for periods of time to work with local academics and, increasingly, return home permanently, when conditions are favorable. These returning students bring with them to their native countries considerable expertise and often assume leadership positions in the local scientific and academic communities. With few exceptions, knowledge and institutional patterns are transferred from the major industrialized nations to the Third World—or even to more peripheral industrial countries—with very little traffic in the other direction.[18]

The knowledge network is complex and multifaceted; while its centers remain extraordinarily powerful, there is a movement toward greater equalization of research production and use. Japan, for example, already has a powerful and increasingly research-oriented university system, and some of the newly industrializing countries of East and Southeast Asia are building research capacity in their universities.[19] But while hegemony may be slowly dissipating, inequality remains endemic in the world knowledge system.

Expansion: Hallmark of the Postwar Era

Postsecondary education has expanded since World War II in virtually every country in the world. This growth has, in proportional terms, been more dramatic than that of primary and secondary education. Writing in 1975, Martin Trow spoke of the transition from *elite* to *mass* and then to *universal* higher education in the context of the industrialized nations.[20] The United States enrolled some 30 percent of the relevant age cohort (eighteen- to twenty-two-year-olds) in higher education in the immediate postwar period, while European nations generally maintained an elite higher education system, with fewer than 5 percent attending postsecondary institutions. By the 1960s, many European nations were educating 15 percent or more of the age group; in 1970, Sweden enrolled 24 percent, France 17 percent. That year, the United States increased its proportion to around 50 percent and was approaching universal access. By the 1990s, most European countries enrolled more than 30 percent of the age group, but the United States increased by only a few percentage points. Thus, while American patterns of access have stabilized, Europe and many newly industrializing countries continue to expand.

In the Third World, expansion has been similarly dramatic. Building on tiny and extraordinarily elitist universities, Third World higher education expanded rapidly in the immediate postindependence period. In India, enrollment grew from approximately 100,000 at the time of independence, in 1947, to more than 4 million in the 1990s. Expansion in Africa has also been rapid, with the postsecondary student population growing from 21,000 in 1960 to 437,000 in 1983; growth has stagnated in the 1990s as a result of the economic and political difficulties experienced by many sub-Saharan African countries.[21] Recent economic difficulties in much of sub-Saharan Africa have meant that per student expenditure has dropped, contributing to a marked deterioration in academic standards. Enrollment growth has also slowed.

Similar trends can be seen among other non-Western countries. In a few instances, such as the Philippines, where more than one-third of the age cohort enters postsecondary education, enrollment ratios have reached those of industrialized nations, although in general the Third World lags far behind in terms of proportion of the population attending higher education institutions. For example, despite China's student population of more than two million, only about 1 percent of the age cohort attends postsecondary institutions—about 4 percent of those who graduate from secondary school. Expansion in the Third World has, in general, exceeded that in the industrialized nations, at least in proportional terms. Among the highest rates of expansion and participation are in Asian newly industrializing countries such as South Korea and Taiwan.

Regardless of political system, level of economic development, or educational ideology, the expansion of higher education has been the single, most important trend worldwide. About 7 percent of the relevant age cohort attends postsecondary educational institutions, a statistic that has increased each decade since World War II. Higher education expanded first in the United States, then in Europe, and later in the Third World and the newly industrializing countries. Women now constitute approximately 40 percent of university enrollment, with considerable variation by country. The industrialized nations, with a few exceptions, have a higher proportion of the age cohort in postsecondary education than Third World countries. Generalized statistics concerning enrollments in postsecondary education mask many key differences. For example, industrialized nations have, in general, a higher proportion of students in technological and scientific fields than in liberal arts, which tend to predominate in the developing nations—although even here there are exceptions, such as China.

There are many reasons for the expansion of higher education, a central one being the increasing complexity of modern societies and economies, which demands a more highly trained workforce. Almost without exception, postsecondary institutions have been called upon to provide the required training. Indeed, training in many fields that was once imparted on the job has become formalized in institutions of higher education. Whole new fields, such as computer science, have come into existence and rely on universities as a source of research and training. Nations now developing scientific and industrial capacity, such as Korea and Taiwan, depend on academic institutions to provide high-level training as well as research expertise.[22]

Not only do academic institutions provide training, they also test and provide certification for many occupations in contemporary society. These roles have been central to universities since the medieval period but have been vastly expanded in recent years. A university degree is a prerequisite for an increasing number of occupations in most societies. Indeed, academic certification is necessary for most positions of power, authority, and prestige in modern societies, which places immense power in the hands of universities. Tests to gain admission to higher education are rites of passage in many societies and are important determinants of future success.[23] Competition within academe varies from country to country, but in most cases stress is also placed on high academic performance and tests. There are often further examinations to permit entry into specific professions.

The role of the university as an examining body has grown for a number of reasons. As industrial and economic expansion has taken place, more sorting mechanisms have been needed. The older, more informal, and often more ascriptive means of controlling access to prestigious occupations no longer provide the controls needed, nor are they perceived as fair. Universities are seen as meritocratic institutions, which can be trusted to provide impartial tests to measure accomplishment and, therefore, to determine access. When such mechanisms break down—as they did in China during the Cultural Revolution—or when they are perceived as subject to corrupt influences—as in India—universities are significantly weakened. Furthermore, entirely new fields have developed for which no sorting mechanisms exist, and academic institutions are frequently called upon to provide not only training but also examination and certification.

Expansion has also occurred because the growing segments of the population of modern societies demand it. The middle classes, seeing that academic qualifications are necessary for success, demand access to higher education, and governments generally respond by increasing enrollment.[24] When governments do not move quickly enough, private initiative frequently establishes academic institutions to meet the demand. In countries like India, the Philippines, and Bangladesh, a majority of the students are educated in private colleges and universities.[25] At present, there are powerful worldwide trends toward imposing user fees in the form of higher tuition charges, increasing the stress on private higher education, and in general considering higher education as a private good, in economic terms. These changes are intended to reduce the cost of postsecondary education for governments while maintaining access, although the long-term implications for the quality of, access to, and control over higher education remain unclear.

In most societies, higher education is heavily subsidized by the government, and most, if not all, academic institutions are in the public sector. While there is a growing trend toward private initiative and management sharing responsibility with public institutions, governments will likely continue to be the main source of funding for postsecondary education. The dramatic expansion of academic institutions in the postwar period has proved very expensive for governments. Nonetheless, the demand for access has been extraordinarily powerful.[26]

Many analysts writing in the 1960s assumed that the world, and particularly Western industrialized nations, would move from elite to mass and finally to universal access to higher education, generally following the American pattern, but the path to universal access has proved to be circuitous.[27] For a period in the 1970s, expansion slowed, only picking up again in the late 1980s. The nations of the European Union are in general moving toward U.S. levels of access. The causes for the slowdowns were in part economic, given the problems in the Western economies that followed the oil shocks of the 1970s; in part demographic, resulting from a significant drop in the birth rate and a smaller cohort of young people; and in part philosophical, as countries became less sympathetic to the growth of public institutions, including universities. Generally, the proportion of the age cohort going on to higher education in Western Europe stabilized at under 20 percent in the 1970s; it began to increase again in the late 1980s and continues to expand.[28] This expansion has taken place in a context of steady population trends and has been impelled by changes in European economies, which have moved to the postindustrial stage.

In sharp contrast to Western industrialized countries, Third World universities have, in general, continued to expand without interruption. The exception is Africa, where enrollment and access have slowed. With only a very few exceptions, such as the Philippines, Third World enrollment ratios remain significantly lower than those in the industrialized nations, but there continues to be a strong commitment to continued expansion and access. This is the case even in countries like India, where there is severe unemployment of graduates and a brain drain of university graduates. In sub-Saharan Africa, there has been a slowing of expansion, not so much because demand

for higher education has decreased but because of severe economic
problems, which have limited the ability of governments to pay the
costs of continued growth. In many Third World countries, it remains impossible for local universities to absorb all of those qualified
to attend, creating an exodus of students abroad. This is the case in
Malaysia, where close to half of the country's students are abroad.[29]
As in the industrialized nations, there is a notable trend toward shifting the burden of funding for higher education from the state to the
individual.

While common worldwide trends exist, such as the increasingly important role of technology, the Third World presents a specific set of
circumstances. While it is likely that expansion in higher education
in some Third World countries will slow in the coming decade, it will
continue to be a factor. Regional variations will be important, with
economic factors dominating. Universities will very likely grow more
slowly in less successful economies. Rapidly expanding economies,
such as those of the newly industrializing countries in East Asia,
will have the resources to expand higher education and at the same
time maintain a demand for graduates. Taiwan and South Korea, for
example, can generally absorb university graduates as well as the
expenditures needed for large, well-equipped universities, especially
since a majority of students study in private universities. Yet, even
where evidence exists that higher educational growth could slow or
even stop, it is unlikely that this will take place, since demand remains high, and political authorities will rather provide more access
than less, especially since the cost has increasingly been shifted from
government to individuals and families.

The situation in Western industrialized nations is more difficult
to predict. A variety of factors argue for a resumption of growth, although probably not at the levels of the 1960s. Modest upturns in
population in some age categories are in evidence in some Western
nations, although demographers predict that this will be relatively
short-lived. The large numbers of graduates trained in the 1960s and
now occupying positions in schools and universities as well as in government and industry will soon be retiring, triggering a significant
demand for university-trained personnel. It is also recognized that
university-based research is an important ingredient for scientific and
technological strength in an increasingly competitive world economy.
Much, however, will depend on broader economic trends. It is also
difficult to predict whether resistance to governmental spending in

general—and for education in particular—will continue to be an important political factor. The 1990s have brought a renewed growth in access to postsecondary education, although this has been combined with significant financial problems.[30]

Change and Reform: The Legacy of the Sixties

The demands placed on institutions of higher education to accommodate larger numbers of students and to expand their functions resulted in reforms in higher education in many countries. Much debate has taken place concerning higher education reform in the 1960s, and a significant amount of change did take place.[31] Without question, the student unrest of the period contributed to disarray in higher education. This unrest was in part precipitated by deteriorating academic conditions, which were the result of rapid expansion. In a few instances, students demanded far-reaching reforms in higher education, especially an end to the rigid, hierarchical organization of the traditional European university.[32] The chair system was modified or eliminated, and the responsibility for academic decision making, formerly a monopoly of full professors, was expanded—in some countries, to include students. At the same time, the walls of the traditional academic disciplines were broken down by interdisciplinary teaching and research.

Reform was greatest in several traditional Western European academic systems. Sweden's universities were completely transformed: decision making was democratized, universities were decentralized, educational access was expanded to previously underserved parts of the country, interdisciplinary teaching and research was instituted, and the curriculum was expanded to include vocational courses.[33] Reforms also took place in France and the Netherlands, where reformers stressed interdisciplinary studies and the democratization of academic decision making. In Germany, the universities in states dominated by the Social Democratic Party were also reformed, with the traditional structures of the university giving way to more democratic governance patterns.

In the 1990s, the major trend in restructuring European universities has been improving administrative efficiency and accountability. Many of the reforms of the 1960s were modified or even eliminated. Students, for example, have less power now. In the Netherlands, national restructuring increased the power of administrators. Similar trends can be seen in Germany, Sweden, and other countries.

In many industrialized nations, structural change was modest. In the United States, for example, despite considerable debate during the 1960s, there was very limited change in the structure or governance of higher education.[34] Japan, where unrest disrupted higher education and spawned a number of reports on university reform, experienced virtually no basic change in its higher education system, although several "new model" interdisciplinary institutions were established, such as the science-oriented Tsukuba University near Tokyo. Britain, less affected by student protest and with a plan for expansion in operation, also experienced few reforms during the 1960s.[35] Some of the changes implemented at that time have been abandoned. In Germany, reforms in governance that gave students and junior staff a dominant position in some university functions were ruled unconstitutional by German courts.[36]

Many of the structural reforms of the 1960s were abandoned after a decade of experimentation or were replaced by administrative arrangements that emphasized accountability and efficiency. Outside authorities, such as government—but also including business, industry, and labor organizations—came to play a more important role in academic governance. Curricular innovations have proved more durable; interdisciplinary programs and initiatives and the introduction of new fields such as gender studies remain.

Vocationalization has been an important trend in the past two decades. Throughout the world, there is a conviction that the university curriculum must provide relevant training for a variety of increasingly complex jobs. The traditional notion that higher education should consist of liberal, nonvocational studies for elites or a broad but unfocused curriculum has been widely criticized for lacking relevance to the needs of contemporary students. Students, worried about obtaining remunerative employment, have pressed universities to focus more on job preparation. Employers have also demanded that the curriculum become more relevant to their needs. Enrollment in the social sciences and humanities, at least in industrialized nations, has declined.

Curricular vocationalism is linked to another worldwide trend in higher education: the increasingly close relationship between universities and industry.[37] Industrial firms have sought to ensure that the skills they need are incorporated into the curriculum. This trend also has implications for academic research, since many university/industry relations are focused largely on research. Industries have established formal linkages and research partnerships with universities to obtain help with research of interest to them. In countries such as Sweden, representatives from industry have been added to the governing councils of higher education institutions. In the United States, formal contractual arrangements have been made between universities and major corporations to share research results. In many industrialized nations, corporations provide educational programs for their employees, sometimes with the assistance of universities.

Technical arrangements with regard to patents, confidentiality of research findings, and other fiscal matters have assumed importance as university/industry relations have become crucial. Critics also point out that the nature of research in higher education may be altered by this relationship, as industrial firms are not usually interested in basic research. University-based research, which has traditionally been oriented toward basic research, may be increasingly skewed to applied and profit-making topics. There has also been some discussion of research orientation in fields like biotechnology, in which broader public policy matters may conflict with the needs of corporations. Specific funding arrangements have also been questioned. Pressure to serve the training and research requirements of industry has implications for the organization of the curriculum, the nature and scope of research, and the traditional relationship between the university and society.[38]

The traditional idea of academic governance stresses autonomy, and universities have tried to insulate themselves from the direct control of external agencies. However, as universities expand and become more expensive, there is immense pressure by those providing funds for higher education—mainly governments—to expect accountability. The conflict between autonomy and accountability has been a flashpoint for controversy in recent years. Without exception, university autonomy has shrunk, and administrative structures have been put into place in such countries as Britain and the Netherlands to ensure greater accountability.[39] The issue takes on different implications in different parts of the world. In the Third World, traditions of autonomy have not been strong, and demands for accountability, both political and economic, are especially troublesome.[40] In the industrialized nations, accountability pressures are more fiscal in nature.

Despite the varied pressures on higher educational institutions for change and the significant reforms that have taken place in the past two decades, there have been few structural alterations in universities. One of the few places where this has occurred is Sweden. Elsewhere, curricula have been altered, expansion has taken place, and there have been continuing debates concerning accountability and autonomy, but universities as institutions have not changed significantly. As Edward Shils has argued, the "academic ethos" has been under strain, and while in some ways it has been weakened, it has survived.[41]

The Millennium

The university is a durable institution. The modern university retains key elements of the historical models from which it sprang even while evolving to serve the needs of societies during a period of tremendous change.[42] There has been a convergence of ideas and institutional patterns and practices in higher education, due in part to the implantation of European-style universities in developing areas during and after the colonial era and in part to universities' having been crucial to the development and internationalization of science and scholarship. Many of the changes chronicled here are the result of great external pressure and were instituted despite opposition from within the institution. Some scholars argue that the university has lost its soul.[43] Others claim that the university is irresponsible because it uses public funds without meeting the needs of industry and government. Pressure from governmental authorities, militant students, and external constituencies have all placed great strains on academic institutions.

The period since World War II has been one of unprecedented growth in universities, and higher education has assumed an increasingly central role in virtually all modern societies. While growth may continue, the dramatic expansion of recent decades is at an end. It is unlikely that the position of the university as the most important institution for training in virtually all of the top-level occupations in modern society will be weakened, although other institutions have become involved in training. The university's research role is more problematical because of the fiscal pressures of recent years. There is no other institution that can undertake basic research, but the consensus that has supported university-based basic research has weakened.[44]

The challenges facing universities are, nonetheless, significant. The following issues are among those that will be of concern in the coming decade and beyond.

Access and Adaptation

In many countries, issues of access will be among the most controversial in debates concerning higher education. Although in a few countries, access to postsecondary education has been provided to virtually all segments of the population, in most countries a continuing unmet demand exists. The broadening of the social class base of higher education has slowed, and in many industrialized countries it ended in the 1970s, but with the arrival of democratic governments in Eastern Europe, the reemergence of demand in Western Europe, and continuing pressure for expansion in the Third World, demand for access—and thus expansion of enrollment—will continue. Limited funds and a desire for "efficient" allocation of scarce postsecondary resources will come into direct conflict with these demands for access. In many countries, racial, ethnic, or religious minorities will thus play a role in shaping higher education policy.

Administration, Accountability, and Governance

As academic institutions become larger and more complex, there is increasing pressure for professional administration, as in the United States. At the same time, the traditional forms of academic governance are increasingly criticized for being unwieldy and, in large and bureaucratic institutions, inefficient. As the administration of higher education increasingly becomes a profession, an "administrative estate" will be established. Growing demands for accountability will cause academic institutions considerable difficulty. And as academic budgets expand, there will be inevitable demands to monitor and control expenditures. At present, no general agreement exists concerning the appropriate level of governmental involvement in higher education. The challenge will be to ensure that the traditional—and valuable—patterns of faculty control over governance and basic academic decisions are maintained in a complex and bureaucratic environment.

Knowledge Creation and Dissemination

Research is a central part of the mission of many universities and of
the academic system generally. Decisions that will be in contention
in the future will concern the control and funding of research, the
relationship of research to the broader curriculum and teaching, the
uses made of university-based research, and related issues. Further,
the system of knowledge dissemination, including journals and books
and computer-based data systems, is rapidly changing. Who should
control the new data networks? How will traditional means of communication, such as journals, survive in this new climate? How will
the scientific system avoid being overwhelmed by the proliferation of
data?[45] Who will pay for the costs of knowledge dissemination? The
needs of peripheral scientific systems, including both the Third World
and smaller academic systems in the industrialized world, have been
largely ignored but are, nonetheless, important.[46]

While the technological means for rapid knowledge dissemination
are available, issues of control and ownership, the appropriate use of
databases, problems of maintaining quality standards in databases,
and related questions are important. It is possible that the new technologies will lead to increased centralization rather than wider access.
It is also possible that libraries and other users of knowledge will be
overwhelmed both by the cost of obtaining new material and by the
flow of knowledge. At present, academic institutions in the United
States and other English-speaking nations, along with publishers and
owners of communications networks, stand to gain. Major Western
knowledge producers currently constitute a kind of cartel of information, dominating not only the creation of knowledge but also most of
the major channels of distribution. Simply increasing the amount of
research and creating new databases will not ensure a more equal and
accessible knowledge system. Academic institutions are at the center,
but publishers, copyright authorities, funders of research, and others
are also necessarily involved.

The Academic Profession

In most countries, the professoriate has been under great pressure in
recent years. Demands for accountability, the increased bureaucratization of institutions, fiscal constraints in many countries, and an
increasingly diverse student body have all challenged the professori-

ate. In most industrialized nations, a combination of fiscal problems and demographic factors led to a stagnating profession. Now, demographic factors and a modest upturn in enrollment are beginning to turn surpluses into shortages.[47] In the newly industrializing countries, the professoriate has in recent years significantly improved its status, remuneration, and working conditions. In the poorer nations, however, the situation has, if anything, become more difficult, with decreasing resources and increasing enrollments. Overall, the professoriate will face severe problems as academic institutions change in the coming period. Maintaining autonomy, academic freedom, and a commitment to the traditional goals of the university will be difficult.

In the West, it will be hard to lure the "best and brightest" into academe when positions are again relatively plentiful, for in many fields, academic salaries have not kept pace with those in the private sector, and the traditional academic lifestyle has deteriorated. Pressure on the professoriate not only to teach and do research but also to attract external grants, do consulting, and the like is great. In Britain and Australia, for example, universities have become "cost centers," and accountability has been pushed to its logical extreme. British academics who entered the profession after 1989 no longer have tenure but are periodically evaluated. In the newly industrializing countries, the challenge will be to create a fully autonomous academic profession in a context in which traditions of research and academic freedom are only now developing. The difficulties faced by the poorer Third World countries are perhaps the greatest—to maintain a viable academic culture under deteriorating conditions.

Private Resources and Public Responsibility

In almost all countries there has been a growing emphasis on increasing the role of the private sector in higher education. One of the most direct manifestations of this trend is the role of the private sector in funding and directing university research. In many countries, private academic institutions have expanded or new ones have been established. Students are paying an increasing share of the cost of their education as a result of tuition and fee increases and through loan programs. Governments try to limit their expenditures on postsecondary education. Privatization has been the means of achieving this broad policy goal.[48] Inevitably, decisions concerning academic developments will move increasingly to the private sector, with the possibility that broader public goals may be ignored. Whether private interests will support the traditional functions of universities—including academic freedom, basic research, and a pattern of governance that leaves the professoriate in control—is unclear. Some of the most interesting developments in private higher education can be found in such countries as Vietnam, China, and Hungary, where private institutions have recently been established. Private initiatives in higher education will bring a change in values and orientation, but it is not clear that these values will be in the long-term best interests of the university.

Diversification and Stratification

While diversification—the establishing of new postsecondary institutions to meet diverse needs—is not new, it is of primary importance and will continue to reshape the academic system. In recent years, the establishment of research institutions, community colleges, polytechnics, and other academic institutions designed to meet specialized needs and to serve specific populations has been a primary characteristic of growth. At the same time, the academic system has become more stratified—individuals in one sector of the system find it difficult to move to a different sector. There is often a high correlation between social class (and other variables) and participation in a particular sector. To some extent, the reluctance of traditional universities to change is responsible for some of the diversification. Perhaps more important is the belief that limited-function institutions are more efficient and less expensive. An element of diversification is the inclusion of larger numbers of women and other previously disenfranchised segments of the population. Women now constitute 40 percent of the student population worldwide and more than 50 percent in fifteen countries.[49] In many countries, students from lower socioeconomic groups and racial and ethnic minorities are entering postsecondary institutions in significant numbers.

Economic Disparities

The substantial inequalities among the world's universities are likely to grow. Major universities of the industrialized nations generally have the resources to play a leading role in scientific research, in a context in which it is increasingly expensive to keep up with the expansion of knowledge.[50] Universities in much of the Third World, however, simply cannot cope with the increased enrollments, budgetary constraints, and in some cases, fiscal disasters. Universities in much of sub-Saharan Africa, for example, have experienced dramatic budget cuts and find it difficult to function, not to mention to improve quality and compete in the international knowledge system.[51] Academic institutions in the Asian newly industrializing countries, where significant academic progress has taken place, will continue to improve. Thus, the economic prospects for postsecondary education worldwide are mixed.

Conclusion

Universities share a common culture and a common reality: in many basic ways, there is a convergence of institutional models and norms. At the same time, there are significant national differences, which will continue to affect the development of academic systems and institutions. It is unlikely that the basic structures of academic institutions will change dramatically: the Humboldtian academic model will survive, although administrative structures will grow stronger and the traditional power of the faculty will diminish. Open universities and other distance education institutions may provide new institutional arrangements, and efforts to save money may yield further organizational changes. Unanticipated change is also possible; while the emergence of significant student movements, at least in industrialized nations, do not seem likely, circumstances may change.[52] The situation for universities in the first part of the twenty-first century are not, in general, favorable. The realities of higher education as a "mature industry" in industrialized countries, with stable rather than growing resources, will affect not only the funds available for postsecondary education but also academic practices. Accountability, the impact of technologies, and the other forces discussed in this chapter will all affect colleges and universities, although patterns will vary. Some academic systems, especially those in the newly industrializing countries, will continue to grow. In parts of the world affected by significant political and economic change, the coming decades will be ones of reconstruction. Worldwide, the coming period is one of major challenge for higher education.

NOTES

I am indebted to Robert Arnove, the late Gail P. Kelly, and Lionel Lewis for their comments on an early version of this chapter and to Lalita Subramanyan and Patricia Murphy for their help with editing.

1. For a historical perspective, see Charles Haskins, *The Rise of Universities* (Ithaca: Cornell University Press, 1957).

2. Philip G. Altbach, *The Knowledge Context: Comparative Perspectives on the Distribution of Knowledge* (Albany: State University of New York Press, 1987).

3. For further discussion of this point, see A. B. Cobban, *The Medieval Universities: Their Development and Organization* (London: Methuen, 1975).

4. The history of British higher education expansion in India and Africa is described in Eric Ashby, *Universities: British, Indian, African* (Cambridge: Harvard University Press, 1976).

5. See Philip G. Altbach and Viswanathan Selvaratnam, eds., *From Dependence to Autonomy: The Development of Asian Universities* (Dordrecht, Netherlands: Kluwer, 1989).

6. Irene Gilbert, "The Indian Academic Profession: The Origins of a Tradition of Subordination," *Minerva* 10 (1972): 384–411.

7. For a broader consideration of these themes, see Lawrence Stone, ed., *The University in Society*, 2 vols. (Princeton: Princeton University Press, 1974).

8. Joseph Ben-David, *Centers of Learning: Britain, France, Germany, the United States* (New York: McGraw-Hill, 1977), 16–17.

9. Friedrich Lilge, *The Abuse of Learning: The Failure of the German University* (New York: Macmillan, 1948).

10. Charles E. McClelland, *State, Society, and University in Germany, 1700–1914* (Cambridge: Cambridge University Press, 1980). See also Joseph Ben-David and Awraham Zloczower, "Universities and Academic Systems in Modern Societies," *European Journal of Sociology* 3 (1962): 45–84.

11. In the German system, a full professor was appointed as head (chair) of each discipline, and all other academic staff served under his direction; the position was permanent. Many other countries, including Japan, Russia, and most of Eastern Europe, adopted this system. On developments in America, see Laurence Veysey, *The Emergence of the American University* (Chicago: University of Chicago Press, 1965); E. T. Silva and S. A. Slaughter, *Serving Power: The Making of the Academic Social Science Expert* (Westport, Conn.: Greenwood, 1984).

12. For a discussion of the contemporary Islamic university, see H. H. Bilgrami and S. A. Ashraf, *The Concept of an Islamic University* (London: Hodder and Stoughton, 1985).

13. Philip G. Altbach, "The American Academic Model in Comparative Perspective," in *Comparative Higher Education*, ed. Philip G. Altbach (Greenwich, Conn.: Ablex, forthcoming).

14. See David Lelyveld, *Aligarh's First Generation: Muslim Solidarity in British India* (Princeton: Princeton University Press, 1978).

15. Michio Nagai, *Higher Education in Japan: Its Take-off and Crash* (Tokyo: University of Tokyo Press, 1971). See Altbach and Selvaratnam, *From Dependence to Autonomy*, for case studies of Asian universities.

16. See Philip G. Altbach, David Kelly, and Y. Lulat, *Research on Foreign Students and International Study: Bibliography and Analysis* (New York: Praeger, 1985).

17. Hyaeweol Choi, *An International Scientific Community: Asian Scholars in the United States* (Westport, Conn.: Praeger, 1995).

18. The number of American students studying abroad is only a small proportion of the number of foreign students studying in the United States, and the large majority of Americans who do study in other countries go to Canada and Western Europe. See also Robert Arnove, "Foundations and the Transfer of Knowledge," in *Philanthropy and Cultural Imperialism*, ed. Robert Arnove (Boston: Hall, 1980).

19. For a discussion of higher education development in the newly industrializing countries, see Philip G. Altbach et al., *Scientific Development and Higher Education: The Case of Newly Industrializing Countries* (New York: Praeger, 1989).

20. Martin Trow, "Problems in the Transition from Elite to Mass Higher Education," paper prepared for a conference on mass higher education held by the Organization for Economic Cooperation and Development, 1975.

21. See World Bank, *Education in Sub-Saharan Africa: Policies for Adjustment, Revitalization, and Expansion* (Washington, D.C.: World Bank, 1988), esp. chap. 6.

22. Altbach et al., *Scientific Development and Higher Education*.

23. Max A. Eckstein and Harold J. Noah, "Forms and Functions of Secondary School Leaving Examinations," *Comparative Education Review* 33 (1989): 295–316.

24. Academic institutions serve as important sorting institutions, sometimes diverting students from highly competitive fields. See, for example, Steven Brint and Jerome Karabel, *The Diverted Dream: Community Colleges and the Promise of Educational Opportunity in America, 1900–1985* (New York: Oxford University Press, 1989).

25. Roger L. Geiger, *Private Sectors in Higher Education: Structure, Function, and Change in Eight Countries* (Ann Arbor: University of Michigan Press, 1986). For a focus on Latin America, see Daniel C. Levy, *Higher Education and the State in Latin America: Private Challenges to Public Dominance* (Chicago: University of Chicago Press, 1986).

26. World Bank, *Education in Sub-Saharan Africa,* strongly argues against continued expansion of higher education, believing that scarce educational expenditures could be much more effectively spent on primary and secondary education. See also D. Bruce Johnstone, *Sharing the Costs of Higher Education: Student Financial Assistance in the United Kingdom, the Federal Republic of Germany, France, Sweden and the United States* (Washington, D.C.: College Board, 1986).

27. Trow, "Problems in Transition."

28. See Ladislav Cerych and Paul Sabatier, *Great Expectations and Mixed Performance: The Implementation of Higher Education Reforms in Europe* (Trentham, England: Trentham Books, 1986), pt. 2.

29. Jasbir Sarjit Singh, "Malaysia," in *International Higher Education: An Encyclopedia,* ed. Philip G. Altbach (New York: Garland, 1991).

30. There are also significant national variations. For example, Britain under Margaret Thatcher's leadership consistently reduced expenditures for postsecondary education, with significant negative consequences for higher education. See, for example, Sir Claus Moser, "The Robbins Report 25 Years After: And the Future of the Universities," *Oxford Journal of Education* 14 (1988): 5–20.

31. For broader considerations of the reforms of the 1960s, see Cerych and Sabatier, *Great Expectations;* Ulrich Teichler, *Changing Patterns of the Higher Education System* (London: Kingsley, 1989); Philip G. Altbach, ed., *University Reform: Comparative Perspectives for the Seventies* (Cambridge, Mass.: Schenkman, 1974).

32. For an example of an influential student proposal for higher education reform, see Wolfgang Nitsch et al., *Hochschule in der Demokratie* (Berlin: Luchterhand, 1965).

33. Jan Erik Lane and Mac Murray, "The Significance of Decentralization in Swedish Education," *European Journal of Education* 20 (1985): 163–72.

34. See Alexander W. Astin et al., *The Power of Protest* (San Francisco: Jossey-Bass, 1975), for an overview of the results of the ferment of the 1960s on American higher education.

35. "The Legacy of Robbins," *European Journal of Education* 14 (1988): 3–112.

36. For a critical viewpoint, see Hans Daalder and Edward Shils, eds., *Universities, Politicians, and Bureaucrats: Europe and the United States* (Cambridge: Cambridge University Press, 1982).

37. See, for example, "Universities and Industry," *European Journal of Education* 20 (1985): 5–66.

38. Of course, this is not a new concern for higher education. See Thorstein Veblen, *The Higher Learning in America: A Memorandum on the Conduct of Universities by Business Men* (New York: Viking, 1918).

39. See Klaus Hufner, "Accountability," in *International Higher Education: An Encyclopedia,* ed. Philip G. Altbach (New York: Garland, 1991).

40. Philip G. Altbach, "Academic Freedom in Asia: Learning the Limitations," *Far Eastern Economic Review*, June 16, 1988.

41. Edward Shils, *The Academic Ethic* (Chicago: University of Chicago Press, 1983).

42. See Ben-David and Zloczower, "Universities and Academic Systems."

43. See, for example, Robert Nisbet, *The Degradation of the Academic Dogma: The University in America, 1945-1970* (New York: Basic Books, 1971). Allan Bloom, in his *The Closing of the American Mind: How Higher Education has Failed Democracy and Impoverished the Souls of Today's Students*(New York: Simon and Schuster, 1987), echoes many of Nisbet's sentiments.

44. In those countries that have located much of their research in non-university institutions, such as the academies of sciences in Russia and some Central and Eastern European nations, there has been some rethinking of this organizational model, a sense that universities may be more effective locations for major research. Since the collapse of the Soviet Union, there have been some moves to abolish the academy model. See Alexander Vucinich, *Empire of Knowledge: The Academic of Sciences of the USSR (1917-1970)* (Berkeley: University of California Press, 1984).

45. See Thomas W. Shaughnessy et al., "Scholarly Communication: The Need for an Agenda for Action—A Symposium," *Journal of Academic Librarianship* 15 (1989): 68-78. See also *Scholarly Communication: The Report of the National Commission* (Baltimore: Johns Hopkins University Press, 1979).

46. These issues are discussed in Altbach, *The Knowledge Context*. For a different perspective, see Irving Louis Horowitz, *Communicating Ideas: The Crisis of Publishing in a Post-Industrial Society* (New York: Oxford University Press, 1986).

47. For an American perspective, see Howard Bowen and Jack Schuster, *American Professors: A National Resource Imperiled* (New York: Oxford University Press, 1986).

48. Levy, *Higher Education*. See also Geiger, *Private Sectors in Higher Education*.

49. Gail P. Kelly, "Women in Higher Education," in *International Higher Education: An Encyclopedia,* ed. Philip G. Altbach (New York: Garland, 1991).

50. A possible exception to this situation are universities in Britain, where a decade of financial cuts by the Thatcher government sapped the morale of the universities and made it difficult for even such distinguished institutions as Oxford and Cambridge to continue top-quality research. See Geoffrey Walford, "The Privatization of British Higher Education," *European Journal of Education* 23 (1988): 47-64.

51. World Bank, *Education in Sub-Saharan Africa,* 68-81.

52. For a survey of student movements, see Philip G. Altbach, ed., *Student Political Activism: An International Reference Handbook* (Westport, Conn.: Greenwood, 1989).

Chapter Two

The Ten Generations of American Higher Education

Roger Geiger

Two powerful reasons exist for the serious study of the history of higher education: because things change and because some things do not change. Continuity is evident in individual institutions, in which circumstances or self-images of origin and development serve to shape current conditions. Basic forms persist as well, perhaps most notably in the intractable centrality of the American college. Issues also recur, particularly those concerned with curriculum, institutional mission, and student development. But change also is an irreducible reality and must, by its nature, be analyzed in a temporal dimension. The key elements here are understanding the processes of change and aggregating such changes to discern fundamental transformations in the entire system of higher education. This last element forms the premise of the analysis that follows: that the character of American higher education has perceptibly shifted in each generation, or approximately every thirty years. The exploration of these successive generations is intended to illuminate these historical dynamics as well as the underlying processes of which they are composed.

The ten generations of American higher education, from the founding of Harvard to the current era, are characterized here in terms of what was taught, the experience of students, and the array of institutions. Extant knowledge is screened by institutions and their faculty for certified acceptance into the curriculum. That curriculum, in turn, has an implied relationship with subsequent uses. The place of higher education in the lives of students can be captured in the phrase "origins and destinations." The expansive nature of American higher education has meant that student origins have tended to be broad and diverse. Yet, expectations about ultimate destinations have largely motivated college attendance, and these same expectations have inspired crucial interventions by third parties—whether governments, churches, foundations, or individuals. Between origins and destinations lies the college experience itself, certainly one of the most critical variables. Finally, there is the institutional order—all the institutions offering higher education and their internal makeup. This scheme is intended to be heuristic, highlighting central features for monitoring change over time without excluding any factors impinging on higher education.

Generation 1: Reformation Beginnings, 1636–1740s

Each of the first three colleges in the British colonies of America was unique, but all may be described as "schools of the Reformation."[1] Harvard, William and Mary, and Yale were established as adjuncts of their respective churches, which in turn were integrally related to their respective civil governments. The long head start enjoyed by Harvard gave it a special, settled character. A true product of the Wars of Religion when it was chartered in 1636, it evolved in the eighteenth century into a more cosmopolitan and tolerant institution. This evolution away from strict Calvinism reflected the spreading heterodoxy of Puritan society and the support of the more secular and mercantile elements in that community. William and Mary was formally linked with the Church of England. Its founder, James Blair, and his successors were titular heads of the church in Virginia. William and Mary did not offer regular collegiate instruction until the 1740s. It then embodied the relative tolerance of official Anglicanism, a stance congenial to the planter families who governed the colony.[2] Only Yale preserved and cultivated the sectarian zeal of the Reformation era into the middle of the eighteenth century.

Some original features persisted long after the Reformation era. External governance was a natural outgrowth of viewing the colleges as an emanation of the polity. Both Harvard and William and Mary had dual structures, consisting of corporations and boards of overseers or visitors. Yale was guided by a single board, originally consisting of ten Congregational ministers, but it looked to the General Assembly of Connecticut for financial support and legal backing.[3] This combination of provincial authority external to the college and the clerical authority lodged within it generated recurring conflicts. Control of Harvard was contested among old-line Puritans and more liberal Congregationalists. Yale's minister-trustees, left to themselves, could not agree where to locate the college. And at William and Mary, the inability of the board of visitors to control the faculty was a perpetual problem. All three colleges nevertheless received financial support from their respective colonies.

A relatively powerful college president eventually emerged as the natural complement to lay authority. A circumscribed role remained to be played by the faculty of tutors, who were usually recent graduates preparing for the ministry. The curriculum of the colleges in this era was little changed from that of the Middle Ages. Its aim was to provide students with a liberal education, which meant facility with classical languages, grounding in the three basic philosophies of Aristotle—ethics, metaphysics, and natural philosophy or science—and a smattering of general worldly knowledge. In order to be admitted, students had to show some knowledge of Latin, a bit of Greek, and arithmetic. The first two years were spent for the most part mastering the classical languages and, particularly, achieving a working knowledge of Latin. Philosophy, general subjects, and divinity were taught in the final two years. Although these colleges lagged well behind Europe, the education offered was a practical one for the seventeenth and early eighteenth centuries, when most learned texts were in Latin. The process of education was undoubtedly as valuable as the content. The collegiate way of living and the constant presence of tutors gave students complete immersion in a learning environment. Composing declamations and engaging in disputations inculcated a facility with language that was indispensable to the oral public culture they would enter.

The founding documents of all three schools speak to the aim of educating ministers. Indeed, except at William and Mary, this was the chief expectation associated with college matriculation. Actual ministerial training, nevertheless, followed upon a liberal education. Nearly two-thirds of the graduates of seventeenth-century Harvard entered the ministry. But nonministerial students were both welcomed and expected. William and Mary sought to make youths "piously educated in good Letters and Manners"; and the founders of

Yale intended to provide education "for Publick employment both in Church & Civil State."[4]

The nexus between college and the ministry would erode slowly during the eighteenth century. Under John Leverett (1708–24), Harvard already possessed a clientele of young gentlemen who took scant interest in studies or piety. At William and Mary, where a ministerial career required a journey to England for ordination, most sons of the Virginia gentry sought only a patina of liberal education, and almost none graduated.

Harvard surmounted the narrow role of a Reformation college in another way by the third decade of the eighteenth century. Gifts from Thomas Hollis created two professorships, in divinity (1721) and in mathematics and natural philosophy (1727). The hiring of individuals who could specialize over the years in a single field of knowledge overcame an important curricular limitation. By the next generation, learned professors in addition to young tutors would be sought by the colonial colleges.[5]

Generation 2: Colonial Colleges, 1745–1775

The mold of Reformation colleges was broken with the founding of the College of New Jersey in 1746. A compromise between Presbyterians and the colony of New Jersey produced a board of trustees having twelve ministers, ten laymen, and the governor of the colony as ex officio presiding officer. The college was rooted in the colony yet served a far wider constituency of Presbyterians; it was denominational in nature yet tolerant of other Protestant sects. The next four colleges to be founded followed this same pattern of "toleration with preferment," although for somewhat different reasons. King's College (1754), as an Anglican founding, had to assuage fears of institutionalizing a state religion. The College of Philadelphia (1755), successor to the academy that Benjamin Franklin had helped to found, continued the tradition of toleration in a context of considerable religious diversity. Baptists, too, believed in toleration, even while insisting upon control over the College of Rhode Island (1765). New Hampshire's eagerness to have a provincial college, above all, prompted it to entice Eleazer Wheelock to found Dartmouth (1769). Only the creation of Queen's College (1771), by and for the Dutch Reformed community, introduced an exclusive (and unsuccessful) model at the end of this period.[6]

Harvard and William and Mary also conformed to the new model of provincial colleges. Yale under Thomas Clap (1740–66), however, resisted this form in the name of doctrinal purity but, in doing so, demonstrated that the theocratic ideal of the Reformation was no longer tenable. Clap's rearguard action to defend Yale against the doctrines of the Great Awakening, against an Anglican presence in Connecticut, and finally against the Connecticut General Assembly ended, ironically, when he lost control of the college to rebellious students.

On the eve of the Revolution, the colonial colleges enrolled nearly 750 students, but three-quarters of them attended the four oldest colleges.[7] The latter, in particular, exemplified instruction that had become more secular in curriculum and purpose. Fewer than half of the graduates of Princeton pursued careers in the ministry. In the small but vital urban centers of the colonies, a sizable class of gentlemen now existed, consisting of professional men and successful merchants. At King's College perhaps 40 percent of the students originated from that milieu, and the proportion at Harvard may well have been higher. Still, many students clearly came from more humble circumstances, chiefly sons of farmers. They no doubt were more likely to be destined for the ministry, while gentlemen's sons more typically followed the path that led to law and public life.[8]

At the outset of this period, the curriculum was an incoherent amalgam of works predicated on both the old, theocentric universe and the new, enlightened views reflecting the writings of John Locke and Sir Isaac Newton. The doctrines of the "Moderate Enlightenment" gradually prevailed.[9] The enlightened spirit also included a more thorough teaching and appreciation of the classical authors. Latin and Greek thus remained at the heart of the curriculum, but Latin ceased to be a language of instruction. Classical authors introduced the generation of the Founding Fathers to the political forms and lessons of the ancient world. Scottish "common-sense philosophy," as taught by John Witherspoon (1768–95) at Princeton, reconciled Christian doctrines and the new knowledge. Students also received more competent instruction in these decades as college teaching became a settled occupation, attracting men of genuine learning.[10]

In sum, during the colonial generation the colleges balanced duties to both church and province, offered a richer and more secular intellectual fare, and served, among others, a constituency of aspiring gentlemen. The new nation soon called upon them to make a still larger contribution.

Generation 3: Republican Education, 1776-1800

The revolution against England was clearly a spark for igniting political feelings in the colleges. However, college life was disrupted for much of the War for Independence and then developed slowly before the nation was united under the Constitution in 1788. Despite this triumph of federalism, political passions rose to a crescendo at the end of the century.

The ideal for collegiate education in this period sought a harmonious joining of disparate elements. First was the notion of republican education—instilling selflessness, patriotism, and virtue in the citizens and leaders of the new republic. Such an outlook was conveyed through the choice of texts, topics for student oratory, and the widely touted (though unsuccessful) introduction of the study of law. Second, Enlightenment learning was welcomed as never before, although the fiscal limitations of colleges made realization fall far short of aspirations. Indeed, these years mark the zenith of Enlightenment influence in American colleges, a time in which theology sought to accommodate the truths of science and reason. Samuel Stanhope Smith (1795-1812), who succeeded Witherspoon at Princeton, epitomized both the ascendancy and the fragility of this "republican Christian Enlightenment": learning was valued in the colleges, and higher education was valued in the polity.[11]

After independence, the newly sovereign states made provision for collegiate education for their citizens. States that had no colleges chartered new institutions—Maryland (1782 and 1784), Georgia (1785), South Carolina (1785), North Carolina (1789), and Vermont (1791)—although some years passed before most of these institutions were able to open. Elsewhere, this same impulse sometimes became entwined with controversial changes in existing colleges. The board of visitors of William and Mary imposed a reorganization of the faculty in 1779. The same year, Pennsylvania supplanted the College of Philadelphia with a "public" institution (the two were merged in 1791 to form the University of Pennsylvania). The superstructure of the University of the State of New York was erected in the 1780s to counter the conservative influence of Columbia. Where continuity was the rule, state officials were made ex officio trustees of colleges (Massachusetts, Connecticut, New Hampshire, and New Jersey), and financial support was sporadically provided. Denominationally sponsored colleges found few students and little influence in these years. The new colleges founded near the frontier often reflected close-knit denominational communities, but they too assumed a public outlook.

The vision of republican higher education was undermined considerably by the material weaknesses of the colleges. The nation's most solid institution, Harvard University, had just three professors at the turn of the century, but that was two more than Yale or Princeton could manage. Collegiate enrollments for the last quarter of the century did not keep pace with population growth, despite the proliferation of new institutions. Where roughly 1 percent of a four-year male cohort attended college in 1775, the corresponding figure for 1800 was 0.75 percent. In some new colleges, like North Carolina, the absence of experienced teachers for a time fomented chaotic conditions. Student unruliness was a particular blight at institutions associated with Jeffersonian Republicanism, like William and Mary and Dickinson. Public subsidies for state-sponsored colleges were soon terminated, leaving these institutions in an exceedingly weak state. At the end of the eighteenth century, there was no functioning model of a state college.[12]

Ironically, popular sentiment now began to turn decisively in support of religion, but the religion of the heart, not the head. In this respect, as in others, the consequences of the dissolution of republican education were realized after 1800.

Generation 4: The Passing of Republican Education, 1800–1820s

The first generation of the nineteenth century is perhaps the least understood in American history. It has largely been associated with negative developments. Indeed, the most widely known historiographical treatment interprets it as the beginning of a "great retrogression."[13] Signs of trouble are not hard to find. The underpinnings of republican education were dislodged by the election of Thomas Jefferson, to the horror of Federalists, who dominated most colleges, and by the upsurge of religious spirit known as the Second Great Awakening, to the detriment of rational Christianity. In addition, many institutions were in a parlous state. In a plea some other colleges might have echoed, Columbia trustees described the college's sorry state as "mortifying to its friends, [and] humiliating to the city."[14] The Universities of Maryland and North Carolina lost their state support; and such major institutions as Princeton and William and Mary began prolonged declines.

Such a picture, however, portrays only misfortunes. Harvard, Yale, Brown, and Union all strengthened notably, and even Columbia was much improved by the 1820s. Moreover, an important group of institutions opened their doors shortly after 1800 — Transylvania, Bowdoin, and the state colleges of Georgia and South Carolina. College enrollments outpaced the rapid population growth, except during the depression caused by the War of 1812, bringing male participation back to 1 percent by the end of the 1820s. Underlying the fortunes of individual institutions, nevertheless, lay fundamental questions stemming in large measure from the obsolescence of the putative republican model: Who owned the colleges? What was their mission? What should students be taught? And how could they be controlled?

In the first three decades of the century, colleges experienced the worst student violence of their histories. Unruliness had long been endemic in all-male residential colleges, but these years were distinguished by episodes of collective resistance to college authority.[15] They invariably began with some minor or major transgression of college rules, but what followed was the key. In certain cases, students deemed disciplinary action, based upon measured degrees of public disgrace, to be unjustly severe. Believing their rights and dignity to have been violated, they would either remonstrate or commit further acts of insubordination. The colleges invariably won these contests of will, but at considerable cost. Numerous unrepentant students were expelled, and the college's reputation was invariably besmirched. Such riots at Princeton and William and Mary were factors in precipitating their declines; Harvard endured its periodic riots more stoically; North Carolina forfeited public support.

Steven Novak interpreted student riots as the stimulus for college leaders to shift the emphasis of the curriculum back toward the ancient languages. Latin and Greek were considered safe, and their difficult study promoted behavioral as well as mental discipline. However, "having embraced [this] curriculum for the wrong reasons — as a bulwark against dangerous ideas — academics were never able to bring it to life."[16] Other factors played a role here as well. Most

conspicuous was the collapse of efforts to construct a republican curriculum of scientific and professional subjects due to lack of suitable
teachers or interested students. Moreover, attempts to deemphasize
classical languages threatened to undermine the entire enterprise. At
Transylvania University the course without Latin and Greek lasted
just two years; and Dickinson students in 1800 demanded, and were
granted, a reduction of the course to a single year. Socially, some
knowledge of the classical languages was a badge of cultural distinction appropriate to gentlemen. As a practical matter, lax entrance requirements brought immature and poorly prepared students to campus. Most established colleges thus made concerted efforts to raise
their entrance requirements, impose a minimum age, and strengthen
instruction in Latin and Greek.

This restandardization of the classical curriculum corresponded to
a refocusing of institutions on their collegiate missions. In a reciprocal development, the links between professional education and the
colleges were dissolving. This trend has seldom been noted. Yale and
other colleges sprouted professional schools during these years and
appeared to become fledgling universities. Few institutions followed
this path, however, and in those that did professional schools were
largely proprietary undertakings with little organic connection to the
parent college. They resembled, in fact, the independent professional
schools that began to flourish in this era.

The most vigorous law school after 1800 operated independently—
in Litchfield, Connecticut. Unlike earlier attempts to teach law in the
colleges, which were intended for civic education, Litchfield prepared
students for professional practice. In medicine, the dominant institution was the University of Pennsylvania. With enrollments exceeding
four hundred, this medical school was the largest higher education
unit in the country. But its students paid the professors directly for
lectures, making the school virtually independent of the university.
Other medical schools either sought similar arrangements, or else
they collapsed. The Columbia medical school faltered and was absorbed by another school; Harvard's medical school achieved greater
autonomy by moving to Boston; and Brown's medical school folded
when the college sought to control its faculty.[17] The most consequential change for the colleges, nevertheless, concerned the training of
ministers.

The preparation of ministers was an integral mission of the colleges, even though ministerial training per se fell outside the under-

graduate course. When New England Congregationalists reacted to the Unitarian capture of Harvard by establishing Andover Theological Seminary (1808), a new alternative became available. During the next two decades, more schools for ministerial training were opened than new colleges. These institutions were in a sense alternatives to collegiate education and, as in the case of the Princeton Theological Seminary (1812), were votes of no confidence in the colleges. Seminaries became the locus for serious scholars of language and philology (and hence, German learning); and they attracted substantial gifts that might have gone to colleges.[18] Most seriously, they distanced colleges from the function of ministerial preparation because, like future lawyers and medical doctors, aspiring ministers increasingly dispensed with collegiate degrees.

The final issue hanging over the colleges was the ambiguous mix of public function and private control. Controversies arising from this situation had plagued the colleges since the Revolution. What proved to be a definitive resolution had to await the justly celebrated Dartmouth College case (1819). When the Supreme Court ruled that New Hampshire could not without cause alter the charter of an "eleemosynary corporation" like Dartmouth College, it effectively provided colleges with a shield against unwanted intrusions of democratic legislatures. More significantly, it resolved an implicit question of ownership that had plagued virtually every college. In Massachusetts, for example, the composition of the board of overseers had been altered by the legislature three times in the 1810s. Justice Joseph Story, a member of that board, was undoubtedly as concerned with the autonomy of Harvard as with that of Dartmouth when he voted on the case. Years passed before the import of the Dartmouth College case became fully apparent; the colleges continued to present both public and private persona, but an agenda of privatization clearly triumphed. Not only did the eastern provincial colleges become fully private institutions, but the way was cleared for the establishment of a new type of unambiguously private denominational college.[19]

Generation 5: The Classical, Denominational Colleges, 1820s–1850s

Generation 5 began in the 1820s, with widespread challenge to the classical college, and was superseded in the 1850s by new waves of reform. The first efforts largely failed, but the second produced permanent change. In between, the private, denominational college emerged as the characteristic institution of American higher education. Its success drove a rapid expansion in both the number of colleges and total enrollments. At the same time, sectional differences created distinctive patterns for higher education in the Northeast, the South, and the transappalachian West.

Criticism of the classical college in the 1820s in part reflected the success of efforts to bolster the curriculum. Now colleges were attacked for their obsession with dead languages, for neglecting practical subjects and science, and for the continued unruliness of apparently disgruntled students. A flurry of specific reforms occurred in the middle of the decade.[20] George Ticknor, after a student insurrection at Harvard, managed to reform his own modern languages department, offering advanced courses outside the rigid boundaries of the separate classes. Thomas Jefferson's University of Virginia (1824) provided an entirely new departure, aimed at achieving the nation's first true university. And Eliphalet Nott created a parallel course for a bachelor of science degree at Union College (1827). Little lasting change resulted from this ferment of reform. The efforts of Ticknor and Nott remained isolated achievements, and the University of Virginia proved an incongruous setting for the sons of southern planters. Instead, the reforms provoked a magisterial defense of the classical college—the Yale Report of 1828.

In defending the classical curriculum, the report defined the purpose of college as "to lay the foundation of a superior education."[21] The object, above all, was to discipline the mind and only secondarily to provide content, or "furniture." The classical languages were championed as the ideal vehicle for instilling mental discipline as well as culture and "balance." From these premises, the report could argue that all other forms of education—for practical training or advanced learning—should be relegated to other kinds of institution. This position rationalized the de facto undergraduate focus of the colleges. The cogency of the Yale Report, moreover, seemed to grow over time and became the principal defense of the classical course for the next sixty years.

The classical college drew upon deeper strengths than the arguments of the Yale Report. Furthermore, it had rather different histories on the eastern and western sides of the Appalachians. In the Northeast, generally, the colleges preserved their narrow focus on preprofessional, liberal education and were content to serve the relatively limited clientele who valued such an expensive badge of cultural distinction. Student life in these institutions changed profoundly during this era and served to fortify this sense of distinction. As the colleges relaxed their oppressive discipline, the students themselves developed a rich extracurriculum of their own. Student life was transformed into a self-contained world of activities and social ceremony that engendered deep loyalties instead of intense hostility.[22] In the West, the most salient development of this era was the proliferation of denominational colleges in territories that had, only short years before, been considered the frontier.

The prototypical denominational college nevertheless emerged in the East in the 1820s. The definition given by the Lutherans of Pennsylvania College (Gettysburg, 1832) cut to the heart of the matter: noting that its students, teachers, trustees, and benefactors all were church members, they concluded that the college "may then with truth be said to belong to that Church."[23] The denominational college was thus consciously established as an alternative to the mixed ownership of "provincial colleges." These colleges were established by religious minorities (some of whom had previously disdained advanced education for their ministers) so that they might have educational institutions that fully belonged to their church. Regional church organizations generally played an important role in their founding as well as in their governance. Thus, Baptists established Waterville College (Colby, 1820) and Columbian College (George Washington, 1821). Episcopalians finally broke the Yale monopoly in Connecticut in 1826 (Trinity). And Methodists joined the collegiate movement by founding Randolph-Macon (1830) and Wesleyan (1831). State legislators required that the charters of these colleges impose no religious tests. The conditions described by the Gettysburg Lutherans nevertheless defined the foremost reality of the denominational colleges.

On the western side of the Appalachians, where colleges were virtually nonexistent in 1820, denominational colleges soon proliferated. The earliest exemplars were founded by Congregational or Presbyterian missionaries almost as soon as the frontiers were settled. Later foundings tended to be sponsored by regional church organizations. In both cases, a crucial role was played by local boosters, who believed that a college would enhance the cultural and economic standing of their towns.[24] The western colleges were capable of notable experiments, especially where student access was concerned. Manual labor schemes were tried repeatedly in the 1830s and 1840s, and Oberlin became the first college to admit women. Pedagogically, though, they initially replicated the classical curriculum. Given denominational sponsorship and clerical leadership (often from graduates of Yale or Princeton), this path was a natural course to follow. Colin Burke argues that these institutions need to be viewed in a different framework from the established colleges of the East: they served the basic need for educational upgrading for their localities. Nearly all found it necessary to establish preparatory departments, for example. Over time, they tended to add diverse educational programs to the classical core in spite of limited means. The average size of western colleges in 1860 was about 56 students (compared with 174 in New England), and costs were kept low for their far-from-wealthy students. By 1860, the Southwest and Midwest contained 59 percent of colleges and 43 percent of students.[25]

A somewhat different institutional pattern, characterized by dominant state universities, emerged in the South during this era. The College of South Carolina (1803) and the University of Virginia (1824) were the region's strongest institutions and the only universities in the country to receive regular state appropriations before the Civil War. Both institutions catered to sons of the planter aristocracy, which dominated their states politically and socially. Such students, with exaggerated notions of personal honor, made student unrest endemic in southern universities. Denominational colleges in such milieus developed later and attracted a more humble clientele. The pattern of strong state universities spread throughout the Cotton Belt but conspicuously failed in states like Kentucky and Tennessee, where social and religious fragmentation favored denominational colleges.

The 1820s and 1830s were two of the most expansive decades for higher education. Enrollments jumped by roughly 80 percent in each decade, fueled by the establishment of denominational colleges. The 1840s, however, were years of comparative stagnation: they were no doubt hampered by the severe economic downturn that followed the crash of 1837 and by the limited appeal of the classical college. Exasperation with these conditions prompted one last spasm of reform. Brown president Francis Wayland (1827–56) accurately diagnosed the weakness of the eastern colleges: they catered solely to the professional class and furnished students with only a preprofessional education—precisely the narrow focus advocated in the Yale Report. Entirely neglected were practitioners of industry and commerce, who were responsible for the transformation taking place in the American economy.[26] However, these were the polemics of the 1820s in more sophisticated guise. Wayland's attempt to restructure Brown in order to appeal to this new class proved disastrous. Ironically, his failure occurred at the opening of one of the most dynamic eras of American higher education, but change in the ensuing generation, rather than displacing the classical college, would complement it with new institutions and studies.

Generation 6: New Departures, 1850s-1890

The Civil War has long been the conventional dividing line for the history of American higher education. However, most of the new departures associated with the postbellum years emerged in preliminary form in the 1850s, if not earlier. German-style universities, offering graduate education, are associated with the opening of Johns Hopkins in 1876, but Henry Tappan (1853–63) transformed the University of Michigan in these same directions. The Morrill Land-Grant Act of 1862 can lay exclusive claim to neither "schools of science" nor agricultural colleges. Daniel Coit Gilman estimates that twenty such institutions existed before 1860, including Yale's Sheffield Scientific School, which had evolved from a few extracurricular courses into a department in which both practical and advanced subjects could be studied.[27] In addition, at least four agricultural colleges were chartered in the 1850s, in Pennsylvania, Michigan, Maryland, and Ohio.

In the same decade, collegiate education was broadened to include other than white males. More than forty women's institutions were chartered to offer collegiate degrees before Matthew Vassar presumed to give women "a college in the proper sense of the word." [28] Ashmun Institute (1854, Lincoln University) in Pennsylvania and Wilberforce University (1856) in Ohio provided college education for free African Americans.

Perhaps the greatest continuity from antebellum to postbellum years existed for denominational colleges. They began a second period of proliferation in the 1850s, which carried through to the early 1870s. The dynamics of this expansion derived from a dual process of extension and elaboration. Through extension, colleges followed close behind the ever moving frontier into the trans-Mississippi West. Once again, the agents of these initial foundings were largely missionaries from the principal denominations. In the wake of this movement, and indeed throughout the Midwest, a second process of elaboration occurred as denominations without colleges made provision for the education of their church members. These colleges differed from their earlier counterparts in being multipurpose in nature. They still preserved the classical core but added degree courses in English and science as well as practical courses in business and teaching. In keeping with this impulse to serve their denominations broadly, these multipurpose colleges were usually coeducational, except for denominations opposed in principle (Roman Catholics, Presbyterians, German Lutherans). This great expansion of denominational colleges proceeded unfazed by the dawning age of the university, until conditions changed radically after 1890.[29]

The Morrill Land-Grant Act still largely determined the character of the new utilitarian education. Enthusiasm among the industrial classes for education in agriculture or the mechanical arts turned out to be sparse. True, well-publicized Cornell attracted the nation's largest entering class in 1868, but these initial students were mixed in aspirations and qualification. Only 10 percent eventually graduated. Outside of New England, preparatory departments overshadowed collegiate ones in the new land-grant colleges. After a slow start, enrollment in the mechanical arts (engineering) grew in the 1880s and then accelerated after 1890. Matriculants in agriculture, however, remained few and far between. Reformers simply misjudged the nexus between farming and advanced education.

Contrary to the conventional view, land-grant colleges did not meet an exigent popular demand, nor did they appreciably democratize higher education. Had they been dependent on enrollment, like other colleges, many undoubtedly would have failed. However, the circumstances of their beginnings gave them an assured, if meager, income as well as an implicit relationship with their respective states. They were thus sustained long enough through their sickly infancy for social and economic conditions to catch up to the expectations that had prompted their premature founding. In 1890, after intensive lobbying by land-grant presidents, the Second Morrill Act gave them direct annual infusions of federal funds, a crucial advantage at a time when universities were entering their most dynamic era of growth.[30]

The first Morrill Act nevertheless set the most important precondition for utilitarian education when it stipulated the establishment of "at least one *college*" in which these subjects would be taught, "without excluding other scientific and classical studies."[31] Unlike in continental Europe, where modern languages and useful subjects were taught in less prestigious institutions than those offering classical and theoretical studies, in the United States the progeny of the industrial classes would eventually study in the same institutions as those from the professional classes.

Despite the salience of the Morrill Act, these years were characterized far more by private initiatives and, particularly, single acts of philanthropy. Gifts of hitherto unprecedented size sought to fill lacunae in American higher education. Matthew Vassar, Henry Wells, Sophia Smith, and Henry Durant created colleges for women between 1861 and 1875 that were intended to equal the best men's colleges.[32] Ezra Cornell and John Purdue enhanced the effectiveness of land-grant colleges. Trustees of estates were responsible for establishing the Stevens Institute of Technology and the Johns Hopkins University. The end of this era was marked by the most spectacular new institutions (after Hopkins)—Clark and Stanford Universities and the University of Chicago.

The American university is the most enduring legacy of these developments, even though its ascendancy over American higher education would have to await the next generation. Charles Eliot said in 1869 that no university yet existed in the United States, and prior to 1890 it was uncertain what form an American university would assume. Indeed, Daniel Coit Gilman, G. Stanley Hall, David Starr Jordan, and William Rainey Harper each independently attempted to invent such an institution (at Hopkins, Clark, Stanford, and Chicago, respectively). The chief conundrum was the relationship between advanced learning, or graduate education, and the American college.

The true paradigm of the American university evolved instead at the country's paramount institution. Charles W. Eliot assumed the presidency of Harvard in 1869 with a clear sense of the changes that were needed in both college and professional schools. For the college, he sought to replace recitations and the classical curriculum with an elective system that could accommodate true learning. This reform took a decade and a half, but by then the old regime was vanquished at Harvard and in retreat at other eastern colleges. Eliot also attacked the decadence of the professional schools at the outset of his presidency. A learned, full-time faculty replaced practitioner-teachers; a mandatory curriculum was put in place; and professional education was eventually defined as requiring a bachelor's degree.

Eliot's instincts were by no means as sure when it came to graduate education. But as the elective system allowed him to appoint many more learned professors, a distinguished faculty emerged, capable of scholarship, research, and advanced instruction. In 1890 the scientific school and the college faculty were merged into the faculty of arts and sciences. The Graduate School of Arts and Sciences was its other face. Finally, Eliot felt that Harvard was "now well on the way to the complete organization of a university in a true sense." The American university would be an institution in which the instruction of large numbers of undergraduates would support a numerous, specialized faculty, who would also teach graduate students. Not even the ingenious William Rainey Harper could devise anything better. Moreover, this model was a natural one for the more vigorous state universities, whose growth was about to explode. The next generation of American higher education would see the efflorescence of this powerful combination of mixed purposes.[33]

Generation 7: Growth and Standardization, 1890 to World War I

The character of growth in American higher education changed profoundly around 1890. During the previous generation, enrollment growth had been absorbed into an increasing number of institutions, but during the generation 7 the net number of institutions remained fairly stable while enrollments swelled. The average institution in 1870 had 10 faculty and 98 students; in 1890, these figures had grown to just 16 faculty and 157 students; but in 1910, they were up to 38 faculty and 374 students. Moreover, the largest institutions led this growth: in 1895 the ten largest universities averaged nearly 2,000 students; in 1910 they approximated 4,000 and in 1915, 5,000.[34] At the other end of the spectrum, colleges that failed to grow were threatened with extinction. The institutional order was anything but stable; the founding of new colleges continued unabated into the 1890s, but many institutions expired during these years.

One important source of growth was the assimilation of women into higher education. In 1890 the majority of female students were found in single-sex colleges, most of which were regarded by contemporaries as inferior. This situation changed abruptly with the opening of the elective curriculum and the expansion of universities. The proportion of women students grew slowly, from 32 to 37 percent (1890–1913), but those in coeducational institutions nearly doubled, to 68 percent. The gulf between the educational experiences of women and men narrowed much further in the next generation.[35]

The standardization of the universities after 1890 is the central theme of Laurence Veysey's classic study. His deliberate emphasis on the cerebral aspects of this subject, however, may slight some of the more mundane features, largely caused by similar adaptations to a common environment. The rapid growth of universities resulted from the growth of their several parts. Most added units in engineering, business, education, plus different combinations of other smaller specialties (e.g., mining, forestry, dentistry, pharmacy, veterinary medicine, art, architecture, and music), in addition to schools for graduate study, medicine, and law. Universities became compartmentalized institutions, whose parts shared little common intellectual ground. Administrative structures were necessary to serve these autonomous compartments and especially to secure ever more resources to fulfill their needs.[36]

By 1908 it was possible to define the standard American university. It admitted only bona fide high school graduates. It provided them with two years of general education followed by two years of advanced or specialized courses. It offered doctoral training in at least five departments, appropriately led by Ph.D.s, and had at least one professional school. A sizable list of desirable options might be added: summer sessions, extension work, correspondence courses, a university press, and the publication of learned journals. Idiosyncrasies faded away in this environment: Eliot's unconstrained elective system and proposed three-year bachelor's degree. Outliers moved closer to the norm: Johns Hopkins enrolled more undergraduates and lengthened the bachelor of arts course to four years; the Massachusetts Institute of Technology established units for research and graduate education.

The universities, in turn, were the most powerful force in generating standards for the rest of higher education, chiefly by defining academic knowledge and the academic profession. From about 1890 to 1905 all of the major disciplinary associations assumed their modern form. In a parallel development, the departmental structure of colleges and universities replicated these contours. Academic disciplines henceforth possessed a dual structure, whereby scientific recognition was embodied in disciplinary organizations while the most consequential positions, those commanding the means to advance these fields, were in university departments. As teaching positions were increasingly reserved for faculty who contributed to the knowledge base of disciplines, the universities imposed a definition on the academic profession. University faculty then took this definition a step further by organizing the American Association of University Professors (1915) to champion their professional rights, particularly academic freedom.[37]

Probably much more apparent to contemporaries was the spread of a set of practices that can best be called the collegiate ideal. Church ties were weak threads for sustaining liberal arts colleges. An alternative emerged from younger alumni with business careers in urban centers. They appreciated the social qualities that were instilled by extracurricular activities, including athletics. Their ability to contribute badly needed funds gave their wishes weight among college trustees and eventually influenced the selection of modernizing presidents. Denominational doctrines were soon deemphasized in favor of broad, middle-of-the-road Protestantism. New kinds of students began to matriculate, eager to throw themselves into campus activities and consciously destined for careers in the business world. Intercollegiate athletics tended to be the catalyst in this process, galvanizing the enthusiasm of students and the loyalties of alumni.[38]

The collegiate ideal developed first out of the unique traditions of the Ivy League schools, especially Harvard and Yale. It quickly captured the principal eastern colleges and spread to include state universities. The older generation of university leaders, like Charles Eliot, had scant regard for such activities, but the next generation—Eliot's successor Abbott Lawrence Lowell (1909–33) and above all Woodrow Wilson (1902–10) at Princeton—sought to amalgamate the collegiate ideal with their own solicitude for undergraduate learning. The collegiate ideal projected clear normative standards about the nature of the college experience, while another form of standardization found champions after 1900.

In 1905 the Carnegie Foundation for the Advancement of Teaching was chartered to provide pensions for college teachers. The same year, the General Education Board reoriented its activities toward promoting "a comprehensive system of higher education in the United States." Both foundations sought to alleviate the "chaos" and "confusion" they perceived in American higher education. The former promulgated stringent criteria of eligibility for its pensions, and institutions scrambled to conform. The latter worked more subtly by providing matching endowment grants that forced colleges to turn to their alumni.[39] Neither required an institution to have a football team, but they validated the types of schools that did: residential colleges with strong alumni support.

Following the model of the Land-Grant College Association (1887), successive associations were formed in this era, and their efforts also furthered standardization. The National Association of State Universities formulated the definition of the "standard American university." The Association of American Universities, formed to set standards for graduate education, soon became, in effect, an accrediting agency for colleges.[40]

A generation of standardizing activities gave much greater definition to the American system of higher education, even if it left the system still highly diverse and decentralized. By World War I, American colleges and universities by and large conformed to a single pattern in terms of admissions, credit hours, offerings, majors, and so on. The large difference among institutions pertained chiefly to the level of resources each commanded for the fulfillment of this pattern. Differences in resources would henceforth produce an increasingly steeper hierarchy among American institutions of higher education.

Generation 8: Hierarchical Differentiation between the Wars

Enrollments in higher education approximately doubled during the 1920s, and this expansion triggered qualitative changes analogous to what Martin Trow would later identify as the transition from elite to mass higher education.[41] Elite patterns are characterized by full-time, residential students, by cultural ideals of liberal learning and character formation, and by destinations in high-status professions. In contrast, mass forms of higher education cater to part-time or commuting students, convey applicable knowledge, and prepare students for employment in technical or semiprofessional positions. American higher education had always been somewhat hierarchical in terms of resource levels and admissions requirements. Between the two world wars, however, it became much more explicitly so. Emergent forms of higher education fulfilled "mass" roles, and educational leaders directly addressed the issue of offering qualitatively different kinds of instruction for different levels of student.

The growth of a mass sector in American higher education was apparent in the burgeoning junior colleges, teachers colleges, and urban, service-oriented universities.[42] Teachers colleges resulted from the process of continuously upgrading normal schools. This process began in the 1900s, although the majority of normal schools converted in the 1920s. Many teachers colleges remained for years confined to education degrees. In addition, they faced competition in this sphere from traditional universities. But as heirs to the normal schools they provided access to higher education for a broad segment of the population, especially women.

The expansion of higher education to serve city dwellers included both new and existing institutions. The free municipal university established in Akron (1913) exemplified the former. Typically with programs in engineering, home economics, commerce, and teaching, it aimed to produce employable graduates for the region. The College of the City of New York was perhaps the most spectacular exemplar of this phenomenon, growing to more than 24,000 students during the 1920s. Private municipal universities shared in this growth, largely by creating special programs for part-time students. In 1930, for example, part-time and summer students exceeded full-time students at New York, Northwestern, Southern California, Boston, and Western Reserve universities. By that date, the biggest American institutions were no longer research universities but municipal universities with large irregular enrollments.

True junior colleges first appeared in the decade of the 1900s but multiplied in the 1920s. They provided local access to higher education for both sparsely populated areas of the West and cities. By 1940, 11 percent of college students were enrolled in junior colleges, many of which were still attached to local high schools. The emergence of junior colleges nevertheless profoundly affected thinking about the structure and purpose of American higher education.

The waves of mass higher education lapping the shores of traditional institutions produced largely defensive reactions. President Ernest Hopkins of Dartmouth caused a stir by declaring that "too many young men are going to college." Probably the most vehement critic was Abraham Flexner, who charged that universities had become " 'service' stations for the general public."[43] A number of educators took inspiration from the apparent success of junior colleges and concluded that democratic access should extend through the sophomore year of college. The University of Minnesota created a two-year

General College for students deemed unfit for its regular programs. Another clear rationalization of hierarchical differentiation was the Carnegie Foundation's 1932 report, *State Higher Education in California,* which defined separate roles for the university in Berkeley, regional state colleges, and largely vocational junior colleges. This document was representative of a crystallization of opinion that sought to redefine the most open sector of higher education—the junior colleges—as terminal programs.

Determined efforts by the leaders of higher education had the effect of hardening the outlines of the mass sector of higher education, which had emerged almost spontaneously. Similarly, purposeful actions were required to define the upper reaches of American higher education. As with the mass sector, this was a matter at once of social origins and destinations, manner or style of attendance, and links with higher learning.

Three general criteria could be used to claim elite status. The *collegiate ideal,* especially popular in the 1920s, was determined by the peer society of students, by extracurricular activities, and by expectations of subsequent careers in the business world. *Quality of undergraduate learning* was a persistent concern, and not only did colleges attempt to raise their standards but also many educators sought to recreate the elusive ideal of liberal education. In universities, the imperative of *advancing knowledge* was an end in itself, the touchstone of research and graduate education but also a distinguishing feature of only a handful of institutions.

At the leading private institutions, financial constraints and rising applications prompted limits on the number of students after World War I. At the same time, these institutions became more sensitive to the social composition of their students and to the implications it had for their collegiate image. Columbia pioneered a form of selective admissions in which social criteria were used to limit the proportion of Jewish students, and the same discriminatory procedures were soon copied by Princeton, Yale, and Harvard.[44] Selective admissions was part of a larger pattern of fashioning elite status. These institutions shaped the peer society and collegiate environment not only by excluding supposedly nonconforming social types but also by widening their recruitment pool to encompass the entire country. They simultaneously became national rather than regional institutions, culling the weakest academic performers from among their traditional clientele and raising the level of study, at least in part. As these institutions prospered in the 1920s, they vastly increased educational spending on each student. When Yale launched the largest endowment drive in university history in 1927, it promised "to make a finer, not a bigger Yale."[45]

For elite universities, additional wealth was invested in more and better faculty—in scientists and scholars actively engaged in the advancement of knowledge. This phase of development was strongly assisted by philanthropic foundations, particularly the Rockefeller trusts. Participation in research also conferred prestige and elite status. Recognition in this dimension lay outside of universities, in international communities of scholars. It thus created an altogether different set of imperatives, which universities could scarcely ignore. It was no paradox, then, that a Jew could be a physics professor at Princeton but not an undergraduate: universalism prevailed in the former sphere but not in the latter.

Probably the most difficult course for sculpting an elite status was to excel in only undergraduate education. However, Swarthmore under president Frank Aydelotte (1921–39) was a notable success in this regard. Inspired by his Oxford experience as a Rhodes scholar, Aydelotte established an honors program to provide a rigorous course of study for able and motivated students. At the same time, he progressively deemphasized the underpinnings of the collegiate ideal— sororities, fraternities, and big-time football. The honors program was used to attract academically ambitious students and soon made Swarthmore one of the most selective colleges in the country. The high cost of this education was met with help from supporters of elitism, Abraham Flexner and the General Education Board.[46]

The hierarchical differentiation of the institutional order between the wars moved American higher education simultaneously in several different directions with respect to elite and mass sectors, access, and curriculum. American higher education became open to virtually all high school graduates, a category that grew from 9 to 51 percent of age cohorts between 1910 and 1940. Yet, social exclusiveness among many elite institutions increased, too, as nativist prejudice strengthened. The system was only weakly meritocratic and largely mirrored the social biases prevailing in the workplace. In curricular matters, the expanding mass sector was dominated by vocationally oriented programs, including attempts to define terminal tracks. A preoccupation of the era was nevertheless the persistent desire to fashion a true liberal education. At the same time, the implacable advancement of the academic disciplines weighed ever more heavily on the structure of college courses. Which trends predominated? The answer would become apparent during the next generation of American higher education: democratic access triumphed over social exclusiveness; academic development raised the stature of mass institutions, even as elite ones became strongly meritocratic; and an academic revolution confirmed the ascendancy of the academic curriculum.

Generation 9: The Academic Revolution, 1945–1975

The thirty years following the end of World War II were possibly the most tumultuous in the history of American higher education. Two fundamental movements nevertheless underlie these myriad developments: expansion and academic standardization. Beginning with the flood of returning soldiers, supported by the Servicemen's Readjustment Act of 1944 (the GI Bill), and concluding with the tidal wave of community college students of the early 1970s, this period was the most expansive in the American experience. The proportion of young people attending college tripled from 15 to 45 percent; undergraduates grew almost fivefold, graduate students almost ninefold (1940–70); the 1960s alone registered the largest percentage growth of any decade.[47]

While previous growth spurts, like the 1920s, were associated with new types of institutions reaching new clienteles, the postwar period was characterized by an implacable movement toward common academic standards. Not only did institutions become more alike in terms of curricular offerings, faculty training, and administrative practices, but students migrated toward studies in the arts and sciences. The principal dynamics of this era fortified these developments.

Most generally, an excess demand for college places existed through most of the era. This phenomenon arose when returning veterans took advantage of the GI Bill in unprecedented and unanticipated numbers. In 1947, 1.1 million ex-GIs were enrolled, compared with 1.5 million total students before the war. This surge did little to raise standards, though, as overcrowded institutions were forced to run year-round, to shorten courses, and to curtail requirements. This interlude nevertheless rebuilt depleted institutional treasuries and boosted morale as well. In the wake of this experience, most institutions sought to consolidate and bolster their programs.

Enrollment backtracked only slightly in the early 1950s, before larger cohorts began coming of age and seeking college places. Student numbers grew by approximately 50 percent in the 1950s. By the end of the decade, however, the baby-boom generation had already filled the high schools. The 1960s experienced a double effect: participation rates increased by half (from 30% to 45%), and the eighteen-to-twenty-one-year-old age cohort grew even more (from 9 million to 15 million). This flood of students flowed into flagship state universities, which expanded to their limits and then became increasingly selective. Private institutions, without generous appropriations to fund expansion, largely sought to optimize their efforts by building stronger academic programs for a more select student body. A large portion of the new students found places at burgeoning regional state institutions. Formerly teachers colleges, they eagerly expanded academic programs, ventured into graduate education, and became regional universities. The final component of this growth came from new public community colleges, which from 1965 to 1972 were opened at a rate exceeding one per week.

The idealism suffusing higher education after the war lent support for the basic arts and sciences. Institutions emphasizing these subjects had assumed preponderant prestige in the interwar years. Now, a consensus formed endorsing the *Harvard Report on General Education,* which pronounced that a judicious sampling of the basic disciplines would compose the foundation for a liberal education.[48] The pattern of institutional expansion also supported this trend toward arts and sciences. Service institutions that had embraced vocational/professional programs (or were confined to teacher education) in the interwar years gradually fortified disciplinary departments. A shift in student majors ensued in the 1960s, when bachelor's degrees awarded in the arts and sciences rose to a peak of 47 percent.[49]

These trends were powerfully fortified by a prodigious expansion of research and graduate education, largely due to federal support.[50] Federal sponsorship of research largely extended, under different organizational headings, the channels established for the wartime emergency. For more than a decade after World War II, the bulk of the increased funding for academic research came from the defense establishment and was skewed toward the physical sciences. However, a new federal relationship with higher education emerged from the Sputnik crisis of 1957. For about a decade after Sputnik, funding growth for academic science came from the civilian side of the federal government: the National Science Foundation, the National

Aeronautical and Space Administration, and most prolifically, the National Institutes of Health. Moreover, this bounteous support was accompanied by assistance for universities to support graduate students, build laboratories, and develop new science programs. Sputnik also provoked Washington to support higher education directly, first through the National Defense Education Act and later through direct aid for buildings and students. The federal largess, superimposed on mushrooming enrollments and state support, produced an ephemeral golden age in American higher education.

Christopher Jencks and David Riesman characterized the transformation that occurred during this era as "the academic revolution."[51] They meant the process by which the theoretical and specialized academic outlook of graduate schools was conveyed throughout the institutional order. It was a process that transcended the sciences, ultimately affecting virtually every school and department. The agents were the new Ph.D.s, trained in burgeoning graduate programs, who staffed the expanding universities. Their teaching and their writings brought the most current and specialized academic knowledge into the classrooms of all types of institution. Ultimately, however, the expectations and idealism of the academic revolution set the stage for a backlash that arose in the late 1960s. Its chief manifestation was the great student rebellion.

The student movement crystallized from the Free Speech Movement at Berkeley and Students for a Democratic Society. The larger national issues of the war in Vietnam and racial injustice largely propelled its evolution toward increasing radicalism and militancy. Although the major campuses suffered their greatest disruption from 1967 to 1969, the enduring impact was to alter the prevailing atmosphere of higher education. The momentum of the academic revolution was checked. The university's relation to its students was profoundly altered, from paternalism to exaggerated permissiveness. And universities retreated for a time to a heightened aloofness. The student rebellion was the crescendo to the tumultuous postwar generation, but it only partially foreshadowed the dawning new era.

Generation 10: Regulation, Relevance, and the Steady State

To extend historical analysis beyond the point in which documentation is available and ensuing consequences can be known is perilous.

But even if the ultimate shape and meaning of generation 10 of American higher education is as yet unfathomable, important features may still be identified. It is now apparent in retrospect that in the first half of the 1970s significant discontinuities occurred in the demographics, the politics, and the social relations of American higher education.

In 1975, enrollments in higher education topped 11 million for the first time, but then an unprecedented change occurred: student numbers for the first time ceased to grow. In the ensuing years there was an upward creep, but twenty years later the number of full-time students had grown by just 20 percent. Never before had enrollments been so stagnant for so long. One important dynamic was nevertheless at work: whereas 55 percent of students were male in 1975, 55 percent were female in 1995.

Higher education's relationship with the federal government changed in these years. Support for academic research was essentially capped in 1968, and aid for infrastructure and graduate education was largely phased out. However, direct support for research remained at high levels and, eventually, expanded once more in the 1980s. Still, the federal investment in higher education increased significantly in the 1970s, with the new funds being used to support student access. The 1972 amendments to the Higher Education Act were a watershed in two respects. First, they formalized a major commitment to provide aid to students on the basis of financial need. The centerpiece of this commitment was what are now called Federal Pell Grants, which provide direct support for the neediest low-income students. During the 1980s, however, the bulk of federal student aid was altered from Pell grants to guaranteed student loans. Nevertheless, the emergence of financial need as the dominant rationale for student support, by institutions as well as government, has been a distinguishing feature of generation 10.

The 1972 amendments also extended the government's regulatory control over higher education. The student rebellion of the 1960s had, in effect, staked the claim for a greater presence in higher education for minorities and women. Title IX now provided the means for legal enforcement. It was perhaps the most significant of a number of measures by which federal regulation became an inescapable presence in higher education.

One clarion call of the student rebellion was for relevance in university studies. Relevance indeed became a hallmark of the new era but in ways not anticipated by student activists. They had advocated a tendentious relevance predicated on the university's role as an aloof critic of society. Thus, they urged universities to study and seek to ameliorate problems stemming from the Vietnam War, racial inequality, poverty, and the environment. These topics long remained preoccupations on campuses, but more powerful trends toward relevance were welling up. Students sought a more tangible form of relevance by turning away from the arts and sciences and toward more vocational or professional majors. Bachelor's degrees in arts and sciences plummeted to just over one quarter of the total, barely more than the number awarded in business alone. Elsewhere, the conviction that academic knowledge should remain in the ivory tower slowly ebbed in the 1970s. A decisive change of attitude occurred in the early 1980s, when universities embraced the notion of economic relevance, specifically furthering economic development through technology transfer and closer involvement with the productive economy.

In the closing decade of the twentieth century, American higher education has endured another storm of public criticism. Yet, from the perspective of this historical analysis, the contemporary vista appears unusually clear. Although the value of a college education was called into question frequently in the 1970s, higher education has become increasingly recognized since then as essential for acquiring the skills and adaptability needed in the modern workplace. The middle-class social destinations made possible by higher education are now so widely recognized that they are undoubtedly the principal force behind rising participation rates. The contributions of academic knowledge were similarly disparaged at the beginning of generation 10. However, the economic relevance of at least some academic research has become widely accepted as a major factor in the strong performance of the U.S. economy. The advancement of basic knowledge, the special province of universities, should now be recognized as a national asset of inestimable value. The institutional order, finally, has remained stable throughout generation 10. Despite formidable financial pressures in the 1990s and demographic pressures looming in the next century, the immeasurable contribution of colleges and universities to American life should sustain them through the inevitable challenges lying ahead.

NOTES

This chapter is a substantially revised version of "The Historical Matrix of American Higher Education," *History of Higher Education Annual* 12 (1992): 7-28, which benefited from the comments of E. D. Duryea, Jurgen Herbst, and W. Bruce Leslie published in the same volume. New material has come from my current study of nineteenth-century colleges, which has been assisted by the Spencer Foundation. Comments from Karen Paulson and Roger Williams were greatly appreciated. References have been reduced to principal secondary works and quotation sources.

1. Jurgen Herbst, *From Crisis to Crisis: American College Government, 1636-1819* (Cambridge: Harvard University Press, 1982), 1-61.

2. Samuel Eliot Morison, *Three Centuries of Harvard, 1636-1936* (Cambridge: Harvard University Press, 1936), 53-82; Richard Hofstadter, *Academic Freedom in the Age of the College* (New Brunswick, N.J.: Transaction, 1996 [1955]), 98-113; Susan H. Godson et al., *The College of William and Mary: A History,* 2 vols. (Williamsburg, Va.: King and Queen Press, 1993), 3-80.

3. Herbst, *From Crisis to Crisis,* 38-47; Richard Warch, *School of the Prophets: Yale College, 1701-1740* (New Haven: Yale University Press, 1973).

4. Bruce A. Kimball, *The "True Professional Ideal" in America: A History* (Cambridge, Mass.: Blackwell, 1992), 75-84; Herbst, *From Crisis to Crisis,* 1.

5. William D. Carrell, "American College Professors: 1750-1800," *History of Education Quarterly* 8 (1968): 289-305.

6. Herbst, *From Crisis to Crisis,* 82-137; Howard Miller, *The Revolutionary College: American Presbyterian Higher Education, 1707-1837* (New York: New York University Press, 1976), 65-75.

7. Beverly McAnear, "College Founding in the American Colonies: 1745-1775," *Mississippi Valley Historical Review* 42 (1952): 24-44.

8. David C. Humphrey, *From King's College to Columbia, 1746-1800* (New York: Columbia University Press, 1976), 199; Morison, *Three Centuries,* 102-3; James McLachlan, introduction to *The Princetonians, 1748-1768: A Biographical Dictionary* (Princeton: Princeton University Press, 1977).

9. Edmund S. Morgan, *The Gentle Puritan: A Life of Ezra Styles, 1727-1795* (Chapel Hill: University of North Carolina Press, 1962), 47-57; Henry F. May, *The Enlightenment in America* (New York: Oxford University Press, 1976).

10. Mark A. Noll, *Princeton and the Republic, 1768-1822: The Search for a Christian Enlightenment in the Era of Samuel Stanhope Smith* (Princeton: Princeton University Press, 1989), 16-98; Miller, *Revolutionary College,* 82-94.

11. Noll, *Princeton and the Republic,* 185-213, 297-99; David W. Robson,

Educating Republicans: The Colleges in the Era of the American Revolution, 1750-1800 (Westport, Conn.: Greenwood, 1985), 143-77.

12. Robson, *Educating Republicans,* 247.

13. Hofstadter, *Academic Freedom,* 209-53.

14. *A History of Columbia University, 1754-1904* (New York: Columbia University Press, 1904), 100.

15. Steven J. Novak, *The Rights of Youth: American Colleges and Student Revolt, 1798-1815* (Cambridge: Harvard University Press, 1977); Leon Jackson, "The Rights of Man and the Rites of Youth: Fraternity and Riot at Eighteenth-Century Harvard," *History of Higher Education Annual* 15 (1995): 5-50.

16. Novak, *Rights of Youth,* 166.

17. Alfred Z. Reed, *Training for the Public Profession of the Law* (New York: Scribner, 1921), 116-60; William F. Norwood, *Medical Education in the United States before the Civil War* (Philadelphia: University of Pennsylvania Press, 1944).

18. Natalie A. Naylor, "The Theological Seminary in the Configuration of American Higher Education: The Ante-Bellum Years," *History of Education Quarterly* 17 (1977): 17-30; Glenn T. Miller, *Piety and Intellect: The Aims and Purposes of Ante-Bellum Theological Education* (Atlanta: Scholar's Press, 1990).

19. Herbst, *From Crisis to Crisis,* 232-43; Leon Burr Richardson, *History of Dartmouth College* (Hanover, N.H.: 1932), 287-346; John S. Whitehead and Jurgen Herbst, "How to Think about the Dartmouth College Case," *History of Education Quarterly* 26 (1986): 333-50.

20. Stanley M. Guralnik, *Science and the Ante-Bellum American College* (Philadelphia: American Philosophical Society, 1975), 18-46.

21. *Report on the Course of Instruction in Yale College; by a Committee of the Corporation and the Academical Faculty* (New Haven, 1828).

22. Frederick Rudolph, *Mark Hopkins and the Log: Williams College, 1836-1872* (New Haven: Yale University Press, 1956); Roger Geiger with Julie Ann Bubolz, "College as It Was: Review Essay," *History of Higher Education Annual* 16 (1996): 105-15.

23. Charles H. Glatfelter, *A Salutary Influence: Gettysberg College, 1832-1985,* 2 vols. (Gettysburg: Gettysburg College, 1987), 175.

24. David B. Potts, " 'College Enthusiasm' as Public Response: 1800-1860," *Harvard Education Review* 47 (1977): 28-42.

25. Colin Burke, *American Collegiate Populations: A Test of the Traditional View* (New York: New York University Press, 1982).

26. Francis Wayland, *Report to the Corporation of Brown University on Changes in the System of Collegiate Education* (Providence, 1850).

27. Daniel Coit Gilman, "Our National Schools of Science," *North Ameri-*

68   Roger Geiger

can Review (Oct. 1867): 495–520. Richard J. Storr, *The Beginnings of Gradu-ate Education in America* (Chicago: University of Chicago Press, 1953), 60–65, 112–17.

28. Thomas Woody, *A History of Women's Education in the United States,* 2 vols. (New York, 1929), 145–47; Christie Anne Farnham, *The Education of the Southern Belle: Higher Education and Student Socialization in the Ante-bellum South* (New York: New York University Press, 1994); Sidney Sher-wood, *The University of the State of New York* (Washington, D.C., 1900), quo-tation on 447.

29. Roger L. Geiger, "The Era of Multipurpose Colleges in American Higher Education, 1850–1890," *History of Higher Education Annual* 15 (1995): 51–92.

30. Roger L. Williams, *The Origins of Federal Support for Higher Educa-tion: George W. Atherton and the Land-Grant College Movement* (University Park: Pennsylvania State University Press, 1991).

31. Richard Hofstadter and Wilson Smith, eds., "The Morrill Act, 1862," in *Higher Education: A Documentary History,* vol. 2 (Chicago: University of Chicago Press, 1961).

32. Helen Lefkowitz Horowitz, *Alma Mater: Design and Experience in the Women's Colleges from Their Nineteenth Century Origins to the 1930s* (Bos-ton: Beacon, 1984).

33. Hugh Hawkins, *Between Harvard and America: The Educational Leadership of Charles W. Eliot* (New York: Oxford University Press, 1972); Morison, *Three Centuries,* 323–99, quotation on 361; Laurence Veysey, *The Emergence of the American University* (Chicago: University of Chicago Press, 1965).

34. Roger L. Geiger, *To Advance Knowledge: The Growth of American Re-search Universities, 1900–1940* (New York: Oxford University Press, 1986), 270–71.

35. Barbara Miller Solomon, *In the Company of Educated Women: A His-tory of Women and Higher Education in America* (New Haven: Yale Univer-sity Press, 1985); Lynn D. Gordon, *Gender and Higher Education in the Pro-gressive Era* (New Haven: Yale University Press, 1990).

36. Veysey, *Emergence;* Geiger, *To Advance Knowledge,* 14–19; enroll-ments by professional school or department are given in Edwin E. Slosson, *Great American Universities* (New York: Macmillan, 1910).

37. Geiger, *To Advance Knowledge,* 30–39; Walter P. Metzger, "Origins of the Association," *AAUP Bulletin* 51 (1965): 229–37.

38. W. Bruce Leslie, *Gentlemen and Scholars: College and Community in the "Age of the University," 1865–1917* (University Park: Pennsylvania State University Press, 1992); Ronald A. Smith, *Sports and Freedom: the Rise of Big-Time College Athletics* (New York: Oxford University Press, 1988).

39. Geiger, *To Advance Knowledge,* 45–47; Ellen Condliffe Lagemann, *Pri-*

vate Power for the Public Good: A History of the Carnegie Foundation for the Advancement of Teaching (Middletown: Wesleyan University Press, 1983), 3–53.

40. Hugh Hawkins, *Banding Together: The Rise of the National Associations in American Higher Education, 1887–1950* (Baltimore: Johns Hopkins University Press, 1992), 107–10.

41. Martin Trow, *The Transition from Elite to Mass Higher Education* (Paris: OECD, 1974).

42. The following draws on David O. Levine, *The American College and the Culture of Aspiration, 1915–1940* (Ithaca: Cornell University Press, 1986).

43. Geiger, *To Advance Knowledge;* Abraham Flexner, *Universities: American, English, German* (New Brunswick, N.J.: Transaction, 1994 [1930]).

44. Harold Wechsler, *The Qualified Student: A History of Selective Admissions in America* (New York: Wiley, 1977); Marcia G. Synnott, *The Half-Opened Door: Discrimination in Admissions to Harvard, Yale, and Princeton, 1900–1970* (Westport, Conn.: Greenwood, 1977); Geiger, *To Advance Knowledge,* 129–39.

45. Geiger, *To Advance Knowledge,* 206; see appendixes for institutional finances.

46. Burton R. Clark, *The Distinctive College* (New Brunswick, N.J.: Transaction, 1992 [1970]), 184–232.

47. Enrollment data are from the *Digest of Education Statistics.* For postwar academic development, see Richard M. Freeland, *Academia's Golden Age: Universities in Massachusetts, 1945–1970* (New York: Oxford University Press, 1992); Roger L. Geiger, *Research and Relevant Knowledge: American Research Universities since World War II* (New York: Oxford University Press, 1993).

48. Harvard University, *General Education in a Free Society* (Cambridge: Harvard University Press, 1945).

49. Sarah E. Turner and William Bowen, "The Flight from the Arts and Sciences: Trends in Degrees Conferred," *Science* 250 (1990): 517–21; Roger L. Geiger, "The College Curriculum and the Marketplace: What Place for Disciplines in the Trend Toward Vocationalism?" *Change,* Nov. 1980.

50. The following draws on Geiger, *Research and Relevant Knowledge.*

51. Christopher Jencks and David Riesman, *The Academic Revolution* (Chicago: University of Chicago Press, 1968); Geiger, *Research and Relevant Knowledge,* 198–203.

Chapter Three

Autonomy and Accountability

Who Controls Academe?

Robert O. Berdahl and T. R. McConnell

If a college or university is effectively to define its goals and select or invent the means of attaining them, it must have a high degree of substantive autonomy. Howard Bowen observed that the "production process" in higher education is far more intricate and complicated than that in any industrial enterprise.[1] Turning resources into human values defies standardization. Students vary enormously in academic aptitude, in interests, in intellectual dispositions, in social and cultural characteristics, in educational and vocational objectives, and in many other ways. Furthermore, the disciplines and professions with which institutions of higher learning are concerned require diverse methods of investigation, intellectual structures, means of relating methods of inquiry and ideas to personal and social values, and processes of relating knowledge to human experience. Learning, consequently, is a subtle process, the nature of which may vary from student to student, from institution to institution, from discipline to discipline, from one scholar or teacher to another, and from one level of student development to another. The intricacy and unpredictability of both learning and investigation require a high degree of freedom from intellectually limiting external intervention and control if an institution of higher education is to perform effectively.

Autonomy and Academic Freedom

On first thought, one might identify academic freedom with autonomy. Certainly, a high degree of intellectual independence is necessary for faculty and students in choosing the subjects of study and investigation, in searching for the truth without unreasonable or arbitrary restrictions, and in expressing scholarly conclusions without censorship. Some forms of external control or even subtle efforts to influence teaching, learning, or research may endanger intellectual freedom. However, academic freedom and university autonomy, though related, are not synonymous. Academic freedom as a concept is universal and absolute, whereas autonomy is of necessity parochial and relative.

Presumably, state boards of higher education designating the missions of sectors or particular institutions after appropriate studies and consultation would not be an unwarranted invasion of autonomy. But specifying the academic programs, academic organization, curriculum, and methods of teaching for the attainment of designated missions is likely to be considered unjustified intervention. A coordinating or governing board might phase out a doctoral program at a particular campus (after appropriate study and consultation) without unwarranted invasion of institutional autonomy or violation of academic freedom. The federal government might impose antidiscrimination procedures in admitting students or in appointing and promoting faculty members without interfering unjustifiably in academic affairs, provided the means do not make unreasonable demands on the institutions or violate necessary confidentiality of records. If appropriate safeguards are followed, no invasion of academic freedom need be suffered.

Requirements for accountability may impose onerous procedures on an institution (e.g., accounting for the use of research grants, as noted later in this chapter), but even these restraints may not endanger academic freedom. Whether restrictions on DNA research, referred to below, put an undesirable limit on choice of problems for investigation remains to be seen. In this case, public protection may justify what seems to be an infringement of academic freedom. In any event, Paul Dressel, in an analysis of the autonomy of public institutions, came to the following conclusion: "Academic freedom is not ensured by institutional autonomy, and recent restrictions of insti-

tutional autonomy have had relatively little effect on academic freedom."[2] One may agree that the absence of external controls does not
guarantee academic freedom and that certain elements of external
control do not endanger intellectual independence, but an institution's right to mobilize its intellectual resources—and within reasonable limits, even its financial resources—toward the attainment of its
agreed-upon purposes is at least strongly fortified by a relatively high
degree of autonomy.[3]

The Nature of Accountability

Intellectual freedom in colleges and universities is not under special
threat, but autonomy is being steadily eroded. Financial austerity
causes legislatures, state coordinating boards, and even consolidated
governing boards to look more critically at institutional roles, at
the availability and distribution of functions and programs, at effectiveness, and at educational and operational costs. As the federal
government extends support for higher education, it prohibits discrimination in the admission of students and in the appointment and
promotion of faculty members. The public at large is becoming more
conscious of its institutions of higher education. States and localities
are more demanding of education and service, more critical of what
they perceive institutions to be doing, and more vocal in expressing
their criticisms and desires. Public institutions, always answerable to
the general interest, will no longer be excused from defending what
they do or do not do. No longer can a university shunt public criticism aside as a mere expression of intellectual shallowness. It will
increasingly have to explain itself, defend its essential character, and
demonstrate that its service is worth the cost. It will become increasingly answerable (i.e., accountable) to its numerous constituencies
for the range of its services and the effectiveness of its performance.
"The extension of substantive autonomy to an individual, organization, or group implies responsibility and accountability," in Dressel's
words.[4] He outlined the elements of accountability as follows:

> Responsible performance, then, involves using allocated resources le-
> gally and wisely to attain those purposes for which they were made
> available. Responsible performance requires continuing accumulation
> of evidence of the extent to which purposes are achieved; reviewing

the evaluation evidence to clarify the avowed goals and their interpretation; consideration of the relevance, effectiveness, and costs of the
processes used to achieve the goals; and continuing effort directed at
improving the educational processes used or finding more effective processes.[5]

Relationships between the federal government and research universities have recently become strained, as the former has attempted
to impose techniques of accountability for federal research grants
that the institutions have considered unreasonable, onerous, and
unnecessarily expensive. In 1978 the National Commission on Research was organized for the purpose of proposing means of resolving
the differences between the two parties. The commission recognized
three forms of accountability: financial and administrative, involving
evidence of financial propriety and compliance with administrative
regulations; scientific, concerned with achievement of results and
progress toward scientific objectives; and social, referring to the
extent to which specific social goals are fulfilled. The commission
concluded that, "When well designed, the system of accountability
involves an appropriate balance between independence and control,
between incentives and constraints, and between the costs and benefits of the various procedures and requirements used."[6]

Accountability is not confined to an institution's external relationships. Internally, a college or university is a complex of mutual responsibilities and reciprocal pressures for accountability. Important
as these bases of accountability are, this chapter is devoted to a discussion of accountability to external agencies. External accountability
often emanates from external intervention, but intervention often
goes well beyond reasonable requirements for accountability. In any
event, intervention and accountability should be discussed together.

Accountability to the Public

Ultimately, public institutions of higher education are broadly answerable to the people who support them. After California voters
failed to approve a state bond issue providing large sums for the construction of medical school facilities and gave other evidences of dis-
affection, the president of the University of California recognized the
ultimate public accountability of the university: "Make no mistake,"

he said to the Assembly of the Academic Senate, "the university is a public institution, supported by the people through the actions of their elected representatives and executives. They will not allow it to be operated in ways which are excessively at variance with the general public will. By various pressures and devices, the university will be forced to yield and to conform if it gets too far away from what the public expects and wants."[7]

At one time, the people were relatively remote from their public institutions, but citizens now find their future economic, social, and cultural lives increasingly influenced, in some cases virtually determined, by their colleges and universities. Consequently, the public university has had to become responsive to a wider range of economic interests and to a more diverse pattern of ethnic and cultural backgrounds and aspirations. Minority groups are pressing for financial assistance, for remedial programs when necessary for admission or attainment of academic standards, and for academic programs that will meet their interests and perceived needs. As special interest groups have pressed the university to provide the services they believe they need, students have organized to promote their interests. With the prospect of declining enrollments, many colleges and universities have responded to that student market by establishing new vocational and professional programs of study, and most institutions are struggling to redistribute faculty, equipment, and resources as students shift from liberal arts courses to vocational and professional curricula. This trend has been especially observable in community colleges, and the effect will change the pattern of enrollment in four-year institutions to which community college graduates in the past have transferred in large numbers.

Serving the public interest has become a complicated process; not all institutions will undertake the same missions or serve common purposes. Accountability is further complicated by a question of what special interests should be served and what should be put aside. Only when an institution's goals are defined, the groups to be served identified, and the relevant programs of teaching, research, and public service determined can an institution's effectiveness be estimated. Thus, accountability is both general (responding to the broad public interest) and particular (responding to more limited constituencies).

Accountability to the public is mediated by the operation of several layers of representation between it and the institutions in question. Colleges and universities are answerable most immediately to their governing boards. Most boards have statutory status: they were created by legislatures and are in nearly all respects under legislative control. Seven or eight states have given constitutional status to their public universities: "The idea was to remove questions of management, control, and the supervision of the universities from the reach of politicians in state legislatures and governors' offices. The universities were to be a fourth branch of government, functioning co-authoritatively with the legislature, the judiciary, and the executive."[8]

Governmental Intervention

The purpose in creating their constitutional position was to give universities a much greater degree of autonomy and self-direction than statutory status would provide. Their autonomy, however, has been materially eroded over the years. A study of statutory and constitutional boards shows that the supposedly constitutionally autonomous university "is losing a good deal of its ability to exercise final judgment on the use not only of its state funds but also of those derived from other sources. It now undergoes intensive reviews of budgets and programs by several different state agencies, by special commissions, and by legislative committees, all of which look for ways to control."[9]

Whether an institution has statutory or constitutional status, or even whether it is public or private, it is moving into the governmental orbit. As Burton Clark put it: "In the changing relation between higher education and government, higher education . . . moves inside government, becomes a constituent part of government, a bureau within public administration."[10]

The State Government

Most students of university governance believe that government officials should not serve on governing boards, since this identifies the institution too closely with political and governmental agencies. In California the governor, the lieutenant governor, the superintendent of public instruction, the president of the state board of agriculture, and the speaker of the legislative assembly are among the ex officio voting members of the board of regents of the University of California. Governors may also use their appointive power to attempt to influence governing boards, although most boards have staggered terms that prevent governors from appointing a majority of members until they have served several years in office.

However, sometimes governors can accomplish through other means what they lack the power to do through direct appointment of trustees or regents. For example, when Ronald Reagan was governor of California, he heartily disapproved of the way President Clark Kerr was handling the mid-1960s student uprisings. A minority of university regents agreed with Governor Reagan; to them he added a few appointments to seats that had fallen vacant. He still lacked a majority who agreed with him, however, until he emphatically noted that the university's budget did not have constitutional autonomy and that he would not look kindly at continued resistance to his point of view. Consequently, Clark Kerr, as he later commented, left the university as he had come to it, "fired with enthusiasm!" Enough additional regents had been intimidated by the governor's statements to swing opinions over to his side.

Although governors may thus influence institutions via their governing boards, they make their greatest impact "through the executive budget process."[11] The state finance or budget officer, who is ordinarily responsible to the governor, may also exercise an important element of authority by controlling shifts or changes in line-item budgets. Some state finance departments conduct preaudits of expenditures that not only pass on the legality of the use of itemized funds but also give the state officer the opportunity to rule on the substance or purpose of the expenditures. In recent times the long arms of state finance officers have reached into academic affairs by conducting program audits or even program evaluations.[12]

But important as the executive officers of state government may be to public colleges and universities, state legislatures are more so. The institutions are dependent on the legislature's understanding of their broad missions and programs, its financial support, and its judgment of the institutions' educational effectiveness. Even a constitutionally autonomous public university is ultimately accountable to the legislature for the ways in which it uses its state-appropriated funds and for the effectiveness of its educational services. Legislators have become increasingly restless in the face of what some regard as the continuing neglect of undergraduate teaching and the overemphasis on research. Studies of faculty workload are becoming more common, with some legislatures considering mandated faculty teaching loads.

Issues raised in program evaluation include the consistency of the program with the assigned institutional role and function; the adequacy of planning in regard to the objectives, program structure, processes, implementation, and evaluation of outcomes; the adherence of program operation to the objectives, structural features, processes, sequence, and outcome appraisal originally specified or the presentation of a sound rationale for any deviations from the original prescription; an evaluation of planning and operation and use of feedback for alteration and improvement; and provision for cost benefit analyses.[13]

In legislatively mandated program evaluations in Wisconsin and Virginia, academic programs, quality considerations, course content, and faculty evaluation have always been considered too close to the heart of academe to be subjected to normal state accountability measures.[14] If institutions, systems, or statewide coordinating boards, in company with colleges and universities under their surveillance, do not keep their academic programs under periodic appraisal, external agencies will take over this function.

Three broad kinds of agency have been organized for statewide or systemwide planning and coordination: the advisory coordinating board, the regulatory coordinating board, and the consolidated governing board. Among the states, there are ten advisory coordinating boards, eighteen regulatory coordinating boards, twenty consolidated governing boards, and two executive planning agencies (see chap. 7).

Consolidated governing boards literally govern the institutions that they also plan and coordinate. Their identification as advocates for the institutions is pretty clear in most states with these consolidated boards. In contrast, regulatory coordinating boards, with which we are mainly concerned here, have a more ambivalent status, poised as they are between consolidated governing boards and state offices. John Millett, who once served as chancellor of the Ohio board of regents, a regulatory coordinating board, believes that such an agency is a part of state government and is "identified primarily with state government officials and processes," while the consolidated governing board is identified with state institutions of higher education.[15] Others believe that these boards should be "suspended at a strategic—and extremely sensitive—point between the institutions and sectors, on the one hand, and the public and its political representatives, on the other," and that "coordinating agencies have the responsibility for helping protect institutions (and sectors) from ill-advised

influences and incursions by the legislative and executive branches of
government and from unwise public pressures and the responsibility
of leading the system of higher education to serve demonstrable and
appropriate public needs—all the while retaining the confidence of
both sides."[16]

This view brings the nature of the regulatory coordinating board
closer to that of the consolidated governing board, although the latter
is in most cases more intimately identified with the institutions. The
primary function of regulatory coordinating boards is to plan the development of higher education in their states in cooperation with
institutions of postsecondary education and their basic constituencies. Then, according to Lyman Glenny, the board should provide a
thorough analysis and evaluation of systemwide or statewide academic programs in relation to long-range strategy. Proposed budgets
should be appraised in relation to educational priorities, differential institutional functions, and relevant allocation of financial resources.[17] Thus, boards may exert their influence and authority by
holding institutions or systems accountable for the effective performance of the functions for which they have accepted responsibility.
Dressel believes that coordination is here to stay and that it will continue to confront institutions of higher education with issues of autonomy and sometimes debatable requirements for accountability.[18]

The Federal Government

With increasing federal financial support and numerous federal laws
and regulations governing use of the funds, both public and private
educational institutions find themselves increasingly accountable to
agencies of the federal government. Total federal support in fiscal
1992 reached about $29 billion, awarded and controlled by a variety
of governmental bureaus. It was inevitable—and appropriate—that
higher education institutions should be held accountable for the way
in which they expend these funds. However, tension between universities and federal granting agencies has steadily increased as the
institutions are subjected to regulations and accounting procedures
they consider extensive, expensive, and inappropriate.

One of the major causes of strain between the federal government
and the universities is the failure of governmental agencies to recognize that, in the words of the report of the National Commission
on Research, "universities carry out teaching, research, and service

as an integrated whole, not as separate functions." [19] The commission went on to say that since teaching, research, and perhaps public service are closely related, accurate costs cannot be assessed for each of the related outcomes. Nevertheless, the commission recognized the necessity for accountability. The commission called for a joint effort by research universities and governmental bureaus to devise methods of accountability that recognize the peculiar characteristics of the academic enterprise.

An example of the federal government's demand for accountability is its regulation of DNA research. After an international group of 150 scientists met to discuss how DNA research should be conducted, the National Institutes of Health appointed a committee that promulgated regulations governing the safety of recombinant DNA research done with NIH funds. It was not long until a university faculty member experienced firsthand the new strictures of DNA investigation. A biosafety committee of the University of California, San Diego, forbade a faculty member in biology to conduct any further cloning experiments after he was charged with copying genetic material from a virus that had been banned from use in such investigations. The university's biosafety committee reported its action to the NIH, which said that it would form a committee to study the university's report and consider what action to take against the university or the professor. The NIH committee found the faculty member guilty of violating the federal guidelines.

It would be an exaggeration to say that research universities have become departments of federal and state governments, but it is not too much to say that they have become more directly accountable to governmental agencies in manifold ways and that it has become difficult to distinguish governmental intervention in university affairs from reasonable governmental requirements for accountability. It is clear, however, that recent issues and events have accelerated invasions of university autonomy. Senator Daniel Patrick Moynihan has warned that "universities must now expect a long, for practical purposes permanent, regimen of pressure from the federal government to pursue this or that national purpose, purposes often at variance with the interests or inclinations of the universities themselves." [20]

Although governmental intervention, regulation, and incipient control of certain activities may threaten public more than private institutions of higher education, the latter are increasingly held accountable by governmental agencies. Private research universities, like publicly supported ones, are accountable for the way they use federal grants. Furthermore, private institutions are required to comply with other federal regulations, such as those prohibiting discrimination in employment. The Carnegie Council on Policy Studies in Higher Education recommended that "financial aid to students should be the primary (though not necessarily the exclusive) vehicle for the channeling of state funds to private institutions." Some state governments, however, do make direct grants to private colleges and universities. An Illinois commission recommended that, as a means of avoiding government intervention in private higher institutions, direct state grants should be channeled to them in the form of contracts administered by the statewide coordinating board.[21]

Judicial Intervention

The increasingly intimate relationship between government and higher education means that colleges and universities are in and of the world, not removed and protected from it. Toward the end of the period of student disruption on college campuses it was observed that "judicial decisions and the presence on campus of the community police, the highway patrol, and the National Guard symbolize the fact that colleges and universities have increasingly lost the privilege of self-regulation to the external authority of the police and the courts. . . . It is apparent that colleges and universities have become increasingly accountable to the judicial system of the community, the state, and the national government."[22]

William Kaplin's book on higher education and the law summarizes legal conditions bearing on higher education institutions and gives numerous examples of court decisions involving trustees, administrators, faculty members, and students, as well as cases involving relationships between institutions and both state and federal governments.[23] Recourse to the courts to settle disputes has increased greatly during the past decade. Faculty members may sue over dismissal, appointment, tenure, and accessibility to personnel records. Students may sue to secure access to their records, over discrimination in admissions (e.g., the DeFunis case at the University of Washington and the Bakke case at the University of California in Davis), and over failure by an institution to deliver what it promised from the classroom and other academic resources. Institutions may take governments to court for the purpose of protecting their constitutional status and, as we illustrate above, in contention over the enforcement of federal regulations.

The traditional aloofness of the campus has been shattered. Kaplin pointed out that "higher education was often viewed as a unique enterprise, which could regulate itself through reliance on tradition and consensual agreement. It operated best by operating autonomously, and it thrived on the privacy which autonomy afforded."[24] The idea of the college or university as a sanctuary was once considered necessary to protect the institution and its constituencies from repressive external control and invasions upon intellectual freedom. Now, other means must be devised to protect an institution's essential spirit while it bows to the world of law and tribunal.

Accountability to Other External Actors

Accrediting Agencies

Accreditation is a process for holding postsecondary institutions accountable to voluntary agencies for meeting certain minimum educational standards. Recently, however, both federal and state governments have entered this arena, too.

Institutional and program accreditation are the two types usually noted. Six regional agencies are responsible for accrediting entire institutions' schools, departments, academic programs, and related activities. Program accreditation, extended by professional societies or other groups of specialists or vocational associations, is extended to a specific school, department, or academic program in such fields as medicine, law, social work, chemistry, engineering, and business administration. A variation is an agency for accrediting single-purpose institutions, such as trade and technical schools. These kinds of accrediting bodies are independent, voluntary agencies.

Two of the principal factors that have brought accreditation to the fore in discussions of accountability are the consumer movement and the allocation of state and federal aid to postsecondary education. Certain federal laws require the secretary of education to publish a list of nationally recognized agencies considered to be "reliable" evaluators of academic quality as a basis for distributing federal aid. An account of the federal government's attitude toward voluntary accrediting bodies notes that the head of the Division of Eligibility and Agency Evaluation of the U.S. Department of Education urged that federal oversight of accreditation should be strengthened: "Stressing the need for greater public accountability, he and his supporters say it is more important than ever for the government to know how its money is being spent, especially in light of some institutions' widely reported abuses in handling student-aid funds."[25] The recent self-closure of the Council on Postsecondary Accreditation leaves a vacuum, which a task force of the American Council on Education is trying to make recommendations to fill.

In the meantime, state governments have become parties to the debate, as they determine eligibility for state aid to both public and private postsecondary institutions. Most states charter and license degree-granting institutions, but some observers believe that in most instances the standards specified are insufficient to ensure quality. The Education Commission of the States has urged that the states establish minimum quality standards for all postsecondary institutions.

Students

It is apparent that educational institutions are increasingly to be held answerable for the attainment of their professed goals in the form of demonstrable changes in students. Howard Bowen declared that "the idea of accountability in higher education is quite simple. It means that colleges and universities are responsible for conducting their affairs so that the outcomes are worth the cost."[26] This view may be simple in conception, but it is extremely difficult in implementation. First, it is essential to translate goals into relevant outcomes. An even more complicated task is to devise means of determining the extent to which students have attained these outcomes. The first question to be asked is, How has the student changed at a given point in relation to this characteristic at entrance? This requires information on how students vary at the starting point not only in previous academic achievement but also in general and special academic aptitude; information on students' intellectual dispositions, such as a theoretical or pragmatic orientation; and information on students' interests, attitudes, values, and motivations, to mention only some of the dimensions relevant to the educational process. These attributes establish baselines for estimating the amount of change over stated periods, and some are indicative of students' educability.

Studies of the influence of institutions on student development also require means of measuring or describing college characteristics, "the prevailing atmosphere, the social and intellectual climate, the style of a campus," as well as "educational treatments."[27] One of the complications involved in describing college environments is that student characteristics and institutional qualities are by no means unrelated. Furthermore, most institutions are not all of a piece and the total environment may have less influence on particular students than the suborganizations or subcultures of which they are members.

It is even more difficult to determine the impact of the environment on students. First, environmental variables probably do not act singly but in combination. Second, changes that occur in students may not be attributable to the effect of the college environment itself. Developmental processes established early in the individual's experience may continue through the college years; some of these processes take place normally within a wide range of environmental conditions, and in order to alter the course and extent of development, it would be necessary to introduce fairly great changes in environmental stimulation. Third, changes that occur during the college years may be less the effect of college experience as such than of the general social environment in which the college exists and the students live.[28]

For these and many other reasons it is extremely difficult to relate changes in behavior to specific characteristics of the college or to particular patterns of educational activity. Studies of change in students' characteristics reveal wide differences from person to person and detectable differences from institution to institution. Bowen summarizes the evidence on change in students in both cognitive and noncognitive outcomes and also differences in the effects of different institutions: "On the whole, the evidence supports the hypothesis that the differences in impact are relatively small—when impact is defined as value added in the form of change in students during the college years."[29] Nevertheless, institutions are accountable for stimulating the development of students in ways that give evidence that colleges and universities have attained their professed goals in reasonable measure.

To date, the research on changes in students has been done mainly in undergraduate education. Fundamental studies on outcome also need to be made in professional and graduate education, as well as in research and public service. Bowen discussed at some length the social benefits that flow from professional training and the social outcomes from research and public service. He also emphasized the interaction of liberal and professional studies and the contribution of research and public service to education of various kinds and levels. Learning is an integrated process that may involve scholarship, investigation, and the relationship of knowledge to personal enrichment and social welfare. Although the definition and measurement of outcomes are especially difficult at higher educational levels, and the environmental forces involved are hard to determine, studies of student development in such fields as professional training, graduate education, and research should be pursued.

State Assessment Programs

Notwithstanding the complexity of the processes described above, a number of states have established policies seeking to assess student learning. The early pathbreakers were Florida, Virginia, New Jersey, and Ohio, followed by about ten other states with differing forms of program. In a very few states, mandated testing of undergraduates was required, some of them serving as a gateway to upper-division study. But in most states, policy makers were persuaded to place the responsibility for developing the assessment program on each public institution, allowing each one to develop a program appropriate to its particular role and mission. Only by allowing for such diversity is it likely that any institution will gain a sense of ownership of the process and be encouraged to use the results for self-improvement. In its 1986 report, *Time for Results,* the Task Force on College Quality of the National Governors' Association revealed an awareness of this problem, but it also made forceful recommendations about moving the process along more quickly.[30]

Educational Costs

Although "a tidy dollar comparison of costs and benefits is conspicuously absent," Bowen goes on to list the financial value of higher education.[31] First, the monetary returns from higher education alone are probably sufficient to offset all the costs. Second, the nonmonetary returns are several times as valuable as the monetary returns. And third, the total returns from higher education in all its aspects exceed the cost by several times.

It is usually said that institutions should be accountable for both effectiveness and efficiency, the latter having to do with the cost of the outcomes attained. But costs are extremely difficult to compute in analyzing differences in student change, both within and among institutions. And, as pointed out above, it is extremely difficult to relate changes to significant features of educational environments. Nevertheless, as enrollment in postsecondary education levels off or declines, institutions will be increasingly held accountable for the attainment of goals inherent in their assigned or professed missions. "Accountability accentuates results," wrote Mortimer. "It aims squarely at what comes out of an educational system rather than what goes into it." [32] Perhaps it would be more telling to say that accountability aims squarely at what comes out of an educational system in relation to what goes into it. The outcomes to be attained must be more explicitly defined and the means of determining accomplishment must be more expertly devised. Then resources must be distributed among institutions and among academic services in accordance with chosen educational values and defensible costs of their attainment. Bowen has made a significant contribution to the analysis of institutional costs, including expenditures per student, cost differences among institutions, and the implications of cost data for administrative policies and decisions. [33] But we have a long way to go before sound means of determining cost effectiveness are developed.

Conclusion

Although autonomy cannot be absolute, only a high degree of independence will permit colleges and universities to devise and choose effective academic means of realizing their professed goals. First of all, institutions must ensure academic freedom to faculty and students. Autonomy does not guarantee intellectual independence, but some forms of external intervention, overt or covert, may undermine such freedom.

While intellectual fetters must be opposed, institutions may legitimately be expected to be held accountable to their constituencies for the integrity of their operations and, as far as possible, for the efficiency of their operations. Colleges and universities are answerable to the general public, which supports them and needs their services. Responding to the public interest, federal and state governments are increasingly intervening in institutional affairs. At times, government pressure may induce an institution to offer appropriate services; at other times, government agencies may attempt to turn an institution, or even a system, in inappropriate directions. Only constructive consultation and requirements for accountability that recognize the fundamental characteristics of academe will effectively serve the public interest and give vitality to the educational enterprise.

Most institutions, including those supported by legislatures, are not immediately controlled by the general public. Public accountability is mediated by several layers of representation. Institutions are directly answerable to their governing boards. They may be responsible to a consolidated governing board. They may be first responsible to institutional or systemwide governing boards, and these in turn may be under the surveillance of statewide coordinating boards. Institutions thus may be controlled by a hierarchy of agencies, an arrangement that may complicate their procedures for accountability but that may provide a measure of protection from unwise or unnecessary external intervention.

Colleges and universities are moving into a period when they will be expected to provide not only data on the attainment of defined outcomes, including changes in students during undergraduate, graduate, and professional education, but also evidence that results have been gained at "reasonable" cost. Institutions of higher education will have to specify their aims, stand ready to justify activities by demonstrating their contribution to objectives, and defend the cost of the enterprise.

NOTES

This chapter is a revision of a previously published chapter by T. R. McConnell, now deceased. It is dedicated to his memory.

1. Howard R. Bowen, *Investment in Learning* (San Francisco: Jossey-Bass, 1977), 12.

2. Paul L. Dressel, ed., *The Autonomy of Public Colleges* (San Francisco: Jossey-Bass, 1980), 13

3. Eric Ashby discusses the relationship between academic freedom and

autonomy in *Universities: British, Indian, African* (Cambridge: Harvard University Press, 1976), chap. 10.

4. Dressel, *Autonomy of Public Colleges,* 5.

5. Ibid., 96.

6. National Commission on Research, *Accountability: Restoring the Quality of the Partnership* (Washington, D.C.: NCR, 1980), 17.

7. C. J. Hitch, "Remarks of the President," address delivered to the Assembly of the California Academic Senate, June 15, 1970.

8. Lyman A. Glenny and Thomas K. Dalglish, *Public Universities, State Agencies, and the Law: Constitutional Autonomy in Decline* (Berkeley: University of California, Center for Research and Development in Higher Education, 1973), 42.

9. Ibid., 143.

10. Burton R. Clark, "The Insulated Americans: Five Lessons from Abroad," *Change,* Nov. 1978.

11. John W. Lederle, "Governors and Higher Education," in *State Politics and Higher Education,* ed. Leonard E. Goodall (Dearborn: University of Michigan Press, 1976), 43–50.

12. Dressel, *Autonomy of Public Colleges,* 40.

13. Ibid., 43.

14. Robert O. Berdahl, "Legislative Program Evaluation," in *Increasing the Public Accountability of Higher Education,* ed. John K. Folger (San Francisco: Jossey-Bass, 1977), 35–65.

15. John D. Millett, "Statewide Coordinating Boards and Statewide Governing Boards," in *Evaluating Statewide Boards,* ed. Robert O. Berdahl (San Francisco: Jossey-Bass, 1975).

16. Kenneth P. Mortimer and T. R. McConnell, *Sharing Authority Effectively* (San Francisco: Jossey-Bass, 1978), 225.

17. Lyman A. Glenny, *State Budgeting for Higher Education: Interagency Conflict and Consensus* (Berkeley: University of California, Center for Research and Development in Higher Education, 1976), 148–50.

18. Dressel, *Autonomy of Public Colleges,* 99–100.

19. National Commission on Research, *Accountability,* 3.

20. Daniel Patrick Moynihan, "State vs. Academe," *Harpers,* Dec. 1980.

21. See Robert O. Berdahl, "The Politics of State Aid," in *Public Policy and Private Higher Education,* ed. David W. Breneman and Chester E. Finn Jr. (Washington, D.C.: Brookings, 1978); Carnegie Council on Policy Studies in Higher Education, *The States and Private Higher Education* (San Francisco: Jossey-Bass, 1977), 63; Commission to Study Nonpublic Higher Education in Illinois, *Strengthening Private Higher Education in Illinois: A Report on the State's Role* (Springfield: Board of Higher Education, 1969).

22. T. R. McConnell, "Accountability and Autonomy," *Journal of Higher Education* 42 (1971): 446–63.

23. William A. Kaplin, *The Law of Higher Education* (San Francisco: Jossey-Bass, 1983).

24. Ibid., 4.

25. *Chronicle of Higher Education,* June 16, 1980.

26. Howard R. Bowen, "The Products of Higher Education," in *Evaluating Institutions for Accountability,* ed. Howard R. Bowen (San Francisco: Jossey-Bass, 1974).

27. C. R. Pace, "When Students Judge Their College," *College Board Review* 58 (Spring 1960): 26–28.

28. McConnell, "Accountability and Autonomy."

29. Bowen, *Investment in Learning,* 257. Other evidence on changes in students over the college years is presented in Alexander W. Astin, *Four Critical Years* (San Francisco: Jossey-Bass, 1977); Patrick Terenzini and Ernest Pascarella, *How College Affects Students* (San Francisco: Jossey-Bass, 1991).

30. Task Force on College Quality, *Time for Results* (Washington,D.C.: National Governors Association, 1986).

31. Bowen, *Investment in Learning,* 447–48.

32. Kenneth P. Mortimer, *Accountability in Higher Education* (Washington, D.C.: American Association for Higher Education, 1972), 6.

33. Howard R. Bowen, *The Cost of Higher Education* (San Francisco: Jossey-Bass, 1980).

Chapter Four

Academic Freedom

Past, Present, and Future

Robert M. O'Neil

The subject of academic freedom has been a central theme throughout the history of American higher education. Within the academic community, there have been differing perspectives on some key issues— for example, whether academic freedom applies as fully to students as to professors and how far beyond or outside the classroom that freedom extends. This chapter explores the meaning and scope of academic freedom in three phases: its origins and historical development, its current status in the courts and in institutional policy, and some challenges that are certain to arise as academic expression and communication occur increasingly in cyberspace.

Academic Freedom's Legacy

The roots of the doctrine of academic freedom lie deep in the history of teaching and scholarly inquiry.[1] German universities long recognized the concept of *Lehrfreiheit,* or freedom to teach, with a corollary *Lernfreiheit,* or freedom of students to learn. Other countries recognized in different ways the distinctive status of university teachers and students. Yet in the United States, what is striking is the recency of any form of systematic protection of academic freedom. As late as the second decade of this century, some of our most eminent universities could discharge—or refuse to hire—professors because their views on economic or social issues were deemed radical or subversive. While many within the academic community found such actions abhorrent, and many governing boards took a more liberal view, the establishment of clear principles protecting outspoken and politically active professors occurred surprisingly late.

The formal origins of academic freedom in this country almost certainly lie in the issuance in 1915 of a "declaration of principles" by a committee of senior scholars convened by the fledgling American Association of University Professors (AAUP). The declaration, some twenty pages in length, canvassed a range of issues. Walter Metzger, the preeminent historian of academic freedom, described the declaration: "Utilitarian in temper and conviction, the theorists of 1915 did not view the expressional freedoms of academics as a bundle of abstract rights. They regarded them as corollaries of the contemporary public need for universities that would increase the sum of human knowledge and furnish experts for public service—new functions that had been added to the time-honored one of qualifying students for degrees."[2] The drafters of the declaration thus characterized the emerging university of their time as an "intellectual experiment station, where new ideas may germinate and where their fruit, though still distasteful to the community as a whole, may be allowed to ripen until finally, perchance, it may become part of the accepted intellectual food of this nation and the world."[3]

Such an institution must, the declaration insisted, be prepared to tolerate a wide range of views on controversial issues. It must also tolerate those members of its faculty who expressed such aberrant views. Institutions that sought to repress or silence such views simply did not deserve respect in the community of higher education. Thus, concluded the declaration, any university that lays restrictions on the intellectual freedom of its professors proclaims itself a proprietary institution and should be so described whenever it makes a general appeal for funds, and the public should be advised that the institution has no claim whatever to general support or regard.

The reception of these views was not entirely harmonious. The *New York Times*, in an editorial fairly representative of the more conservative press, scoffed at the newly declared principles: " 'Academic freedom,' that is, the inalienable right of every college instructor to make a fool of himself and his college by . . . intemperate, sensational prattle about every subject under heaven . . . and still keep on the payroll or be reft therefrom only by elaborate process, is cried to the winds by the organized dons."[4] The reference to "elaborate process" was not unfair. A major element of the declaration was the cornerstone of what was to become the concept of academic tenure; Metzger terms it "a new working plan, a series of concrete proposals concerning the acquisition and disposition of tenure citizenship that, when refined and broadly adopted, would represent a very great reform."[5]

Thus, by the time of the U.S. entry into World War I—an event that would create new strains in relations between professors and society—three vital elements were already in place. There was a rather elaborate and forceful declaration of the principles of academic freedom. There was the nucleus of a guarantee of tenure, in the form of procedures that should be followed in the event of demands for the removal of a professor. And there was an organization, created by and for university faculty, committed not only to disseminating the new principles but also to implementing and enforcing those principles by investigating egregious departures from them. In a remarkably short time, the roots of modern academic freedom had thus been put firmly in place.

The next major milestone in the evolution of academic freedom was a shorter statement, adopted in 1925 by a conference that the American Council on Education convened. The new version was immediately endorsed by the Association of American Colleges (AAC), which from that time has been a close partner of the AAUP in defining and seeking wider support for principles of academic freedom and tenure. This collaboration set the stage for a drafting process over the next decade and a half, culminating with the issuance in 1940 of what is essentially the current charter of academic freedom. A joint effort by the AAUP and the AAC, the 1940 "Statement of Principles on Academic Freedom and Tenure," has gained the endorsement of virtually every scholarly society, presidential organization, and learned organization—well over 150 signatories at that level—and of many hundreds of university administrations and governing boards.[6] A set of "interpretive comments" added in 1970, and the removal of gender-based language in 1990, have kept current a set of principles that have proved remarkably durable through dramatic changes in the academic environment.

The 1940 statement opens with a declaration, brief and deceptively simple, that college professors are entitled to academic freedom in three core dimensions: freedom in research and in the publication of the results; freedom in the classroom in discussing their subject and when they speak or write as citizens; and freedom from institutional censorship or discipline. Each freedom contains limits: with regard to research, the statement cautions that "research for pecuniary return should be based upon an understanding with the authorities of the institution." In the classroom, college teachers "should be careful not to introduce . . . controversial matter which has no relation to their subject." Teachers speaking as citizens "should at all times be accurate, should exercise appropriate restraint, should show respect for the opinions of others, and should make every effort to indicate that they are not speaking for the institution." The balance of the 1940 statement defines the elements of tenure, including the need for a clear statement of the terms and conditions of appointment, a finite probationary period during which the probationer enjoys academic freedom, and rigorous procedures for considering charges that might lead to dismissal for cause. The statement also envisions that tenured and continuing appointments might be terminated for "financial exigency," though only when such a condition is "demonstrably bona fide."

Of the 250 pages in the current issue of the AAUP's *Policy Documents and Reports* (styled the *Redbook,* and most recently reissued in 1995), the 1940 statement occupies but 7, even with interpretive comments. The bulk of the book consists of myriad documents dealing with procedures for dismissal or nonreappointment, a host of important faculty issues such as extramural utterances, artistic freedom, access to personnel files, and the status of part-time and non-tenure-track faculty. Other sections of the *Redbook* cover matters of professional ethics, research, discrimination, university government, collective bargaining, student rights and freedoms, accreditation, and collateral benefits. Hardly a year passes without either a new statement or a major revision of an existing one—most recently, for example, a much needed reconciliation of long-standing principles of free expression with newer concerns about sexual harassment in verbal forms.

An especially meaningful addition to the AAUP policy collection is the "Statement on the Relationship of Faculty Governance to Academic Freedom" adopted in 1994. This statement notes the link between faculty participation in the governance of a university and the condition of academic freedom. Central to that freedom is the right of a faculty, without fearing reprisal, to criticize the administration and the governing board on matters of concern. Thus the nexus between governance and academic freedom is vital, as this recent statement recognizes.

It is not only the endorsement of virtually all learned societies and so many universities that has made the 1940 statement a recognized source of academic common law. The U.S. Supreme Court in one major case, and lower federal and state courts in numerous instances, have cited the statement as a guide, template, or exemplar of academic freedom principles.[7] "Probably because it was formulated by both administrators and professors," observed a federal appeals court in a 1978 case, "all of the secondary authorities seem to agree [that the 1940 statement] is the 'most widely accepted academic definition of tenure.'" Another appeals court cited approvingly the AAUP policy on nonrenewal of continuing appointments, noting that "it strikes an appropriate balance between academic freedom and educational excellence on the one hand and individual rights to fair consideration on the other." Judges have also recurrently invoked the AAUP standards for determining financial exigency as a prelude to dismissal of tenured faculty. On most such issues, there simply are few if any other credible and widely accepted sources. Moreover, AAUP standards tend to come out of practical experience at the campus level and have often been revised in light of further experience in the field. Thus, it is hardly surprising to find such a degree of judicial reliance on these policies.

The practices and actions to which the standards are addressed have, of course, varied continually and dramatically over time. In the early years, the faculty at greatest risk tended to be economists and others in the social sciences who had spoken or written about social problems in ways that made business leaders acutely uncomfortable. Since those leaders played prominent roles as governing board members and in alumni and donor groups, their pejorative views about particular outspoken professors could not easily be discounted. The pressures they brought to bear led even so illustrious an institution as the University of Pennsylvania to discharge a nonrevolutionary Marxist (Scott Nearing) from the faculty of its Wharton School; Nearing was for the next several years unemployed in academia, until the University of Toledo hired him.[8] There were other egregious cases of outspoken critics of the early-twentieth-century social order who were either dismissed or not hired because of their publicly expressed views, even by the most prestigious universities.

Of course there were also many cases to the contrary; some universities fought to keep, and to protect, "radical" or "subversive" professors, even without the full force of academic freedom and tenure. The coming of World War I created another set of tensions; a small number of visible and vocal professors who opposed U.S. entry into the war became targets of legislative and alumni demands for their removal. Again, some institutions acceded while others stood firm. Harvard's example was notable. President A. Lawrence Lowell refused in 1916 to discipline a prominent professor for his pro-German statements, noting that a university that officially disapproved faculty views it disliked would quickly find attributed to it virtually all professorial utterances it did not officially condemn.[9]

The gravest challenge to academic freedom and tenure occurred during the McCarthy era of the early to mid-1950s. Many professors (as well as screenwriters, actors, and others) were summoned to hearings by federal and state antisubversive investigations. Often, there was no evidence that the target of inquiry had personally engaged in subversive activity, much less actually been a member of the Communist Party; rather, such a person might have befriended, or worked with, or simply met casually, one or more suspected Communists or front groups. Many summoned professors either declined to appear (fearing that their mere presence in the committee room would put them at risk) or appeared but refused to name names, expose friends or colleagues, describe political gatherings at which they had been present, or in other ways jeopardize long-standing relationships within the academic community.

Recalcitrance led in many cases to demands for reprisal. Few of even the strongest and most principled of institutions—their presidents and governing boards—were able to resist these pressures completely. The stakes were too high, the publicity too strident, the anti-Communist fervor too intense. The histories of Harvard, Michigan, and many other leading research universities include at least one incident of accommodation if not capitulation, with resulting grievous harm to academic careers. At other great institutions, like the University of California, the damage to academic careers resulted not so much from investigations as from mandated loyalty oaths. Faculty, even those of impeccable and demonstrable loyalty, were required to declare that they did not, and would not, belong to organizations that advocated the violent overthrow of the government. Such requirements caused many a conscientious professor to pause long before signing, and a few simply could not sign at all—not because they were disloyal but because they could not really know what they were being

asked to disclaim. By the late 1960s, these oath laws had been univer-
sally held in violation of the First Amendment.[10] They had, however,
taken their toll—forcing many people to sign against conscience and
a few to give up academic careers because they would not sign.

Since the McCarthy era purges followed by about a decade the
adoption of the 1940 statement, it is fair to ask whether academic
freedom and tenure failed their first critical test. The question is an
exceedingly difficult one, on which the judgment of history probably
cannot be reliably rendered for at least another generation. There
are at least two contrasting views. One holds that the academic community, being especially vulnerable and suspect, would have fared
far worse without such safeguards as existed. The evidence for this
more sanguine view rests in closed meetings between presidents and
trustees, at which guarantees of academic freedom and tenure were
quietly but successfully invoked to protect professors who otherwise
would have been wholly without recourse. The contrary view recounts
the undeniable carnage that Senator McCarthy and his minions in-
flicted. Skeptics would add that the record of the most secure institutions (at which, admittedly, the most controversial faculty tended to
teach) was often no better than that of the less secure places. These
critics also point to the somewhat equivocal role of the AAUP; this
was surely not its proudest moment, though judgments cannot fairly
be made based solely on the hindsight of those who did not experience
the devastating threats of those times. Suffice it to say that, while an
ideal system of safeguards would surely have afforded better protection, the damage would undoubtedly have been even worse but for
the principles and procedures that were in place during this perilous
time.

The end of the McCarthy era brought a period of relative calm
to the academic world. The 1960s launched a massive expansion of
higher education. With dramatic growth in faculties, intense competition for young scholars, and a marked lessening of repression, conditions improved. The tumult of the Vietnam War era brought some
institutional pressures on outspoken faculty, both for their publicly
expressed views on issues of the day and for such collateral actions as
reconstituting courses or turning regular class time over to teach-ins
about such issues as Vietnam, poverty, racism, and the environment.

The more recent history of academic freedom has brought one
other source of hope and promise. While those who teach in private
colleges and universities cannot claim (against their institutions) the

protection of the First Amendment, state university professors enjoy not only the speech rights of citizens but also a special solicitude that courts have recently shown for the academic setting. Starting with a 1950s case that barred a government demand for a teacher's lecture notes, through key loyalty oath cases in the next decade, and on to later judgments invalidating laws that endangered free expression in the campus setting, courts have repeatedly noted the centrality of academic freedom. Perhaps the strongest statement is that of Justice William Brennan in striking down New York state's loyalty oath in 1967:

> Academic freedom . . . is of transcendent value to all of us and not merely to the teachers concerned. That freedom is therefore a special concern of the First Amendment, which does not tolerate laws that cast a pall of orthodoxy over the classroom. . . . The classroom is peculiarly a marketplace of ideas. The Nation's future depends upon leaders trained through wide exposure to that robust exchange of ideas which discovers truth out of a multitude of tongues, [rather] than through any kind of authoritative selection.[11]

While there remain vital differences between court-defined free speech and collegially shaped principles of academic freedom, as William Van Alstyne noted in his review of their relationship, each has reinforced the other over the past half century.[12] Today, most major private universities, though they are not legally bound to adhere to First Amendment precepts, pride themselves on voluntary adherence to standards at least as rigorous as those by which their public counterparts are bound. The history of academic freedom, covering most of the twentieth century, reflects gradual, and at times checkered, progress toward enhanced security for professorial speech and activity. Along the way there have been (and continue to be) some truly chilling casualties. Yet that history suggests how much less well the American professoriate would have fared without some widely accepted principles and a commitment to due process for terminating or removing faculty appointments.

Academic Freedom Faces New Tests

University professors are no longer required to sign oaths or to demonstrate their loyalty in other ways. Rarely these days are lecture notes subpoenaed by legislative bodies seeking to prove that campuses are radical enclaves. Save for an occasional professor who may still become embroiled in a political controversy, most of today's academic freedom issues are subtler—if no less urgent for those whose careers may be at risk.

The emergence of sexual harassment as a campus concern illustrates the shift. Disparaging and insensitive remarks by male professors to and about female colleagues and students were surely prevalent a decade and more ago. Yet such transgressions went largely unredressed in the absence of harassment policies and procedures. Only within the past decade has the academic community given adequate attention to such practices. The implications both for gender equity and for academic freedom are profound.

A recent court case illustrates how different are the current challenges to academic freedom. Dean Cohen had for many years been a tenured English teacher at a California community college. He used a teaching style that he conceded to be "abrasive" and "confrontational." He also read excerpts in class from such sources as *Penthouse* and *Hustler* and occasionally used vulgarity, profanity, and sexual themes to "enliven" discussion. Many colleagues and students lauded his ability to reach and excite slower learners. But in 1993, one female student charged Cohen with sexual harassment. A campus committee agreed with the charges and ordered Cohen to "become sensitive to the needs of his students" and to "modify his teaching strategy when it becomes apparent that his techniques create a climate which impedes the students' ability to learn." Cohen went to federal court, claiming that such sanctions abridged his free speech and academic freedom. The trial judge disagreed, though recognizing that the college's harassment policy was not a model of clarity and might give a veto over course content and class discussion to "the most sensitive and easily offended students." The appeals court reversed that decision late in August 1996, finding in the sexual harassment policy a "legalistic ambush" because the terms were too vague to afford adequate guidance, especially to a professor whose classroom style had for many years "been considered pedagogically sound and within the bounds of teaching methodology permitted at the College." [13]

This is the first appellate judgment dealing with the growing tension between academic freedom and sexual harassment. The Cohen court did not say that use of vulgarity and profanity or sexual themes are necessarily within the scope of a professor's free speech; given the narrow basis for the decision in Cohen's favor, there was no occasion to address broader issues. Thus, determining the scope of free speech in regard to purely verbal harassment—and how far a professor may go in using sexually charged language—remains for another case and another day. The AAUP has, however, sought to reconcile its advocacy of academic freedom with its realization that sexual harassment not only exists but may be the least tolerable form of professorial expression. At its 1995 annual meeting, the association approved a policy that defines as forbidden harassment such relatively easily identified verbal abuses as offering a grade in exchange for sex or targeting and embarrassing an individual student with sexual insults or epithets. The policy also addresses the much harder case of nontargeted classroom speech of the kind the Cohen case raises. Before it may be punished as harassment, "speech . . . of a sexual nature . . . directed against another" must be shown to be "abusive" or "severely humiliating" or to "persist . . . despite objection," or alternatively, that it be "reasonably regarded as offensive and substantially impair the academic work opportunity" of students. This last option carries a vital corollary: "If [speech] takes place in the teaching context, it must also be persistent, pervasive, and not germane to the subject matter." [14]

Would such a policy help in cases like that of Professor Cohen (or the similar case of Professor Ron Silva at the University of New Hampshire a few years earlier)? [15] It almost certainly would help in two distinct ways. For one, such a policy would avoid the vagueness and lack of notice that so troubled the Cohen court. It would also enable institutions to distinguish between the merely salty teaching style and unacceptable classroom sexism. One example may suffice: if a professor begins every other class with a round of sexist jokes, the conditions of the AAUP policy would seem to be met. Assuming it offended some students enough to evoke a complaint, such material could be found to be "persistent, pervasive and not germane to the subject matter."

There is one other feature of the current landscape that such a policy addresses: the matter of process. Many institutions, including the two that have been to court, have adopted special and less formal procedures for handling sexual harassment cases. Where other serious charges of faculty misconduct (e.g., plagiarism) would require a peer panel of senior faculty, strict secrecy, and full due process, the separate harassment process often dispenses with such safeguards and entrusts the fate of a senior professor to a panel that includes nonfaculty members and that follows much more casual rules. Such procedures would not be accepted as the basis for any other charge that could lead to a professor's dismissal. The federal court that ruled in favor of Professor Silva, and ordered his reinstatement at the University of New Hampshire, faulted on many due process grounds the special and informal process for handling harassment cases. However different the sexual harassment area may be, and however compelling the case for informality and flexibility in the investigative process, the use of informal methods for trying such charges seems unacceptable. In the one case where the due process issue was central, that was precisely the ruling.

If sexual harassment has been the most painful academic freedom arena of the 1990s, several other catalysts have created major concern. Professors' expression and activity remain less free in certain kinds of institution, notably those with weak traditions of faculty governance and academic freedom, and at certain church-related institutions, where curbs on faculty speech not only serve theological needs but occasionally go well beyond theology in ways that find no acceptable secular counterpart. Yet, new and small and religious colleges have no monopoly on academic freedom violations; in recent years the AAUP's list of censured institutions has added, for example, New York University and the University of Southern California. Major institutions placed on censure (like the University of Florida and the University of California Regents some years ago) tend to be far quicker to work their way off the censure list—though the State University of New York remains on the list for untimely faculty terminations in the late 1970s.

The censure list increasingly involves procedural violations rather than (as in earlier times) direct reprisal for professorial views or activities. Yet hardly a year passes in which substantive academic freedom rights are not involved in at least one cause celebre—whether it be jarring public statements, letters critical of the administration or the governing board, or unorthodox research projects. And many of the cases that turn mainly on process have a substantive side as well; the person who has been inadequately charged or tried became a target of a deficient process in part because of speech-based concerns. Thus, even when the cases seem technical or legalistic, old-fashioned academic freedom concerns may lie not too far below the surface.

Termination of faculty appointments for financial reasons continues to invite AAUP scrutiny and, occasionally, litigation as well. Ironically, there is an acceptable way to downsize a university if financial pressures become acute; what AAUP policy requires (and accepts) is a faculty-involved process for bringing to the governing board a declaration of financial exigency, with accompanying safeguards for faculty whose appointments lapse, including a right of recall if the position reopens.[16] Some beleaguered institutions have done it the right way; several University of Wisconsin campuses in the 1970s, for example, provided a model of how to declare and apply financial exigency and how to protect the interests of affected faculty during and after the trauma of layoff. Yet others—most visibly, Bennington and St. Bonaventure in 1994—may have had financially adequate grounds for making major personnel changes but simply failed to follow the guidelines; they incurred censure not so much for what they did but for how they went about it. Similarly, an institution may effect a "bona fide elimination of a program or department" if the judgment is "based essentially upon educational considerations, as determined primarily by the faculty as a whole or an appropriate committee thereof."

Some institutions have targeted an unproductive unit for elimination but have either failed to develop the requisite "educational considerations" or have soon hired new faculty in closely related fields, suggesting something less than bona fides in the initial action. Once again, there is a right way to proceed, which supports the termination of tenured or continuing faculty appointments, and there are wrong ways, which risk censure even when an adequate basis for taking drastic action exists. The longest standing and most widely recognized basis for terminating a tenured appointment is, however, none of the above but, rather, the elusive concept of "cause." The AAUP has consistently declined to offer what many would find a convenient checklist of transgressions that constitute cause. Reports of investigations give limited, case-by-case insight into the prevailing view of cause, but there is no guideline or definition that encompasses it. Instead, the relevant AAUP recommendation says only that "adequate cause for a dismissal will be related, directly and substantially, to the fitness of faculty members in their professional capacities as teachers or researchers. Dismissal will not be used to restrain faculty members in their exercise of academic freedom or other rights of American citizens."

One other current issue of a rather different sort merits attention here: Does academic freedom require or depend upon tenure? Pros and cons have been vigorously debated in the 1990s, with several studies undertaken by the American Association for Higher Education and other groups. Tenure has been under attack in several states, notably through the creation of new, non-tenure-track campuses in Arizona and Florida and through legislative proposals in several states to eliminate or curtail tenure. In the summer of 1996, the Texas Senate Education Committee, for example, approved a proposal that would permit terminating the tenure of a professor who was rated poorly for two consecutive years. Such a policy would of course depart dramatically from the prevailing assumption that (absent program elimination or demonstrated financial exigency) cause must be shown and that substandard performance, whether for two years or ten, simply would never constitute cause for dismissal or loss of tenure. Yet Texas would be free to make such a change, at least prospectively, for new faculty. Indeed, the Permian Basin campus of the University of Texas opened in the 1970s without tenure, though by the late 1980s the board of regents gave faculty there the same protections that tenured and tenure-track faculty had at other UT campuses. Washington's Evergreen State College, long a rare example of a non-tenure-track institution, in the late summer of 1996 adopted a tenure system for the first time in its thirty-year history. Such actions suggest that, while alternatives to tenure do exist, their use has been limited and their acceptance modest.

The AAUP and other faculty groups do not claim that academic freedom can be protected only by formal tenure. There has never been any thought about imposing censure on the few administrations that never adopted tenure, notably Hampshire College in Massachusetts and (until recently) Evergreen State. As long as such colleges do not use the absence of tenure as a way to abridge academic freedom or due process, they are free to refuse to renew faculty appointments beyond the seven-year probationary period that is nearly universal for tenure-track campuses. Rather, the AAUP argument is that tenure not only is the best means of ensuring academic freedom but also has other virtues. Tenure provides continuity and stability of employment in a profession whose members often engage in long-term research, which could be seriously harmed by the prospect of nonrenewal. It also forces (toward the close of the probationary period) a critical choice about the performance and potential of younger faculty, a mandate that has no counterpart in alternative faculty personnel systems.

Yet even the strongest supporters of tenure would make three concessions. First, the current system is far from perfect. More rigorous review of tenured professors, for example, may improve the system, as long as it offers no subterfuge for biased or selective review. Even greater care in the granting of tenure is also appropriate. When faculty fall seriously short of expectations, to the detriment of students and colleagues, there may not be cause for dismissal, but some lesser sanction may be warranted on the basis of commensurate procedures. Second, alternative safeguards for academic freedom may exist and should be studied. The overwhelming adoption of, and adherence to, tenure by most baccalaureate and graduate institutions may reflect the paucity of known alternatives but surely does not close the book on the subject. Indeed, as one looks ahead to the status of academic freedom in the next century and beyond, one of the clearest impressions is that the quest for alternatives will be as vigorous as the defense of tenure systems and principles. Third, tenure has created (or at least buttressed) hierarchy within the academic profession. Undoubtedly, there have been abuses of the authority and influence that senior scholars enjoy. Junior colleagues, including some who are clearly eligible for tenure under the most rigorous standards, may have some ambivalence about a system that qualifies one facet of their academic freedom in the very process of obtaining fuller protection. To what extent these concerns are tied to tenure, rather than to seniority and hierarchy, remains a fair question.

The Future of Academic Freedom in the Electronic Age

As new technologies become a growing factor in campus communications, this seems a fitting time to ask whether freedom of speech and press apply to electronic messages.[17] The short answer is, Why not? Over the 205 years since the adoption of the Bill of Rights, the First Amendment's provisions have come to encompass motion pictures, radio, television, facsimile machines, and cable television and should thus be able to embrace the newest of technologies. But a better and more thoughtful answer is just beginning to emerge from the courts.[18] In the Communications Decency Act cases decided in 1996 by two three-judge federal courts, the analogy between digital and printed or spoken expression seems compelling. Comparable reasoning also produced a judgment striking down, on free speech grounds, certain provisions of the federal encryption laws. Those courts less ready to move the First Amendment into the electronic age seem to be a dwindling minority.

Indeed, there may even be a case now for greater protection. Certain time-tested exceptions to free speech in familiar forms may simply not apply to cyberspace or may apply differently. For a half century, free expression has contained an exception for "fighting words." Epithets, slurs, and insults shouted in someone's face—speech, to be sure—may be punished if they create a high risk of physical violence. Yet there simply is no electronic counterpart. By definition, protagonists at their keyboards cannot engage in fighting words. Not even the most intemperate and adversarial "flaming" creates the incendiary conditions that would justify an arrest to avert a street brawl. Much the same may be true for other exceptions to free speech, most notably the "clear and present danger" doctrine. While an electronic incitement is not beyond the realm of possibility, the risks of an imminent uprising seem far more remote when communication is by modem than by more personal and more proximate means. So when one applies the basic principles of free speech to cyberspace, the case for at least a comparable degree of liberty seems compelling.

Academic freedom is bound to be different in cyberspace. The sanctity of the classroom, and of the speech that occurs there, is at the core of academic freedom. If, however, an instructor creates a home page for a course, and if much class discussion between teacher and students takes place electronically, are the home page and the discussion groups simply an extension of the classroom, for academic freedom purposes? Further, it is widely accepted that professors must avoid any implication that they speak for their institutions when they do not. That injunction is clear enough when it affects writing to legislators or the local newspaper on university letterhead, but other issues of attribution may be raised by the electronic use of the university logo on a personal home page, for example, or the identification of e-mail addresses and points of origin. One other area of potential difficulty is the disparate treatment of on- and off-campus speech in traditional modes. In the print world, physical location may be crucial. In the virtual world, however, it may be meaningless. To such issues as these—the boundaries of the virtual classroom, restraint in extramural utterances, and the use of institutional symbols—others will surely be added as electronic communication in the academic world becomes more complex and creative.

There have already been several criminal charges against university professors for downloading child pornography in electronic form. Undoubtedly, existing institutional policies would recognize the universal illegality of such material, leaving only the question (not affected by the medium) of how directly such criminality bears on a professor's continuing fitness to teach. The same cannot be said, however, of sexually explicit material that may not even be legally obscene, much less child pornography. Even the most puritanical administration would be unlikely to move against a professor for bringing a personal copy of *Penthouse* or *Hustler* to the campus or for taking to his office the library's copy of the same magazine. Here, we seem to have somewhat different, media-shaped, views.

Carnegie-Mellon University (the nation's first fully wired campus) shocked the academic world by announcing late in 1994 that it would restrict access to the "alt.sex" internet newsgroups. After an initial outcry, the policy was modified; text materials would remain accessible, though sexually explicit graphics would be off limits, pending a committee's review. The administration's credible concern was that "local servers carrying newsgroups may make the University complicit in the provision of materials to the CMU community" and that, as part of a global network, "university servers provide feeders to other locations." The review body proposed that "in cases where the university has decided to carry a newsgroup that is illegal . . . carrying of this newsgroup on computer equipment owned and operated by the university is prohibited." The policy would also bar the university from carrying or retaining newsgroups under two other conditions: where "the stated purpose and content violate the law" (with specific reference to child pornography and copyright infringement) and where "the newsgroup consistently violates over a reasonable trial period legal canons, regardless of the stated purpose of the newsgroup." It remains unclear how effective any such restrictions would be in practice; an ingenious group of CMU students circumvented the ban by creating a "censorship page" that does not itself contain the proscribed material (thus avoiding the policy) but that provides links to pages beyond the reach of the ban.

The wonder is that so few other universities have followed Carnegie-Mellon's lead. Stanford briefly adopted a similar restriction early in the digital age but promptly rescinded it. Most campus computer center directors recognize the risks but either believe or have been advised that merely providing a passive conduit to suspect material is not likely to trigger criminal sanctions. They also tend to reject a premise advanced by Carnegie-Mellon's administration, that the target materials can be obtained through other channels. Such a response seems a bit like saying that if Carnegie-Mellon removes certain books from its library, faculty may still obtain them by inter-library loan from Pittsburgh, Duquesne, or Penn State. Given the rapidly growing importance to scholarship and inquiry of university-sponsored and -serviced computer networks, there should be a presumption that academic freedom protects unfettered access to all electronic material that does not violate criminal law.

Two other intriguing electronic issues deserve attention. Recently, the Simon Weisenthal Center urged U.S. universities to adopt policies to reduce the risk of further and wider dissemination of such anti-Semitic material as the diatribes of Canadian Ernst Zundl that had recently appeared on several students' campus-based home pages. Such a request comes from a private organization and thus carries no threat of sanctions. Yet there is an obvious risk that voluntary compliance (even if control were feasible) could replicate the Carnegie-Mellon problem. Surely, university libraries in this country would refuse requests that they limit circulation of *Mein Kampf* (as German libraries are required by law to do). Presumably, most computer center directors would follow a similar path with regard to digital hate material—however abhorrent—that might have any interest for members of the academic community. Academic freedom argues strongly for parity of policy across media.

The final issue—inevitable in the electronic age—is privacy of faculty e-mail. Professors certainly view their physical mail as private and inviolable, and most probably make similar assumptions about their e-mail. Yet, they are also increasingly aware that much of what they send and receive (and some of what they believe has been deleted) is retained for some time in university computer files, usually for benign reasons. Faculty also realize that external demands (such as subpoenas) or internal needs could arise that would sorely test the privacy of campus e-mail. Indeed, the first such case may already be on its way. Late in the fall of 1995, a University of California, Irvine, librarian found that some of her e-mail had been diverted to her supervisor during a prolonged medical leave. That disclosure revealed not only the physical and electronic capacity to make such a diversion but also the pending policy that would permit doing so under

certain conditions—such as a faculty member on extended leave—
when opening a physical mailbox or a desk or file drawer would not
be remotely acceptable. The proposed UC policy would empower campus officials to divert and access a faculty or staff member's e-mail
"as required by university legal and audit purposes and for legitimate university operational purposes." Such a provision is obviously
at variance with the safeguards that protect physical mail and that
arguably should apply to digital communications.

Privacy may not ever be complete. There are times when a university simply cannot avoid a subpoena or other demand for material
in its possession. In such a case, though, something more than un-
critical delivery would seem to be in order. A conscientious custodian
should, for example, afford any affected professor adequate notice and
time to take protective steps. When such a claimed need for access
arises internally, only the clearest exigency would seem to justify in-
vading digital privacy and, then, only after a full hearing at which the
strength of the asserted interest would be tested against countervail-
ing interests. In any event, such obvious differences as exist between
print and electronic mail and other files do not seem to warrant dis-
pensing with established safeguards and privacy protections.

Many other intriguing academic freedom issues await us in cyberspace. Students are far ahead of faculty in their use of digital communication and, not surprisingly, have already tested some of the limits.
The first major student case alerts us to some of the differences: when
University of Michigan undergraduate Jake Baker was arrested for
posting on the internet a work of sexually violent fiction (a tale of
torturing a female fellow student with a hot curling iron), he was at
first denied bail because the magistrate said he feared for the safety
of his twelve-year-old daughter. The university, in turn, suspended
him through a summary procedure normally reserved for persons
so potentially violent to themselves or others that a normal hearing
cannot be held. The contrast between print and electronic material
becomes starkest here: had such a story appeared in an underground
journal, there would have been concerns and possibly even a stern
word from a dean but hardly federal criminal charges or suspension
from the university.

Issues of academic freedom in cyberspace are just beginning to
reach the courts. Novel legal issues and disparate facts discourage
easy generalization. The early results have not yet yielded adequate

guidance to universities and their faculties. Additional time, and more cases, will undoubtedly shape new principles of academic freedom in cyberspace. As that process evolves, institutions may reasonably rely on precepts that have well served the world of higher education for nearly a century.

NOTES

1. See Walter Metzger, "The 1940 Statement of Principles on Academic Freedom and Tenure," in *Freedom and Tenure in the Academy,* ed. William W. Van Alstyne (Durham: Duke University Press, 1993).

2. Ibid., 13.

3. "General Report of the Committee on Academic Freedom and Academic Tenure," *AAUP Bulletin* 17 (1915): 1.

4. Quoted in "The Professors' Union," *School and Society* 175 (1916): 3.

5. Metzger, "The 1940 Statement," 9.

6. American Association of University Professors, *Policy Documents and Reports* (Washington, D.C.: AAUP, 1995), 3–10.

7. See *Tilton v. Richardson,* 403 U.S. 672, 681–2 (1971); *Jiminez v. Almodovar,* 650 F.2d 363, 369 (1st Cir. 1981); *Krotkoff v. Goucher College,* 585 F.2d 675, 679 (4th Cir. 1978); *Gray v. Board of Higher Education,* 692 F.2d 901, 907 (2d Cir. 1982); *Levitt v. Board of Trustees of Nebraska State Colleges,* 376 F. Supp. 945, 950 (D. Neb. 1974). See also Matthew W. Finkin, ed., *The Case for Tenure* (Ithaca: Cornell University Press, 1996); Ralph S. Brown Jr. and Matthew W. Finkin, "The Usefulness of AAUP Statements," *Educational Record* 59 (1978): 30–44.

8. See "Report of the Committee of Inquiry on the Case of Professor Scott Nearing of the University of Pennsylvania," *AAUP Bulletin* 127 (1916): 2.

9. Abbott Lawrence Lowell, "Annual Report to the Harvard Corporation, 1916–17," quoted in Henry Aaron Yeomans, *Abbott Lawrence Lowell, 1856–1943* (Cambridge: Harvard University Press, 1948), 311–12.

10. *Keyishian v. Board of Regents,* 385 U.S. 589 (1967).

11. Ibid., 603.

12. William W. Van Alstyne, "Academic Freedom and the First Amendment in the Supreme Court of the United States," in *Freedom and Tenure in the Academy,* ed. William W. Van Alstyne (Durham: Duke University Press, 1993).

13. *Cohen v. San Bernardino Valley College,* 92 F.3d 568 (9th Cir. 1996).

14. AAUP, *Policy Documents and Reports,* 171–73.

15. *Silva v. University of New Hampshire,* 888 F. Supp. 293 (D.N.H. 1994).

16. The following is from AAUP, *Policy Documents and Reports,* 23–26.

17. See Robert M. O'Neil, "Academic Freedom in Cyberspace," speech given at the President's Convocation on Academic Freedom, California State University, Apr. 1996.

18. See *ACLU v. Reno*, 929 F. Supp. 824 (E.D. Pa. 1996), cert. granted, U.S. Supreme Court, Dec. 6, 1996; *Bernstein v. U.S. Department of State*, 922 F. Supp. 1426 (N.D. Cal. 1996).

Chapter Five

Issues Facing Higher Education in the Twenty-first Century

Ami Zusman

Higher education in the United States is facing profound challenges as the twenty-first century approaches. Societal expectations and public resources for higher education are undergoing fundamental shifts. Changes both within and outside the academy are altering the nature and makeup of higher education—its students, faculty, governance, curriculum, functions, and its very place in society. As Clark Kerr and Marian Gade have noted, crisis and change in higher education "have been the rule, not the exception."[1] Nevertheless, current changes are transforming higher education to an extent perhaps greater than in the past half century.

This chapter focuses on major external influences on U.S. higher education and, conversely, on how institutional decisions in matters such as tuition or the conduct of research affect the broader society. The seven issues addressed cover a gamut of critical dependencies that will influence higher education in the next century; by necessity, of course, other significant changes are omitted from discussion, and still others have yet to emerge. A common thread runs through these issues: public challenges to the nature of colleges' and universities' "social contract." These challenges are apparent in ongoing conflicts between the ideals of equality and merit, the balance between teaching and research in the university, and the expectation that higher education serve as an engine for the nation's economic growth, among others.

The New Reality: Ongoing Fiscal Constraints

Shrinking Public Support

In the new reality of the twenty-first century, state and federal funding levels for higher education will almost certainly continue to be more constrained and unpredictable than they were as recently as the 1980s. Public institutions, which enroll nearly 80 percent of all students, will be particularly hard hit by state funding constraints, but federal support of public and private universities is at risk as well.

Private colleges will also continue to feel the effects of budget constraints, as a result of rising costs, market limits on the extent to which tuition can be increased, reduced corporate giving, cuts in allowable federal research overhead costs, and in some states, reduced state financial support for students in private colleges.

Declining State Funding

The U.S. economic recession of the early 1990s resulted in cuts to public higher education unequaled since at least World War II. In 1992/93, for the first time since record keeping began in the late 1950s, overall state appropriations were lower than they had been two years earlier, despite a 5 percent increase in public enrollments.[2] By the mid-1990s, state economies and state funding for higher education had rebounded in most states, rising 8 percent overall between 1993/94 and 1995/96.[3] Yet this apparent rebound is deceptive. If we control for inflation, total state appropriations in 1995/96 were 8 percent below appropriations a full five years earlier, as figure 5.1 shows, despite an increase in public enrollments of about 6 percent.

More important, long-term prospects for state higher education funding are not favorable. Higher education faces increasing competition for state funds from other state services, especially K–12 education, Medicaid, and prisons. Between 1988 and 1994, Massachusetts increased Medicaid funding by 103 percent and funding for adult corrections by 69 percent; by contrast, state funds for higher education dropped 12 percent.[4] Other states showed similar patterns. Over the next decade, growth in K–12 enrollments, increases in the prison population as a result of "three strikes" laws, and the health care needs of growing numbers of the elderly will all require large in-

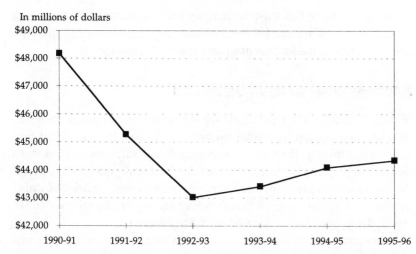

Figure 5.1 State Higher Education Appropriations, 1990/91 to 1995/96 (in constant 1996 dollars)

Source: Edward R. Hines and Gwen B. Pruyne, "State Higher Education Appropriations, 1992–93," *Grapevine* (Normal: Illinois State University, Center for Higher Education, 1992).

Note: Amounts are state funds used for higher education operating expenses in fifty states.

creases in state expenditures. Yet voters in a number of states have imposed tax constraints and spending limits on state and local expenditures. Higher education will remain vulnerable to state cuts or, at best, to funding below inflation levels, because it is one of the few large discretionary items in state budgets other than corrections.

Shrinking capital dollars (i.e., funding for building construction, maintenance, and repair) are often ignored in discussions of state budgets. Yet in some states, lack of funds to construct or renovate buildings for classrooms or research may be a bigger constraint on institutions' ability to accommodate enrollment growth, recruit faculty, and conduct research than are state appropriations for operating expenses. In California, because further expansion of state bonds (a common way to finance capital construction) could lower the state's credit rating, far fewer state dollars for capital projects at the state's public colleges are expected over the next decade than were available in the previous decade. Although many policy makers are looking to instructional technology to overcome space limitations, technology costs will likely be at least as high as traditional ways of delivering instruction in the near future; nor will computers and the internet supplant the needs for teaching and research laboratories.

Uncertain Federal Research Funding

Federal funding is critical to higher education in two areas: research funding and student financial support, both directly to students and indirectly, mainly through research assistantships associated with federal research grants and contracts. In fiscal year 1995, federal funds to universities for research and development (R&D) totaled nearly $16 billion (over 60% of university expenditures for R&D), while direct student aid totaled over $15.5 billion.[5]

Commitments by both Congress and the president to balance the federal budget by the year 2002 present a major threat to university research funding. Balancing the federal budget in an era when large tax increases are politically unsalable would require big cuts in discretionary programs, and most analysts believe that nondefense R&D funding would be a prime target of such cuts. For example, the American Association for the Advancement of Science projected in 1996 that, if the president's plans to balance the budget were implemented, the overall R&D budget for the National Science Foundation, a key source of university research funds, would decrease by 18 percent.[6] Such cuts would have a major impact on universities' ability to conduct research, especially in those fields subject to the greatest prospective cuts—the physical sciences, engineering, and the social and behavioral sciences. Continuing threats to eliminate the National Endowments for the Humanities and the Arts could wipe out what little federal funding now exists in these fields. Only the biomedical sciences seem relatively secure because of their strong political support. In turn, federal R&D cuts could have a major impact on graduate training by sharply reducing both research assistantships and research opportunities for graduate students.

Whether a balanced federal budget will actually be implemented in the next five or even ten years is unclear, since doing so would require large and perhaps politically unpalatable cuts. Moreover, as of fall 1996, support for basic research (the focus of most university research) remained strong. Nevertheless, given strong pressures to reduce, if not eliminate, the budget deficit without increasing taxes, threats to university research funding remain very real.[7]

Privatization

One consequence of the decline in state funding, already well under way, is the increasing privatization of public colleges and universities, as funding shifts from the state to student fees and to federal or corporate sources. At the nine-campus University of California, for example, state funds dropped from 37 percent in 1981/82 to 26 percent in 1996/97, with much lower percentages at some campuses. Nor are these declines just at research universities. In Virginia, the state percentage of the instructional budget for ten four-year colleges dropped from two-thirds in 1988 to under one-half four years later.[8] Although the declining proportion of state funding is due in part to public institutions' success in obtaining extramural funding, it is primarily due to the substitution of tuition and fee income in place of state support. In 1980, tuition and fees composed 13 percent of current-fund revenues of public higher education institutions; by 1993, they composed more than 18 percent. A number of states have imposed far higher tuition levels, especially for graduate or professional students.

These state funding reductions may reflect a profound shift in public attitudes toward the value of higher education. Two demographic trends deserve particular note: the aging of the general population and the declining proportion of white, middle-class students in the eighteen-to-twenty-four-year-old population. As a result, a smaller proportion of individuals with economic and political power may see itself as having a direct stake in higher education. When current public dissatisfaction with undergraduate education and decreased public trust resulting from perceived wasteful practices and highly publicized academic scandals are added to these long-term trends, the result is likely to be continued financial stress for U.S. colleges and universities.

Many public institutions are themselves pursuing privatization as a means to raise revenues. One such strategy is to require academic programs, especially high-demand, high-return professional programs like law or business, to be fully funded by clients (students) or business. At a number of institutions, including the Universities of Michigan, Virginia, and North Carolina, graduate and especially such professional programs as business and law have approached or reached self-supporting levels. Even teacher or school administrator training programs (which are not usually considered high return) have been privatized in some cases. Community colleges and other institutions are expanding contract education programs with specific businesses or industries. Both public and private universities also are adopting commercial technology transfer and other for-profit collaborations with industry. Still another strategy is the "outsourcing" of institutional functions to private vendors or other education institutions, including operation of residential dorms, employment training, and even academic functions such as remedial education and beginning language instruction. University hospitals are forming partnerships with both nonprofit and for-profit health organizations. Other institutions are planning shared-use facilities with private enterprise. These strategies raise several questions: On what basis will states or institutions determine that some programs warrant continued state support while others do not? How will such shifts affect access, diversity, faculty equity, and the curriculum? How can institutions ensure that outsourcing, especially of academic functions, does not undermine overall institutional coherence and accountability?

Institutional Retrenchment and Reallocation

During previous periods of fiscal constraints, most institutions under financial stress responded primarily by deferring maintenance and construction, freezing new hires, increasing tuition, and making across-the-board cuts. However, if budgetary constraints continue, higher education institutions may be forced to make long-term cuts to programs and faculty and to restructure programs and narrow institutional priorities. Some institutions have begun making more selective and more extensive cuts. Experiences to date and prospective future actions raise questions and concerns about the long-term impact of institutional retrenchment and reallocation. How will tuition increases affect access to higher education? How will retrenchment affect faculty, academic programs, and the educational system as a whole?

Impact on Students, Faculty, and Academic Programs

Unless sufficient financial aid is provided, low-income students and historically underrepresented ethnic groups may be excluded from institutions of higher education. Middle-class families are also finding it more difficult to pay for college, because college costs as a percentage of family income have risen to a twenty-year high. Will public

institutions cap or even reduce enrollments, despite growing enrollment demands, if they cannot raise tuition or other funds enough to
offset the declining proportion of state funding (as some did during
the early 1990s recession)?

To date, relatively few tenured faculty have been terminated. However, institutions have cut faculty in other ways: reducing new hires,
offering early retirement incentives, and terminating non-tenure-
track faculty. Conversely, many institutions have hired more part-
time, temporary faculty at lower salaries and benefits as well as full-
time faculty ineligible for tenure. About half of all college instructors
are now ineligible for tenure, including about 15 percent of full-time
faculty at four-year institutions. Thus, two contrary trends appear
to be occurring: the elimination of many temporary faculty and the
hiring (or rehiring) of other temporary faculty, often on a part-time
basis. Growing use of temporary faculty presents both advantages
and problems. On the one hand, it reduces institutions' costs and
increases their ability to respond to changing student demand. On
the other hand, it creates a two-tier academic labor force. According
to the American Association of University Professors, the increasing
reliance on part-time, temporary, and adjunct faculty threatens the
tenure system and may harm the quality of higher education.[9] Faculty cuts and reallocations may also affect the ethnic, gender, and age
distribution of faculty. Together with the termination of affirmative
action programs in California and (potentially) elsewhere, these cuts
may undermine efforts to create a more diverse faculty. The challenge to higher education is to ensure that faculty cuts do not reduce
quality or equity, the range of faculty perspectives, or institutions'
ability to respond to changing fields. Colleges and universities also
have a responsibility not to use a buyer's job market to take unfair
advantage of nontenured faculty.

The impact on academic programs to date remains largely un-
planned. In some cases, disproportionate numbers of faculty in certain fields have accepted early retirement, leaving an imbalance
between faculty expertise and institutional needs. In terminating
non-tenure-track faculty, institutions have indirectly made decisions
to reduce or eliminate programs such as remedial education, beginning language courses, and teacher education, which often depend
heavily upon non-tenure-track faculty. Repetitive across-the-board
cuts have gradually weakened once viable programs until they become obvious candidates for termination. As fiscal constraints con-

tinue, more public and private institutions are intentionally reducing, consolidating, or eliminating specific programs. By the mid-1990s, the board of regents for the University of Maryland system had approved plans to discontinue, suspend, or consolidate large numbers of bachelor's and master's degree programs and seven Ph.D. programs and to reallocate over $10 million in monies saved to areas defined as high priority. The Universities of Chicago, Pennsylvania, and Rochester, among others, had also begun phasing out academic programs, especially doctoral programs, in areas such as American civilization, anthropology, chemical engineering, education, and linguistics. State policy makers have at times been the driving force behind institutional restructuring. Statewide coordinating agencies in Ohio, Virginia, and Illinois, in response to pressures from governors or legislators, have encouraged or required institutions to eliminate scores of programs, especially doctoral programs, or to reduce graduate enrollments sharply.

Generally, the programs cut have been identified as academically weak, high cost, and duplicative and as having low market demand or as being less central to institutional mission or state need. Deciding what programs are low quality or less important, however, may be subjective. Based on faculty retrenchment cases in the 1980s, Sheila Slaughter suggested that departments serving primarily women or fields unable to tie themselves to market needs may be disproportionately cut.[10] In the late 1990s, humanities and social science programs may be at increasing risk, as more universities implement budget systems that require departments to generate income equal to their costs. By contrast, science and professional programs that can continue to attract extramural funding or charge high tuition will be more secure. As institutions cut academic offerings, they need to maintain program quality and balance and to protect programs and functions crucial to state and national interests. This will require several efforts: revising program review processes to address existing programs as well as new ones; reallocating scarce dollars to support important areas unlikely to be sustained by extramural dollars; finding ways to implement new initiatives to meet changing needs and new research directions, through intercampus collaboration, for example; and ensuring that students in programs being eliminated are given adequate resources or alternatives to complete their degrees.

Impact on Governance, Infrastructure, and the Educational System

Budget constraints may lead to greater centralization of authority. Some university presidents and trustees have argued that when budget cuts must be made quickly and require faculty and staff to cut their own programs, traditional participatory processes become difficult if not impossible. Slaughter concluded that retrenchment "generally undermined faculty participation in governance and faculty authority over the direction of the curriculum." [11] Conversely, Donald Kennedy, former president of Stanford University, has argued that an overreliance on consensus has resulted in the reservation of final decisions to the top level. [12] Without faculty and staff agreement, major program reductions and reallocations will likely lead to resistance, lower morale, and ultimately lower productivity.

Building construction, maintenance, and repair have been among the areas most hard hit by budget constraints. According to a survey by the National Association of State Universities and Land-Grant Colleges, 79 percent of member institutions had deferred building repair or rehabilitation in 1996. [13] Ultimately, these repairs will cost more than if maintenance and replacement had been made on schedule. As noted above, failure to construct or renovate buildings and laboratories may impair institutions' ability to enroll new students or conduct research.

If tuition at public institutions continues to rise, higher education could see enrollment shifts from public to private higher education, as well as from four-year to less expensive two-year institutions. In fact, there have been some small shifts in these directions in the last few years. However, enrollment shifts to public two-year colleges assume both that two-year colleges will have the resources to enroll more students and that students can afford their rising fees. If insufficient resources force institutions and students to make choices, nontraditional students, including returning adults and those whose initial preparation precludes admission at other institutions, may well be shut out of traditionally open-door community colleges.

A more subtle impact is the adoption of the language and values of business: downsizing (i.e., workforce reduction), the growing use of temporary employees, privatization, and commercialization. These changes threaten traditional academic values. Their proponents, however, argue that institutions must give marketplace approaches more emphasis, in order to meet "fundamental changes—in the goods and services the public seeks; in the nature and needs of students; in faculty work and ambitions."[14] Finally, the gloomy picture presented by ongoing budget constraints is not without its positive side. Budget cuts are forcing many institutions to reexamine their missions and priorities; this assessment may lead to more coherent institutional missions and a reinvigorated sense of purpose and academic community.

Who Will Attend Institutions of Higher Education?

U.S. college enrollments have nearly doubled over the past twenty-five years, to over 14 million students in 1994. As we approach the twenty-first century, however, shifting demographic, political, and economic forces are challenging past assumptions about who will—and even who should—enroll in our colleges and universities.

A Changing Student Pool

Students in U.S. colleges and universities today are very different from those of even twenty years ago.[15] Nearly one-quarter of all college students are ethnic minorities, up from about 15 percent in the mid-1970s. Latino and Asian enrollments nearly doubled between the mid-1980s and the mid-1990s. More than one-third of the traditional college-age population and 60 percent of recent high school graduates are enrolled in college (table 5.1). In addition, a larger proportion of college students are women, part-time, and older students. In 1993, students aged twenty-five years and older composed 44 percent of total college enrollments and 22 percent of full-time enrollments, primarily because of the large numbers of baby boomers (now thirty to fifty years old) in the U.S. population.

Despite the growth in numbers, African American, Latino, Native American, and low-income students remain significantly underrepresented in higher education. Many Latinos are eliminated from the college pool even before high school graduation; nearly one-third drop out before completing high school, although some proportion of these are immigrants who were never enrolled in U.S. schools. By contrast, although the proportion of African Americans completing high school increased significantly over the past twenty years, only half

Table 5.1

High School Completion and Participation in Higher Education, by Race and Ethnicity (%)

Year	African American	Latino	White	Total[a]
	High school drop-out rates of 16–24-year-olds			
1974	21.2	33.0	11.9	14.3
1984	15.5	29.8	11.0	13.1
1994	12.6	30.0	7.7	10.5
	College enrollment rates of recent high school graduates[b]			
1976	41.9	52.6	48.9	48.8
1984	40.2	44.3	57.9	55.2
1994	50.9	48.9	63.6	61.9
	College enrollment rates of 18–24-year-olds			
1974	17.6	18.0	25.8	24.6
1984	20.3	17.9	28.9	27.1
1994	27.7	18.8	38.1	34.6

Source: National Center for Education Statistics, *Digest of Education Statistics, 1995* (Washington, D.C.: U.S. Department of Education), tables 101, 177, 180.

a. Includes Asian, Native American, and other population groups.

b. Rates are for individuals aged 16 to 24 who graduated from high school during the preceding 12 months. Data for African Americans and Latinos, which was first collected for 1976, are subject to relatively large sampling errors, due to small sample size. Latinos are also included in figures for African Americans and whites.

of these graduates enter college, compared to nearly two-thirds of white high school graduates. Underrepresented students who do attend college enroll disproportionately in two-year colleges. Consequently, an even smaller proportion receive bachelor's or higher degrees. In 1993/94, African Americans received only 7 percent of all bachelor's degrees, and Latinos received only 4 percent. Low-income students of all ethnic backgrounds are especially underrepresented. Young adults from families in the bottom income bracket are eight times less likely than others in their age group to complete a bachelor's degree.[16]

The twenty-first century will bring continued change in the student pool. Over the next decade, most states will see increases in their traditional college-age populations, as many in the baby boom "echo" generation reach adulthood. Some states (notably large Sunbelt states like Florida, California, and Texas) will see large increases in these populations. Because of the baby boomers, older students will remain a significant part of college enrollments as well. There will also be further shifts in the ethnic composition of the college-age population, with students of color comprising over one-third of this population nationally. Shifts will be dramatic in some states, especially the growth of Latino populations in the Southwest and Asian populations in the West. By the year 2004, for example, California projects that Latino students will compose 49 percent of public K–12 enrollments and Asian/Pacific Islander students another 12 percent. In 1996, 16 percent of California's public high school students were identified as limited-English-proficient. Despite major immigration policy changes, many future students will likely have limited English proficiency.[17]

These changes have important implications for higher education and especially for access. First, growth in the college-age pool will increase demand for higher education. Public institutions will face pressures to enroll more students with less funding and to shift admission priorities—to reduce the number of graduate students and deny admission to students needing remedial assistance, for example. Many private institutions and some public ones will have a seller's market, allowing them to become more selective. More institutions may leverage financial aid funds by directing more of their limited dollars to well-off, tuition-paying students. Second, at a time when a larger proportion of the pool will be composed of historically underserved groups, it will be more difficult than in the past for them to enroll. This will be especially true if affirmative action programs are eliminated. Unless higher education cooperates with schools and communities to increase these students' college participation, U.S. society will lose the talents of a growing segment of the population. Moreover, without countersteps, relatively few such students will attend four-year colleges and universities. Third, the increasingly diverse student body will continue to change the face of the campus. Colleges will need to develop ways to respond effectively to these students, especially low-income, first-generation African American and Latino students, who drop out of college at higher rates than do middle-class white students. This may mean more support for English as a second language, as more non-native-English speakers enter college. It will also require college climates and curricula that welcome students' differing backgrounds and perspectives as opportunities to enlarge the range of voices and experiences and to build upon students' diverse language and cultural backgrounds in preparing them for a more interdependent global society.

Changing Public Expectations

The growing demand for higher education will collide with other forces limiting enrollment: budgetary demands on government to meet other social needs, increased public readiness to consider higher education a private good, and consequent reduction in public funding. Since 1980, student fees have increased significantly, especially at public institutions. During the same period, federal financial aid has undergone two major changes: it has shifted overwhelmingly toward loans, rising from about half to about three-quarters of all federal aid, and aid eligibility has been expanded to include more middle-class students. Low-income students are most affected by these changes because they are less willing to incur large amounts of debt to finance college, and federal programs have not increased enough to cover the expanded pool.

The backlash against affirmative action has occurred in this context of scarce resources. Under affirmative action programs, institutions admitted students using criteria that supplemented standardized academic measures with criteria that recognized both previous discrimination or disadvantage and the special value that women and students of color (along with musicians, athletes, and others with diverse backgrounds and talents) could bring to the campus. In California, Texas, Maryland, and other states, college affirmative action programs, which by and large have long had broad support, have been terminated by the electorate, the courts, or university governing boards, and they are being challenged elsewhere. As a result, the numbers of underrepresented students could drop sharply, especially in highly selective institutions. For example, an analysis by the University of California, Berkeley, estimates that underrepresented groups could drop from 23 percent of the freshman class to 12.5 percent or less, as a result of the 1995 decision by the university's governing board to eliminate affirmative action in admissions and other areas. Moreover, the backlash against affirmative action has radically changed the debate over equity and access. While supporters see affirmative action as a means to "level the playing field" and enhance valued diversity, critics portray it as creating new inequities and giving access to unqualified individuals. In turn, the latter view is creating a more hostile campus climate for minorities, which could discourage some from even applying to many colleges and universities. In this new environment, how colleges identify ways to maintain and increase access by all segments of the population will be a critical test.

Public views of who should be admitted to college are changing in other ways as well. Over the past decade, high school students of all ethnic backgrounds completed substantially more college preparatory and advanced courses than in previous generations, as states raised graduation and college admission requirements in response to national and state reports on K–12 education. Having achieved higher levels of academic preparation, however, students may find themselves shut out of four-year colleges, if these institutions reduce enrollments or raise admission standards further.

As powerful as the anti-affirmative action backlash appears to be in altering past consensus on access and equity, reduced public funding and changing public expectations pose even more serious threats to higher education participation. If policy makers and higher education leaders, in effect, change the rules just when a new generation of students—less white, less middle class—is prepared to enter college, questions are raised about equity in a democratic society as well as about risks to social stability. Reducing access to higher education also raises concerns about meeting society's economic and civic needs at a time of increasing technological, economic, social, and political complexity and interdependence. Slowing or even reversing the country's historic movement toward universal access to higher education is especially problematic because it is being driven largely by state and institutional decisions made on financial grounds, rather than by explicit policy decisions on higher education access and participation. Both policy makers and institutional leaders have a responsibility to address the long-term implications of their responses to budget constraints.

School/College Interdependence

The changing student pool, new demands on both K–12 and higher education, and ongoing concerns about the fit between high school and college education have led schools and colleges to a growing recognition of their interdependence and their shared responsibility for student success. Colleges and universities have a direct stake in the quality of K-12 education because they depend on the public schools to provide the academic preparation that students entering college need to succeed. For higher education to flourish also requires effective public education for all students, because education contributes to the economic health and social stability of the larger society. Even if it were not in higher education's self-interest to do so, state policy makers are demanding that colleges play a larger role in strengthening K-12 education—through teacher preparation and professional development, curricular support, programs to recruit and better prepare underrepresented students, and other areas.

Preparation and Reform in K-12 Education

Many critics argue that the schools too often do not prepare students well for college. Ten years after the 1983 publication of *A Nation at Risk,* the report that mobilized national efforts to reform K-12 education, former secretary of education Terrel Bell concluded that those ten years had been "a splendid misery for American education." [18] Scholastic Assessment Tests (SAT I) scores for college-bound high school seniors are lower today than they were in the early 1970s, and the gap between white students' performance and that of African American and Latino students remains significant. Nearly 30 percent of college freshmen take remedial courses in mathematics, reading, or writing, and even the most elite institutions spend substantial resources to offer them.[19]

Yet the past decade has also seen substantial overall improvements in K-12 education and achievement. SAT mathematics scores are the highest they have been in nearly twenty-five years, and verbal scores have remained relatively stable since the late 1970s, even though larger numbers of students in the bottom 60 percent of their classes are taking the SAT. High school graduates are also completing more mathematics, science, English, and history courses than did earlier graduates. The belief that previous generations of entering college freshmen were better prepared than current students may be more myth than fact.[20]

Serious problems still do exist in K-12 education, and overall improvements mask great disparities among students. Large numbers of public school students have limited proficiency in English and live below the poverty line, conditions that correlate with low academic achievement. Over 20 percent of children in the United States live in poverty, with double these rates for African American and Latino children. Unless current trends are reversed, these percentages are expected to increase, especially in large industrialized states. The disparities between rich and poor extend to school districts as well. Unless school financing is reformed, low-income students in poor school districts will continue to receive much lower quality education, by almost every measurable indicator, than that provided middle-class and upper-class students in wealthier districts—what Jonathan Kozol has characterized as "savage inequalities" in how the United States supports its school children.[21]

While colleges and universities continue to focus on K–12 students' SAT scores and high school courses, they have been slow to recognize the implications for higher education of K–12 reforms under way in curricula, instructional methods, and assessment. California and other states are developing statewide K–12 curriculum frameworks designed to promote interdisciplinary curriculum, activity-based instruction, and collaborative learning. State K–12 leaders are also engaged in developing assessments based in part on student performance and portfolios. These reforms may conflict with higher education's traditional admissions requirements, undergraduate content, instructional approaches, and assessment practices. These developments raise several questions: How can higher education institutions work with their high school colleagues to ensure appropriate articulation between high school and college requirements and curricula? What role should college faculty play in helping to develop state and national curriculum content and standards? How should changes in K–12 education affect teacher preparation? Finally, what lessons do K–12 initiatives provide for higher education's own efforts to reconceive undergraduate education to include more emphasis on collaborative learning, interdisciplinary curricula, and alternative approaches to student assessment?

School/College Collaboration

School/college partnerships have been one response to schools and colleges' growing recognition of their interdependence. Over the past decade, collaborations across institutions have blossomed, in programs ranging from student achievement initiatives and faculty alliances to development of new curriculum, articulation of vocational education, and schoolwide reforms. State policy makers have often played important roles in promoting collaboration through financial incentives, mandated programs, and threats to reduce funding if institutions fail to work together. Because many legislators see collaboration as a way to save money by reducing redundant programs, they will likely encourage more collaboration in the future.[22]

School/college partnerships are also changing. First, new collaborations are more likely to be real partnerships that recognize the needs, strengths, and shared values of both sides. Although most university educators still consider schools as the partner that needs to change, there is growing recognition within higher education that colleges, too, must change—for example, by revising admissions criteria to address reformed K–12 curricula and assessments. Second, school/college partnerships have become more comprehensive. Initially, most partnerships involved programs to assist individual elementary and secondary students or teachers. While these still predominate, more and more collaborations involve multiple elements of the school system—students, teachers, curriculum, and administration. Third, a growing number of collaborations involve statewide and even national collaborations. The National Writing Project, for example, has created a system of more than 150 project sites across the United States that promote sustained, peer-oriented, professional development for teachers and an ongoing professional network. Such large-scale collaborations not only have the resources to facilitate change at the local level but can help create a coherent vision of teaching and learning across the state or nationally and across education levels. Finally, school/college partnerships have begun to include organizations outside education, such as business, social service agencies, and minority community organizations, in an effort to develop a comprehensive, integrated system for children's services. These more comprehensive partnerships recognize that sustained, significant improvements in student learning are likely only by integrating health, nutrition, and other factors that affect children and by incorporating the resources that other organizations can provide.

School/college partnerships present several challenges. For partnerships to succeed, sustained university participation and leadership are essential. New initiatives need time for participants to learn how to implement change effectively, adjust to new structures and procedures, and develop commitment and trust, especially between partners from different organizations, before change can be institutionalized. Especially in the early years of a new initiative, colleges and universities can offer unique resources to help conceive, develop, and implement educational reforms. Several barriers to school/college partnerships must also be overcome. Chief among these are the differences in cultures, perceptions, and priorities between schools and colleges and the lack of institutional rewards for participation in collaborations. Higher education can encourage faculty participation in K–12 activities through such means as funding for collaborative research on schooling issues and faculty promotion criteria that better recognize faculty research and service to the schools.[23]

Challenges to the Teaching/Research Balance

Undergraduate education is under intense scrutiny from both within and outside the academy. Battles over the content of the curriculum, governmental regulations for assessing student learning, and changing technologies, among others, are challenging the nature of undergraduate education. This section discusses a central issue within higher education: the continuing conflict over the balance between undergraduate education, on the one hand, and research and graduate education, on the other.

Over the past twenty-five years, faculty involvement in undergraduate teaching has diminished, as universities and colleges have sought to strengthen their research and graduate education missions. According to several studies, faculty members teach fewer undergraduate courses than they did twenty-five to thirty years ago, temporary part-time instructors and graduate teaching assistants meet a larger part of the teaching load, and institutions have largely delegated advising, mentoring, and tutoring responsibilities to student services staff. These shifts have been prompted by changing incentives. Faculty tenure and promotion decisions, especially at universities but increasingly at four-year colleges as well, have come to depend much more heavily on research excellence and publications than on teaching. In science and technology fields, research universities' growing reliance on federal research dollars has led them to provide additional incentives, including reduced teaching loads, to faculty who can generate these funds. As a result, large disparities in faculty teaching responsibilities have developed both between and within institutions. According to William Massy and Andrea Wilger, faculty and institutional norms are caught in an "academic ratchet," in which research norms gradually rise while expected teaching loads decline.[24]

While state policy makers have expressed dissatisfaction for many years with what they see as the neglect of undergraduate teaching, current budgetary constraints have increased their readiness to intervene. At a time when undergraduates are paying more tuition but are receiving more of their education from temporary faculty or teaching assistants, political authorities and other stakeholders, especially tuition-paying students and parents, are pressuring institutions to make undergraduate education and teaching their top priority. In many states, policy makers have initiated reviews of higher education's functions and priorities.

Faculty teaching workloads have become a prime target of these reviews, prompted in part by budget constraints. As James Mingle noted, because faculty salaries are the largest single expenditure in state higher education budgets, "the costs of faculty stand out as a target of opportunity" for budget cutting.[25] By 1995, twenty-three states had mandated some kind of action regarding faculty workloads. In most states, these mandates simply required institutions to report on their faculty workload policies and practices, but ten states imposed more substantive requirements. In Ohio, for instance, the legislature mandated that the board of regents increase undergraduate teaching by 10 percent.[26] Although few states have yet done so, political authorities are becoming more willing to mandate minimum faculty course loads, an action that previously would have been considered an inappropriate political intrusion into institutional authority over academic matters. More often, the threat of budget cuts or legislative intervention has prompted public institutions to adopt revised teaching policies and practices on their own. At private institutions, rising tuition and enrollment competition have had a similar impact in encouraging many to give more emphasis to undergraduate teaching.

The challenge to higher education institutions from these trends is twofold. First, institutions need to reassess their priorities, rather than allowing either outside actors or institutional drift to determine them, and to adopt approaches to support undergraduate teaching appropriate to their missions. In particular, faculty reward structures will need to recognize scholarship in teaching more adequately.

Ernest Boyer's call for expanding the definition of scholarship to include not only discovery but also integration, application, and teaching has stimulated much discussion. Others have argued that departments should be held responsible for teaching by allocating resources based on departmental teaching participation and excellence.[27] Institutions are implementing a range of policies to encourage undergraduate teaching or to increase teaching productivity. These include developing departmental workload policies to ensure fair and reasonable teaching loads, eliminating low-enrollment courses and programs, and providing financial rewards for demonstrated teaching excellence.

Second, institutions need to persuade policy makers and the public not only that they are now doing a better job of teaching undergraduates than is frequently perceived but that research, graduate education, and public service functions are important as well. Institutions will need to demonstrate more clearly how faculty research activities not only infuse the content of undergraduate courses but also contribute to students' understanding about how to acquire knowledge. To do this, institutions will need to identify the criteria and measures by which they believe they should be evaluated and to shift the discussion from how much faculty teach to how well students are learning. Indeed, nearly half of all states already require public institutions to establish student assessment programs.[28] Here too, however, colleges and universities will need to press for appropriate criteria.

The Changing Nature of University Science

In the past twenty years, universities have both witnessed and initiated significant changes in the nature of scientific research.[29] These include the development of fields and techniques not even imagined twenty years ago; growing university/industry collaboration in the commercial marketing of research discoveries; an increase in the proportion of federal research funding targeted toward specific projects; greater political involvement in funding denials in politically charged areas; and a movement toward "big science" projects involving hundreds of researchers and billions of dollars. The question is, Will these trends continue over the next ten to twenty years, and if so, how will they impact universities?

University/Industry Collaboration

During the 1980s, industry funding for university R&D in science and engineering grew much more rapidly than any other funding source, nearly doubling as a percentage of total university research dollars, from 4 to 7 percent. While this is a small percentage of total dollars, industry support plays a much larger role in certain fields, such as civil engineering and biotechnology. In addition, large numbers of faculty receive at least some industry support; in engineering, for example, 79 percent of university faculty receive industry funding. If federal research funding is cut back, researchers may seek industrial sponsorship much more aggressively.

University/industry partnerships, in which both parties are actually involved in research activities, have grown dramatically over the past decade. This trend reflects an increasing permeability of boundaries between the two sectors, as universities engage in more commercial marketing and as more new Ph.D.s take jobs in industry but maintain ties with their former faculty advisers. One indicator of this is the growth in the number of university-based research centers with close ties to industry, which increased nearly two and one-half times between 1980 and 1990.[30] Federal and state agencies have further stimulated these partnerships by linking research funding to industry participation; as a result, even public funding takes on characteristics of industry sponsorship.

University/industry collaboration can provide additional sources of support for university research, access to a broader range of talent, and more rapid development and transfer of useful products like vaccines. However, it also presents potential problems, including hindering the flow of research information, because industrial sponsors often require researchers to delay release of potentially marketable results.

Commercialization

A still more problematic trend is the growing involvement of university researchers and of universities themselves in the commercial marketing of scientific and technological discoveries. During the 1980s, leading university researchers established or became associated with for-profit biotechnology and other high-technology companies based on their federally funded university research, a development that prompted Congress to enact conflict-of-interest regulations. Nevertheless, this trend has continued during the 1990s.[31] Moreover, many universities have encouraged spin-off companies based on faculty research and have established for-profit technology transfer units, designed to speed the flow of scientific discoveries and products to the private sector and bring dollars into the institution. Universities have moved aggressively to secure commercial patents as well as to negotiate royalty and licensing arrangements with private companies. Between 1984 and 1994, the number of patents awarded to academic institutions tripled.

Although these initiatives have sometimes run into strong faculty opposition, they are likely to grow, especially during a period of cutbacks in state and federal funding, because they promise universities increased revenues. But they also pose threats, among them the possibility that they will create conflicts of interest for individuals and institutions, restrict the flow of information, increase the university's fragmentation into entrepreneurial fiefdoms, and shift power to nonacademic personnel, who typically control for-profit enterprises within the university. Commercialization may further shift research priorities toward more marketable areas in science and technology fields and distort traditional academic missions.[32]

"Big Science"

The past two decades have seen a growing emphasis on megascience: long-term, multi-billion-dollar research projects that involve hundreds and even thousands of researchers across disciplinary fields and multiple locations and even across countries. The human genome project, the global change research program, and the defunct superconducting supercollider are examples. Because of their vast scale, most have been funded by the U.S. government.[33]

These projects have generated great controversy within the scientific community. Large, long-term projects offer great promise for facilitating scientific breakthroughs that individual investigators could not accomplish, achieving national missions that integrate science and application and providing economies of scale. Some argue they provide better training for graduate students because they offer more opportunities for interaction with other researchers not only in the same field but also in emerging interdisciplinary fields. On the other hand, large-scale collaborations provide fewer opportunities for individuals to design their own experiments, to see an experiment through to completion, or to pursue an unorthodox direction. As a result, they risk alienating creative young scientists and discouraging scientific experimentation that does not conform to existing paradigms. Because such collaborations often result in papers with dozens of coauthors listed alphabetically, they make it difficult either to evaluate faculty members' research contributions, for determining promotions, or to hold particular individuals responsible for research findings.[34] Some observers also argue that big-science grants may divert funding from individual research, resulting in greater competition and smaller grants to individual researchers.

In sum, these changes in the nature of scientific research provide opportunities for universities to develop new revenue streams and to serve economic and other public needs more effectively, but they also pose threats to university missions, priorities, academic integrity, and faculty control. The challenge for research universities, and for government and private funders of university research, will be to address more fully the public's legitimate needs, while implementing policies and decisions to maintain university support for core academic areas; to develop clear accountability mechanisms to prevent conflicts of interests or submitting to external pressures; and to take a more active role in informing and shaping public discussion about national priorities.

The Uncertain Job Market for Ph.D.s

Projecting labor market needs for new Ph.D.s has perhaps never been more difficult than it is in the current fluid economic, political, and demographic environment. There is growing debate over whether U.S. universities are training more Ph.D.s than the labor market can absorb. Policy makers assert that we are overproducing Ph.D.s at the expense of undergraduate access. Young scientists struggling to find permanent employment argue passionately for Ph.D. "birth control" (i.e., reductions in Ph.D. enrollments). Other scholars argue that the demand for Ph.D.s in many fields remains strong and that employment needs by the time new Ph.D. students complete their degrees in six to ten years could be far different.

Past Projections and Current Realities

As recently as the early 1990s, labor market analysts predicted critical shortages of higher education faculty and other Ph.D.-trained scientists and engineers after 1997, if not earlier. Expected high retirement rates among faculty and scientists, rising enrollments, and cold war–related and health-related needs for scientists and engineers, coupled with projected slow or no growth in the number of new Ph.D.s were expected to lead to serious shortfalls.[35]

By the mid-1990s, it became clear that these shortfalls were not materializing. Ongoing state funding constraints have meant that public colleges have hired fewer faculty than expected, despite early retirement programs at a number of institutions. The end of the cold war brought about the downsizing of the defense industry, which had employed many doctoral scientists and engineers. Other reductions in private sector R&D and in business and government employment have further reduced demand. At the same time, partly in response to earlier shortfall projections, doctoral production, which had been expected to remain level, increased more than 30 percent between 1984 and 1994—more than twice the growth in four-year college enrollments.

As a result, by the mid-1990s, the job market for new Ph.D.s was worse than it had been in two decades, as figure 5.2 shows. This was true not only for Ph.D.s in the humanities and social sciences, many of whom have long faced lengthy job searches after graduating, but for new engineering and physical science Ph.D.s as well. Moreover, more than half of all physical scientists and nearly two-thirds of life scientists now seek postdoctoral study positions after graduating, rather than immediate employment, and the number of years they spend in postdoctoral positions appears to be lengthening. While the rise in "postdocs" reflects a dramatic change in expectations about how scientists are prepared, it is also a response to the weaker job market.[36]

Most Ph.D.s, in both science and nonscience fields, eventually find jobs. However, a recent study of science, social science, and engineering Ph.D.s (known as the COSEPUP study) concluded that "in some fields the process is taking much longer than it did for their predecessors," and surveys by a number of professional associations have reached similar conclusions.[37] Part-time, out-of-field, or tempo-

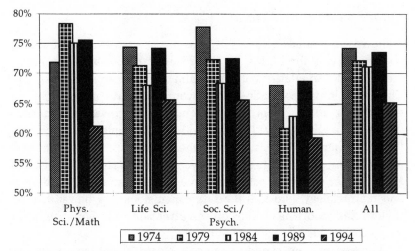

Figure 5.2 Job Placement Rates of New Ph.D. Recipients, Selected Fields
Source: Derived from National Research Council, "Surveys of Earned Doctorates," in *Summary Report: Doctoral Recipients from United States Universities* (Washington, D.C.: National Academy Press, 1974–94).
Note: Numbers exclude those planning postdoctoral study.

rary employment among recent Ph.D.s has also been rising across many disciplines. In the humanities, 14 percent of recent (1988–92) Ph.D.s were involuntarily working part-time or outside their field, and 11 percent were in temporary positions.[38] There are also questions whether the high proportion of new science Ph.D.s now in postdoctoral positions will in fact secure permanent, full-time jobs appropriate to their training.

The types of job that doctoral recipients are taking have undergone major changes in recent years as well. Most U.S. science and engineering Ph.D.s and nearly half of all social science Ph.D.s no longer work in four-year colleges or universities, the traditional employer of Ph.D.s. Rather, by 1991, business and industry had become the largest single employment sector for both engineering and physical science Ph.D.s. Even in the humanities, only two-thirds of all employed Ph.D.s worked in four-year colleges or universities, compared to 74 percent in 1985.[39] As the COSEPUP study concluded, "Ph.D.s are increasingly finding employment outside universities and more and more are in types of positions that they had not expected to occupy."[40]

Future Supply and Demand

Some recent studies give highly pessimistic assessments of the job market outlook for Ph.D.s. In a 1995 draft report based on econometric model simulations of supply and demand, William Massy and Charles Goldman concluded that, given conditions prevailing in the early 1990s, about 22 percent of science and engineering doctorates in the United States could fail to find suitable employment—ranging from a 44 percent labor surplus in mechanical engineering to no or negligible surpluses in chemistry, psychology, and computer science.[41] Many higher education scholars argue that the study's assumptions and methodology, and therefore its conclusions, are flawed. Nevertheless, the report has received wide attention from both the media and policy makers.[42]

However, present conditions may not hold. Some factors suggest that demand for Ph.D.s could rise over the next decade. For example, the traditional college-age population will increase slightly in the next ten to fifteen years, which could require colleges to hire more faculty to meet enrollment demand. Since nearly half of all full-time faculty were aged fifty or older as of 1992, colleges will also need to hire new faculty to replace retirees.[43] In the nonacademic sector, expanding industries in biotechnology, microelectronics, health care, and other fields could generate demand for more Ph.D.-trained professionals, and these fields will have replacement needs, too.

Yet it is unclear whether these factors will lead to a significantly better Ph.D. job market in the near future. Even if enrollments increase and many faculty retire, colleges and universities may not hire new faculty in the numbers once expected. Rather, in the face of public funding constraints and limits on tuition increases, institutions may raise the student/faculty ratio, rely more heavily on instructional technology, or hire more temporary and part-time faculty at lower salary levels. All of these responses appear to be happening now.[44] In addition, if college access and affordability decline as the proportion of the college-age population from poor families and underrepresented minority groups increases, college participation rates could drop. In the nonacademic labor market, prospects remain uncertain as well, given the downsizing in military-related industries and private sector R&D. Finally, if Ph.D.s now in postdoctoral or other temporary positions are drawn into the permanent labor market, if older faculty stay on beyond traditional retirement age, or if there is an influx of immigrant scientists and engineers, there will be fewer openings for new doctorates.

On the supply side, if fewer Ph.D.s are prepared, those who do pursue doctoral training should find a better job market. Since graduate enrollments in public universities depend on state policy makers' willingness to fund expensive doctoral training at current levels, such state support is not assured. Prospective cuts in federal research funds that support graduate research assistantships could also affect applications and admissions, especially in the sciences. And word of poor job prospects may dissuade individuals from pursuing graduate studies. In the 1970s, Richard Freeman concluded that a boom and bust cycle exists in the academic labor market: when Ph.D. jobs appear plentiful, growing numbers of individuals apply to graduate programs, but fewer apply when jobs are in short supply.[45] The problem is that a lag exists between job market needs and Ph.D. production, so job shortages are inevitably followed by surpluses, and surpluses by shortages. Moreover, universities and departments respond differently to these patterns. Some departments, especially in the sciences, have reduced their graduate admissions because they could not provide students full financial support, but other departments have dug more deeply into their applicant pools or increased foreign admits in order to maintain enrollments.[46]

The Impact on Graduate Education and Graduate Students

The uncertain job market outlook for Ph.D.s, combined with competing demands for scarce public dollars, has prompted widespread demands for changes in graduate training, ranging from a radical restructuring of the doctoral curriculum to sizable reductions in doctoral programs and enrollments. A number of different "solutions" have been proposed, including the following:

—*Broaden the Ph.D. curriculum to prepare students for alternative careers.* The COSEPUP report recommends that universities prepare Ph.D.s for nonacademic (as well as academic) careers, in applied R&D positions in industry as well as in areas such as K–12 teaching or science writing.[47] However, Ph.D. training is a long and expensive route toward K–12 teaching or science writing, and it is unclear if faculty would admit students with such career goals or if they would be able to provide such preparation. How many additional openings there will be in industrial R&D, let alone in the underfunded K–12 system or in science writing, is also uncertain.

—*Shift the graduate balance toward master's programs.* Others urge that we reinvent the master's degree in the sciences so that it serves as a gateway to science careers rather than as a consolation prize for failed Ph.D.s. Professionally oriented master's programs, these advocates argue, hold the most promise.[48]

—*Impose academic "birth control."* A more radical solution is zero population growth in doctoral enrollments and, in fields with an oversupply of Ph.D.s, a moratorium on admissions, at least until the reserve pool of unemployed or underemployed Ph.D.s is significantly reduced. Critics, both within and outside of higher education, argue that unrestrained growth of doctoral enrollments and programs has been a major cause of the Ph.D. surplus and that Ph.D. enrollments are driven less by workforce needs than by internal university interests and pressures—for graduate students to teach introductory undergraduate courses and help faculty do their research, to attract top faculty eager to work with talented professionals-in-training, and to raise institutions' standing in prestige rankings.[49] Foreign students, who now compose more than 40 percent of new engineering Ph.D.s and more than 25 percent of Ph.D.s in physical sciences and business, are a particular target of those who would reduce graduate enrollments, because they are seen as artificially propping up graduate enrollments and worsening the job market for U.S. citizens.

—*Eliminate weaker Ph.D. programs.* Many favor this solution—for universities other than their own. Few institutions voluntarily close doctoral programs. Still, in the face of budgetary constraints, some universities are cutting weaker programs on their own campuses, and some state agencies have forced the termination of doctoral programs judged weak or duplicative.

—*Retain the current system, which has served the United States well.* Other scholars urge caution. Unemployment rates among Ph.D.s remain low. Moreover, students entering doctoral programs now will graduate in six to ten years, when employment needs may be far different. If market difficulties are temporary and we turn away promising individuals, the ability of academia, industry, and government to conduct essential teaching, research, and other services could be impaired. These scholars urge that students should be better advised about current and prospective market conditions, to the extent they are known, but argue that externally mandated cuts are undesirable.

—*Restructure demand.* Finally, many in the research community argue that higher education and its allies must not only identify new roles that Ph.D.s can and should play to enhance society but must make a strong public case for the value of Ph.D.-trained professionals in contributing to national goals.

What then should be done? The costs—to individuals, higher education, and society—will be high if we significantly misjudge labor and societal needs in either direction. Universities and faculty members must take a more proactive role in advising prospective doctoral students about job prospects, encouraging and preparing students for careers both within and outside of academia, and helping them find jobs. But this is not enough. Given what appear to be permanent federal and state funding realignments, educators need to undertake a fundamental reassessment of the size, quality, and effectiveness of individual programs and the Ph.D. enterprise. This should include asking questions such as the following: How should we measure quality and effectiveness in doctoral programs? Should programs with high attrition or low placement rates be either strengthened or eliminated? What are the implications for admissions, curriculum, and faculty promotion of the recommendations to broaden doctoral training or to shift some doctoral enrollments into master's programs?

Revisiting the Social Contract: Accountability, Governance, and Leadership

Institutional Autonomy and Accountability

All of the trends discussed above have profound implications for the relationship between higher education, the public, and governmental authorities. As state budgets have become more constrained and student tuition fees have increased, for example, governors and legislators have become more interested in controlling institutional costs by regulating such core academic matters as faculty workloads and aca-

demic programs. At the federal level, government officials have begun
using student financial aid dollars to regulate institutional actions in
admissions and other areas, under the aegis of accountability. The
growing power of advocacy groups and the use of the political process
by higher education institutions have led to research funding targeted
more on specific projects and to pressures for earmarked funding that
bypasses peer review. At both state and federal levels, demands for
institutional accountability will almost certainly continue. The kinds
of accountability that institutions must meet are changing as well.
Policy makers are demanding that institutions not only demonstrate
fiscal responsibility but also achieve explicit governmental goals, including increased productivity, minimum faculty contact hours, and
specified student outcomes.

Although the federal government will continue to have a major
impact on higher education, especially through research funding and
student financial aid, state governments will remain the dominant
players in higher education in the foreseeable future because public
institutions enroll nearly 80 percent of all college students. Ironically,
this is so even though the proportion of public institutions' budgets
that is state funded is declining, because states continue to fund most
of public colleges' basic operating costs, including faculty and staff
salaries. In addition, states retain extensive regulatory authority over
most public institutions, ranging from authority over institutional
missions and degrees to regulation of purchasing procedures.

State governors and legislators have been actively involved in
higher education in recent years.[50] This seems to be true even when
(some argue, because) there are strong statewide coordinating or governing boards for higher education. Governors and legislators have
been key catalysts for reform initiatives in a number of states, implementing major program review, resource reallocation, and restructuring plans. Legislatures have enacted requirements for assessment
of student learning, faculty workload studies, and requirements for
English-language competence for teaching assistants. Most important, governors and legislators have used the budgetary process directly to compel or indirectly to induce institutions to pursue desired
actions. Higher education will remain a target for state control in the
coming years because it is one of the few discretionary items in the
state budget. In addition, legislative term limits, now in place in more
than twenty states, put pressure on legislators to make their mark
quickly, before many of them develop in-depth expertise; and new
legislators often bring with them inexperienced staff.

Nevertheless, the threat of governmental intervention into core academic affairs should not be overstated. To date, most states' demands for evidence of student learning, increased faculty workload, and institutional performance on state-determined criteria have left much discretion to institutions to determine appropriate responses. Moreover, higher education institutions, especially universities with strong alumni support, alternative revenue sources, and complex, loosely coupled structures, have considerable ability to adopt strategies to help retain institutional autonomy.[51] Of course, when institutions adopt actions desired by policy makers under threat of regulatory or budgetary action, it is difficult to say whether or not political authorities are wielding inappropriate influence. Three points should be noted here. First, governmental regulation and centralization of decision making in higher education tend to wax and wane over time in response to budgetary crisis, salience of higher education vis-à-vis other social needs, and particular incidents or situations.[52] Second, each of the fifty states will follow its own path based on its particular conditions and history. Some states may grant institutions greater autonomy in return for greater institutional privatization, as Maryland and Oregon recently did for selected institutions. Third, institutional autonomy and public accountability need not be in conflict, if accountability is broadly and appropriately defined.[53] Given higher education's important role in U.S. society, there are legitimate public demands for institutional accountability. The challenge for higher education is a long-standing one: to respond forthrightly to public needs while establishing with political authorities appropriate expectations for institutional accountability and autonomy.

Changing Structures and Governance

The past thirty years have seen a revolutionary transformation in the governance of higher education, from single-campuses to large, complex, and heterogeneous multicampus systems.[54] Nearly three-fourths of all students enrolled in U.S. public higher education institutions are at campuses that are part of a multicampus system (i.e., two or more campuses with a single, systemwide governing board and a central administration).[55] These students are enrolled in about 120 systems, numbering more than 1,000 campuses. By contrast, in 1968, barely half of public college students were enrolled in multicampus systems, which then had about 550 campuses. Although the functions and powers of these systems vary substantially, systemwide governing boards and administrations have the potential for exercising broad leverage over their campuses through budget and program review powers. Systems may act as buffers against political intervention or as channels for it. On the one hand, system boards and administrations may reduce campus autonomy and flexibility if they impose inappropriately standardized priorities or expectations. Systems also increase bureaucratization and make shared governance more difficult to achieve. On the other hand, systemwide leaders can bring to bear broader perspectives on the overall needs of the campuses and the state. System leadership (boards, administrators, and faculties) may be especially important in matters that have relatively weak campus constituencies but are important to the system or to the state, such as undergraduate general education or improved K–12 education. Moreover, when a system office does not exercise adequate quality control, other actors, such as the state's executive branch, may step into the vacuum.[56]

Statewide boards or commissions for higher education (both governing boards for public systems and coordinating agencies with more limited powers but often broader scope) have become key higher education players in many states. In the late 1980s and the first half of the 1990s, nearly half of all states made some change in their statewide governance or coordination of higher education.[57] Some states, such as Maryland, gave statewide boards greater authority. But other states weakened or even eliminated statewide coordination, most notably New Jersey, where the governor abolished the once powerful coordinating board and replaced it with a much weaker agency. Although in many cases these reorganizations sought to use structural changes to solve what were fundamentally budgetary, not governance, problems, nevertheless large-scale structural changes make a difference. James Hearn and Carolyn Griswold found that, independent of other social, educational, and economic factors, states with relatively centralized higher education structures (whether governing boards or strong coordinating boards) were more likely to adopt certain academic policy changes, such as mandatory student assessment, than were states with more decentralized structures.[58]

Will states implement additional structural and governance changes in the next decade? If they do, the individual state context will largely determine whether these changes result in more centralization or more decentralization (or in a mix of centralization and decentralization at different levels). Change itself has costs, however. Structural reorganizations disrupt settled processes and relationships and create greater uncertainty, as new players establish their authority, priorities, and rules of interaction.

Nevertheless, both system-level and statewide higher education leadership will have critical roles in the twenty-first century. Systemwide leadership may be needed to address issues of student access during extended periods of budgetary constraints, and systemwide decisions, involving the key parties at all levels, may be needed to affirm or to revise individual campus missions. During retrenchment periods, this may mean greater specialization among campuses as well as greater focus on intercampus programs. Both multicampus and statewide leadership will be important in ensuring that higher education as a whole maintains an appropriate balance and range of programs and flexibility to respond to new needs.

On the campuses, too, there will be conflicting pressures for greater centralization, as a means to make tough budget decisions, and for decentralization of departments and task groups, as a means to center accountability in the units directly responsible for instruction and research. Responsibility-centered management, which rewards entrepreneurship and priority setting, is creating new approaches to, and new questions about, priorities, governance, and administrative functions. Its impacts on departments that typically have not had the slack that comes with large amounts of external funding, as well as on institutions as a whole, remain uncertain. The possibility of further faculty unionization is yet another unknown.

Leadership

During the difficult period that lies ahead, higher education will need greater leadership at all levels: administrative, faculty, trustee, student, and public. Yet the exercise of effective leadership may become more difficult, especially at public universities. According to a study for the National Association of State Universities and Land-Grant Colleges (NASULGC), the average tenure of presidents of member universities declined from 4.6 years in 1980 to 3.2 years in 1992. By comparison, the overall average tenure for higher education presidents remained relatively stable, at about 7 years, over the previous eight-year period, according to a study for the Association of Governing Boards of Colleges and Universities. William Davis, who collected the NASULGC data, speculates that the high turnover rates

for NASULGC presidents, who represent many of the country's public research universities, reflects the intense public scrutiny and increasingly politicized governing boards under which they work.[59]

Faculty leadership in determining academic priorities and ensuring academic control over the conduct of research will also be greatly
needed. Yet it, too, may be more difficult to obtain. Clark Kerr concluded that over the past decades faculty loyalties have shifted away
from the institutions in which they work and toward their research
and professional associations.[60] Faculty members not only are teaching less but have become less willing to serve on institutional committees, less willing to protect the institution from political disruption,
and less careful to avoid exploiting the institution's name or facilities for economic gain. This decline in "academic citizenship" has
serious implications for shared governance of universities and colleges. Finally, in the face of difficult budgetary decisions, public policy
makers will need to exercise leadership in support of higher education, to ensure that the social and economic benefits and quality of
higher education in the United States are not eroded.

Revisiting the Social Contract

The twenty-first century will bring new and continuing challenges
to U.S. society, among them economic constraints and organizational
restructuring, further demographic shifts, increasing technological
complexity, potential threats to the nation's social fabric, the recon-
figuring of nations, and changes in international economic and power
relationships. In this environment, higher education will not be able
to ignore demands that it help society meet these changes through
developing a highly skilled workforce, mediating social mobility, and
advancing research, development, and service directed toward economic and social considerations. At the same time, it will face increasing competition from other claimants for public support and will be
called upon to be more accountable, and in new ways, for the funding it receives. In short, policy makers, as well as students, parents,
and the private sector, are demanding changes in the social contract
between higher education and its constituencies. The challenge for
colleges and universities will be to take the initiative in determining
their priorities (including deciding what they cannot do during an era
of constraints), assessing the outcomes of their goals and programs,
and strengthening their contributions to larger societal needs. The

challenge for policy makers will be to provide institutions with sufficient support, autonomy, and flexibility to accomplish critical social and economic needs, including such long-range needs as basic research and the maintenance of colleges and universities as centers of academic thought and quality.

NOTES

1. Clark Kerr and Marian L. Gade, "Current and Emerging Issues Facing American Higher Education," in *Higher Education in American Society,* ed. Philip G. Altbach and Robert O. Berdahl (Buffalo: Prometheus, 1987), 129.

2. Edward R. Hines and Gwen B. Pruyne, "State Higher Education Appropriations, 1992–93," *Grapevine* (Illinois State University, Center for Higher Education, 1992).

3. Edward R. Hines and Gwen B. Pruyne, "State Higher Education Appropriations, 1990–91 through 1995–96," World Wide Web, http://coe.ilstu.edu/grapevine.

4. Bruce A. Wallin, "Massachusetts: Downsizing State Government," in *The Fiscal Crisis of the States: Lessons for the Future,* ed. Steven D. Gold (Washington, D.C.: Georgetown University Press, 1995).

5. National Center for Education Statistics, *Digest of Education Statistics, 1995* (Washington, D.C.: U.S. Department of Education, 1995), table 353, 1995 estimates. Research funds include federal obligations for R&D centers administered by colleges and universities.

6. Testimony of Albert H. Teich, director of science and policy programs, American Association for the Advancement of Science, before the House Science Committee, July 23, 1996.

7. Further cuts in federal reimbursement rates for research overhead costs also remain a concern. Recent cuts have already affected the research enterprise, especially at private universities, where rates had been high.

8. Office of the President, *1997–98 Budget for Current Operations* (Oakland: University of California, 1996), excludes the system's three federally funded Department of Energy laboratories; Goldie Blumenstyk, "College Officials and Policy Experts Ponder Implications of 'Privatizing' State Colleges," *Chronicle of Higher Education,* May 13, 1992.

9. American Association of University Professors, "The Status of Non-Tenure-Track Faculty," *Academe* 79 (1993): 39–46; Robin Wilson, "Scholars off the Tenure Track Wonder If They'll Ever Get On," *Chronicle of Higher Education,* June 14, 1996; American Association of University Professors, *Policy Documents and Reports* (Washington, D.C.: AAUP, 1995); Elaine El-Khawas and Linda Knopp, *Campus Trends, 1996* (Washington, D.C.: American Council on Education, 1996).

10. Sheila Slaughter, "Retrenchment in the 1980s: The Politics of Prestige and Gender," *Journal of Higher Education* 64 (1993): 250–82.

11. Ibid., 276.

12. Catherine Gardner, Timothy R. Warner, and Rick Biedenweg, "Stanford and the Railroad: Case Studies of Cost Cutting," *Change*, Nov./Dec. 1990. See also Commission on the Academic Presidency, *Renewing the Academic Presidency: Stronger Leadership for Tougher Times* (Washington, D.C.: Association of Governing Boards of Universities and Colleges, 1996).

13. National Association of State Universities and Land-Grant Colleges, *Survey of Selected Institutions* (Washington, D.C.: NASULGC, 1996). See also Association of Higher Education Facilities Officers and National Association of College and University Business Officers, *A Foundation to Uphold* (Washington, D.C.: APPA, 1996), which estimates that colleges and universities in 1996 had an estimated $26 billion backlog in deferred maintenance of existing facilities, of which $5.7 billion required urgent attention.

14. Robert Zemsky, "A Call to Meeting," *Policy Perspectives* 4 (1993): 1A–10A, quotation on 1A.

15. Much of the data in this section is drawn from the National Center for Education Statistics, including *Digest of Education Statistics, 1995; Condition of Education* (Washington, D.C.: U.S. Department of Education, 1996); and *Projections of Education Statistics to 2006* (Washington, D.C.: U.S. Department of Education, 1996).

16. Arthur Levine and Jana Nidiffer, *Beating the Odds: How the Poor Get to College* (San Francisco: Jossey-Bass, 1995).

17. Adalberto Aguirre, "Ethnolinguistic Populations in California: A Focus on LEP Students and Public Education," *Journal of Educational Issues of Language Minority Students* 15 (1995).

18. National Commission on Excellence in Education, *A Nation at Risk: The Imperative for Educational Reform* (Washington, D.C.: U.S. Department of Education, 1983); Terrel Bell, "Reflections One Decade after *A Nation at Risk*," *Phi Delta Kappan* 74 (1993): 592–97, quotation on 597.

19. College Board, press release, Aug. 22, 1996; National Center for Education Statistics, *Remedial Education at Higher Education Institutions in Fall 1995* (Washington, D.C.: U.S. Department of Education, 1996).

20. David C. Berliner, "Mythology and the American System of Education," *Phi Delta Kappan* 74 (1993): 632–40.

21. Jonathan Kozol, *Savage Inequalities: Children in America's Schools* (New York: Crown, 1991).

22. Franklin P. Wilbur and Leo M. Lambert, eds., *Linking America's Schools and Colleges: Guide to Partnerships and National Directory* (Washington, D.C.: American Association for Higher Education/Anker, 1995); Kenneth A. Sirotnik and John I. Goodlad, eds., *School-University Partnerships in Action: Concepts, Cases, and Concerns* (New York: Teachers College

Press, 1988); Elizabeth M. Hawthorne and Ami Zusman, "The Role of State Departments of Education in School/College Collaborations," *Journal of Higher Education* 63 (1992): 418–40.

23. Hawthorne and Zusman, "The Role of State Departments of Education."

24. William F. Massy and Andrea K. Wilger, "Productivity in Postsecondary Education: A New Approach," *Educational Evaluation and Policy Analysis* 14 (1992): 361–76. See also Charles T. Clotfelter, *Buying the Best: Cost Escalation in Elite Higher Education* (Princeton: Princeton University Press, 1996).

25. James R. Mingle, "Faculty Work and the Costs/Quality/Access Collision," *AAHE Bulletin* 45 (1993):4.

26. Edward R. Hines and J. Russell Higham III, *State Policy and Faculty Workload* (Normal: Illinois State University, Center for Higher Education, 1996).

27. Ernest Boyer, *Scholarship Reconsidered: Priorities of the Professoriate* (Princeton, N.J.: Carnegie Foundation for the Advancement of Teaching, 1990); Robert Zemsky, "Testimony from the Belly of the Whale," *Policy Perspectives* 4 (1992): 1A–8A.

28. "Nine Issues Affecting Colleges: Roll Call of the States," *Chronicle of Higher Education,* Sept. 2, 1996.

29. Data on research trends in this section draw heavily on National Science Board, *Science and Engineering Indicators, 1996* (Washington, D.C.: Government Printing Office, 1996).

30. Harvey Brooks, "Current Criticisms of Research Universities," in *The Research University in a Time of Discontent,* ed. Jonathan R. Cole, Elinor G. Barber, and Stephen R. Graubard (Baltimore: Johns Hopkins University Press, 1994).

31. David Blumenthal, Eric Campbell, Nancyanne Causino, and Karen Seashore Louis, "Participation of Life-Science Faculty in Research Relationships with Industry," *New England Journal of Medicine* 335 (1996): 1734–39.

32. Roger L. Geiger, "Research Universities in a New Era: From the 1980s to the 1990s," in *Higher Learning in America, 1980-2000,* ed. Arthur Levine (Baltimore: Johns Hopkins University Press, 1993).

33. Albert H. Teich, "Megascience Projects in the United States: Cost, Funding, and Budget Issues," in *AAAS Science and Technology Policy Yearbook, 1995,* ed. Albert H. Teich, Stephen D. Nelson, and Celia McEnaney (Washington, D.C.: AAAS, 1995).

34. Kim A. McDonald, "Physicists in Large Collaborations Find That 'Big' Is Not Always Better," *Chronicle of Higher Education,* Dec. 9, 1992; Roy F. Schwitters, "The Substance and Style of 'Big Science,'" *Chronicle of Higher Education,* Feb. 16, 1996.

35. See William G. Bowen and Julie Ann Sosa, *Prospects for Faculty in the*

Arts and Sciences: A Study of Factors Affecting Demand and Supply, 1987 to 2012 (Princeton: Princeton University Press, 1989); Richard Atkinson, "Supply and Demand for Scientists and Engineers: A National Crisis in the Making," *Science* 248 (1990): 425–32; William G. Bowen and Neil L. Rudenstine, *In Pursuit of the Ph.D.* (Princeton: Princeton University Press, 1992).

36. National Research Council, "Surveys of Earned Doctorates," in *Summary Report: Doctoral Recipients from United States Universities* (Washington, D.C.: National Academy Press, 1974–94).

37. Committee on Science, Engineering, and Public Policy of the National Academy of Sciences, the National Academy of Engineering, and the Institute of Medicine, *Reshaping the Graduate Education of Scientists and Engineers* (Washington, D.C.: National Academy Press, 1995), 2–6. See also recent surveys of new Ph.D.s or of job market openings by professional associations such as the American Mathematical Society, the American Institute of Physics, and the Modern Language Association.

38. National Science Board, *Science and Engineering Indicators*, 3–6.

39. COSEPUP, *Reshaping the Graduate Education* (based on 1991 data for those employed five to eight years after receiving a U.S. Ph.D., to account for time in postdoctoral study); National Research Council, *Humanities Doctorates in the United States, 1985 Profile* and *1993 Profile* (Washington, D.C.: National Academy Press, 1986 and 1995).

40. COSEPUP, *Reshaping the Graduate Education*, 2–3.

41. William Massy and Charles Goldman, "The Production and Utilization of Science and Engineering Doctorates in the United States," draft report to the Alfred P. Sloan Foundation, May 1995, with August 1995 revised executive summary and authors' corrections.

42. For example, the Massy/Goldman model ignores differences among fields in industrial demand and retirement rates; nor does it account for major changes in the National Research Council's definitions of field of study and employment, which affect overall numbers. Among the model's surprising conclusions are an estimated labor shortage in chemistry, a relatively small surplus in physics, and large surpluses in electrical engineering and bioscience—all the reverse of findings drawn by professional association surveys and other studies. See Peter D. Syverson, "When Simulation Becomes Reality: Press Reaction to Massy/Goldman Study Creates Erroneous Message," *CGS Communicator* (newsletter of the Council of Graduate Schools), Aug. 1995; Charlotte Kuh, "Is There a Ph.D. Glut? Is That the Right Question?" *CGS Communicator* Aug./Sept. 1996.

43. Jack H. Schuster, "Whither the Faculty? The Changing Academic Labor Market," *Educational Record* 76 (1995): 28–33; National Center for Education Statistics, *National Study of Postsecondary Faculty* (Washington, D.C.: U.S. Government Printing Office, 1993).

44. National Center for Education Statistics, *Digest of Education Statistics, 1995;* El-Khawas and Knopp, *Campus Trends.*

45. Richard Freeman, *The Overeducated American* (New York: Academic, 1976).

46. Recent and in-progress studies will improve our understanding of the career paths of doctoral recipients and of the particular difficulties faced by ethnic minority Ph.D.s. See, for example, Daryl G. Smith, Lisa E. Wolf, and Bonnie E. Busenberg, *Achieving Faculty Diversity: Debunking the Myths* (Washington, D.C.: Association of American Colleges and Universities, 1996). Maresi Nerad and Joseph Cerny are completing a study, "Ph.D.s—Ten Years Later," which will look at the career paths of more than six thousand doctoral recipients in six fields from sixty-one universities.

47. COSEPUP, *Reshaping the Graduate Education.*

48. Sheila Tobias, Daryl E. Chubin, and Kevin D. Aylesworth, *Rethinking Science as a Career: Perceptions and Realities in the Physical Sciences* (Tucson: Research Corporation, 1995).

49. See, for example, David Goodstein, "Scientific Ph.D. Problems," *American Scholar* 62 (1993): 215-20; Cary Nelson, "Lessons from the Job Wars: What Is to Be Done?," *Academe* 81 (1995): 18-25, quotation on 18. Goodstein calculates that, in physics, each research university professor on average produces about fifteen new Ph.D.s in a career, an exponential growth rate that cannot continue indefinitely.

50. Edward R. Hines, *Higher Education and State Governments: Renewed Partnership, Cooperation, or Competition?* (Washington, D.C.: Association for the Study of Higher Education, 1988); Paula L. W. Sabloff, "Another Reason Why State Legislatures Will Continue to Restrict Public University Autonomy," *Review of Higher Education* 20 (1997): 141-62.

51. Ami Zusman, "Legislature and University Conflict: The Case of California," *Review of Higher Education* 9 (1986): 397-418.

52. Lois Fisher, "State Legislatures and the Autonomy of Colleges and Universities: A Comparative Study of Legislatures in Four States, 1900–1979," *Journal of Higher Education* 59 (1988): 133-62; Carol Everly Floyd, "Centralization and Decentralization of State Decision Making for Public Universities: Illinois, 1960-1990," *History of Higher Education Annual 1992* 12 (1992): 101-18.

53. See Frank Newman, *Choosing Quality: Reducing Conflict between the State and the University* (Denver: Education Commission of the States, 1987), for a discussion of what constitutes appropriate public policy versus inappropriate governmental intrusion.

54. Clark Kerr and Marian L. Gade, *The Guardians: Boards of Trustees of American Colleges and Universities: What They Do and How Well They Do It* (Washington, D.C.: Association of Governing Boards of Universities and Colleges, 1989), 116.

55. Where multicampus systems include all public four-year institutions in a state, they also carry out statewide governance and coordination functions for the state.

56. Kerr and Gade, *Guardians;* Marian L. Gade, *Four Multicampus Systems: Some Policies and Practices that Work* (Washington, D.C.: Association of Governing Boards of Universities and Colleges, 1993); Ami Zusman, "Multicampus University Systems: How System Offices Coordinate Undergraduate and K-12 Education," paper prepared for the annual meeting of the Association for the Study of Higher Education, Oct. 1992; Robert O. Berdahl and Frank Schmidtlein, "Restructuring Maryland Higher Education: An Analysis of the 1988 Reorganization," paper prepared for the annual meeting of the Association for the Study of Higher Education, Nov. 1994.

57. Laurence R. Marcus, "State Systems in Flux," paper prepared for the annual meeting of the Association for the Study of Higher Education, Nov. 1995.

58. James C. Hearn and Carolyn P. Griswold, "State-Level Centralization and Policy Innovation in U.S. Postsecondary Education," *Educational Evaluation and Policy Analysis* 16 (1994): 161–90.

59. Carolyn J. Mooney, "Presidents' Tenure Fluctuated Little over Past 8 Years," *Chronicle of Higher Education,* Dec. 2, 1992; Patrick Healy, "Activist Republican Trustees Change the Way Public Universities Seek Presidents, *Chronicle of Higher Education,* Aug. 9, 1996.

60. Clark Kerr, *Higher Education Cannot Escape History: Issues for the Twenty-first Century* (Albany: State University of New York Press, 1994).

Part Two

External Forces

Chapter Six

The Federal Government and Higher Education

Lawrence E. Gladieux and Jacqueline E. King

The framers of the U.S. Constitution lodged no specific responsibility for education with the national government, yet the federal influence on American colleges and universities has been enduring and pervasive. From sponsorship of land-grant colleges in the nineteenth century to the underwriting of student loans and university-based research and development in the twentieth century, the federal government has actively and extensively supported higher education to serve a variety of national purposes.

Today, the federal government provides less than 15 percent of all college and university revenues. But in two types of spending, direct aid to students and funds for research and development (R&D), federal outlays far exceed those of the states, industry, and other donors. Higher education is also affected by federal tax policies, both in the financing of institutions and in family and student financing of the costs of attendance. Moreover, as a condition of federal spending and tax support, Congress and the executive agencies of the government impose a variety of rules and mandates on postsecondary institutions and students. The federal impact on campuses and on students is substantial, diverse, and constantly changing. It is the product of deeply rooted traditions but also short-term decisions. This chapter analyzes the federal government's relationship to higher education, beginning with the historical underpinnings and current means and dimensions of support. It then discusses issues in research support, student aid, tax policy, and regulation, and concludes with thoughts on federal policy directions for the balance of the 1990s and beyond.

The Responsibility for Higher Education in the American System

That the states have the basic responsibility for education at all levels is an American tradition. The Tenth Amendment, reserving powers not delegated to the central government to the states, coupled with the fact that "education" is nowhere mentioned in the Constitution, pointed toward a secondary role for the federal government in this field. While some of the Founding Fathers urged a national system of education run by the federal government, the majority favored state, local, and private control, perhaps with a national university to cap the system. All proposals to establish such a university in the capital city failed, despite the fervent support of George Washington and several of his successors in the presidency. To this day, the federal government does not directly sponsor institutions of higher learning apart from military academies and a few institutions serving special populations. Still, early federal policy was crucial in promoting higher education as an adjunct of western migration and public land development in the late-eighteenth and nineteenth centuries. The Morrill Land-Grant College Act of 1862 fostered the creation and development of what are now some of the nation's great public and private universities.[1]

Federal investment in university-based R&D and in student aid via the GI Bill soared following World War II. Beginning with the Soviet challenge of Sputnik, Congress created a variety of aid-to-education programs in the late 1950s and 1960s, and by the 1970s the federal government became the largest source of direct assistance to individual students for financing their college expenses. Fundamentally, however, federal expenditures have remained supplementary to state subsidies and private support of higher learning. Terry Sanford, former governor of North Carolina, U.S. senator, and president of Duke University, once put it this way: "The money for the extras came from the national funds. . . . This is the glamour money. . . . It is needed, it has improved the quality. . . . It is proper to remember, however, for all the advantages brought by the extras, the train was

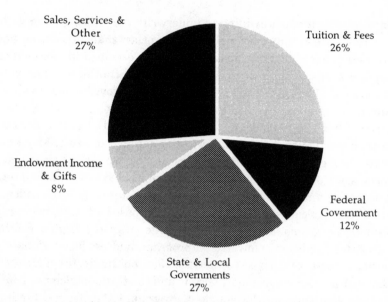

Sales, Services &
Other
27%

Tuition & Fees
26%

Endowment Income
& Gifts
8%

Federal
Government
12%

State & Local
Governments
27%

Figure 6.1 Sources of Revenue for Higher Education Institutions, 1992/1993 (total = $171 billion)

Source: National Center for Education Statistics, *Digest of Education Statistics, 1995* (Washington, D.C.: U.S. Department of Education, 1995).

put on the track in the first place by the states, and continues to be moved by state fuel and engineers."[2]

Over the past two centuries, the states have moved with varying speed to create and expand public systems of higher education and, more recently, to assist private colleges and universities or to purchase educational services from them. Although state funding as a percentage of total higher education revenues has declined in the 1980s and 1990s, the lion's share of government support for post-secondary institutions continues to come from the states. Figure 6.1 shows the sources of funding for higher education in 1992/93.

The traditional division of responsibilities between the federal and state governments was reaffirmed in the early 1970s, when Congress debated and ultimately rejected proposals for general purpose federal institutional aid. In passing the 1972 amendments to the Higher Education Act, "Congress pulled up short of a plan that amounted to federal revenue sharing with institutions of higher education— across-the-board general operating support distributed on the basis of enrollments. It was unwilling to underwrite the entire system without reference to any national objective other than preserving and strengthening educational institutions. The responsibility for general support of institutions, it was decided, should continue to rest with the states."[3] This is not to say that the federal government has been unconcerned about the health and capacity of institutions. Certain types of institutions have received special federal attention because of their particular contributions to the national interest. Major research and graduate-oriented universities, particularly their medical schools, are one such category. They are supported by grants and contracts from multiple federal agencies. The historically black colleges are also beneficiaries of federal institution-based support, primarily through programs authorized under Title III of the Higher Education Act. In addition, a few federal programs address institutional capacity for research. These include the National Institutes of Health's Biomedical Research Support Grants and the National Science Foundation's Institutional Development Program. Other federal funding goes to support the arts and humanities, occupational and vocational education, international exchanges and studies, the provision of military training, and other purposes. Although the amounts are relatively small, they are significant for some institutions and certain parts of the education community.

Meanwhile, student aid represents at least an indirect subsidy of consequence to nearly every institution in the country.[4] About a third of the 21 million students who attend postsecondary education each year are estimated to receive some federal aid, in the form of grants, loans, or work/study programs.[5] Aid programs benefit all sectors of postsecondary education, but the rate of participation is by far the highest in proprietary schools (67%), followed by private nonprofit colleges (38%), public four-year institutions (31%), and public two-year institutions (18%). Whenever the Higher Education Act comes up for reauthorization in Congress, the stakes are high for institutions. Representatives of all the postsecondary sectors—two-year, four-year, public, private, proprietary—struggle over scores of amendments that determine who gets what under Title IV of the statute, which authorizes the federal student aid programs. Likewise, when federal budget cutbacks threaten, the higher education community tends to close ranks to defend the programs.

In sum, while federal education moneys are much sought after, the historical parameters of the federal role continue to prevail in the

1990s. The states retain the fundamental responsibility for higher education, primarily through provision of operating support for public systems of colleges and universities. The federal role is to provide particular kinds of support to meet perceived national objectives, generally without distinguishing between public and nonpublic higher education. The federal government provides this support in three ways:

— Purchasing R&D services, thereby supporting universities' research capacity as well as graduate-level training programs
— Filling gaps and meeting special needs, such as college library support, foreign language and area studies, and health profession development
— Directing almost half its aid to students rather than institutions, with the aim of removing barriers facing individuals who aspire to postsecondary education

In the nineteenth century, states served as intermediaries in federal patronage of higher education. Proceeds from the sale of public lands provided endowments that helped the states establish and finance the early land-grant institutions, agricultural extension programs, and other forerunners of today's public colleges and universities. These federal grants to the states were broad and carried few restrictions.

Toward the beginning of the twentieth century, however, the pattern began to change. Federal support became piecemeal and started going directly to institutions themselves, bypassing state governments. In recent decades, nearly all federal moneys have been channeled to institutions (or to departments, schools, and faculty members within institutions) or to individual students. For this reason, a federal/state partnership in supporting higher education is meaningful only in a general sense. In fact, there is virtually no conscious meshing of funding purposes and patterns between the two levels of government. By and large, federal activity proceeds independently. One observer concluded that "with a few modest exceptions, federal postsecondary spending arrangements make no attempt to stimulate state spending, to compensate for differences in state wealth or effort, or to give state governments money to allot as they see fit."[6] Nor, it might be added, would it be easy to implement a program or funding formula that would effectively achieve any combination of such objectives.

The federal government's activities affecting higher education are

Table 6.1

Federal Financial Assistance to Higher Education, by Type and Source, Fiscal Year 1995

Type and Source	Millions of Dollars	Percentage
Student aid	15,565	46.3
Department of Education	12,850	
Department of Veterans Affairs	1,219	
ROTC scholarships and other military assistance	573	
Health professions scholarships/fellowships	786	
Programs for Native Americans	128	
Other scholarship/fellowship programs	9	
Research and development	15,926	47.4
Other institutional support	2,125	6.3
Department of Education	884	
Special institutions	369	
Military academies	169	
National Science Foundation	265	
International education/cultural exchange	237	
Other	201	
Total federal aid	33,616	100.0

Source: National Center for Education Statistics, *Digest of Education Statistics 1995,* (Washington, D.C.: U.S. Department of Education, 1995), table 353.

Note: Some amounts differ from those in figure 6.2 and table 6.3. Figure 6.2 provides total aid available to students for academic year 1995–96, including the volume of borrowing generated by federal loan guaranties and subsidies, as well as amounts contributed by states and institutions. Military training assistance is included here but not in figure 6.2. Research and development figure includes federal obligations for research and development centers administered by colleges and universities, unlike federal R&D figures in table 6.3.

so decentralized and so intermixed with other policy objectives that simply enumerating the programs and tallying total investment is problematic. Creation of the U.S. Department of Education in 1979 consolidated only about a fourth of the more than four hundred programs that existed then and less than a third of total federal expenditures for higher education—not substantially more than were encompassed by the old Office of Education in the U.S. Department of Health, Education, and Welfare. The remaining programs and funds are still scattered across a number of federal agencies, from the Departments of Defense, Energy, Agriculture, Transportation, and Health and Human Services to the Veterans Administration,

Environmental Protection Agency, National Aeronautics and Space Administration, and Smithsonian Institution. This diffuse pattern within the executive branch is mirrored in Congress, in which committee responsibilities tend to follow agency structures. Thus, the fragmentary nature of federal influence and support for higher education seems likely to persist.

Table 6.1 provides an overview of federal support for higher education. In fiscal year 1995, federal spending totaled $33.6 billion, with 47 percent of this amount for university-based R&D, 46 percent for the cost of student aid, and the balance for assorted categorical assistance and payments to colleges and universities. The more than $15 billion spent on student aid programs is considerably less than the $37 billion in federal aid actually made available to students through these programs in academic year 1995/96, because the federal government guarantees and subsidizes private loans and requires nonfederal matching in certain programs.[7]

Federal Research Support

Federal spending on R&D and other aspects of science at colleges and universities predates the federal commitment to student aid, going back to an 1883 law to support agricultural experiment stations. But the investment in academic science was fairly small until the needs of World War II caused federal spending for campus-based research to skyrocket. The boom in federally sponsored research continued through the 1950s and early 1960s. Though such support has not continued to grow as fast in subsequent decades, the federal government remains the largest source of financing for campus-based research, supplying more than $13 billion in 1995.

Unlike student aid, federal research funding is highly concentrated on a relatively small number of institutions, most of them major research universities. According to the National Science Foundation (NSF), a hundred doctorate-granting institutions receive more than 80 percent of all federal R&D obligations to academia, a proportion that has remained quite stable over the years.[8] This support flows from multiple federal agencies and policy objectives. When NSF was created in 1950, presidential science adviser Vannevar Bush envisioned a single agency having broad purview over federal funding of research in the physical sciences, medicine, and defense, with a separate science advisory board to evaluate and integrate technical research sponsored by other government departments.[9] This vision is far from today's diffuse reality, with more than a dozen mission-oriented agencies funding academic science for a variety of purposes.

R&D expenditures at colleges and universities are summarized in table 6.2. In constant dollars, the federal contribution increased by 50 percent between 1980 and 1995. Contributions from industry and other sources also grew faster than inflation. Overall, this was a robust period for investment in university-based science. According to one observer, "If the 1960s were the golden age of research, then the 1980s were the gilded age."[10] This growth curve continued despite the end of the cold war and the dissolution of the former Soviet Union, which diminished public interest in military research and the "big science" projects that were a hallmark of competition between the superpowers. Can such spending persist into the next century? What priorities will the federal government set for its research investment? How will it award, and what constraints will it impose, on this money?

For most of the past fifty years, America invested disproportionate resources and dedicated many of its best minds to defense-related science and technology. The challenge of the 1990s and beyond is to reorient the country's research enterprise toward investments that promise benefits to the American economy and quality of life. Policy makers now stress economic security and competitiveness, rather than military preparedness, as the rationale for research budgets. The fastest-growing area of federal research funding is biomedical research, a field in which breakthroughs yield economic and "quality of life" returns. The Clinton administration's plan for R&D also assigns high priority to projects with clear potential for "technology transfer," commercial applications, and job creation. Republican leaders of Congress share this enthusiasm for the promise of advanced commercial technologies but tend to favor deregulation and tax credits for businesses investing in R&D rather than direct federal spending on technology projects. There have been worries in the scientific community that, carried too far, the focus on bottom-line results and economic competitiveness will shortchange investment in fundamentally important scientific studies that have no obvious commercial appeal but that could bring greater returns over the long haul. The Clinton administration argues, on the other hand, that basic and applied research should be viewed as interdependent, not competing, branches of science, which along with technology must be more sharply focused on areas of national need.

Table 6.2

R&D Expenditures at Universities and Colleges, by Source of Funds, Fiscal Years 1980 and 1995

	Constant Dollars (millions)		
Source	1980	1995	Increase (%)
Federal government	8,864	13,442	51.6
State and local governments	1,062	1,654	55.8
Industry	510	1,551	203.8
Institutional funds	1,806	4,033	123.3
All other sources	872	1,654	89.8
Total	13,114	22,334	70.3

Source: National Science Board, *Science and Engineering Indicators, 1996,* (Washington, D.C.: Government Printing Office, 1996).

Note: Federal government dollars do not include amounts for federally funded research and development centers.

Meanwhile, federal policy makers are divided over how federal dollars for academic science should be awarded. In 1980, Congress earmarked a total of roughly $10 million for specific projects and institutions, bypassing formal competition and merit review. By 1993 such earmarking had ballooned to more than $750 million, sparking intense debate between congressional critics of "pork barrel science" and appropriators grown accustomed to awarding research grants to campuses in their home districts. Since 1993, the volume of earmarks has receded, totaling $300 million in fiscal year 1996. But the congressional infighting on this issue is bound to continue.[11] Traditionally, federal campus-based research funds have been distributed on the basis of competition, with experts evaluating grant proposals in their field. Peer reviews, along with considerations of cost effectiveness, largely determine which proposals receive funding. Proponents of the peer review system argue that it ensures that the best research is supported. Opponents argue it is an old boys' network, which precludes many worthwhile projects because the researchers are not tied into the network and which discriminates against younger faculty members, women, and minorities.[12]

In part, congressional earmarking is a reaction to the heavy concentration of federal R&D spending on a relatively few institutions. Institutions outside this group go to their elected representatives and plead their case, often hiring expensive lobbyists. Earmarking is also a response to a long-term problem affecting virtually all research universities—the deterioration and obsolescence of scientific equipment and facilities. Only a small proportion of federal research funds support renovation, new construction, or the purchase of equipment. In the 1950s and 1960s, separate appropriations were made for such things, but in recent decades the federal government has persisted in a policy of procuring R&D from universities and leaving the institutions to their own devices for maintaining the necessary infrastructure. In reaction, some institutions have gone directly to the congressional appropriations committees to fund the construction or renovation of particular facilities.

Budget constraints, however, may limit the federal contribution to both competitively based research and pork barrel science for the foreseeable future. Virtually all R&D funding for universities comes from the shrinking portion of the federal budget that is discretionary, which means what is left after mandatory (entitlement) spending and interest on the national debt. Excluding defense as well, this share of the budget is now down to 17 percent. The country's investment in science and technology will compete with interstate highways, national parks, environmental protection, housing, and a host of other domestic needs for a smaller and smaller piece of the federal pie. On the bright side, academic science, especially biomedical research, continues to enjoy broad bipartisan support and largely has been protected during recent rounds of federal budget cutting.

Not only will budgets be tight, but questions surrounding the management and conduct of university research may have weakened the case for academic science support in the 1990s. The nation's investment in science during the past half century has been repaid many times over in the form of pathbreaking discoveries and practical applications. The computer, radar, polio vaccine, America's world leadership in agriculture can all be traced to academic science. Yet, controversy and skepticism have beset the university research establishment in recent years. Publicized cases of research fraud and other ethical breaches by federally sponsored researchers, including violations of protocols for the use of human subjects and treatment of laboratory animals, have triggered investigations and doubts about the integrity of scientific research.

In the late 1980s and early 1990s, indirect-cost recovery on government grants and contracts also clouded the outlook for federal support of campus research. Stanford University became the lightning rod for public and legislative concern when it was revealed that expenses for a number of questionable items had been charged to the government over the years as part of Stanford's indirect costs of federally sponsored research.[13] Adverse publicity and congressional hearings led to investigations of other research universities. Several institutions were required to return millions of dollars in questionable billings.

The existing system of indirect-cost recovery, developed by the Office of Management and Budget (OMB) over thirty years ago, is based on the principle that an institution's indirect-cost recovery should be tied to the share of research-related costs in an institution's total budget. Such a system gives institutions great incentive to categorize as much of their spending as possible as research related. Several reforms in the OMB regulations were instituted in the wake of the problems at Stanford and elsewhere, but indirect-cost recovery remains an arena of ongoing negotiation. On the one hand, the government always wants to pay as low a price as possible for the research it supports. On the other hand, faculty are interested in diverting as many funds as possible from indirect to direct costs, and there is always a risk that the rules will be stretched too far.

All these issues take on particular significance in light of the dependence of universities on federal research dollars. While federal grants and contracts constitute less than 10 percent of total revenues to higher education, at some major research institutions, federal dollars represent 25 percent or more of revenues, and indirect-cost reimbursements have in some cases exceeded 10 percent of a university's budget.

In sum, tight federal budgets and questions about academic research practices will stir continued debate on the federal responsibility for R&D in the 1990s and beyond. Universities will be challenged to do more with less, to identify their comparative advantages, to consolidate efforts with other research institutions, and to articulate more clearly how research contributes to societal goals.

Federal Student Aid

While the national investment in science helped establish the world preeminence of U.S. research universities, the federal government's investment in student aid has helped extend college opportunities to a larger segment of the population than any other system of higher education in the world.[14] Starting with the Servicemen's Readjustment

Act of 1944, or GI Bill, federal student assistance has helped transform attending college in America from an elite to a mass activity. Congress passed the GI Bill to reward veterans who had served their country during wartime and to help them catch up with their peers whose lives had not been interrupted by military service. During the 1940s and 1950s, the GI Bill sent thousands of men and women to college who otherwise would not have had the opportunity.

The GI Bill was so successful that it inspired broader proposals for scholarship assistance unrelated to military service. But federal aid-to-education proposals of all kinds faced an uphill struggle in the early postwar years, blocked in Congress by civil rights and church-state controversies, fear of federal control of education, and (in the case of college scholarships) resistance from those who believed students should not get "a free ride." Many members of Congress of that era had worked their way through college. The Soviet launch of Sputnik, the first unmanned space satellite, gave Congress the occasion to justify a limited form of student assistance in the name of national security and cold war competitiveness. The National Defense Education Act of 1958 provided low-interest loans for college students, with debt cancellation for those who became teachers after graduation.

The big breakthrough, however, came during the crest of the civil rights movement and the War on Poverty of the mid-1960s. As part of President Lyndon Johnson's Great Society, the Higher Education Act of 1965 embodied, for the first time, an explicit federal commitment to equalizing college opportunities for needy students. Programs were designed to identify the college-eligible poor and to facilitate their access with grants, replacing contributions their families could not afford to make. Colleges and universities that wanted to participate in the new Educational Opportunity Grant program were required to make "vigorous" efforts to identify and recruit students with "exceptional financial need." The legislation also authorized the College Work-Study program to subsidize the employment of needy students and the federally guaranteed student loan program to ease the cash-flow problems of middle-income college students and their families. Pell Grants and State Student Incentive Grants were enacted in the early 1970s, rounding out the principal student aid programs under Title IV of the Higher Education Act.

Thus began more than a quarter century of dramatic growth in federal financial aid for students enrolled in postsecondary education and training. In 1963, the federal government invested approximately

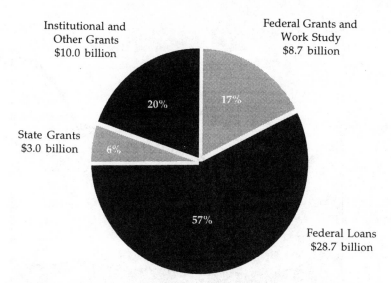

Institutional and
Other Grants
$10.0 billion

Federal Grants and
Work Study
$8.7 billion

State Grants
$3.0 billion

Federal Loans
$28.7 billion

20%

17%

6%

57%

Figure 6.2 Aid to Postsecondary Students, by Type, 1995/1996 (total = $50.5 billion)
Source: College Entrance Examination Board, *Trends in Student Aid: 1986 to 1996*
(Washington, D.C.: CEEB, 1996).

$200 million in a handful of graduate student fellowships and the newly established National Defense Education Act student loan program. More than thirty years later, the federal government generated more than $35 billion in student assistance annually, either through direct appropriations or loan guarantees and subsidies—a thirtyfold increase after adjusting for inflation. Figure 6.2 summarizes the types and amounts of aid to postsecondary students from federal as well as nonfederal sources in academic year 1995/6.

For most of this period, the federal commitment to student aid has had wide bipartisan support. This commitment was tested following President Reagan's election; in the budget retrenchment of the early 1980s, grant support dropped, as did the overall purchasing power of student aid before gradually resuming upward growth (see figure 6.3). It was also tested in the late 1980s, when student loan defaults and widespread abuse by for-profit vocational trade schools put the federal student aid programs on political trial; legislative and regulatory reforms helped address these problems, and the programs survived. The commitment to student aid was tested again in the mid-1990s, when Republican leaders of Congress advanced their Contract with America. And it surely will be tested in the years ahead, as fed-

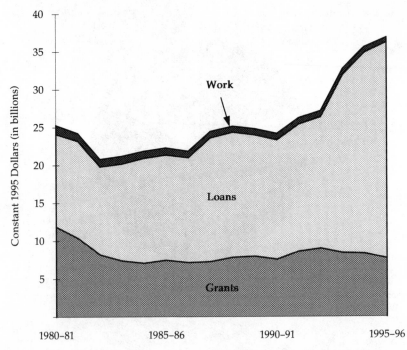

Figure 6.3 Federal Aid Awarded to Postsecondary Students, by Type, 1980–1995 (constant 1995 dollars)
Source: See figure 6.2.

eral policy makers struggle to balance the budget. The federal grant and work/study programs will be vying for the same shrinking discretionary portion of the federal budget for which university-based research must also compete. The guaranteed and direct student loan programs, on the other hand, operate as entitlements in the federal budget and are thereby less subject to the vagaries of annual budgeting and appropriations, though entitlement programs will also be under intense pressure in a budget-balancing environment.

While there may be little room for maneuver in the federal budget, policy makers in the 1990s are nonetheless clamoring to address the public's anxieties about financing higher education. After all the polls told politicians in 1996 that voters were concerned about rising college costs, both national party platforms put a spotlight on the issue, and President Clinton proposed a new program of tuition tax credits and deductions as a centerpiece of his reelection campaign. His tuition tax proposals will be debated by Congress, and the outcome could reshape the federal role in higher education into the next century (see discussion of tax policy later in this chapter).

Trends in Aid, Affordability, and Access

What has pushed the issue of college affordability so high on the national policy agenda? Alarmist coverage by the media has been a factor. The media tend to focus on the most expensive institutions in the country, obscuring the fact that college remains highly affordable for many Americans at a range of institutions. But public alarm is also rooted in real economic trends of the past fifteen years. The tuition price spiral has been unabated during this period. Adjusted for inflation, average tuition has risen almost 90 percent at private, and 100 percent at public, four-year institutions. And what has happened to the principal resources available to pay these rising prices? Median family income has essentially stagnated, growing only 5 percent in the past fifteen years. At the same time, income disparities have widened during the 1980s and 1990s, which means that the share of family income required to pay rising college costs has gone up the most for those on the bottom rungs of the economic ladder. Student aid has increased in real value but not enough to keep pace with growth in tuition or in the eligible student population, and most of the growth in aid has come in the form of loans.

By contrast, during the 1970s tuition rose roughly in step with the consumer price index, income inequality was less, increases in federal aid outstripped growth in tuition and growth in the eligible student population, and grant aid was more common than borrowing. After 1980, all these trend lines shifted for the worse from the standpoint of keeping college affordable.

Yet, overall, college participation rates have risen in the 1980s and 1990s. The potential investment returns to the individual are high, demand has been robust, more people have been going to college. The problem is that enrollment growth is not spread evenly across society by income and race. Wide gaps persist in who benefits from higher education in America. The goal of equalizing college opportunities emblazoned in national policy thirty years ago has proved elusive. The data suggest that measurable progress was made in closing some of these gaps during the late 1960s and 1970s, but the story of the 1980s and 1990s has been one of losing ground. For a student from a family in the bottom 25 percent of the income distribution, the chances of going to college remain far less than for a student in the top income quartile. That gap is widening, and the disparities are even more pronounced when one examines not just enrollment but also degree completion.[15]

Policy Drift

One must look well beyond economics to explain the continuing gaps in opportunity. Enrollment and success in higher education are determined by many factors—differences in prior schooling and aptitude, family and community attitudes, student motivation and awareness of opportunities, campus environment and support. However, the underpinnings of federal aid policy have clearly shifted over the past quarter century:

—In its conception, federal student aid primarily was about helping those who otherwise might not be able to attend college. In their evolution, federal policies have become as much (or more) about relieving the cost burden for those who probably would go without such aid. The antipoverty origins of the 1960s legislation have faded into history, as eligibility for federal assistance has been extended up the economic scale.

—At the same time, student aid has evolved from a grant-based to a loan-based system. The original Higher Education Act called for need-based grants for the disadvantaged, while helping middle-class families with government-guaranteed but minimally subsidized bank loans. Figure 6.4 shows how the balance of loan and grant aid has shifted over time. Loans accounted for 21 percent of federal aid in 1975/76 and 77 percent in 1995/96, while grants and work/study dropped from 79 percent to 23 percent over the same period. Today, loans are far and away the largest source of aid. Federal student and parent loans totaled over $28 billion in 1995/96, five times more than the Pell Grant program, which was meant to be the system's foundation. Even those most at risk—low-income students, students in remediation, students taking short-term training with uncertain returns—increasingly must borrow to gain postsecondary access.

The drift toward a loan-centered aid system dates back to 1978, when Congress passed the Middle Income Student Assistance Act, which modestly expanded eligibility for Pell grants but, more signifi-

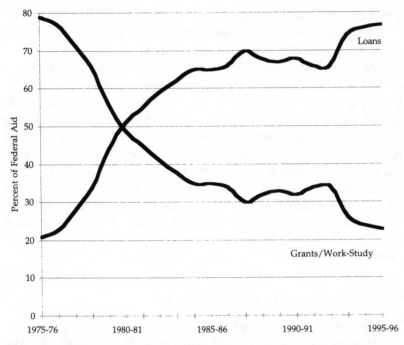

Figure 6.4 Grants, Work/Study, and Loans as Shares of Federal Aid, 1975–1995
Source: See figure 6.2.

cantly, made subsidized guaranteed loans available to any student regardless of income or need (the major subsidy to the borrower being
government payment of interest during the period of enrollment).
A year later, Congress ensured banks a favorable rate of return on
guaranteed student loans by tying their subsidies to changes in trea-
sury bill rates. With the economy moving into a period of double-digit
inflation and interest rates, student loan volume and associated federal costs mushroomed. During the retrenchment of the early Reagan
years, loan eligibility and subsidies were scaled back, but as an entitlement that had become popular with the middle class, guaranteed
student loans proved the most resilient form of aid. Loan volume continued to grow, although at rates slower than between 1978 and 1981.

   When Congress reauthorized the student aid programs in both
1986 and 1992, the borrowing trend was a major focus of concern.
Congressional leaders said they wanted to restore a better balance between grants and loans, but the legislative outcome in both years continued the policy drift in the opposite direction. In 1992, the prospect
of a post–cold war peace dividend had fueled hopes that Pell grants

might be turned into an entitlement or mandated spending program, with automatic annual increases for inflation. But the peace dividend never materialized, leaving no room under the budget rules for such an expansion. After the Pell entitlement failed, Congress followed a path of less resistance in boosting the dollar ceilings in the existing loan programs. The 1992 reauthorization bill also established an unsubsidized loan option not restricted by need, intended to make loans available to middle-income students who had been squeezed out of eligibility for the regular subsidized loan (*unsubsidized* meaning that the government does not pay interest costs while the borrower is in school). All told, the principal impact of the 1992 legislation is clear: far from correcting the grant/loan imbalance, it expanded borrowing capacity for students and parents at all income levels, spurring a 70 percent increase in borrowing through the main federal loan programs in the three years since the law took effect.

Reforming the Delivery of Student Aid

The 1992 reauthorization law, along with legislation the Clinton administration proposed and Congress passed in 1993, changed the way student need is calculated, mandated a stand-alone federal application form for determining eligibility, added a new state-based oversight mechanism intended to reduce fraud and abuse of federal student aid funds, and called for major changes in the way student loans are financed, originated, serviced, and repaid. In the mid-1990s, policy makers and aid administrators have been preoccupied with implementing these major legislative changes and making the new delivery systems work for students.

The most daunting challenge for the government and the student aid community has been to launch a system of direct federal lending through institutions to compete with traditional bank-based student loans. The promise of the Clinton reform program is a streamlined loan system that serves students better, promotes improvements in the bank-based system through competition, and saves tax dollars by reducing subsidies to private lenders and guarantee agencies. Republicans, however, are skeptical that the Department of Education can successfully run such a system, and they predict that any potential savings will be more than offset by the larger federal bureaucracy that will be required.

At the same time, policy makers hope to mitigate the potentially adverse effects of debt financing on students' career choices and on equity of access to higher education by providing greater flexibility in repayment. Borrowers are now offered graduated and extended repayment terms and may also repay loans as a percentage of their future income. The majority of borrowers will probably continue to repay without difficulty on the standard ten-year schedule. But for those students who know in advance that they want to pursue relatively low-paying service occupations, as well as those who later fall on hard times, alternative repayment schemes will probably become increasingly important in the 1990s and beyond.

Special Initiatives and Populations

Community Service

The Clinton administration is also committed to expanding opportunities for students to pay for their education through performance of service to the nation or community. While falling well short of the ambitious program the president had initially proposed, legislation passed in 1993 aims to enable individuals to earn postsecondary education or training benefits by serving in areas of public need for up to two years. The benefits could be used either to pay postservice educational expenses or to repay educational debts already incurred. The Clinton service initiative has many historical antecedents, including the Civilian Conservation Corps of the 1930s, the Peace Corps, VISTA, the National Health Service Corps, and a number of loan forgiveness and deferment provisions written into the student aid legislation over the past thirty years. The Clinton program also has strong critics in the Republican Congress who object on principle to payment for volunteer service and charge that the per student costs of the program are exorbitant.

Nontraditional Students

Many policy makers and analysts worry that the existing aid system, designed primarily for families whose dependent children attend college full time, is not sensitive to the wide-ranging needs and circumstances of nontraditional students. Increasing numbers of adults beyond traditional college age are returning to higher education for a second chance, retraining, or midcareer change. They often attend less than full time and have continuing family and work responsibilities while in school. Whether and how to support these students will be an ongoing policy concern in the 1990s. It may be that conventional aid programs are not the best way to reach nontraditional students. The expanding eligibility of independent adult students for existing levels of aid will reduce the dollars available to dependent students from low-income families. And need-based grants and loans may not fit with the needs of many nontraditional students attending college on a sporadic basis. Policy makers are considering mechanisms outside the traditional forms of student assistance, including expanded tax incentives to employers for facilitating and supporting employee training and retraining.

Counseling and Outreach

Policy makers also recognize that student aid dollars alone are not sufficient to ensure greater access to higher education by underrepresented groups. Earlier, larger, and more sustained interventions in the education pipeline are necessary. This need has been addressed through the so-called TRIO programs of counseling, outreach, and special support services for the disadvantaged, created as a complement to the student aid programs in the original Higher Education Act. Congressional appropriations for the TRIO programs have grown steadily over the years, but funding of these efforts still falls far short of the need. The 1992 reauthorization called for additional initiatives inspired by Eugene Lang's "I Have a Dream" movement in cities around the country, which seeks to mentor disadvantaged junior high students, widen their horizons, and see them through to high school graduation and postsecondary opportunities. Such federal incentives have yet to be funded by Congress.

Graduate Student Assistance

While the bulk of federal student aid goes to undergraduates, and the policy debates in Washington focus largely on issues of educational access and choice at the undergraduate level, a portion of the aid available through loan and work/study programs goes to graduate and professional students. Federal support for graduate students also comes in the form of research assistantships, fellowships, and traineeships, and much of this support is built into the funding of R&D administered by institutions.

Overall, fellowship and other grant money for graduate students has declined since the 1960s, and universities have looked to alternative sources. The federal work/study program, for example, requires only a 20 percent match by institutions and has been increasingly used to fund teaching assistants. But the most common recourse for filling the gap has been student borrowing. Federally guaranteed loans have become an integral part of financing graduate and professional education, and many privately sponsored supplemental loan programs have been created to serve students in high-cost fields such as the health professions. It is at this level that concerns about mounting student indebtedness can become acute, especially among students who have already accumulated substantial loan obligations as undergraduates. Traditionally, graduate institutions and departments have awarded aid primarily on the basis of academic merit. But recent financing trends indicate a dual system. Research assistantships and what remains of fellowship support from federal and private sources continue to be awarded on competitive academic criteria, whereas the great proportion of subsidized work, loan, and other aid to graduate and professional students is directed to students according to their financial need. In general, graduate students are experiencing increased difficulty financing their education when financial rewards accruing to an advanced degree, especially in traditional academic disciplines, are uncertain at best. Many observers worry about the quality and numbers of students pursuing graduate work and the adequacy of federal policies to meet national needs for highly trained personnel in the 1990s and beyond.

Access to What?

For most of the past quarter century, federal policy under Title IV of the Higher Education Act has consistently emphasized access. But policy makers in the 1990s also want assurances that they are supporting access to *quality* academic and vocational programs. Are dollars being directed effectively to those who really need help and who have a reasonable chance of benefiting from the education and training that is being subsidized? Do federal aid recipients complete their programs? Do they secure jobs in the fields for which they have prepared? In short, are students and taxpayers receiving their money's worth?

A principal though not exclusive object of concern regarding quality and standards has been the proprietary trade schools. In the 1970s, Congress substituted the term *postsecondary* for *higher* in student aid statutes, and eligibility was broadened to include short-term vocational training provided by for-profit schools, as well as the traditional programs of public and private nonprofit institutions. Congress embraced a marketplace philosophy: students would "vote with their feet," taking their federal aid to institutions that met their needs. But the marketplace rationale begged important questions of institutional effectiveness and accountability. Few foresaw the burgeoning of the trade school industry that would be stimulated by the new federal incentives. Many for-profit programs came to be subsidized almost entirely by tax dollars, setting their prices based on the aid package available to students from the federal government. For quality control, the federal student aid programs have traditionally relied on a so-called triad of institutional accreditation, state review, and federal oversight. The federal responsibility, as carried out by the Department of Education, has included certifying accreditation agencies as well as ultimately approving institutions to participate in the federal aid programs. Over time, however, the triad arrangement has proven inadequate to the task.

Restoring "integrity" to the student aid process was a principal theme of the 1992 reauthorization of the Higher Education Act. Congressional sponsors recognized that these issues had to be addressed if the programs under Title IV of the act were to be viable in the intense competition for federal appropriations in the years ahead. The principal new thrust in the 1992 legislation was to rely more on state agencies to help determine which postsecondary institutions should be eligible to participate in the federal Title IV programs. Ultimately, however, the higher education community balked at the authority that the 1992 law vested with so-called state postsecondary review entities (SPREs), and states themselves proved to be reluctant partners in such an endeavor. State officials responsible for licensing and reviewing postsecondary programs have long complained they should not bear the brunt of regulatory problems that the federal government helped create, in part by subsidizing the proprietary sector so substantially. The SPRE initiative has been abandoned.

Meanwhile, the Department of Education has tried to crack down on institutions with excessively high default rates, and this effort has helped to reduce the overall level of defaults and eliminate schools that were clearly abusing the system. Some of the worst problems have been remedied: the default rate has dropped from a high of 22 percent in 1990 to 11 percent in 1994. But establishing default-rate cutoffs is arbitrary and problematic in many respects, and institutions have great incentive to manipulate their numbers to stay below the cutoff level. In addition, the due process entailed in withdrawing federal approval has proved to be so cumbersome that many institutions manage to participate for many years after being targeted.

So the fundamental issues of institutional eligibility and quality control in the federal aid programs remain to be effectively addressed. The Clinton administration is considering fresh approaches in this area, including new performance and compliance standards that would condition institutional eligibility to participate in the aid programs, and the issue will no doubt resurface in the next reauthorization of the Higher Education Act, scheduled for 1998.

The Cost Side of the Equation

Finally, questions about quality ultimately are linked to concerns about cost and price. Policy makers along with the general public worry about the tuition spiral, where it will lead, and whether it will ever end. Federal student aid seems unlikely to catch up any time soon. Might the government at some point try to intervene on the other side of the affordability equation, namely, try to curb growth in the price of a college education? In the final analysis, making college affordable again will depend on controlling the tuition spiral, but it is far from clear that the federal government has either a mandate or sufficient leverage to impose price controls (thus realizing some of the worst fears of the higher education community about the potential for federal intrusion). Federal policy makers, however, will surely use congressional hearings and press conferences to urge colleges to rein in their price increases.

Tax Policies

In addition to direct funding of students and institutions, the government indirectly assists higher education through a variety of tax policies. A number of exclusions, exemptions, and deductions in the federal tax code over the years have benefited education at all levels. Some of these provisions—for example, the personal exemptions parents may claim for dependents who are students aged nineteen to twenty-four, and a tax break on proceeds from U.S. savings bonds that are used for higher education — affect individual and family ability to save for and pay college costs. Other provisions affect the revenue and financing arrangements of colleges and universities; for example, their charitable (501[c]3) status allows them to receive tax-deductible contributions. The monetary benefits to institutions and students of these tax provisions (tax expenditures, in federal budgetary parlance) are measured by the estimated amount of federal revenue that would be collected in the absence of such provisions. Prior to the passage of the Tax Reform Act of 1986, estimated annual tax expenditures for higher education totaled more than $4 billion.

Corporate investment in university-based research was promoted by the tax legislation of 1981, which gave tax credits to industry for investment in cooperative, applied research projects with universities and permitted enhanced deductions for gifts of research and research training equipment. The 1986 tax bill amended these provisions to balance the tax incentives for corporate investment in basic and applied research. But overall, the reform legislation of 1986, a watershed in federal tax policy, had adverse implications for higher education. For colleges and universities, particularly private nonprofit institutions, the principal setback came in the form of limitations on charitable giving. The legislation both tightened tax deductions for gifts of stock, land, works of art, and other appreciated property and terminated the deductibility of gifts by nonitemizing taxpayers. The 1986 law also changed the rules for tax-exempt bond financing, placing a $150 million cap on such borrowing by private colleges and universities.

Other changes legislated in 1986 have affected students and parents:

— The elimination of tax-deductible Clifford Trusts designed for very high-income families and changes in taxation of unearned income of children under the age of fourteen have reduced the advantage of transferring income from parent to child as a means of saving for educational purposes. For the great majority of families, however, a transfer of income remains a viable college savings technique with a tax benefit.
— An individual may not take a personal exemption on his or her own tax return if eligible to be claimed as a dependent on another's

return. Thus, students under the age of twenty-three who up to 1986 were allowed to benefit from such an exemption are no longer able to claim it.

—The deduction for consumer interest, including interest on education loans to students and parents, was phased out. However, home mortgage interest remains deductible, and taxpayers are able to deduct interest payments on home equity loans used to meet educational expenses.

—Scholarships, fellowships, and federal grants to graduate and undergraduate students are counted as taxable income to the extent these awards, either individually or together, exceed the cost of tuition and related expenses. For most students, the increase in the standard deduction has mitigated the impact of this change, producing little or no additional tax liability. Those potentially affected are married students with spouses earning income, athletes receiving full scholarships, and paradoxically, some of the neediest students (those with large grants).

Almost as soon as the Tax Reform Act of 1986 was signed into law, bills were introduced in Congress to restore the exclusion of scholarships and fellowships from taxable income, the deductibility of interest on student loans, and the full deduction for gifts of appreciated property, as well as eliminating the cap on tax-exempt borrowing by private institutions. But recovery of losses in the 1986 law has not come easily for higher education or any other constituency. Other than correcting technical errors, congressional tax-writing committees were determined to let the new law take effect, holding the line on the 1986 reform.

In 1993, higher education won at least one significant concession as part of the five-year Clinton budget package. As passed by Congress, the legislation restores the full tax deductibility of gifts of appreciated property. The 1993 legislation also retroactively restores two tax provisions that expired in 1992: the tax break for corporate spending on university research, mentioned above, and the income tax exemption for individuals who receive educational benefits from their employers. The latter tax exemption, known as Section 127, for its location in the tax code, has been an on-again, off-again legislative item for many years. In 1996, the exemption was restored, but only through tax year 1997 and only for undergraduate students receiving employer-provided tuition benefits.

Tax legislation is high on the agenda of the 105th Congress (1997/98), and the debate will have major implications for higher education. During his 1996 reelection campaign, President Clinton countered Senator Bob Dole's across-the-board tax cut proposal with his own plan of targeted tax relief (including credits and deductions for families paying college tuition), which would cost the federal government an estimated $36 billion in lost revenue over six years. Representatives of higher education are ambivalent toward the Clinton proposals. Cheered by the unexpected commitment of new resources, they worry about a variety of possible unintended consequences, including entanglements with the Internal Revenue Service (IRS), which would have to enforce a B-average grade requirement for tuition credits, among other provisions. Critics also question whether the president's proposal would actually increase investment in education and help equalize opportunity or whether it would just benefit families of students who would have gone to college anyway; whether it would encourage higher tuition, thus benefiting no one; and whether the resources could be more effectively invested in the existing grant, loan, and work/study programs run by the Department of Education, especially the Pell grant program.[16]

On two previous occasions the federal government came close to enacting tuition tax breaks much like the Clinton proposals. In 1965, there was a groundswell of congressional support for tuition tax deductions to help the middle class, but they were countered by the Johnson administration when it added the guaranteed student loan program to the Higher Education Act. Tuition tax bills built another head of steam in the mid-1970s, but President Carter agreed to the Middle Income Student Assistance Act to head them off. On both occasions, instead of trying to deliver educational assistance through the tax code, the response was to expand eligibility and expenditures on direct student aid. The difference in today's debate is that for the first time the president is pushing for, not trying to avert, the enactment of tuition tax breaks. The issues and choices, however, are much the same. What is the most effective way for the government to help students and families finance postsecondary education? Who should be the target of assistance? And should it be delivered via the tax code or through existing student aid programs?

Federal Regulation and Its Impact

Federal regulation of higher education derives from two principal sources: the requirements of accountability that accompany the receipt of federal funds; and the dictates of social legislation, executive orders, and judicial decisions stemming from such legislation.[17] To the degree that government officials insist on accountability for the proper expenditure of funds, and while congressional mandates addressing a range of social problems remain in force, there will be complexity and strain in the relationship of government and higher education. Tensions are inherent, given the traditions of academic autonomy, the mandates of Congress, the missions of federal agencies, and the responsibilities of those agencies for the stewardship of taxpayer dollars.

The academic community has long been wary of entanglement with government, but only a few institutions (mainly independent and religiously affiliated) have consistently refused funds from Washington. The great majority of colleges have accepted federal patronage even though it exacts a price in the expenses of compliance and in the distraction and intrusion of external controls. The federal government influences higher education through scores of statutes and regulations administered by diverse federal agencies. Some mandates, such as the Americans with Disabilities Act or regulations of the Environmental Protection Agency and the Occupational Safety and Health Administration, affect all types of organizations equally. Others, such as the Buckley Amendment on privacy rights of students and Title IX of the Education Amendments of 1972 barring gender bias, are specific to educational institutions. Colleges have long argued that such regulatory burdens contribute to their spiraling costs. But there is no documentation of the extent to which higher education is disproportionately affected by federal requirements, thereby justifying the more rapid increases in college charges during the past decade and a half relative to prices of other goods and services in the economy.

During the 1980s, higher education's concerns on this front receded to some degree. The Reagan administration's widely publicized support for regulatory relief altered the climate of regulation. Enforcement eased in some areas, and over the years colleges learned to accommodate the bureaucratic requirements of the government, tempering previous conflicts. Some institutions actually bargained with the federal government to lessen their regulatory burden. Prior to the highly publicized controversy over indirect costs in the early 1990s, for example, Yale and Stanford had accepted lowered indirect cost reimbursement on research contracts in exchange for reduced federal reporting requirements. But in many respects regulatory burdens have mounted not only for colleges but for all sectors of society in recent years. Higher education, along with other constituencies, has complained about the proliferation of "unfunded mandates" from Washington—legislative and regulatory requirements imposed by the federal government without federal funding to help pay the costs of compliance.

The balance of the 1990s will no doubt be replete with regulatory challenges for higher education. Leaving aside the potential complexity of the Clinton tuition tax proposals should they pass, IRS scrutiny of colleges appears to be intensifying as tax regulations and compliance procedures grow more complex for all nonprofit institutions. In the student aid arena, the unique regulatory dilemma is the sheer number and diversity of schools and kinds of training supported by programs under Title IV of the Higher Education Act. Applying the same rules and simultaneously regulating the use of student aid subsidies by more than eight thousand proprietary and collegiate institutions strains the capacity of an understaffed Department of Education and imposes undue burdens on schools that do a good job of administering federal programs. While the Clinton administration has tried to advance alternative delivery and regulatory mechanisms, Congress has been reluctant to differentiate by postsecondary sector or length and nature of training.

An arena of ongoing debate and litigation will be civil rights enforcement. While the Supreme Court's 1954 decision in *Brown v. Board of Education* applied to collegiate as well as elementary and secondary education, it was not until 1992 that the Court handed down a decision providing guidance for ending patterns of racial segregation in state postsecondary systems. In *U.S. vs. Fordice,* the Supreme Court ordered a lower court to review all policies that "contribute to the racial identifiability" of Mississippi's public colleges and universities. Interpreting and applying *Fordice* will take years, both in the federal courts and in the enforcement activities of the Office of Civil Rights of the U.S. Department of Education. A great deal is at stake not only for Mississippi but also for as many as fifteen other states that have faced legal challenges to their higher education systems on grounds of alleged discrimination.

Paradoxically, at the same time that courts and the Department of Education continue to monitor and rule on the status of desegregation in various states, voters, political leaders, and the courts have taken action to scale back or eliminate the use of affirmative action in admissions, hiring, and student financial aid. U.S. Circuit Courts of Appeal have struck down a race-specific scholarship program at the University of Maryland, College Park, and the law school admissions policy at the University of Texas, Austin. While these decisions apply only to the circuits in which they were handed down, proponents of affirmative action argue that they have had a chilling effect on all institutions. So far, the Department of Education has urged colleges and universities to stand by their current policies, arguing that the Supreme Court's decision in *Regents of the University of California v. Bakke,* certifying the use of race as a "plus factor" in college admissions, is still the law of the land.[18] Nonetheless, this issue will continue to preoccupy college leaders as they await more definitive court decisions and as opponents of affirmative action mount further challenges to campus policies.[19]

Prospects for the Federal Role in Higher Education

In summary, here are some of the issues that will influence the federal role in higher education at the turn of the century and beyond:

— Clouding the generally positive outlook for federal patronage of university-based research are persistent concerns about research practices in academia and unrelenting pressure to reduce federal budget deficits. Some policy makers are calling for science and technology investments that are more sharply focused on areas of national need. Universities will be challenged to articulate more clearly how research contributes to societal goals. Debate will also focus on the balance of funding between research and commercial applications, the need to upgrade the physical infrastructure of scientific research, and the adequacy of government support to train the country's next generation of top-flight scientists and engineers.
— Policy makers will continue to worry about the consequences of growing student indebtedness for individuals and society, and there will be efforts to restore the purchasing power of federal

grant aid. But the policy drift toward a loan-based system seems likely to continue. Much energy and debate will focus on changes in the way student loans are financed, originated, serviced, and repaid. The Department of Education will continue to try to expand direct lending and streamline the student aid process. Issues of quality control, the costs of education, and consumer protection will also continue to concern federal policy makers.

—At least in the near term, tax policy debates will center on proposals to help middle-income families finance postsecondary education. At stake is the fundamental question of how the federal government should deliver aid to students and families: by way of tax relief or through direct-expenditure programs based primarily on need.

— Higher education will continue to petition federal agencies for regulatory relief. But as long as government officials insist on accountability for taxpayer dollars and legislative mandates addressing a range of social problems remain in force, the burden of rules and regulations will be the price universities must pay for federal assistance.

The federal government will undoubtedly continue to make important contributions to enhancing the academic enterprise and equalizing educational opportunities in America. As in the past, federal support will supplement the basic funding provided by state and private sources, and it will spring from objectives such as economic competitiveness, health, and quality of life rather than from an interest in education for its own sake. And funds, along with regulations, will continue to flow from a variety of agencies in Washington. Such support is untidy, piecemeal, and not without headaches for institutions, students, and states. But the pattern serves a variety of national purposes and, in fact, ultimately may better serve to protect institutional diversity, students' freedom of choice, and independent thought in American education than would an overarching federal policy.

NOTES

The authors wish to acknowledge the constructive comments on drafts of this chapter by Robert Durkee, vice president for public affairs, Princeton

University, and Jerold Roschwalb, director of federal relations, National Association of State Universities and Land-Grant Colleges. Any errors of fact or interpretation are the sole responsibility of the authors.

1. For the historical development of the federal role in higher education, see George N. Rainsford, *Congress and Higher Education in the Nineteenth Century* (Knoxville: University of Tennessee Press, 1972). The two private universities benefiting from the Morrill Land-Grant College Act are the Massachusetts Institute of Technology (established in 1861) and Cornell University (1865).

2. Terry Sanford, *Storm Over the States* (New York: McGraw-Hill, 1967), 63.

3. Lawrence E. Gladieux and Thomas R. Wolanin, *Congress and the Colleges: The National Politics of Higher Education* (Lexington, Mass.: Lexington Books, 1976), 226.

4. For an approach to assessing the indirect effects of student aid, see Michael S. McPherson, "Silver Linings: Student Aid's Unintended Good Deeds," paper prepared for the annual meeting of the American Educational Research Association, April 1987.

5. National Postsecondary Student Aid Study (NPSAS), 1993, analysis by authors; National Center for Education Statistics, *Digest of Education Statistics, 1995* (Washington, D.C.: U.S. Department of Education, 1995), table 306. The data from NPSAS are for the 1992/93 academic year. Updated figures for the academic year 1995/96 are likely to show a higher percentage of postsecondary students receiving federal aid.

6. Chester E. Finn Jr., "A Federal Policy for Higher Education?" *Alternative* (May 1975): 18–19.

7. College Entrance Examination Board, *Trends in Student Aid, 1986 to 1996* (Washington, D.C.: CEEB, 1996).

8. National Science Foundation, *Selected Data on Academic and Engineering R&D Expenditures, Fiscal Year 1992* (Arlington, Va.: NSF, 1994).

9. Deborah H. Shapley and Roy Rustum, *Lost at the Frontier* (Philadelphia: Institute for Scientific Information Press, 1985), 39.

10. Congressman Rick Boucher, "Science Policy for the 21st Century," *Chronicle of Higher Education,* Sept. 1, 1993.

11. Colleen Cordes and Siobhan Gorman, "Congress Slashes Earmarks for Academe by 50%, the Biggest Decrease Ever," *Chronicle of Higher Education,* Sept. 13, 1996.

12. U.S. General Accounting Office, *Peer Review: Reforms Needed to Ensure Fairness in Federal Agency Grant Selection* (Washington, D.C.: GAO, 1994).

13. Stanford was later exonerated on charges of mishandling federal funds.

14. See Lawrence E. Gladieux and Arthur M. Hauptman, *The College Aid Quandary: Access, Quality, and the Federal Role* (Washington, D.C.: Brookings, 1995).

15. See Michael Mumper, *Removing College Price Barriers: What Government Has Done and Why It Hasn't Worked* (Albany: State University of New York Press, 1996); Lawrence E. Gladieux, *College Opportunities and the Poor: Getting National Policies Back on Track* (Washington, D.C.: Center for the Study of Opportunity in Higher Education and College Board, 1996).

16. Lawrence E. Gladieux and Robert D. Reischauer, "Higher Tuition, More Grade Inflation," *Washington Post,* Sept. 4, 1996.

17. John T. Wilson, *Academic Science, Higher Education, and the Federal Government, 1950–1983* (Chicago: University of Chicago Press, 1983), 104–6.

18. Patrick Healy, "Education Department Urges Colleges to Keep Affirmative Action," *Chronicle of Higher Education,* May 3, 1996.

19. For more on the affirmative action debate and related legal issues, see chap. 8, this volume.

Chapter Seven

The States and Higher Education

Aims C. McGuinness Jr.

The period of the remaining years of the 1990s and well into the next decade is likely to be one of the most troubling in the history of the nation's higher education enterprise. Relations between state government and higher education are likely to be especially strained because of five broad trends:[1]

— *Escalating demands.* These are driven not only by numbers but also by higher expectations for what an increasingly diverse student population should know and be able to do as the result of a college education. The demands extend to virtually every dimension of higher education, including research and service.
— *Severe economic constraints.* Even with gradual economic recovery, it is unlikely that higher education will see significant improvements in funding, at least on a per student basis, within the next decade. The federal deficit, competing priorities for public funds, public anger about rising student costs, and severe competition for limited corporate and philanthropic funds will all contribute to the continuing financial constraints.
— *The academy's inherent resistance to change.* As demands increase and resources dwindle, institutions are slowly recognizing that, if they continue to do business as usual, their ability to educate students and continue their research and service missions will be seriously compromised. But translating this slow awareness

into changes at the institutional core—in curriculum, in modes of
teaching and learning, and in faculty governance—will be a long-
term, incremental process. The resulting public frustration with
the academy's inability to respond to major societal needs only
intensifies the danger of blunt governmental intervention.

—*Negative climate of public opinion.* Ironically, it is not a feeling that
higher education lacks value to the individual and society that
is driving the negative public view. On the contrary, the problem seems to be that the public values higher education greatly.
But they see it being directed by a largely internal agenda disconnected from major societal priorities and mismanaged in ways
that will make it increasingly inaccessible (especially in terms
of cost).

—*Instability of state political leadership.* The trend toward term
limitations and the demands of political office are contributing
to major changes in the state leadership. This is especially pronounced in state legislatures. As each legislative session begins,
the proportion of new members increases. The 1994 midterm
elections accelerated this change, but the process began earlier,
and its impact will be increasingly evident as time passes. The
relative stability provided by the memory about state higher education policies of long-term legislative leaders is being lost. Other
issues are dominating the agendas. The twenty-year trend toward
larger and more dominant legislative staffs is accelerating.[2]

These conditions are certain to exacerbate already frayed state relationships with higher education. Constructive resolution of these
conflicts is essential both to the continued strength of American
higher education and to its capacity to respond to major societal priorities. The purpose of this chapter is to present a framework and
basic information about the state role as a beginning point for further reading and study.[3]

Assumptions about State and Higher
Education Relationships

Two underlying assumptions are basic to the understanding of state/
higher education relations: first, the essential and legitimate role of

the state and, second, the great variations among states in size, culture, policies, and structure.

For some within higher education even the mention of state government conjures up negative images. There continues to be a widespread sense within the academy that virtually any state involvement, other than providing funding with no strings attached, is an infringement on legitimate institutional autonomy. The relationships are viewed along a continuum: at one end, complete institutional autonomy is good; at the other end, state involvement is seen as bad. Frank Newman suggested a different, more constructive view, that both institutional autonomy and state involvement are important. Governments have a legitimate interest in the responsiveness of the academy to major societal needs. At the same time, it is important for both society and the academy that higher education be able to pursue values and purposes that are different from, and in same cases in conflict with, the prevailing values and priorities of the state. "What becomes clear," Newman stated, "is that the real need is not simply for more autonomy but for a relationship between the university and the state that is constructive for both, built up over a long period of time by careful attention on the part of all parties."[4]

Robert Berdahl made a similar distinction between the concept of academic freedom, which is universal and absolute, and autonomy, which is "of necessity parochial and relative." He continued by emphasizing that, "the real issue with respect to autonomy . . . is not whether there will be interference by the state but whether the inevitable interference will be confined to the proper topics and expressed through a suitably sensitive mechanism."[5]

The key is for the higher education community to recognize that it has a stake, if not a responsibility, to engage actively with state political leaders in defining the nature of the relationship. This includes defining the major societal ends toward which the academy should direct its energies and shaping the policies and other "suitably sensitive" mechanisms that will govern the relationships.

A second point in understanding state/higher education relations is that, despite the appearance of similarity in institutional missions and state structures, states vary significantly in history and culture and in political and economic dynamics. Colleges and universities, as social institutions, reflect and even amplify these important yet often subtle differences. In reports on state policy, one often sees state-by-state listings or figures that convey the false impression that they have evolved in a vacuum, disconnected from unique state circumstances. In a time when multivariate analysis is greatly eased by computers, researchers should be cautioned that the most important variables may not be easily quantified. Variations on tuition policy and student policy illustrate this point:

—States with comparatively high public tuition and strong commitments to need-based student aid tend to be those with historically strong private higher education sectors, reinforced by a pattern across all governmental dimensions to rely upon private entities and forces to meet public needs. These states have a history of recognizing the role of the independent sector in serving public purposes. Public colleges and universities evolved as major forces only since the 1960s, and the states have only recently, and sometimes hesitantly, developed a commitment to the public sector. More often than not, the state's posture on tuition has evolved not through conscious policy choice but through the interaction of culture and politics over many decades.

—States with comparatively low public tuition and modest student aid programs, in contrast, are often those whose higher education systems evolved from a more populist tradition and where the private sector played a limited role in meeting public needs in the states' early history. Again, this pattern is often reflected in many years of action on all public issues.

A particularly informative, yet controversial, way of thinking about state variations is presented by the political science literature on state political cultures. Daniel Elazar, for example, set forth a theory of political subcultures and classified states according to their culture and ethnicity, whether they were moralistic, individualistic, or traditionalistic, and whether their ethos was "public-regarding" or "private-regarding."[6]

The former Washington State Council for Postsecondary Education made a similar but more limited effort to classify state postures toward higher education, ranging from those with a tradition of treating public colleges like state regulatory agencies to those that treated them like state-assisted private corporations, which are largely exempt from state procedural controls.[7]

The "State Period" in American Higher Education

Historically, states have provided the legal framework within which both public and private institutions have operated, but with the dramatic expansion of the public sector since the 1950s and 1960s, this has also become the case in terms of enrollment and financing.[8] From the 1950s to the end of the 1980s, the share of total enrollment in public institutions (including many community colleges partially funded from local revenues) increased from about 60 to 80 percent. The private sector continued to grow, but it was outstripped by increases of one-and-a-half times in public four-year enrollments and five times in public two-year institutional enrollments. The proportion of institutions in the private sector dropped from 65 to 45 percent.

From a comparative perspective, American higher education remains perhaps the most diverse, decentralized, private, market-driven system (if it can even be called a system) in the world. Yet state governments have gradually come to play a more central role than is often conveyed in international comparisons. In fact, there appears to be a worldwide convergence toward the kind of mixed public/private system that has evolved in the United States. While other nations are increasing the private elements in their systems, the United States has been moving for several decades toward a more public system.[9]

In the early 1990s, state and local governments provided approximately 32 percent of the overall financial support for higher education, both public and private. This compared with 16 percent from the federal government, 31 percent from tuition and fees, and 21 percent from other sources (including endowments, private philanthropy and corporations).[10] As Clark Kerr observed in 1985, mid-1980 to mid-1990 (and perhaps beyond) would be a decade of state and private leadership in higher education and that periods of federal leadership have been relatively brief: 1860–90 and 1955–85. He further observed that as the impact of higher education on the states' economies has become more politically important, state governors have emerged as the most important political figures.[11] The late 1980s and early 1990s have confirmed Kerr's observations. In fact, states substantially increased support for higher education in the mid-1980s in all but a few cases. Some increases were as high as 90 percent over the ten-year period ending in 1991/92, even when adjusted for inflation.[12] The state and local share of overall funding increased over the same period from 30 to 32 percent, while the federal share decreased from 20 to 16 percent.[13] While the state share increased in the 1980s, the most dramatic increases in higher education revenue came from students and their parents and from other private sources. This relatively affluent period for colleges and universities was made possible both by substantial increases in state appropriations and by substantial tuition increases, primarily in the private sector.

In the first years of the 1990s, higher education experienced an abrupt downturn in revenues. For the first time in the thirty-three-year history of collection of data on state appropriations by Illinois State University, an actual decline was recorded. By fiscal year 1996/97, state support for higher education had regained strength: state appropriations had increased to $46.5 billion, the highest level ever — a 5 percent increase over the previous year and a 9 percent increase over a two-year period, and the largest one- and two-year increases since 1990.[14] Despite these positive signs, higher education will likely continue to receive a steadily declining share of state revenues. Even though, in absolute terms, state higher education appropriations increased significantly in the 1980s, the percentage of state revenues declined, the strength of state economies offsetting the decline in higher education's share. Now the economy is growing more slowly, and states are faced with largely mandatory increases in funding for health care, prisons, and the public schools. In these conditions, states will find it difficult to provide the increases for higher education for the remaining years of the 1990s necessary to keep up with increased student demands and inflation.

Dramatic increases in public tuition were a consequence of the fiscal crisis of the early 1990s. In the 1980s, double-digit increases were primarily a phenomenon of the private sector. In 1991/92, tuition increased 13 to 15 percent on the average, but some states, such as California, increased fees by 40 percent or more. By the mid-1990s, the rate of public tuition increases moderated considerably, reflecting improved state support. In 1994/95, states increased student aid funding by 7.7 percent over the previous year.[15] Increases from 1995/96 to 1996/97 averaged 5 percent for public four-year and two-year institutions, one of the smallest in fifteen years. This still exceeded the 2.9 percent increase in the consumer price index for the same period.[16] In the longer term, states will abandon their commitment to low tuition, not as policy but out of economic necessity. As these trends suggest, state higher education financing is undergoing fundamental changes.

The resulting tensions will make financing one of the central issues for the next decade.

Even more important than providing financial support, the states have been, and continue to be, national leaders in education reform. Governors have spearheaded this movement, using the Education Commission of the States (ECS) and the National Governors' Association (NGA) as primary vehicles. It was the governors who took the initiative in organizing the 1989 Education Summit with President George Bush in Charlottesville, Virginia, in 1989, and in advocating for the first time in the country's history a series of national goals. The governors continue to pursue these goals and monitor the progress through the national goals panel.

During the 1980s, the states led a fundamental change in the definition of accountability. Up to that point, states focused primarily on issues of resource allocation and utilization and rarely became involved in basic questions about the outcomes of a college or university education. By the end of the 1980s, questions about outcomes, especially student outcomes, dominated states' agendas. More than any other force, state policies requiring institutions to assess student learning and to provide information to the states and the public stimulated higher education's attention to these issues. Many colleges and universities now report that they are making active efforts to assess student learning. While state mandates initially stimulated this attention, it is now being sustained by voluntary accreditation and other forces.[17] The states also led in developing new funding systems, such as competitive, incentive, and performance funding. The use of funding "on the margin" to support centers of excellence in research and technology and to stimulate improvement in undergraduate education was widespread.[18] Relating this to the discussion in chapter 3 on autonomy, since the early 1980s, states have been much more willing to enter into the area Robert Berdahl defines as "substantive autonomy."

There are signs that the "state period" in American higher education is fading and that a new period is coming into being in which all levels of government and both public and private sectors will participate in shaping nationwide policy. Yet the states remain the locus for change. Two governor-led initiatives illustrate this point. The first is the renewed attention to the quality of undergraduate education stimulated by Colorado Governor Roy Romer when he was 1994/95 ECS chairman. The resulting report, *Making Quality Count in Under-*

graduate Education, sheds light on the differences among internal
and external constituents (students, faculty, and business and political leaders) in how they define quality and in what they expect from
colleges and universities. It gives renewed attention to the challenge
of measuring quality and providing students and the public with information to make choices about postsecondary education.[19]

The second major initiative is the 1996 decision of the seventeen
governors who are members of the Western Governors Association to
endorse the development of the Western Governors University (WGU;
initially called the "virtual" university). In making this decision the
governors cited the growing importance of postsecondary education
to their states and the nation but emphasized the barriers of severely
constrained resources and "the inflexibility and high costs of traditional educational practices and . . . outdated institutional and public
policies." They emphasized two potential means to overcome these
barriers: the "exploding availability and capabilities of advanced-technology-based teaching and learning," and "cutting-edge educational
and assessment services." Behind the initiative were two concerns:
first, the challenge of meeting dramatic enrollment increases projected for several western states and, second, the growing demand of
business and industry and many adult learners for a shift to assessment of competency as the basis for recognizing learning and awarding credentials. Two goals of the new university will be, first, to provide a means for learners to obtain formal recognition of the skills and
knowledge they acquire through advanced-technology-based learning
at home, on the job, or through other means outside the formal educational system; and second, to shift the focus of education to the
actual competence of students and away from "seat time" or other
measures of instructional activity.[20]

As envisioned by the governors, WGU will be a regional, nonprofit,
degree-granting, accredited institution. When it begins operation in
late 1997, it will serve primarily as a means to broker learner access
to educational opportunities and degree programs currently available through technology-based learning from existing providers (e.g.,
traditional colleges and universities). In time, it will offer its own degrees but only on the basis of assessment of competencies. The WGU
will not provide instruction itself but will facilitate learners' access to
courses, modules, and programs provided by others. The university
will include an internet-based information and advisement system as
well as a network of service centers in each of the participating west-

ern states. The ECS's national goals initiative and the WGU exemplify the leadership of governors in addressing an issue without the explicit involvement of the federal government. Yet in both cases, a federal role will be essential. The changes proposed by the governors will require complementary changes in federal policies on statistics, student aid, institutional eligibility, and telecommunications, to mention only a few.

State Coordination and Governance

Rising expectations for performance and accountability, coupled with serious budget problems, inevitably led governors and legislators to issues of governance.[21] From 1985 through 1993, about thirty-three states had special studies or blue-ribbon commissions on higher education. In all of these, changes in state structure were an issue. Several other states either enacted or seriously debated reorganization proposals. Changes of some consequence were actually enacted in sixteen states in the period.[22] In the period 1993–96, another four states (Illinois, Minnesota, Montana, and New Jersey) carried out significant governance changes. Other states (e.g., Massachusetts and South Carolina) made important changes to current structures. State structures can be understood from two perspectives: in terms of *public institutional governance,* or how the state governs public institutions; and in terms of *statewide coordination,* or how the state provides for coordination of the overall higher education system.

Public Institutional Governance

All states assign responsibility for the operation of public colleges and universities to governing boards. The responsibility of these boards is much the same as that of a board of directors for any nonprofit corporation. They appoint the campus's chief executive (or the system's chief executive), establish policies, approve actions related to faculty and other personnel, ensure institutional fiscal integrity, and perform other policy and management functions. Clark Kerr and Marian Gade have categorized public governing boards as follows:[23]

—*Consolidated governance systems.* One board covers all two-year and four-year public campuses or one board covers all four-year

campuses, including research universities and other four-year institutions, with separate arrangements for two-year institutions.
—*Segmental systems.* Separate boards cover separate types of campus, such as research universities, comprehensive colleges and
universities, and community colleges.
—*Campus-level boards.* These have full authority over a single campus and are not covered by a consolidated governing board or
multicampus system. In North Carolina and Utah, boards have
authority delegated by the central board and can make some decisions on their own. In the State University of New York and the
University of Maryland systems, boards are largely advisory.

Governing boards of public institutions were modeled after lay
boards of private nonprofit colleges and universities, which in most
instances govern single institutions. Perhaps for this reason, many
retain an impression that the single-board, single-institution pattern
is dominant. The reality is that 75 percent of the students in American public higher education are on campuses that are parts of multicampus or consolidated systems of multiple campuses, all under a
single governing board. Because these systems are important to so
much of the nation's higher education enterprise, their performance
is under increasing scrutiny. Kerr and Gade made the following com-
ment: "The drift in the public sector of higher education, especially
during the past 40 years . . . [is] toward consolidation and toward
control. . . . This tendency toward consolidation and control runs
counter to the development in American national economic policy
toward more competition and autonomy. This economic trend is present in most countries—even in the Soviet Union and China. The general government tendency in the United States has also been toward
decentralization to the states and localities." [24]

Statewide Coordination

Coordination is the term used most often to describe state approaches
for handling the interconnections between the state and the higher
education enterprise. It has become common for the term to refer primarily to the actions of agencies formed explicitly for this purpose. In
a broader sense, however, coordination occurs through a wide array
of mechanisms, from governors' and legislators' actions to institutions' informal networks and associations, their administrative staffs,

faculties, and students.[25] States assign the following eight statewide coordinating functions to governing boards:

—*Planning.* Most states carry out some form of long-range or master planning to examine state needs, establish state goals and objectives, consider the resources of all institutions, and recommend public policy priorities. In some states, the process focuses on a master, or strategic, plan. In others, a conscious decision is made not to produce a master plan but instead to carry out special studies resulting in a series of reports rather than a single document.

—*Policy analysis and problem resolution.* In addition to the analysis carried out in the formal planning process, states undertake special studies on issues that transcend the concerns of any single institution. These may relate to long-term issues (such as the feasibility of authorizing graduate programs at a rural campus or location), or they may concern specific intersector or interinstitutional issues, such as minority participation and achievement, student transfer and articulation, and alternative financing policies or tuition policy. Often these studies are performed at the request of the governor or legislature.

—*Mission definition.* As an outgrowth of the planning process, a number of states define the missions of each public college and university in terms of degrees awarded, programs offered, and clientele served. These are used for both institutional and state-level decision making on new degree and program proposals, budget and financing formula development, and other coordinating functions.[26]

—*Academic program review.* Most states examine proposals from institutions for new academic programs. Since the late 1970s, many states as well as multicampus systems have instituted periodic reviews of existing programs. Now, in serious economic conditions, program review is being used as a strategy to identify programs for termination and areas for quality and productivity improvements.[27]

—*Budget development, funding formulas, and resource allocation.* All states have processes for reviewing and approving institutional operating and capital budgets, moving these budgets through the decision-making process, allocating funds to systems or institutions, and ensuring accountability. The extent of a higher edu-

cation agency's role depends largely on the governor's and legislature's roles. In some states, these bodies delegate authority to
an agency; in others, they maintain direct control of most of the
steps in the budget process.[28]

—*Program administration.* States assign administrative responsibilities for state and federal programs to one or more agencies. The
most common administrative responsibilities relate to state student grant and loan programs.

—*Information, assessment, and accountability systems.* Statewide
data systems are among the most common, core capabilities of
coordinating boards. In the past decade, the emphasis of these
systems has shifted decidedly from resources and inputs toward
outcomes or indicators of performance. Several states require institutions to prepare "report cards" to the state and the public
on their performance in relation to their missions. Most states
now have requirements that institutions establish programs to
assess student learning. The focus of these, however, is primarily
on improvement within the institutions, and requirements tend
to be that institutions demonstrate that they have an assessment
program and that they are using the results for their internal
renewal purposes. There is now a resurgence of state interest in
public reporting on institutional performance. In 1995, about one-
third of the states had issued or were planning to issue a higher
education performance report, mostly for public institutions. By
September 1996, more than half the states were involved, and
about two-fifths were linking or planning to link performance to
funding in some way.[29]

—*Institutional licensure and authorization.* All states have statutes
requiring institutions to be licensed to operate within the state.
States vary greatly in the ways that they organize and carry out
this responsibility. In only a few (e.g., New York) is the responsibility assigned to a single agency. In others, it may be dispersed
across three or four entities, some responsible only for non-
degree-granting proprietary institutions, others responsible for
a specific category of school (e.g., truck driving or cosmetology
schools). Standards applied by these entities also vary greatly. According to federal law, institutions must be licensed to operate by
a state in order for their students to be eligible for federal student
assistance. This has been a requirement of the Higher Education
Act since its enactment in 1965. Because of variations in the rigor

of state oversight, questions have been raised for a number of years about the adequacy of this gatekeeping provision in federal policy. In response to these concerns, Congress in 1992 amended the Higher Education Act to establish a new Part H, requiring states to designate a state postsecondary review entity (SPRE) to be responsible for reviewing postsecondary education institutions for eligibility for federal student aid. When the higher education community became aware of this provision as the Department of Education implemented it in 1993 and 1994, it created a firestorm of protest in the higher education community.[30]

Many, especially representatives of independent colleges and universities, believed that the SPRE legislation would fundamentally change the relationship between higher education and government. In particular, they feared it would empower states (through a provision in federal law) to become directly involved in the internal affairs of institutions in ways that would seriously undermine autonomy. After the dramatic changes in the 1994 midterm congressional elections, there remained little support for implementing SPRE in either Congress or the administration, and funding for the program was eliminated. Implementation was canceled, but the provisions remain in federal law. How to reshape these gatekeeping functions to define appropriate roles for the states, the federal government, and voluntary accreditation will be a continuing issue as the Congress debates future changes in the Higher Education Act.

Classifications of State Structures

A number of classification systems have been developed since the 1960s to describe the variations in state structures. None is entirely satisfactory in reflecting the subtle differences among boards and agencies.[31] Most make a basic distinction among three kinds of state structures:

— *Consolidated governing board states.* Twenty-two states and Puerto Rico assign responsibility for coordinating most, if not all, higher education through a board whose primary responsibilities relate to governing the institutions under its jurisdiction. Most of these boards would be in the category of consolidated governing board

as defined by Kerr and Gade, although in several states, the responsibility is shared between two segmental boards, one for four-
year institutions and the other for community colleges or technical institutions. A consolidated governing board (1) usually heads
a single corporate entity that encompasses all institutions within
the system, (2) carries out coordinating responsibilities in addition to its responsibilities for governing institutions under its
jurisdiction, (3) has authority both to develop and to implement
policy, (4) advocates needs of the institutions to the legislature
and governor, (5) appoints, sets compensation for, and evaluates
system and institutional chief executives, (6) sets faculty personnel policies and usually approves tenure, and (7) has authority to
allocate and reallocate resources between and among the institutions within its jurisdiction.

—*Coordinating board states.* Twenty-four states and the District of
Columbia govern their institutions through single boards, segmental boards, or some combination of these. Governance, as opposed to coordination, is relatively decentralized. Coordination is
assigned to a single board other than one of the governing boards.
Six of these states and the District of Columbia have coordinating entities that, except for their formal statutory status, have
authority not significantly broader than those in the state planning agency states. A coordinating board (1) does not govern institutions, in the sense that this is defined above (e.g., appoint
institutional chief executives or set faculty personnel policies),
(2) usually does not have corporate status independent of state
government, (3) focuses more on state and system needs and priorities than on advocating the interests of the higher education
community,[32] (4) plans primarily for the system as a whole (in
most states with a coordinating board and includes all institutions, both public and private), (5) appoints, sets compensation
for, and evaluates the agency executive officer and staff but not
the institutional chief executives (in several states, the governor
is the final appointing authority but usually with recommendations coming from the coordinating board), (6) may or may not
review and make recommendations on budgets (a few coordinating agencies recommend consolidated budgets for the whole public system, while others simply make recommendations to the
governor or legislature on individual institutional or segmental
budgets), and (7) may or may not review or approve proposals for

new academic programs, and may or may not have authority to require institutions to review existing programs.

—*Planning agency states.* Four states have no statutory entity with coordinating authority beyond a voluntary planning and convening role to ensure good communications among institutions and sectors. Minnesota recently replaced its coordinating board with an entity responsible for administering student aid and maintaining statewide information systems. Its planning role is now limited to providing support for planning undertaken by the two university systems and the staffs of the legislature and executive branch of state government.

Beyond these three formal categories, subtle differences tend to make each state unique, despite what may appear to be a structure similar to those in other states. Differences in state history and culture are especially important. In addition, three other factors should be considered:

—*Role of legislative and executive branches.* In some states, the power is in the legislature, and the governor has only limited authority. In others, the governor wields most of the power.

—*Size of system.* States that have consolidated governing boards usually have comparatively less complex systems and smaller enrollments (less than 100,000 and, in some cases, less than 25,000). Georgia, North Carolina, and Wisconsin are three major exceptions. Most coordinating board states have large enrollments (a third with enrollments over 200,000) and complex systems of multicampus, segmental, and individual governing board arrangements.

—*Tradition and quality of leadership.* While traditions may endure, the leadership qualities of board members, state agency chief executives and staffs, and institutional leaders change. A board recognized as strong and effective at one point may be seen as weak and ineffective at another. The quality of leadership of the governor and key legislators can also make a profound difference. More than formal authority, those variables that tend to define the strength and effectiveness of a higher education board include (1) the prestige and credibility of board members, (2) the board's performance as a cohesive, policy-making group, (3) the reputation of the board and staff for objectivity, fairness, sound judgment, and constructive conflict resolution, and (4) the ability of the board to focus its agenda on major policy issues confronting the state and the higher education system. This means that the board has found ways to organize its work, to delegate and to manage its time effectively.

Changes in State Structures

The basic patterns of state-level organization were in place in the early 1970s. The year 1972 marked the culmination of more than a decade of development of state higher education agencies formed to coordinate the massive expansion in the late 1950s and 1960s. By that year, forty-seven states had established either consolidated governing boards responsible for all senior institutions (and in some cases, community colleges) or coordinating boards responsible for statewide planning and coordination of two or more governing boards. Three small states with a limited number of institutions did not form a special statutory agency but continued to handle statewide higher education issues through existing governing boards, informal coordination, and direct involvement of the governor and state legislature.

Perennial Issues

Throughout the past twenty years, several issues have consistently spurred governors and legislators to make higher education reorganization proposals. These tend to be long-standing irritants whose urgency increases as the public expectations rise or economic conditions worsen.

—*Actual or potential duplication of high-cost graduate and professional programs.* Most states are confronted with intractable political and economic stresses as growing urban centers compete with rural areas and older economic centers. These stresses are amplified and played out in conflicts within the states' higher education systems. The most common pattern is for a growing urban area to press to have accessible graduate and professional programs. In the first stage, the interest usually is simply to have these offered in the area, but this soon leads to demands that a new university be formed. The issue becomes further complicated when the prestige of having university status and graduate programs becomes mixed with issues of community pride and economic development. The reality that the new initiatives would duplicate or threaten support for similar programs at the state's major research university becomes a major issue. That many of the major public universities are located away from urban centers complicates the issue. The same scenario is also played out when isolated rural areas struggle to gain access to programs for place-bound adults. What usually sparks governance controversies are directly asking the governor or legislature for special attention. The ensuing political struggles inevitably lead to major restructuring proposals. Short-term victories gained from bypassing established coordinating structures usually lead in the long run to greater centralization.

—*Visible conflict between the aspirations of two institutions (often under separate governing boards) in the same geographic area.* Again, conflicts tend to be about which institution should offer high-cost graduate and professional programs. Major reorganization proposals (merger or consolidation) usually occur after years of less dramatic efforts to achieve cooperation and coordination.

—*Legislative reaction to intense institutional lobbying.* As governors and legislators face politically difficult and unattractive choices, focused on curtailing rather than expanding programs, intense lobbying by narrow, competing institutional interests can spark demands for restructuring. Political leaders seek ways to push such battles away from the immediate political process by increasing the authority of a state board in the hope that it will resolve conflicts before they get to the legislature. The reverse situation also frequently occurs. A state board will prevent an institutional end run and be faced with a legislative proposal (frequently stimulated by the offending institution) to abolish the board.

—*Frustrations with barriers to student transfer and articulation.* Evidence (usually in the form of constituent appeals to influential legislators) that institutions are making it difficult for students to transfer or are limiting credit transfer often lead to legislative intervention and, in extreme cases, to reorganization proposals.

—*Proposals (and related opposition) to close, merge, or change institutional missions.* At issue may be small, isolated, rural institutions or institutions in close proximity and with similar missions. What sparks the reorganization proposal is the sense that the existing system is unable to address these kinds of problem. Or, once a proposal is made and a political firestorm breaks out, reorganization may be proposed because the existing state board handles the issue poorly.

—*Lack of coordination among institutions offering vocational, technical, occupational, and transfer programs.* Many states have regions or communities where two or more public institutions, each responsible to a different state board or agency, offer similar programs. In the worst situation, this may involve a postsecondary technical institute, a community college, and a two-year lower-division university. Because of differences among the institutions in their educational missions and philosophies, they may resist program coordination and make it difficult for students to transfer. In a larger scale version of the same issue, many states face escalating demand in their two-year sectors that threatens to take resources from the university sectors. When these battles are fought on the floor of the state legislature rather than being resolved within the higher education system, they inevitably lead to proposals for restructuring.

—*Concerns about the effectiveness of the state board.* Major reorganization proposals are often made because of a sense that the existing board (or its staff) either is ineffective or lacks the political influence or judgment to address critical issues or is more focused on detailed administrative, regulatory, or internal management issues than on policy leadership. Ironically, when such criticisms of state boards are made, a previous legislature often has assigned these management or regulatory functions to the board. Reorganization may be proposed not because an agency lacks formal authority but because of a desire to change the leadership.

— *"Super board" proposals.* Almost without exception in governance debates, the option of consolidating all public institutions under a single governing board is raised. Because of the inevitable opposition these proposals generate (primarily from institutions that fear their independence will be threatened), few have been enacted in the past twenty years, which has not deterred others from advancing the idea. In lieu of total consolidation, states often consolidate institutional clusters to form segmental (all institutions with similar missions) systems.[33] As an alternative to forming a single statewide governing board, several states have strengthened the existing state coordinating board to the point that its regulatory powers border on authority to govern institutions.

Debates For and Against Consolidation

Kerr and Gade have cited two underlying reasons for the trend toward consolidation and control in U.S. higher education:

> The government does have a clear interest in centralizing and controlling some decisions, specifically over missions and over budgets, in order to make effective use of resources and to be sure that all important missions are actually and fairly served. ("Missions" include general admissions policies for students). Government also has an interest in effective review of performance.
>
> State authorities, specifically governors and legislative committees, find it helpful to hold one board and one chief executive officer accountable. They prefer to have to place or receive only one phone call rather than to have to deal with several or many competitive and combative institutions, their representatives, and supporters. This can be time consuming and exasperating. Some infighting, often highly counterproductive, can be kept out of the state capitol.[34]

Despite intense debates for and against consolidated systems, conclusive evidence on either side of the argument is difficult to find. Examples can be found of systems that are working well in terms of providing leadership while ensuring highly diverse missions, decentralized governance, and creative use of the benefits of a system to meet the state's educational needs.[35] At the same time, one can find examples of both coordinating and consolidated governing boards that are giving insufficient time to policy leadership, that have lost credibility with the state's political and higher education leadership, that are excessively focused on administrative, regulatory, and internal management issues, that fail to promote mission differentiation, and that give insufficient attention to the major policy challenges facing the state. The greatest danger is that states will adopt one alternative or another without first clarifying the ends to be achieved and without making a serious assessment of whether the alternative is the best means to those ends. The pressure simply to copy another state's structure is often overwhelming. The state's underlying political culture is one of the most important considerations.

In the mid-1990s, two states made significant changes in their structures, each reflecting a break from established patterns in the specific state and for the nation as a whole. In 1994, New Jersey eliminated the State Board and Department of Higher Education and replaced it with a smaller, more policy-focused Commission on Higher Education and a Presidents' Council, composed of the executives of all the public and state-supported independent institutions in the state. The change also decentralized institutional governance by strengthening the authority and responsibility of the governing boards. The change eliminated a state coordinating board that had gained the reputation during the 1980s as being one of the most effective and powerful in the nation. The new Commission on Higher Education retains important coordinating authority and responsibility but has less authority than its predecessor to regulate new programs and other institutional functions.[36]

In 1993, Minnesota consolidated three systems to form the Minnesota State Colleges and Universities system, which consolidates the former state university system, the community college system, and the technical college system. The law provided for a two-year planning period before formal implementation in mid-1995. Also, in 1995, the state replaced the Minnesota Higher Education Coordinating Board with the Minnesota Higher Education Services Board. At the heart of the issues that led to the new system were concerns about conflict, duplication, and years of ineffective coordination among state universities, community colleges, and technical colleges, especially those serving the same geographic area. The new system initially had sixty-six separate campuses, but changes implemented since the merger has reduced this to approximately fifty-four. Further consolidation can be expected.[37]

When economic times worsen, governance proposals seem to increase. Given the prospects for the 1990s, reorganization will clearly be on the agenda. A 1995 survey of state legislators found that nineteen states expected governance reform to be a legislative issue in the upcoming legislative session.[38] Many of these will be framed in terms of the perennial issues, and many of the alternatives will be simply copied from other states. As emphasized later in this chapter, it may be time for states to examine the appropriateness of structures formed for the mid-1900s for the conditions of the next century. It is a time for new, creative thinking about old categories and solutions.

What Issues Are on State Agendas?

Two surveys provide a picture of issues on state agendas.[39] The first, a survey of state legislators conducted under the sponsorship of the National Education Association, involved interviews with fifty-eight house and senate education committee chairs in forty-nine states. Survey objectives were to identify and clarify states' legislative agendas for higher education, their strategies and policy options, and the political, economic, and social factors that influence legislative policy and budgetary decisions. The survey found a high degree of uncertainty among state legislators about the legislative outlook for higher education, an uncertainty shaped by legislators' insecurity over the economy, enrollment growth, escalating costs, and limited state revenues. In terms of expectations for higher education, legislators emphasized the need to set priorities and for higher education not to be all things to all people. Specific priorities focused on undergraduate education and improving K–12 education; legislators exhibited little interest in become directly involved in questions of instructional quality in higher education.

Legislators also expressed concerns about the current organization and governance of higher education. They were interested in greater decentralization, less bureaucracy, and a strengthening of the authority and responsibility of institutional governing boards. This decentralization, in legislators' views, should be balanced by increased accountability and efficiency around state priorities. They were concerned, too, about the capacity of states to respond to new demands for access, especially in light of resource limitations. They saw technology as a primary means to meet these needs and to avoid the need to build new campuses. The efficiency of a student's movement through the system to earn a credential was a major concern. Issues of matriculation, transfer, and time-to-degree were mentioned as serious concerns. Legislators recognized higher education's funding needs but were skeptical about the possibilities for significantly increased funding. Many expressed interest in revising the states' higher education funding policies to give greater emphasis to performance.

The second survey was conducted by the State Higher Education Officers (SHEEO).[40] Respondents were SHEEO members, the executives of state coordinating and governing boards. This sur-

vey, conducted in 1996, was similar to ones conducted in 1989 and
1992. In 1989, the top three priority issues were quality of undergraduate education, minority student access and achievement, and
teacher education and preparation. In 1992, the top three priorities
were adequacy of overall state financial support, effectiveness and
accountability, and quality of undergraduate education. State financial support remained the most important issue for SHEEOs, second
in importance was effectiveness and accountability, and third was instructional technology and distance learning. The issue of technology
had not appeared on previous surveys, underscoring the growing importance of this issue and related concerns to the SHEEOs. The survey also documents for the first time how SHEEO agency funding
and staffing have changed and how the agencies' functions are changing. These changes reflect increasing emphasis on work with external
constituents (legislators and business and corporate leaders), on developing a public agenda, and on performance-oriented accountability
and less emphasis on operational functions and constituencies internal to higher education. Overall, SHEEO members saw their agencies
as being more entrepreneurial and less regulatory and as giving more
emphasis to solving pressing policy concerns.

Looking to the Future

Faced with the realities stressed at the beginning of this chapter — expectations, economic constraints, resistance to change, negative public opinion, and unstable state political leadership — American higher
education will be forced to undergo a restructuring as fundamental
as any attempted in the past fifty years.[41] Higher education faces four
basic choices:[42]

— *To do more with less.* If this choice is not accompanied by dramatic
changes in the core work of the faculty and changes in the modes
of teaching, research, and service, it will mean a decade-long decline in quality and a significant lowering of standards at a time
when the public demands just the opposite.
— *To do less with less.* This choice will mean that thousands of students will be denied access and the nation's worldwide standing
in research and graduate education will decline.

—*To take resources from other basic public services.* These services will include elementary and secondary education, health, public safety, and the environment.

—*To raise additional revenue from other sources.* Most of these sources are already highly taxed and, even according to the most optimistic view, could not replace losses in other revenue sources.

As institutions face these choices, so also must government—especially state government—assess whether its policies provide a constructive environment for institutional change to take place. This will require challenges to some of the basic assumptions that have guided state policy during the past twenty years.

1. How can the nation achieve a closer relationship between high participation rates and high achievement rates?

After several years of intense debate about the quality of American public schools, the focus has shifted to higher education. As suggested earlier, in the mid-1980s the debate about higher education accountability shifted sharply from resources to outcomes, and the rapid spread of assessment, stimulated in part by state mandates, was the result. But the debate is now taking a new turn. These questions are being asked:

—Are too many students simply being processed through higher education institutions with no clear sense of what they should know and be able to do upon graduation?

—Aside from a few, usually highly selective, institutions, are the expectations for student learning for many of the students enrolled in higher education not much higher than those for students in secondary education? [43]

—Should the United States shift its focus away from higher education to education for the non-college-bound student and to vocational/technical and apprenticeship training? [44]

—Why is it taking students longer and longer (now averaging six years) to complete a baccalaureate degree? Could the time-to-degree be significantly shortened? [45]

—Should the states or even the nation set standards or expectations about what students should know and be able to do upon completing a baccalaureate degree (or perhaps at the level of two years of postsecondary education or training)?[46]

— Should the basic structure of postsecondary education in the United States be altered? The basic structure of institutions and degrees that has characterized American higher education since World War II may be on the verge of change. This may include changing the roles of secondary schools, open-access comprehensive community colleges, and four-year colleges and universities, both public and private.

2. How will technology and technology-based teaching and learning transform not only higher education but also state policy?

In just a few years, technology has moved from promise to reality as perhaps the most powerful transforming force in American higher education. WGU is a symbol of this change. Its key dimensions are likely to characterize the future of the nation's higher education system: (1) it is market driven, (2) its focus is on learners and clients, (3) it awards credentials on the basis of an assessment of competency rather than credit hours, and (4) it accounts for the explosive increase in providers, including not only traditional college and universities seeking new types of student but also new private enterprises offering education and training modules over the internet and utilizing a variety of technologies (CD-ROM, video, etc.).

These changes are forcing a fundamental rethinking of many of the roles and responsibilities of states and state higher education agencies. In many respects, the state is no longer a realistic "community of solution" for higher education policy and quality assurance. Traditional state regulatory policies are based on the physical location of institutions and program delivery sites within the state. Licensure and authorization policies, mission definition and service area policies, and program approval policies aimed at reducing unnecessary duplication must all be reconsidered. Perhaps the most profound changes will occur as states and institutions move to competency and away from credit hours as the basis for measuring student process and awarding credentials. This change will require significant changes in state and federal policies for student and institutional financing.

3. How should institutional forms, methods of program delivery, and governance be changed to create a more responsive, cost-effective, and flexible system?

Before the surge in attention to technology in the mid-1990s, severe economic conditions early in the decade had already stimulated serious reconsideration of the traditional structure and management practices of the nation's public and private colleges and universities. A series of reports by the Pew Higher Education Research Program at the University of Pennsylvania has played a leading role in shaping the debate about the need for the fundamental restructuring of higher education, especially the research university.[47] Questions are now being raised that the higher education community would not have dared to consider just a few years ago:

— Should some sectors of public higher education be shifted to largely private nonprofit status, with less public funding and more dependence on student and other nongovernmental revenue?
— Should some large public multicampus systems be broken up into smaller units or radically decentralized to give greater independence to individual units under a smaller central staff?
— Could a higher proportion of the undergraduate population be served off campus through the use of technology at home or on the job, thus avoiding the need to build new facilities (or even allowing institutions to be scaled down or closed)?

4. Should both the sources and the methods of financing for students and institutions be changed in fundamental ways?

As suggested earlier, the prospects for increased revenue from any major source are dim, especially when matched with the realities of increased demand and inevitable cost increases. Survey responses from the states and systems underscore that financing issues cut across all other concerns and are intertwined with issues of quality and access. There is a growing sense that the traditional debates about who benefits and who pays, which characterized the mid-1970s, simply do not fit the conditions of the 1990s. A basic question now on the agenda is whether methods of student and institutional finance could be tied to incentives for both students and institutions to speed up time-to-degree. New questions are being raised about consolidating funding now provided separately for secondary schools, multiple training options, and the first two years of college to create more flexible and powerful approaches to raising the skills and knowledge levels of the population. As suggested earlier, the shift toward competency-based credentials will force fundamental changes in how both the federal and state governments structure their financing policies.

5. How must state government policy change to support the transformation of the higher education system?

Given the political instability and economic pressures facing governors and state legislators, the 1990s could be one of the most pronounced periods of bureaucratic centralization in recent U.S. history, including (1) a return to more detailed, line-item budget controls, (2) an extension of state agency authority over higher education purchasing, personnel and pensions, and management of facilities and equipment, (3) the elimination of state subsidies for private nonprofit colleges and universities (for students or programs), (4) the centralization and consolidation of governance, (5) the elimination of state coordination and planning agencies and a shift of oversight functions to the governor's office and the state legislature, and (6) a restriction on the use of state resources for out-of-state (and especially international) purposes, thereby limiting the movement of both students and higher education faculty and staff.

In other words, while most major private corporations and most other nations seem to be reducing bureaucracy and increasing flexibility, many state governments seem to be moving in the opposite direction. Because of this danger, the ECS, in collaboration with the State Higher Education Executive Officers and the National Center for Higher Education Management Systems, has been designing ways for states to assess the impact of their policies on the capacity of their universities and colleges to respond to the new realities.[48] The aim is to assist states in shaping a new generation of policies to (1) decentralize institutional governance, (2) reconceive and reorient central state functions (emphasizing standard setting, productivity improvement, partnerships, differentiation in institutional missions), (3) provide the public with better information about the performance of students, institutions, and the higher education system as a whole, and (4) establish independent, nongovernmental, third-party entities to monitor the progress of the enterprise in addressing basic societal needs and priorities.

An example of new thinking is the California Higher Education Policy Center, an independent nonprofit entity committed to raising fundamental policy questions about the future of higher education in the states, questions that the current policy and education leadership cannot or will not raise. The aim is to engage the public in the debate in the hope that future directions will be set by conscious policy choice and not by policy drift. New thinking is needed about the policies most likely to stimulate and sustain lasting restructuring of the system to ensure its capacity to serve these ends.

6. Is the nation reaching the end of the "state period" to which Clark Kerr referred in the mid-1980s?

Countering the tendency for states to turn inward in difficult economic times, the United States is experiencing a greater interest in nationwide education leadership than at any time in its history. What is different about the current debate is that leaders are seeking largely nongovernmental mechanisms to provide this nationwide policy framework. At the 1996 Education Summit, the president, governors, and business leaders agreed that educational standards should be pursued by nongovernmental means and by individual states rather than by the federal government. The WGU is another private mechanism through which issues about technology-based learning and competency-based standards for student achievement can be raised outside the framework of formal governmental policy. These changes suggest the need for a renewed discussion about the role of the federal government and of federalism but go far beyond education and beyond the roles of governments.[49]

7. Are today's concepts of policy for nation-states and regional economic blocs inconsistent with, or even barriers to, the internationalization of knowledge and worldwide movement of students and scholars?

Clark Kerr recently addressed the issues of the internationalization of knowledge from the perspective of nation-states and concluded that nation-states have been and continue to be major forces in the advancement of higher education but that this has certainly not always been so.[50] In the case of the United States, international networks have exploded in recent years, largely without and even in spite of government action. In addition to thousands of foreign students and researchers coming to major U.S. research universities each year, international contacts are reflected in a myriad of informal links among scholars and researchers, cooperative agreements among colleges and universities, and telecommunications contacts.[51]

Have the states outlived their usefulness as communities of solution for higher education policy in a global economy? In a subtle way, this question is already on the nation's agenda. Rather than shift back to a federal period, the emphasis will increasingly be on nationwide policy. Using the benefits of modern technology and telecommunications, alternatives will involve all stakeholders: local entities, institutions, states, the federal government, the private sector, and more than ever, the general public.

NOTES

1. Aims C. McGuinness Jr., "Lessons from European Integration for U.S. Higher Education," paper prepared for the Eleventh General Conference of Member Institutions, Programme on Institutional Management in Higher Education, Organisation for Economic Development and Co-operation, Sept. 1992.

2. See Sandra S. Rupert, *The Politics of Remedy: State Legislative Views on Higher Education* (Washington, D.C.: National Education Association, 1996), for the results of a survey of state legislative views in the changing political environment following the 1994 elections.

3. See Edward R. Hines, *Higher Education and State Governments: Renewed Partnership, Cooperation, or Competition?* (Washington, D.C.: Association for the Study of Higher Education, 1988), for a useful overview of the issue. Also, Richard Novak, *State Issues in Higher Education: A Bibliography* (Washington, D.C.: American Association of State Colleges and Universities, 1992).

4. See Frank Newman, *Choosing Quality: Reducing Conflict between the State and the University* (Denver: Education Commission of the States, 1987), xiii.

5. Robert O. Berdahl, *Statewide Coordination of Higher Education* (Washington, D.C.: American Council on Education, 1971), 9.

6. Daniel Elazar, *American Federalism: A View from the States* (New York: Crowell, 1966), chap. 4.

7. Washington Council for Postsecondary Education, *Higher Education in Washington: The Next Six Years* (Olympia: Washington Council for Postsecondary Education, 1983), 4–7.

8. The following statistics are from National Center for Education Statistics, *Digest of Education Statistics, 1989* (Washington, D.C.: U.S. Department of Education, 1989), tables 148, 149, 196.

9. Clark Kerr, "The American Mixture of Higher Education in Perspective: Four Dimensions," *Higher Education* 19 (1990): 1–19.

10. Robert Atwell, "Financial Prospects for Higher Education," *Policy Perspectives* (Sept. 1992): 5B–7B.

11. Clark Kerr, "The States and Higher Education: Changes Ahead," *State Government* 58 (1990): 45–49.

12. State Higher Education Executive Officers, *State Higher Education Appropriations, 1991–1992* (Denver: SHEEO, 1992).

13. Atwell, "Financial Prospects for Higher Education."

14. See State Higher Education Executive Officers, *State Higher Education Appropriations, 1991–92;* Peter Schmidt, "Higher Education Gets Largest Increase from States since 1990," *Chronicle of Higher Education,* Nov. 1, 1996. Data on state appropriations for higher education are available through the Illinois Center for Higher Education by means of the World Wide Web, at http://coe.ilstu.edu/grapevine.

15. Patrick Healy, "Survey Reveals Surge in State Spending on Student-Aid Programs," *Chronicle of Higher Education,* Mar. 15, 1996. Data on state student aid programs are available through the New York State Higher Education Services Corporation, 99 Washington Ave., Room 1438, Albany, N.Y. 12255.

16. Ben Gose, "Undergraduate Tuition Rises by an Average of 5%," *Chronicle of Higher Education,* Oct. 4, 1996.

17. Elaine El-Khawas, *Campus Trends, 1993* (Washington, D.C.: American Council on Education, 1993), 16.

18. For an analysis of these developments in the 1980s, see Newman, *Choosing Quality;* Robert O. Berdahl and Barbara Holland, eds., *Developing State Fiscal Incentives to Improve Higher Education: Proceedings from a National Invitational Conference* (College Park: University of Maryland, National Center for Postsecondary Governance and Finance, 1990); Peter Ewell and Dennis Jones, *Assessing and Reporting Student Progress: A Response to the "New Accountability"* (Denver: State Higher Education Executive Officers, 1991); James R. Mingle, *State Policy and Productivity in Higher Education* (Denver: State Higher Education Executive Officers, 1992).

19. Education Commission of the States, *Making Quality Count in Undergraduate Education* (Denver: ECS, 1995).

20. Western Governors Association, "Western Governors University: Goals and Visions," paper prepared for the Western Governors, fall 1995,

available through the World Wide Web, at http://www.westgov.org/smart/vu/
vuvision.html.

21. This section draws heavily on Aims C. McGuinness Jr., *State Postsecondary Education Structures Handbook, 1994* (Denver: Education Commission of the States, 1994).

22. See John Folger and Robert O. Berdahl, *Patterns in Evaluating Higher
Education Systems: Making a Virtue out of Necessity* (College Park: University of Maryland, National Center for Postsecondary Governance and Finance, 1988), for an analysis and case studies of state approaches to evaluating their higher education boards and systems.

23. Clark Kerr and Marian L. Gade, *The Guardians: Boards of Trustees of
American Colleges and Universities* (Washington, D.C.: Association of Governing Boards of Universities and Colleges, 1989), 116, 128–29.

24. Ibid., 115–18. For further reading on the subject of multicampus sys-
tems, see Marian L. Gade, *Four Multicampus Systems: Some Policies and
Practices That Work* (Washington, D.C.: Association of Governing Boards of
Universities and Colleges, 1993); Edgar B. Schick, Richard J. Novak, James A.
Norton, and Houston G. Elam, *Shared Visions of Public Higher Education
Governance: Structures and Leadership Styles That Work* (Washington, D.C.:
American Association of State Colleges and Universities, 1992); Aims C. Mc-
Guinness Jr., "Perspectives on the Current Status of and Emerging Policy
Issues for Public Multicampus Higher Education Systems" (Association of
Governing Boards of Universities and Colleges, Washington, D.C., 1991).

25. For historical perspectives on statewide coordination, see Ernest
Boyer, *Control of the Campus* (Princeton, N.J.: Carnegie Foundation for the
Advancement of Teaching, 1982); Berdahl, *Statewide Coordination of Higher
Education;* Carnegie Commission on Higher Education, *The Capitol and
the Campus: State Responsibility for Postsecondary Education* (New York:
McGraw-Hill, 1971); Carnegie Foundation for the Advancement of Teaching,
States and Higher Education: A Proud Past and a Vital Future (San Fran-
cisco: Jossey-Bass, 1976); Education Commission of the States, *Challenge:
Coordination and Governance in the 1980s* (Denver: Education Commission
of the States, 1980); Lyman A. Glenny, *Autonomy of Public Colleges* (New
York: McGraw-Hill, 1959; Lyman A. Glenny et al., *Coordinating Higher Edu-
cation for the '70s* (Berkeley: University of California, Center for Research
and Development in Higher Education, 1971); John D. Millet, *Conflict in
Higher Education: State Government versus Institutional Independence* (San
Francisco: Jossey-Bass, 1982).

For more recent commentaries on statewide coordination, see Patrick M.
Callan, *Perspectives on the Current Status and Emerging Issues for State Co-
ordinating Boards* (Washington, D.C.: Association of Governing Boards of
Universities and Colleges, 1991); Lyman A. Glenny, *State Coordination of
Higher Education: The Modern Concept* (Denver: State Higher Education Ex-

ecutive Officers, 1985); James R. Mingle, "Effective Coordination of Higher Education. What Is It? Why Is It So Difficult to Achieve?" *Issues in Higher Education,* no. 23 (1988); State Higher Education Executive Officers, *New Issues—New Roles: A Conversation with State Higher Education Executive Officers* (Denver: State Higher Education Executive Officers, 1989).

26. See Don A. Carpenter, *Role and Mission Development: A Comparison of Different Approaches* (Denver: State Higher Education Executive Officers, 1987); J. Kent Carruthers, *Mission Maintenance: Tools for Change and the Consultative Process* (Denver: State Higher Education Executive Officers, 1987); Ellen Earle Chaffee, *System Strategy and Effectiveness* (Denver: State Higher Education Executive Officers, 1987).

27. The productivity, quality and performance (PQP) initiative of the Illinois Board of Higher Education is perhaps the best example of a comprehensive, aggressive, coordinating board initiative that links program review with a restructuring of institutions to meet the economic realities of the next decade. See Education Commission of the States, *Priorities, Quality, and Productivity: The Illinois PQP Initiative* (Denver: ECS, 1996). For further information on basic program review processes, see Robert J. Barak and Barbara E. Breier, *Successful Program Review* (San Francisco: Jossey-Bass, 1990); Robert J. Barak, *Program Review in Higher Education* (Boulder, Colo.: National Center for Higher Education Management Systems, 1982).

28. See Dennis P. Jones, *Higher Education Budgeting at the State Level: Concepts and Principles* (Boulder, Colo.: National Center for Higher Education Management Systems, 1984); John K. Folger and Dennis P. Jones, *The Use of Financing Policy to Achieve State Objectives* (Denver: Education Commission of the States, 1993).

29. Peter T. Ewell, "The Current Pattern of State-Level Assessment: Results of a National Inventory," in *Performance Indicators in Higher Education: What Works, What Doesn't, and What Next?* ed. Gerald H. Gaither (College Station: Texas A&M University Press, 1996). New York State Education Department, Office of Higher and Professional Education, "Performance Reporting in Higher Education in the Nation and New York State," briefing paper for the Regents Committee on Higher Education and Professional Education, Sept. 1996, is available through the Worldwide Web, at http://unix5.nysed.gov/ohpe/. For further information on performance reporting, see Education Commission of the States, *Charting Higher Education Accountability: A Sourcebook on State-Level Performance Indicators* (Denver: ECS, 1994); Peter T. Ewell, "A Matter of Integrity: Accountability and the Future of Self-Regulation," *Change.* Nov./Dec. 1994; Peter T. Ewell, "Assessment and the 'New Accountability': Challenge for Higher Education's Leadership" (Education Commission of the States, Denver, 1990); Peter T. Ewell, *State Policy on Assessment: The Linkage to Learning* (Denver: Education Commission of the States, 1990).

30. Cheryl D. Lovell, *State Postsecondary Review Entities: One Step Forward and Two Steps Back in State-Federal Relationships?* (Denver: State Higher Education Executive Officers, 1996); Arthur M. Hauptman and James R. Mingle, *Standard Setting and Financing in Postsecondary Education: Eight Recommendations for Change in Federal and State Policies* (Denver: State Higher Education Executive Officers, 1994).

31. For different approaches to classification, see Berdahl, *Statewide Coordination,* 18–19; Millet, *Conflict;* Kerr and Gade, *The Guardians,* 117, 128–29. For a discussion of the advantages and disadvantages of different kinds of state board, see Millet, *Conflict,* 102–7.

32. Berdahl, *Statewide Coordination,* 15, describes these boards as "suitably sensitive mechanisms" for the transmission of the state's interests in higher education.

33. For a discussion of origins of systems, see McGuinness, "Perspectives on the Current Status."

34. Kerr and Gade, *The Guardians,* 118–19.

35. See Gade, *Four Multicampus Systems;* Schick et al., *Shared Visions;* D. Bruce Johnstone, *Central Administrations of Public Multicampus College and University Systems* (Albany: State University of New York, 1992).

36. Aims C. McGuinness Jr., *Restructuring State Roles in Higher Education: A Case Study of the 1994 New Jersey Higher Education Restructuring Act* (Denver: Education Commission of the States, 1995).

37. Terrance J. MacTaggart, "The Human Side of Restructuring: Minnesota," in *Restructuring Higher Education: What Works and What Doesn't in Reorganizing Governing Systems,* ed. Terrance J. MacTaggart (San Francisco: Jossey-Bass, 1996).

38. Rupert, *Politics of Remedy,* 19. See MacTaggart, *Restructuring Higher Education,* for case studies of several major changes and recommendations for states considering changes.

39. For the following, see Rupert, *Politics of Remedy,* 53–54, 19, 41–43.

40. See Rhonda Martin Epper and Alene Bycer Russell, *Trends in State Coordination and Governance: Historical and Current Perspectives* (Denver: State Higher Education Executive Officers, 1996), 15–28.

41. Portions of this section are drawn from McGuinness, "Lessons from European Integration."

42. James R. Mingle, "Funding Higher Education in the 1990s: The Choices We Face," remarks to the Quality Reinvestment Conference of the University of Wisconsin, Apr. 3, 1992.

43. Ray Marshall and Marc Tucker, *Thinking for a Living* (New York: Basic Books, 1992).

44. National Center for Education and the Economy, *America's Choice: High Skills or Low Wages!* (Rochester, N.Y.: National Center for Education and the Economy, 1990).

45. See D. Bruce Johnstone, *Learning Productivity: A New Imperative for American Higher Education* (Albany: State University of New York Press, 1993).

46. National Education Goals Panel, *Report of the Task Force on Assessing the National Goal Relating to Postsecondary Education* (Washington, D.C.: NEGP, 1992).

47. See "The End of Sanctuary," *Policy Perspectives* 3 (1991): 1A–8A; and other issues of *Policy Perspectives*.

48. See Dennis Jones, "A Framework for Devising State Policy Toward Higher Education," background paper prepared for the Education Commission of the States, Oct. 1995. Other relevant publications include these from the State Policy and College Learning Project: Peter Ewell and Dennis Jones, *The Effect of State Policy on Undergraduate Education* (Denver: Education Commission of the States and National Center for Higher Education Management Systems, 1993); Richard B. Heydinger and Hassan Simsek, *An Agenda for Reshaping Faculty Productivity* (Denver: Education Commission of the States and State Higher Education Executive Officers, 1993); Dennis Jones and John Folger, *Use of Fiscal Policy to Achieve States' Educational Goals* (Denver: Education Commission of the States and National Center for Higher Education Management Systems, 1993); Stephen M. Jordon and Daniel T. Layzell, *A Case of Faculty Workload Issues in Arizona: Implications for State Higher Education Policy* (Denver: Education Commission of the States and State Higher Education Executive Officers, 1993); Aims C. McGuinness Jr., *Redesigning the State's Higher Education System for the Twenty-first Century* (Denver: Education Commission of the States, 1992); Richard C. Richardson Jr., *Creating Effective Learning Environments* (Denver: Education Commission of the States, 1993).

49. Alice M. Rivlin, *Reviving the American Dream: The Economy, the States, and the Federal Government* (Washington, D.C.: Brookings, 1992).

50. Clark Kerr, "The Internationalization of Learning and the Nationalization of the Purposes of Higher Education: Two 'Laws in Motion' in Conflict?" *European Journal of Education* 25 (1989): 5–22.

51. El-Khawas, *Campus Trends, 1993*.

Chapter Eight

The Legal Environment

The Implementation of Legal
Change on Campus

Michael A. Olivas

In modern higher education, few major decisions are made without considering the legal consequences, and though the core functions of higher education—instruction and scholarship—are remarkably free from external legal influences, no one would plausibly deny the increase of legalization on campus. We know surprisingly little about the law's effect upon higher education, but virtually no one in the enterprise is untouched by statutes, regulations, case law, or institutional rules promulgated to implement legal regimes.

Lewis Thomas, perhaps our most thoughtful commentator on medicine and science in society, ascribes organic qualities to the university, and his view of a college as a "community of scholars" is grounded in an appreciation of the history of education. Paul Goodman and John Millett also exemplify this perspective. Like a prism refracting light differently depending upon how you hold it up for viewing, higher education can appear differently. For Herbert Stroup and many other sociologists, colleges are essentially bureaucracies, and no student confronting course registration today is likely to be dissuaded from this view. To Victor Baldridge, universities are indisputably political organizations, as they also appear to Clark Kerr and Burton Clark. To critics, higher education is stratified by class (Randall Collins), resistant to legal change (Harry Edwards), and in need of fundamental restructuring (Paolo Freire).[1] As many observers would insist, all are equally close to the truth or truths, depending upon which truth is being refracted. The cases in this chapter reveal many truths and, often frustratingly, few answers. As the following cases reveal, legal considerations can pare governance issues down to the essential question, What is a college?

Legal Governance

Despite the seeming obviousness of the question posed above, a variety of cases probe the fundamental definitional issue. In *Coffee v. Rice University,* the issues were whether the 1891 trust charter founding Rice University (then Rice Institute), which restricted admissions to "white inhabitants" and required that no tuition be charged, could be maintained in 1966.[2] The court held that an "institute" was a postsecondary institution by any other name, and its postcompulsory, collegiate nature rendered it a college. On the issue of whether the trust could be maintained with its racial restrictions and tuition prohibition, the court applied the doctrine of cy pres, which theory allowed the trustees to reformulate the provisions and admit minorities and charge tuition, for to continue the practices would have been impracticable; if the trust provisions can no longer be realistically carried out, a court can reconstitute the trust to make it conform to the changed circumstances.

A court is not always so disposed as the *Coffee* court was. In *Shapiro v. Columbia University National Bank and Trust Co.,* the court allowed a trust reserved only for male students to remain male only, refusing to apply cy pres.[3] My personal favorite is *U.S. on Behalf of U.S. Coast Guard v. Cerio,* in which a judge allowed the Coast Guard Academy to reformulate a major student prize when the endowment's interest had grown to more than $100,000.[4] The judge began, "This is essentially a case of looking a gift horse in the mouth and finding it too good to accept as is" and allowed the academy to use some of the prize interest for other support services.

Sometimes a zoning ordinance raises the issue of what constitutes a college. In *Fountain Gate Ministries v. City of Plano,* a city wished to keep colleges from locating in residentially zoned housing areas.[5] The church argued that its activities were those of a church rather than those of a college. However, the court took notice of the educational instruction, faculty, degree activities, and other collegelike activities

and determined that these constituted a college, protestations to the
contrary notwithstanding. In the opposite direction, a court held that
a consultant firm's use of the term "Quality College" to describe its
activities did not make it a college or subject it to state regulation. In
wry fashion, the court noted that to make use of the word *college* in
an organization's title would make a college bookstore or the Catholic College of Cardinals into institutions!

Sometimes the definition drives a divorce decree. In *Hacker v.
Hacker,* a father who had agreed to pay for his daughter's college
tuition did so while she was a theater major at the University of
California but refused to do so when she moved to Manhattan and
enrolled in the Neighborhood Playhouse (TNP), a renowned acting
school; that it was not degree-granting persuaded the judge that TNP
failed to meet the definition of a college.[6] Occasionally, the definition
turns on accreditation language (*Beth Rochel Seminary v. Bennett*),
while at other times it turns on taxation issues (*City of Morgantown
v. West Virginia Board of Regents*).[7]

Due to the different constitutional considerations between public
and private colleges, such as free speech and due process not applying to private colleges, it is important to distinguish between the two
forms in order to understand the full panoply of rights and duties
owed to institutional community members. Consider the public/pri-
vate distinction as a continuum, with *Trustees of Dartmouth College v. Woodward* at the purely private end and *Krynicky v. University of Pittsburgh* at the other end, that of purely public colleges.[8]
In *Dartmouth,* the first higher education case considered by the U.S.
Supreme Court, the State of New Hampshire had attempted to rescind the private charter of Dartmouth College, which was incorporated in the state nearly fifty years earlier, and to make it a public
college with legislatively appointed trustees to replace the college's
private trustees. The Supreme Court held that the college, once chartered, was private and not subject to the legislature's actions, unless
the trustees wished to reconstitute themselves as a public institution.
At the other end of the spectrum, *Krynicky* held that Temple University and the University of Pittsburgh were public colleges, due to the
amount of money given by the state, the reconstitution of the board
to include publicly appointed trustees (including ex officio elected officials), state reporting requirements, and other characteristics that injected state action into the act of reconstituting the institutions into
the state system of higher education.

Of course, if there are pure archetypes such as Dartmouth and the University of Pittsburgh, there must be intermediate forms, such as Alfred University, where several students were arrested, the court holding in *Powe v. Miles* that regular students were entitled to no elaborate due process, as the institution was private.[9] However, the ceramics engineering students were entitled to hearings before dismissal, as the Ceramics College in which they were enrolled was a state-supported entity; New York contracted with the private college to provide this program rather than establish such a program in a state school. Other hybrid examples of a state-contracted unit within a private school include Cornell University's agricultural sciences program and Baylor's College of Medicine, both of which operate as if they were state institutions.

Other important foundational issues have also resulted in litigation, resulting in a complex definitional process. For example, in *Cahn and Cahn v. Antioch University,* trustees of the institution were sued by co-deans of the law school to determine who had authority for governance decisions; the court ruled that trustees have the ultimate authority and fiduciary duty.[10] In contrast to *Dartmouth,* where there was a "hostile takeover" of the institution by the state, private trustees can close a college or surrender its assets, such as its accreditation (*Fenn College v. Nance* and *Nasson College v. New England Association of Schools and Colleges*).[11] Another important issue involving the definition and legal governance of colleges turns on consortial or collective behavior of institutions: Does their mutual recognition in athletics accreditation and information sharing subject them to state action? In *NCAA v. University of Oklahoma,* the U.S. Supreme Court held that the NCAA was a "classic cartel" engaged in restraint of trade by its negotiated television contract; another court held that the activities of the Overlap Group—a group of elite institutions that share information on financial aid offers with other colleges admitting the same students so as to "coordinate" the awards—similarly violated antitrust law (*U.S. v. Brown University*).[12] However, in accreditation activities, mutual-recognition agreements have been allowed by courts, as not constituting a restraint of trade, as in *Marjorie Webster Jr. College v. Middle States Association* and *Beth Rochel Seminary v. Bennett,* in which an institution that was not yet accredited failed to negotiate the complex exceptions to the accreditation requirement for financial aid eligibility.[13]

In sum, despite the seeming simplicity of legally defining a college, it is not always easy. Cases were cited on which entities not labeled colleges were found to be colleges, while some that resembled colleges were held not to be, including a commercial program ("Quality College") that was held not to be an institution of higher education. For some technical, eligibility-driven issues—such as child support or taxation—the definition was extremely important. The bottom line appears, from these cases, to be that a college is an entity with instructional programs and degree-granting authority. In addition, the definitional issue is raised in the context of who is responsible for governance of the institution. The answer is ultimately the trustees, although the *Yeshiva* case, discussed in the following section, appears to hold the opposite.[14] With this foundational layer in place, we turn to the two major campus actors: faculty and students.

Faculty and the Law

Although there have not been many studies of patterns in postsecondary law, the few that have been undertaken show that faculty bring many of the suits in higher education. A 1987 study of Iowa case law shows that litigation against colleges brought by students totaled 11 percent, while faculty brought 31 percent; a 1988 study of Texas litigation shows that faculty brought 35 percent of all college cases in that state.[15] These numbers are surprising, for two reasons. First, higher education has traditionally been a "gentlemen's club," to use William Kaplin's apt term.[16] This meant that if faculty members did not receive tenure, or were forced to move for another reason, they would simply find another position or fall upon their sword. To do otherwise would brand them as troublemakers or contentious colleagues. Second, there were no civil rights laws or widespread collective bargaining until the 1960s and 1970s, so faculty had fewer opportunities to bring suit or engage in collective protection, such as that afforded by security provisions in collective bargaining agreements.

Tenure

The two leading U.S. Supreme Court tenure cases were decided the same day in 1972, and both *Perry v. Sinderman* and *Board of Regents v. Roth* turn on what process is due to faculty, should institutions wish to remove them.[17] In *Perry,* a community college instructor who had been a thorn in the side of college administrators was fired for "insubordination," without a hearing or official reasons. The college had no tenure policy, except one that said, "the Administration of the College wishes the faculty member to feel that he has permanent tenure as long as his teaching services are satisfactory and as long as he displays a cooperative attitude toward his coworkers and his supervisors, and as long as he is happy in his work." The court held that the instructor thus had a property interest in his continued employment and ordered the lower court to determine whether he had been fired for his protected speech or for cause. In short, the administrators were required to give him notice of the reasons for his firing and an opportunity to explain his side of the matter. This is what tenure grants: a presumption of continued employment, absent certain circumstances (financial exigency, etc.). In *Roth,* the Court held that an untenured professor had no constitutional right to continued employment, beyond the contractual period for which he was hired.

These two cases, together with several others fleshing out the terms of faculty employment, delineate the contours of tenure. For example, in *Wellner v. Minnesota State Junior College Board,* an untenured teacher was removed from his position for allegedly making racist remarks; he was sanctioned without a hearing or an opportunity to explain his behavior.[18] The appeals court ordered that he be accorded a hearing, as his liberty interest had been infringed. That is, his record was stigmatized and his reputation was at stake, so the court ordered a hearing to allow him to clear his name.

In addition to contract and liberty interests, faculty may have property interests as well, as in *State ex rel. McLendon v. Clarksville School of Theology,* in which the court held that Professor McLendon had a property interest in being considered for tenure, since she ostensibly qualified by being in rank the requisite period of time.[19] Although many cases, including *Roth,* have held that no reasons need be given for denying tenure, McLendon had, on the surface, appeared to earn tenure by default, and a hearing was required to show why she was not entitled to tenure. These cases are very grounded in fact and case specific, due to individual institutional policies and each state's contract or employment law.

A surprising number of cases deal with the ambiguities of tenure rights, as in whether or not American Association of University Professors (AAUP) guidelines apply (*Hill v. Talladega College*), exactly when the tenure clock applies (*Honore v. Douglas*), if financial reasons apply once a candidate has been evaluated in the tenure review process (*Spuler v. Pickar*), and whether institutional error can be sufficient grounds for overturning a tenure denial (*Lewis v. Loyola University of Chicago*).[20]

As for discrimination in the tenure process, nearly a hundred cases have been reported, most of which defer to institutional judgments about the candidates. Most find that the plaintiff, whether a person of color or an Anglo woman, did not prove that the institution acted in an unfair or discriminatory fashion. In *Scott v. University of Delaware*, the court held that, "while some of this evidence is indicative of racial prejudice on the University campus, it does not suggest to me that Scott was a victim of racial discrimination by the University in its renewal process, or that he was treated differently than non-black faculty by the University."[21] That this is so is particularly due to the extraordinary deference accorded academic judgments, as in *Faro v. NYU*: "Of all fields, which the federal courts should hesitate to invade and take over, education and faculty appointments at a University level are probably the least suited for federal court supervision."[22]

Even so, occasionally an institution goes too far, as the Claremont Graduate School (CGS) did in the 1992 case of *Clark v. Claremont Graduate School*.[23] In this case, a black professor chanced upon the meeting in which his tenure consideration was being reviewed. From the room, whose door was apparently left ajar, he overheard the committee making racist remarks, such as "us white folks have rights, too" and "I couldn't work on a permanent basis with a black man." When the court and jury reviewed his entire record, compared it with others who had recently been considered for (and received) tenure, and noted that no other minority professor had ever received tenure at CGS, it was determined that Professor Clark had been discriminated against due to his race, and he was awarded $1 million in compensatory damages as well as punitive damages and lawyers' fees.

Women have won several cases in which it was held that they were treated discriminatorily, as in *Sweeney v. Board of Trustees of Keene State College, Kunda v. Muhlenberg College, Mecklenberg v. Montana State Board of Regents,* and *Kemp v. Ervin,* among others, in which courts or juries found for women faculty plaintiffs.[24] Professor Jan Kemp particularly prevailed, winning six years on the tenure clock and more than $2.5 million in compensatory and punitive damages from the University of Georgia.

Recent developments in employment law have made it more difficult for faculty to prevail in state and federal court, particularly by extending cases outside higher education to the college enterprise. Thus, *Hazelwood School District v. Kuhlmeier,* a U.S. Supreme Court decision about school boards' right to control editorial content in a public K–12 school setting, has been cited in college faculty cases such as *Bishop v. Aranov* and *Scallet v. Rosenblum,* while *Waters v. Churchill,* a public hospital case that held that public employees whose speech was "disruptive" could be removed for cause, was cited in *Jeffries v. Harleston.*[25] Professor Leonard Jeffries, removed from his department chair position for his offensive and anti-Semitic speech, had won at trial and upon appeal, but the Supreme Court remanded and ordered the appeals court to review his case in light of *Waters.* After this review, the appeals court overturned and vacated its earlier opinion.

Collective Bargaining

Since the first college faculties were unionized in the 1960s and 1970s, collective bargaining has become widespread in higher education. Union data indicate that 830 of the 3,284 institutions in the United States (25 percent) were covered by faculty collective bargaining agreements; figures for nonfaculty college employees were even higher.[26] By 1984, nearly 200,000 faculty (27% of all faculty) were unionized, 83 percent of them in public colleges and 17 percent in private institutions. Unionized public senior colleges totaled 220, private four-year colleges 69, public two-year colleges 524, and private two-year colleges 13. In the last two decades, there were 138 full-time college faculty strikes (or work stoppages), averaging almost 15 days; the longest, 150 days, was at St. John's University in 1966.

Collective bargaining is governed by federal and state laws, although several states also authorize local boards of junior colleges (hence, local laws) to govern labor. Twenty-six states and the District of Columbia have such authorizing legislation. While state or local laws, if they exist, govern the respective state or local institutions, the National Labor Relations Act (NLRA) governs faculty collective bargaining in private institutions. In 1951, the National Labor Relations Board (NLRB) decided that colleges would not fall under NLRB jurisdiction if their mission was "noncommercial in nature and intimately connected with the charitable purposes and education activities."[27] This refusal to assert jurisdiction remained in force until 1970, when the NLRB reversed itself.[28] After reviewing labor law trends in the twenty years that had passed, the NLRB noted, "we are convinced that assertion of jurisdiction is required over those private colleges and universities whose operations have a substantial effect on commerce to insure the orderly, effective, and uniform application of the national labor policy." The board set a $1 million gross revenue test for its standard, a figure that would today cover even the very smallest colleges.

The NLRB decision to extend collective bargaining privileges to Yeshiva University faculty, however, was overruled by the U.S. Supreme Court, which held that faculty were, in effect, supervisory personnel and therefore not covered by the NLRA. This important decision, of course, reversed a decade of organizing activity and struck a heavy blow to faculty unionizing efforts. Since the decision not to entitle Yeshiva faculty to organize collectively, nearly a hundred private colleges have sought to decertify existing faculty unions or have refused to bargain with faculty on *Yeshiva* grounds. Dozens of faculty unions have been decertified, and an untold number of organizing efforts have been thwarted because of the decision or because of the absence of state enabling legislation.

The decision, which affected only private colleges, has recently been applied to public institutions, such as the University of Pittsburgh. The State of Pennsylvania has a labor law (Public Employment Relations Act) that was construed by a Pennsylvania Labor Relations Board hearing examiner to exclude faculty: "As the faculty of the University of Pittsburgh participate with regularity in the essential process which results in a policy proposal and the decision to [hold a union election] and have a responsible role in giving practical effect to insuring the actual fulfillment of policy by concrete measures, the faculty of the university are management level employees within the meaning of PERA and thereby are excluded from PERA's coverage." [29]

In some instances, a court has found that *Yeshiva* criteria were not met and that the faculty did not govern the institution, as in *NLRB v. Cooper Union* and *NLRB v. Florida Memorial College*.[30] Scholars and courts will continue to sort out the consequences of *Yeshiva* and its successors, and unless legislation is enacted at the federal level (to amend the NLRA, for instance) or in the states (to repeal "right to work" legislation), this issue will remain a major bone of contention between faculty and their institutions, both public and private.

Students and the Law

There are many ways to approach the topic of students and the law, but the most interesting and historically based approach is to track the changes in the common law definition of the legal relationship between colleges and college students. This history, which resembles that of faculty and the colleges, began with few rights but now includes many protections. Private institutions afford students fewer rights than public institutions do, and constitutional rights extend only to students in public institutions. Moreover, there is no evidence of statutory development comparable to Title VII or the Equal Pay Act. Although since *Bakke v. Regents of University of California*,[31] students have used Title VI to gain legal standing and student athletes, especially women, have utilized Title IX to litigate for parity in intercollegiate athletic programs, the status of students is largely the province of constitutional protections.

The traditional status of students relative to their colleges was that of child to parent or ward to trustee: in loco parentis, literally, "in the place of the parent." This plenary power gave colleges virtually unfettered authority over students' lives and affairs. Thus, the hapless Miss Anthony of *Anthony v. Syracuse University* could be expelled from school for the simple offense of "not being a typical Syracuse girl," which, the record reveals, meant that she could be expelled from school for smoking a cigarette and sitting on a man's lap. An earlier case, *Gott v. Berea College,* held that colleges could regulate off-campus behavior, while more recent cases up until the 1970s still held that students were substantially under institutional control. The weakening of this doctrine began with *Dixon v. Alabama State Board of Education,* a case involving black students dismissed from a public college for engaging in civil disobedience at a lunch counter. When the court held that they were entitled to a due process hearing before expulsion, it was the first time such rights had been recognized.[32]

The age of majority changed from twenty-one to eighteen years in 1971, and since that time, student rights have either been grounded in tort law (*Tarasoff v. Regents of University of California, Mullins v. Pine Manor College*) or contract theories (*Johnson v. Lincoln Christian College, Ross v. Creighton University*).[33] An area that has developed recently accords protection to students under legislation addressing consumer fraud and deceptive trade practices. While these arguments have been used primarily for tuition refund or proprietary school (for-profit) cases, they have picked up momentum and in some states can provide for damage awards. For example, courts used the theory of fraudulent misrepresentations against a college in *Gonzalez v. North American College of Louisiana* (1988) and consumer statutes in *American Commercial Colleges, Inc. v. Davis* (1991).[34]

The case studies that follow are excellent proxies for the many cases in admissions, affirmative action, and other student issues that might be appropriate for this review. Two case studies involve subjects that are litigated often and represent important societal developments outside the academy. I situate the case studies in their legal and societal context to suggest alternative ways they could have been decided. In law, as in life, it is not always the end result that is important but the reasoning itself.

Admissions and Race

Hopwood v. State of Texas is arguably the most important postsecondary affirmative action case since the U.S. Supreme Court decision in *Bakke.* The *Bakke* case struck down racial quotas in higher education but allowed race as a discretionary factor in admissions. *Hopwood* is both more and less than *Bakke.* It is more harsh and unyielding in its analysis and result than *Bakke,* but it is also less compelling and intuitive than Justice Lewis Powell's carefully crafted and nuanced plurality opinion, which struck down the use of quotas and set-asides but upheld the use of race as an acceptable criterion in admissions. While some absolutists have since lampooned Powell's balancing act, it served a great purpose in reassuring universities that they still had discretion and latitude in choosing from among their many applicants. *Hopwood,* however, is the opposite. To this panel of the Fifth Circuit, nearly all was black and white (literally, since these justices also seemed to believe that Mexican Americans in Texas never faced any state action to discriminate against them), race or merit, qualified or preferential.

In my reading of *Hopwood,* these justices got it wrong, both in legal terms and in the practicalities of the admissions process. Remarkably, two of the three judges on the Fifth Circuit's panel attempted to overturn *Bakke* or suggested that the Supreme Court abandoned *Bakke:* "The law school places much reliance upon Justice O'Connor's concurrence in *Wygant* for the proposition that Justice Powell's *Bakke* formulation is still viable."[35] They characterize Justice Powell's decision as a "lonely" opinion. Whereas Mr. Powell began his *Bakke* opinion by holding that to seek diversity was clearly "a constitutionally permissible goal for an institution of higher education," this panel opinion stated that, in *Bakke,* "any consideration of race or ethnicity by the law school for the purpose of achieving a diverse student body is not a compelling interest under the Fourteenth Amendment."[36] This opinion is unequivocally wrong.

While it is true that *Wygant, Croson,* and *Adarand* trimmed back the reach of affirmative action, striking down federal minority set-asides unless they are narrowly tailored and, in general, requiring exacting tests for enacting preference programs, *Bakke* remains the law of the land.[37] For instance, Justice O'Connor wrote in *Wygant,* "although its precise contours are uncertain, a state interest in the promotion of racial diversity has been found to be sufficiently 'compelling,' at least in the context of higher education, to support the use of racial considerations in furthering that interest."[38] In *Adarand,* the federal minority set-aside case, O'Connor wrote that, "when race-based action is necessary to further a compelling interest, such action is within the constitutional constraints if it satisfies the 'narrow tailoring' test this Court has set out in previous cases."[39] These opinions hardly sound like the death knell of well-crafted admissions programs.

As this panel misread *Bakke,* so it misread the admissions process. The panel also did not understand that Cheryl Hopwood wanted affirmative action to apply in her case: she was a mother with a child born with cerebral palsy, and the panel found the case one of "unique background," in which Hopwood's "circumstances would bring a different perspective to the law school." But when she applied, the University of Texas (UT) law school committee did not have this information. Incredibly, Hopwood provided no letters of recommendation and no personal statement outlining her unique background.[40] Yet, she was certain she was displaced from her rightful place by lesser-qualified minorities. Another of the plaintiffs had a letter of recommendation from a professor describing the plaintiff's academic performance at his undergraduate institution as "uneven, disappointing, and mediocre."[41] That such students could score high on an index utilizing only grade point averages and LSAT (Law School Admission Test) scores indicates why law schools look to features other than mere scores. Any law school would be wary of incomplete applications or ones in which letters of recommendation singled out a student for "medio-cre" academic achievement.

White beneficiaries of racial practices often assume that they have reached their station in life on their merits and that minority com-munities have advanced only through bending the rules. Critics of affirmative action and some federal judges believe that higher scores translate into more meritorious applications and that "objective" measures are race neutral. The evidence for this proposition is more intuitive than verifiable; indeed, a substantial body of research litera-ture and academic practice refutes it. Heavy reliance on test scores and the near-magical properties accorded them inflate the narrow use to which these scores should be put. Accepted psychometric prin-ciples, testing industry norms of good practice, and research on the efficacy of testing all suggest more modest claims for test scores, whether standing alone or combined with other proxy measures. Test scores are at best imperfect measures to predict first-year grades, and first-year grades are only a small part of the aptitude for law study. More important, the same score means different things for differ-ent populations. For example, studies consistently show that scores on standardized tests are less predictive of minority students' first-year grade-point averages (both underpredicting and overpredicting) than Anglo students' averages. This finding weakens substantially the claim by affirmative action critics that the LSAT and other stan-dardized tests should be given more weight in the admissions process.

The plaintiffs and the Fifth Circuit panel acted as if a massive dislocation of deserving whites had occurred, in which a great many undeserving students of color have taken whites' rightful places. The data contradict this view. The number of white law students today is at an all-time high: more than 120,000, or 85 percent of the total en-rollment in the fifty states and the District Columbia. Blacks consti-tute just over 6 percent, and other minorities an even smaller percent-age. For Mexican Americans and Puerto Ricans, among the fastest growing ethnic minority groups in the country, these enrollments represent an actual numerical and percentage decline from the early 1980s. In 1990, white students took 79 percent of all the LSAT exams administered, and 58 percent of all the whites who applied to law schools were admitted; of other groups, only Asians were admitted in a higher percentage (61%). There is no evidence of slippage here and no hint of unfairness. No law school can afford to admit unqualified students, as its spaces are precious and competitive. Moreover, in the case of the University of Texas law school, more whites were taken off the waiting list than the total number of new minorities enrolled. Virtually all the applicants in the pool could achieve at UT law school, where there is almost no attrition. However, criticism of affirmative action is likely to continue because the transition to a more meritorious and heterogeneous legal profession will inevitably lead to a loss of white privilege, particularly white male privilege.

Current admissions programs at nearly all law schools are more thorough and better administered than at any point in legal education. Most admissions officers and financial aid administrators are capable and dedicated professionals who sift through thousands of papers and files to assemble as accomplished and diverse a class as possible. The sheer crush of applicants—Georgetown receives nearly ten thousand applications per year—means that admissions officers can choose among many exceptionally qualified persons. This is a key point. When they can choose from thousands of applicants, most of whom have the credentials to do the work, admissions committees are doing exactly what they are charged to do: assembling a qualified, diverse student body. *Bakke* sanctions this approach, common sense dictates it, and no anecdotal horror stories or isolated allegations can change this central fact.

On July 1, 1996, the Supreme Court left intact the Fifth Circuit's ruling in *Hopwood v. State of Texas,* a ruling that threatens all affirmative action programs at public colleges in Texas, Louisiana, and Mississippi.[42] In 1997, Dan Morales, Texas attorney general, indicated that the ruling in *Hopwood* extends to financial aid programs, including scholarships. *Bakke* remains the law of the land in all jurisdictions save the Fifth Circuit. Two U.S. Supreme Court justices, while denying certiorari, wrote that the issue was moot inasmuch as the University of Texas had already changed its admissions plan. But Morales has misinterpreted the Title VI ruling that this decision affects scholarships; the Office for Civil Rights, for one, has ruled otherwise.

There has been a virtual retreat from affirmative action in Texas. Even before the Fifth Circuit decided the case and the appeal was due to the U.S. Supreme Court, schools, including private colleges such as Rice University, began to bail out. Rice announced to the world that it would no longer "take into account" race or ethnicity in admissions, reversing a policy that had stood since 1966, when Rice received permission to ignore its own founding trust documents that established a free university for Houston's white citizens. A race to the bottom ensued, with the University of Texas, Texas A&M, and the University of Houston all announcing deracinated admissions policies for fall 1996. Rice even rescinded several admissions slated for black students.[43] The decision, although it was limited to the Fifth Circuit, has begun to leach into other states, as in Georgia, where the attorney general announced that he would follow *Hopwood.*

Race is a fugue that plays throughout U.S. society, including higher education. In the 1990s, there has been a societal backlash against affirmative action, as evidenced by a major political party's platform plank against the principles, California voters' ballot initiative to outlaw affirmative action in state services and employment, the University of California regents' action to overturn admissions affirmative action, and congressional action to dismantle a number of federal education programs. In addition, there is a new and resurgent nativism evident, as in California Ballot Initiative 197 to deny undocumented alien children public education (struck down by the California courts) and in federal initiatives to deny benefits to legal permanent residents. As society has become more conservative on affirmative action, so too have the courts and legislatures.

Faculty Rights versus Student Rights

In several important legal cases, faculty and student rights have come into direct conflict.[44] One involved prayer in the public college classroom, in which the court precluded the practice, finding that the Establishment Clause mandated that the college discontinue the practice. Another religion case, *Bishop v. Aranov,* pitted a public university against an exercise physiology professor who invited students in his class to judge him by Christian standards and to admonish him if he deviated from these tenets.[45] The appeals court held that colleges exercised broad authority over pedagogical issues and that "a teacher's speech can be taken as directly and deliberately representative of the school." This troubling logic, which reached the correct decision to admonish the professor, did so for the wrong reasons and rested upon the erroneous ground that faculty views are those of the institution. The court could have more parsimoniously and persuasively decided the same result by analyzing the peculiar role of religion injected into secular fields of study, especially when the teacher invites a particular religious scrutiny.

In another course, a studio art teacher was dismissed for his habit of not supervising his students; he argued that this technique taught students to act more independently. The court disagreed that his behavior was a protected form of professorial speech, as did a court that considered a professor's extensive use of profanity in the classroom. In a similar view, a basketball coach, dismissed for angrily calling his players "niggers" on the court to inspire them, found an unsympathetic court, which held that the remarks were not a matter of public concern and, therefore, not protected speech. A white professor also lost his position at a black college for making a remark that was interpreted by students as racist and for refusing to go back to teaching until the college administrators removed a student he considered disruptive.[46]

These and other cases have made it clear that students have some rights in a classroom, while well-known cases such as *Levin v. Harleston* and *Silva v. University of New Hampshire* have made it clear that courts still protect professors' ideas, however controversial (*Levin*), and teaching styles, however offensive (*Silva*).[47] A proper configuration of professorial academic freedom is resilient enough to resist extremes from without or within, to fend off the New Hampshire legislative inquiry of *Sweezy* and the proselytizing of *Bishop*.[48] In this view, professors have wide-ranging discretion to undertake their research and to formulate teaching methods in their classrooms and laboratories. However, this autonomy is, within broad limits, contingent upon traditional norms of peer review, codes of ethical behavior, and institutional standards. In the most favorable circumstances, these norms will be subject to administrative guidelines for ensuring requisite due process and fairness. Even the highly optimistic and altruistic 1915 AAUP Declaration of Principles holds that "individual teachers should [not] be exempt from all restraints as to the matter or manner of their utterances, either within or without the university."[49] In short, academic freedom does not give carte blanche to professors but, rather, vests faculty with the establishment and enforcement of standards of behavior, which are to be reasonably and appropriately applied in evaluations. Although I attempt to persuade that the academic common law is highly normative, contextual, and faculty driven, I do not lose sight of the range of acceptable practices and extraordinary heterogeneity found in classroom styles.

Additionally, persuasive research has emerged to show that persons trained in different academic disciplines view pedagogy differently. John Braxton and his colleagues summarize how these norms operate across disciplines:

> Personal controls that induce individual conformity to teaching norms are internalized to varying degrees though the graduate school socialization process. Graduate school attendance in general and doctoral study in particular are regarded as a powerful socialization experience. The potency of this process lies not only in the development of knowledge, skills, and competencies but also in the inculcation of norms, attitudes, and values. This socialization process entails the total learning situation. . . . Through these interpersonal relationships with faculty, values, knowledge, and skills are inculcated.[50]

Moreover, they are all inculcated differently. To grab a student and put my hands on his chest would be extraordinarily wrong in my immigration law class, but it could happen regularly and appropriately in a voice class, physical education course, or acting workshop. Discussing one's religious views in an exercise physiology class may be inappropriate, but certainly it is appropriate in a comparative religion course. Discussions of sexuality, which would be salacious in a legal ethics course, would be appropriately central to a seminar in human sexuality. Each academic field has evolved its own norms and conventions.

However, courts are not in the business of contextualizing pedagogical disputes, as is evident from a current case—*Mincone v. Nassau County Community College*—that is making its awkward way through the judicial system.[51] Although *Mincone* has forbears in other decisions, it is sufficient to make my points: if colleges do not police themselves, others will; disputes between teachers and pupils are on the rise; and poor fact patterns and sloppy practices will lead to substantial external control over the classroom. One other thread is that it arose in a two-year community college, making it likely that the results will be taken by subsequent judges as directly pertinent for higher education in a way that K–12 cases (notwithstanding *Hazelwood*'s leaching into postsecondary cases) have not been held to be controlling. Given the overlap with the mission of senior institutions and their usual transfer function, two-year colleges will not be easily distinguished. If a K–12 case is not in my favor, I can always try to convince a judge to limit it to the elementary/secondary sector; I will not be able to muster such a finely graded distinction in a postcompulsory world, even though two-year colleges are, on the average, more authoritarian and administrator driven than are four-year colleges. The widespread use of part-time and non-tenure-track faculty makes academic freedom more problematic at community colleges, where faculty do not always have the security or autonomy to develop traditional protections of tenure and academic freedom.

This is the second round of a case that began as a request for public records, in this instance, course materials for Physical Education 251 (PER 251), "Family Life and Human Sexuality." The course is taught in several sections to nearly three thousand students each year, and in *Mincone,* a senior citizen auditor (enrolled under terms of a free, noncredit program for adults over sixty-five years of age), who reviewed the course materials before he took the class (to be offered in summer 1995), sued to enjoin the course from using the materials or from using federal funds to "counsel abortion in the PER 251 course materials." Mincone, the representative of a co-plaintiff party, the Organization of Senior Citizens and Retailers (OSCAR), filed in May 1995 a lawsuit with eight causes of action: PER 251, under these theories, violates the strict religious neutrality required of public institutions by the New York State constitution; burdens and violates state law concerning the free exercise clause of the New York State constitution by "disparagement" of Judeo-Christian faiths and by promoting the religious teaching of Eastern religions with regard to sexuality; violates the federal First Amendment; violates the plaintiffs' civil rights guaranteed under Sec. 1983; teaches behavior that violates Sec. 130.00 of the New York State Penal Law (sodomy statutes); violates federal law concerning religious neutrality by singling out one "correct view of human sexuality"; disregards the duty to warn students of course content so they can decide whether or not to enroll in the course; endangers minors who may be enrolled in the course; and violates federal law enjoining abortion counseling.

This broad frontal attack on the course is virtually without precedent, as the plaintiff was not even enrolled in the course for credit and enjoined the course even before the term began and before he took the course as an auditor. While in all likelihood he will be denied standing, in that he suffered no harm and has no cognizable claim, OSCAR could simply enroll a plaintiff to get over that hurdle. But the

wide-ranging claims, particularly those that allege religious bias, are
so vague and poorly formulated that it is difficult to believe they will
survive.

If we begin with the premise that faculty members have the absolute right, within the limits of germaneness and institutional practice, to assign whatever text they wish, subject only to the text being
appropriate for the course and to academic custom, then professors
can pick whichever texts seem best for their courses. Sometimes, this
means a compromise, as in using a central text supplemented by the
extra materials they might wish were in the basic text (not everyone can or is inclined to write their own book). Therefore, materials
could be assigned that are a compromise, or materials may be not assigned because they are inappropriate. Surely, for a course known to
be a lightning rod (by the earlier suit), sex education and physiology
faculty carefully chose the filmstrips and materials; this is the contextual and professional judgment that my theory requires. As AAUP
general counsel, I would have no qualms in defending the course materials: they were picked by professionals with considerable expertise
in this field; the course is widely accepted and regularly fully enrolled;
it does what it sets out to do: expose students to wide-ranging issues
of sexuality; and the materials clearly put students on notice what
the course covers. Except for the personal and moral objections of the
plaintiffs concerning the materials, this course is generically like any
course. Context is all, as is professional authority to determine how
it will be taught.

Cases like this are fraught with implications for higher education
practice, especially for teacher behavior. In *Cohen v. San Bernardino Community College,* the District Court could have gone in the
opposite direction, as it had for Professors Silva and Levin, by stressing their academic freedom rather than by balancing the competing
interests.[52] However, by characterizing the issues as ones of classroom control and students' learning environment, Professor Cohen's
interests are trumped, at least with the admonishment. (His orders
were to do essentially as Professor Silva was ordered by the University of New Hampshire to do: take counseling, alter his class style,
etc.) He had been admonished to stop teaching from *Hustler* and
other "pornographic" materials in his remedial English class. And
the court did suggest that the admonishment was mild: "A case in
which a professor is terminated or directly censored presents a far
different balancing question." But does it? Can there be any doubt

that Cohen considers himself "directly censored" by the formal complaint of one student? Was Levin censored by City University of New York's "shadow section"? Is reading *Hustler* letters a good idea for a remedial English class?

Finally, there is the issue of a solution to the conundrum of faculty autonomy and sexual harassment jurisprudence. The difficulty is acknowledging that a classroom can be a hostile environment in some instances. In the AAUP, we have hammered out a compromise attempt to preserve faculty autonomy and to acknowledge and deal with an environment so hostile that it can stifle learning opportunities. The AAUP Proposed Statement of Policy for Sexual Harassment[53] reads as follows:

> It is the policy of this institution that no member of the academic community may sexually harass another. Sexual advances, requests for sexual favors, and other speech or conduct of a sexual nature constitute sexual harassment when:
>
> 1. Such advances or requests are made under circumstances implying that one's response might affect academic or personnel decisions that are subject to the influence of the person making the proposal; or
>
> 2. Such speech or conduct is directed against another and is either abusive or severely humiliating, or persists despite the objection of the person targeted by the speech or conduct; or
>
> 3. Such speech or conduct is reasonably regarded as offensive and substantially impairs the academic or work opportunity of students, colleagues, or co-workers. If it takes place in the teaching context, it must also be persistent, pervasive, and not germane to the subject matter.

The academic setting is distinct from the workplace in that wide latitude is required for professional judgment in determining the appropriate content and presentation of academic material. In our search for the perfect, clarifying epiphany, this proposed policy falls short: What is "severely humiliating"? Is it more than "humiliating"? How much more? How long does harassment have to persist in order to be found "persistent"? Isn't the classroom a "workplace" for faculty?

To me, in interpreting academic standards, it is not surprising that things work so badly but, rather, that they work so well. My own experiences as a student and as a professor lead me to believe that any comprehensive theory of professorial authority to determine "how it shall be taught" must incorporate a feedback mechanism for students to take issue, voice complaints, and point out remarks or attitudes that may be insensitive or disparaging. At a minimum, faculty should encourage students to speak privately with them to identify uncomfortable situations. Professor Bishop asked his students to point out inconsistencies between his Christian perspectives and his lifestyle. This is excessive and could itself provoke anxiety on the part of both Christian and non-Christian students. But a modest attempt to avoid stigmatizing words and examples is certainly in order for teachers, and schools should have in place some mechanism to address these issues. I cringe when exams consign "Jose", "Maria," or "Rufus" to criminal questions or when in-class hypotheticals use "illegal aliens" or sexist examples and stereotypes to illustrate legal points. Such misuse may be especially prevalent in fact patterns involving criminal activities, such as rape and consent. Students have a right to expect more thoughtful pedagogical practices.

Policy Implications and Conclusion

If events continue as in the past, there can be no doubt that higher education will become increasingly legalized, by the traditional means of legislation, regulation, and litigation as well as the growing areas of informal lawmaking, such as ballot initiatives, insurance carrier policies, and commercial or contract law in research. This cascade will shower down upon institutions, each leaving its residue in the form of administrative responsibility for acknowledging and implementing the responsibilities.

Understanding how legal initiatives become policy, particularly complex regulatory or legislative initiatives, should contribute greatly to improving administrative implementation of legal change on campus. Even with this modest review, it is clear that some legal policies will be more readily adopted than others. It is also clear that academic policy makers have substantial opportunities and resources to shape legal policy and smooth the way for legal changes on campus. Of course, no one can be expected to endorse all legal initiatives with equal enthusiasm or to administer them as if they were all high institutional priorities. Not all will be. Some will be implemented only grudgingly. However, understanding the implementation of legal change will influence the amount of policy output produced, the distribution of policy outputs, and the overall extent of compliance achieved.

The considerable autonomy and deference accorded higher education often translate into institutions designing their own compliance regimes for legislative and litigative change, and increased understanding of this complex legal phenomenon should increase this independence. As no small matter, higher education officials could begin to convince legislators that mandated legal change has a better chance of achieving the desired effects if institutions are allowed to design their own compliance and implementation strategies. This role could ease the sting so many campuses feel when another regulatory program is thrust upon them, or when they lose an important case in court, as happened at the University of Texas in *Hopwood v. State of Texas*. It could also lead higher education officials to seek reasonable compliance rather than exemption, which occurs often in practice. As higher education becomes more reliant upon government support and as colleges offer themselves for hire as participants in commercial ventures and as social change agents, legal restrictions are sure to follow. Understanding the consequences of legalization is a first step toward controlling our fate.

This and the other chapters in this book show how interdependent the higher education system is and reveal why we need to adapt to the times. Our timeless values, such as academic freedom, tenure, institutional autonomy, and due process are in danger of being legislated or litigated away, if we do not remain vigilant and alert and if we do not self-police. There are many police outside the academy all too willing to do it if we do not.

NOTES

1. Lewis Thomas, *The Youngest Science: Notes of a Medicine Watcher* (New York: Viking, 1983); Paul Goodman, *The Community of Scholars* (New York: Free Press, 1962); John Millett, *The Academic Community* (New York: McGraw-Hill, 1962); Herbert Stroup, *Bureaucracy in Higher Education* (New York: Free Press, 1966); Victor Baldridge, *Power and Conflict in the University* (New York: Wiley, 1971); Burton R. Clark, *The Higher Education System* (Berkeley: University of California Press, 1983); Clark Kerr, *The Uses of the University* (Cambridge: Harvard University Press, 1982); Randall Collins, *The Credential Society* (New York: Academic, 1979); Harry T. Edwards, *Higher Education and the Unholy Crusade against Governmental Regulation* (Cambridge, Mass.: Institute for Educational Management, 1980); Paolo Freire, *Education for Critical Consciousness* (New York: Seabury, 1973).

2. *Coffee v. Rice University,* 408 S.W.2d 269 (1966).

3. *Shapiro v. Columbia Union,* 576 S.W.2d 310 (1979).

4. *U.S. on behalf of U.S. Coast Guard v. Cerio,* 831 F.Supp. 530 (E.D. Va. 1993).

5. *Fountain Gate Ministries, Inc. v. City of Plano,* 654 S.W.2d 841 (Tex. App. 5 Dist. 1983).

6. *Hacker v. Hacker,* 522 N.Y.S. 768 (Supp. 1987).

7. *Beth Rochel v. Bennett,* 825 F.2d 478 (D.C. Cir. 1987); *City of Morgantown v. West Virginia Board of Regents,* 354 S.E.2d 616 (W. Va. 1987).

8. *Trustees of Dartmouth v. Woodward,* 4 Wheaton (U.S.) 518 (1819); *Krynicky v. University of Pittsburgh,* 742 F.2d 94 (1984).

9. *Powe v. Miles,* 407 F.2d 73 (1968).

10. *Cahn and Cahn v. Antioch University,* 482 A.2d 120 (D.C. App. 1984).

11. *Fenn College v. Nance,* 210 N.E.2d 418 (1965); *Nasson College v. New England Association of Schools and Colleges,* 16 B.C.D. 1299 (1988).

12. *NCAA v. University of Oklahoma,* 488 U.S.85 (1984); *U.S. v. Brown University,* 5 F.3d 658 (3d Cir. 1993).

13. *Rochel Beth Seminary v. Bennett,* 825 F.2d 478 (D.C. Cir. 1987); *Marjorie Webster Junior College v. Middle States Association,* 139 U.S.App. D.C. 217, 432 F.2d 650 (1970).

14. *NLRB v. Yeshiva University,* 444 U.S.672 (1980).

15. Lelia Helms, "Patterns of Litigation in Postsecondary Education: A Caselaw Study," *Journal of College and University Law* 14 (1987): 99–110; Margaret Lam, *Patterns of Litigation at Institutions of Higher Education in Texas, 1878–1978* (Houston: IHELG, 1988).

16. William Kaplin and Barbara Lee, *The Law of Higher Education* (San Francisco: Jossey-Bass, 1995); Matthew Finkin, *The Case for Tenure* (Ithaca: Cornell University Press, 1996); George LaNoue and Barbara Lee, *Academics in Court* (Ann Arbor: University of Michigan Press, 1985); Patricia Spacks, ed., *Advocacy in the Classroom* (New York: St. Martin's, 1996).

17. *Perry v. Sindermann,* 408 U.S.593 (1972); *Board of Regents v. Roth,* 408 U.S.564 (1972).

18. *Wellner v. Minnesota State Junior College Board,* 487, F.2d 153 (1973).

19. *State ex rel. McLemore v. Clarksville School of Theology,* 636 S.W.2d 706 (1982).

20. *Hill v. Talladega College,* 502 So.2d 735 (Ala. 1987); *Honore v. Douglas,* 833 F.2d 565 (5th Cir. 1987); *Spuler v. Pickar,* 958 F.2d 103 (5th Cir. 1992); *Lewis v. Loyola University of Chicago,* 500 N.E.2d 47 (Ill. App. 1 Dist. 1996).

21. *Scott v. University of Delaware,* 455 F.Supp. 1102 (1978).

22. *Faro v. NYU,* 502 F.2d 1229 (1974).

23. *Clark v. Claremont Graduate Center,* 8 Cal. Rptr. 2d 151 (Cal. App. 2 Dist. 1992).

24. *Sweeney v. Board of Trustees of Keene State College,* 569 F.2d 169

(1978); *Kunda v. Muhlenberg College,* 463 F.Supp. 294 (E.D. Pa. 1978); *Mecklenberg v. Montana State Board of Regents,* 13 EPD 11, 438 (1976); *Kemp v. Irvin,* 651 F.Supp. 495 (N.D. Ga. 1986).

25. *Hazelwood School District v. Kuhlmeier,* 108 S.Ct. 562 (1988); *Bishop v. Aranov,* 926 F.2d 1066 (11th Cir. 1991); *Scallet v. Rosenblum,* unpublished opinion, U.S. Court of Appeals, 4th Cir., Jan. 29, 1997 (C.A. 94-16-c).; *Waters v. Churchill,* 114 S.Ct.1878 (1994); *Jeffries v. Harleston,* 828 F.Supp. 1066 (S.D.N.Y. 1993) 21 F.3d 1238 (2d Cir. 1994), vac. and rem. 115 S.Ct.502 (1995) vac. and rev'd, 52 F.3d 9 (2d Cir. 1995), cert den. 116 S.Ct.173 (1995).

26. Data from Joel Douglas, "Professors on Strike: An Analysis of Two Decades of Faculty Work Stoppages, 1960–1985," *Labor Lawyer* 4 (1988): 87–101.

27. *Trustees of Columbia University,* 29 LRRM 1098 (1951).

28. *Cornell University,* 183 NLRB 329 (1970).

29. *United Faculty v. University of Pittsburgh,* PLRB No. PERAR-84–53W (March 11, 1987).

30. *NLRB v. Cooper Union,* 78 3 F.2d 29 (2d Cir. 1985); *NLRB v. Florida Memorial College,* 820 F.2d 1182 (11th Cir. 1987).

31. *Bakke v. Regents of University of California,* 438 U.S.265 (1978).

32. *Anthony v. Syracuse University* 231 N.Y.S.435 (1928); *Gott v. Berea,* 156 Ky.376, 161 S.W.204 (1913); *Dixon v. Alabama State Board of Education,* 294 F.2d 150 (1961).

33. *Tarasoff v. Regents of University of California,* 551 F.2d 334 (1976); *Mullins v. Pine Manor College,* 449 N.E.2d 331 (Mass. 1983); *Johnson v. Lincoln Christian College,* 501 N.E.2d 1380 (Ill. App. 4 Dist. 1986); *Ross v. Creighton,* 957 F.2d 410 (7th Cir. 1992).

34. *Gonzalez v. North American College of Louisiana,* 700 F.Supp. 362 (S.D. Tex. 1988); *American Commercial Colleges, Inc. v. Davis,* 821 S.W.2d 450 (Tex. App.-Eastland 1991).

35. *Hopwood v. State of Texas,* 78 F.3d 945 (5th Cir. 1996) (reviewing constitutional standards). For a review of this and other higher education cases, see Michael A. Olivas, *The Law and Higher Education* (Durham, N.C.: Carolina Academic Press, 1997).

36. Ibid., 948.

37. *Wygant v. Jackson Board of Education,* 476 U.S.267 (1986); *City of Richmond v. Croson,* 488 U.S.469 (1989); *Adarand v. Pena,* 115 S.Ct.2097 (1995).

38. *Wygant v. Jackson Board of Education,* 476 U.S.267, 286 (1986).

39. *Adarand v. Pena,* 115 S.Ct.2097, 2117 (1995).

40. *Hopwood v. State of Texas,* 78 F.3d 946 (5th Cir. 1996).

41. *Hopwood v. State of Texas,* 861 F.Supp. 551, 566–567 (W.D. Tex. 1994).

42. *Hopwood v. State of Texas,* 78 F.3d 932.

43. "The Short History of Raced-Based Affirmative Action at Rice University," *Journal of Blacks in Higher Education* 18 (1996): 36–38.

240 Michael A. Olivas

44. Michael A. Olivas, "Professorial Academic Freedom: Second Thoughts on the 'Third Essential Freedom,'" *Stanford Law Review* 45 (1993): 1835–58.

45. *Bishop v. Aranov*, 926 F.2d 1066 (11th Cir. 1991).

46. *McConnell v. Howard University*, 818 F.2d 58 (D.C. Cir. 1987).

47. *Levin v. Harleston*, 770 F.Supp. 895 (S.D.N.Y. 1991), aff'd in relevant part, vac. on other grounds, 996 F.2d 85 (2d Cir. 1992); *Silva v. University of New Hampshire.*

48. *Sweezy v. New Hampshire*, 354 U.S.234 (1957); *Bishop v. Aranov*, 926 F.2d 1066 (11th Cir. 1991).

49. "General Report of the Committee on Academic Freedom and Academic Tenure," *AAUP Bulletin* 17 (1915): 1, reprinted in *Law and Contemporary Problems* 393 (1990): 53.

50. John M. Braxton, Alan Bayer, and Martin Finkelstein, "Teaching Performance Norms in Academia," *Research in Higher Education* 33 (1992): 533–70, quotation on 535–36.

51. *Mincone v. Nassau County Community College*, N.Y.S.2d 419 (A.D. 2 Dept. 1992).

52. *Cohen v. San Bernadino Valley Community College*, 883 F.Supp. 1407 (C.D. Cal. 1995), rev'd in part, 92 F.3d 968 (9th Cir. 1996).

53. American Association of University Professors, "AAUP Proposed Statement of Policy for Sexual Harassment," in *Policy Documents and Reports* (Washington, D.C.: AAUP, 1995), 171.

Chapter Nine

The Hidden Hand
External Constituencies
and Their Impact

Fred F. Harcleroad

Postsecondary institutions have endured in the United States for over three and one-half centuries. All except those established recently have been modified over the years and have changed greatly in response to pressures from external forces. Particularly in the last century and a half, literally thousands of diverse institutions have opened their doors, only to close when they were no longer needed by sufficient students or the public and private constituencies that founded and supported them. Those in existence today are the survivors, the institutions that adapted to the needs of their constituencies.

The varied external forces affecting postsecondary education in the United States have grown out of our unique three-sector system of providing goods and services for both collective consumption and private use. First, the *voluntary enterprise sector,* composed of millions of independent nonprofit organizations, often has initiated efforts to provide such things as schools, hospitals, bridges, libraries, environmental controls, and public parks. They are protected by constitutional rights to peaceful assembly, free speech, and petition for redress of grievances. These formidable protections plus their record of useful service led to their being nontaxable, with contributions to them being tax free. Second, the *public enterprise group,* composed of all local, state, and federal governments, administers the laws that hold our society together. Third, the *private enterprise sector,* com-

posed of profit-seeking business and commerce, provides much of the
excess wealth needed to support the other two sectors. This pluralistic and diverse set of organizations implements the basic ideas behind
our federated republic.

Our constitution provides for detailed separation of powers at the
federal level between the presidency, the Congress, and the judiciary.
The Tenth Amendment establishes the states as governments with
"general" powers, delegating "limited" powers to the federal government. Education is not a delegated power and therefore is reserved to
the states, whose constitutions often treat it almost as a fourth branch
of government. In addition, the Tenth Amendment reserves "general" powers to citizens, who operate through their own voluntary
organizations, their state governments, or state-authorized private
enterprise. Consequently, only a few higher education institutions are
creations of the federal government (mostly military institutions, to
provide for the common defense); more than 99 percent are creations
of states, voluntary organizations, or profit-seeking businesses.

Both of the oldest institutions in the country, Harvard (established
in 1636) and the College of William and Mary (established in 1693),
have closed for different reasons but opened up again when changes
were made. Harvard closed for what would have been its second year
(in 1639–40), after Nathaniel Eaton, its first head, was dismissed
for cruelty to students and stealing college funds. After being closed
for the year, government officials determined that the Massachusetts
Bay Colony still needed a college to train ministers and to advance
learning. A new president, Henry Dunster, reopened the college in
1640, and by changing regularly, and sometimes dramatically, the
college has remained in operation ever since. Two small examples
illustrate this process. As Massachusetts grew and secularized, ministerial training at Harvard became only one function, so it was placed
in a separate divinity school. Also, by the late 1700s required instruction in Hebrew was replaced by student choice, a beginning of our
current elective system.

William and Mary was the richest of the colonial colleges, supported
by the Commonwealth of Virginia, which included income from taxes
on tobacco, skins, and hides. Nevertheless, the college had to make
many adaptations in order to remain politically supported. For example, after the Revolution, in 1779, it dropped its chair of divinity
and established the nation's first professorship of law and police. The
college closed during the 1861–65 Civil War, reopened briefly, but

closed again in 1881. It eventually reopened in 1888, when the state agreed to make it a state-supported institution if it would become Virginia's main teacher education college. Thus, it changed from being essentially a private college operated by the Episcopal Church, an excellent example of a government taking over a private institution to meet the developing needs of the society as a whole. Interaction of this type between government and private constituencies is a singular characteristic of the democratic republic established in the United States, and it is important to consider in studying the relationships of colleges and universities to their external environment.

External groups, associations, and agencies from all three sectors impact on the institutions of postsecondary education. This diverse group of external organizations includes everything from athletic conferences and alumni associations to employer associations and unions (or organized faculty groups that function as unions). Of course, the corporate boards that administer all of the private colleges, universities, and institutes authorized to operate in the respective states belong in this group. Their power to determine institutional policies is clear and well known. However, many other voluntary associations can and do have significant effects on specific institutions or units of the institutions. Five of these—private foundations, institutionally based associations, voluntary accrediting associations, voluntary consortia, and regional compacts—are described below in some detail, indicating their backgrounds, their development, and their possible impact on institutional autonomy and academic freedom.

Private Foundations

The beginnings of private foundations in the United States took place over two centuries ago.[1] Benjamin Franklin led in the establishment, in Philadelphia, of a number of voluntary sector organizations, including the American Philosophical Society in 1743, an association with many foundation characteristics. In 1800 the Magdalen Society of Philadelphia, possibly the first private foundation in the United States, was established as a perpetual trust to assist "unhappy females who had been seduced from the paths of virtue." In the 1890s and early 1900s, long before the federal income tax became legal due to the Sixteenth Amendment to the U.S. Constitution, the Carnegie foundations, followed shortly by the Rockefeller foundations, set a

pattern that continues to this day. These foundations established a
high standard of operations and service. Few academics realize that
their current TIAA pensions were developed and are currently administered by a foundation resulting from Andrew Carnegie's feeling
of public service responsibility. Decades before such "contributions"
became tax deductible, he gave several million dollars to set up the
first pension fund for college teachers.

Today, private foundations vary greatly in form, purpose, size,
function, and constituency. Some are corporate in nature, many are
trusts, and others are only associations. Many of them can affect postsecondary institutions through their choice of areas to support. They
can be classified into five types as follows: (1) community foundations, often citywide or regional, which make a variety of bequests or
gifts (local postsecondary institutions often can count on some support from such foundations for locally related projects), (2) family or
personal foundations, often with limited purposes, (3) special purpose
foundations (including such varied examples as the Harvard Glee
Club and a fund set up to provide every girl at Bryn Mawr with one
baked potato at each meal), (4) company foundations established to
channel corporate giving through one main source, and (5) national
independent foundations (including many of the large, well-known
foundations, such as Ford, Kellogg, Johnson, Lilly, and Carnegie, plus
recent additions such as Murdock, MacArthur, and Hewlett). Over
90 percent of private foundation grant funds to higher education
come from these national foundations. They usually are interested
in making grants with national or international implications, often
within carefully determined target areas of interest.

The number of grant-making foundations, estimated at more than
35,000 in 1996, is constantly growing. These foundations award
grants approximating $10 billion yearly, much of it to higher edu-
cational institutions for research, demonstration projects, in-service
training, staffing support, program revisions and expansion, and community improvement efforts. A special report of the Foundation Center in 1991 reported that 228 of the larger foundations made grants
totaling more than $980 million in thirty-eight fields of interest, such
as adult education, environment, history, medical education, public
health, rural development, theater, dance, and vocational education.

Foundations, especially those in the national independent category,
provide significant help to higher education institutions, and by their
choice of areas to finance they entice supposedly autonomous colleges

to do things they might not do otherwise. Institutional change continues to be a prime goal of foundations, as it has been for most of the past century. Thus, although their grants provide a relatively small proportion of the total financing of institutions, they have had significant effects on program development and even operations. Important support has been provided for such critical activities as the upgrading of medical education, the development of honors programs, and the international exchange of students. Grants from foundations have been instrumental in the establishment of new academic fields such as microbiology and anthropology and the redirection of the fields of business and the education of teachers. Significant support has been provided particularly for the increasing opportunities for minority students to attend at both undergraduate and graduate levels, especially in professional fields. Complaints that private foundations limit their significant funding efforts to "establishment" activities fail to recognize the many critical social changes in which private foundations have led the way. Often, foundation funds have encouraged colleges and universities to take forefront positions in some social causes.

It is important to stress, however, that private foundations affect institutional freedom only if the institutions voluntarily accept the funds for the purposes prescribed by the foundation. The redirection of programs and even of private institutional goals is possible and has occurred on occasion. Nevertheless, the private foundation model has been so successful that government has adopted it in forming and funding such agencies as the National Science Foundation, the Fund for the Improvement of Postsecondary Education, and the National Endowments for the Arts and for the Humanities. Clearly, private foundations have been and undoubtedly will continue to be important external forces affecting postsecondary education.

Institutionally Based Associations

Voluntary membership organizations of this type are almost infinite in possible number.[2] Although formed by institution officials for their own purposes, the associations often end up having indirect or direct effects on the institutions themselves. The American Council on Education, probably the major policy advocate for postsecondary education at the national level, plays a critical coordinative role as an umbrella organization, composed of a wide spectrum of institutions. Other major national institutional organizations include the Association of American Colleges and Universities, the American Association of Community Colleges, the American Association of State Colleges and Universities, the Association of American Universities, the Council of Independent Colleges, the National Association of Independent Colleges and Universities, and the National Association of State Universities and Land-Grant Colleges. The American Council on Education also coordinates a larger group, of thirty-seven higher educational associations, known as the Washington Higher Education Secretariat; it convenes monthly to exchange information and to discuss current or projected activities, many of them national policy issues, often regarding federal financing or control. These organizations represent most of the public and private nonprofit postsecondary institutions in the United States, with some institutions belonging to two or three of them. Based for the most part in Washington, they represent the differing interests of the varied institutions. Also, especially when they work together as a united front, they can influence congressional committees and government agencies on key issues affecting higher education.

The strength of these national associations will continue to grow along with taxes, the federal budget, and federal purchase of selected services from their member institutions. Even though most postsecondary institutions are state chartered and many are basically state funded, the increasing power of the federal tax system will make such national associations even more necessary.

Many specialized voluntary membership associations contribute in diverse ways to the development and operations of functional areas within institutions. For example, the American College Testing Program and the College Entrance Examination Board (its service bureau, the Educational Testing Service, is not a membership organization) provide extensive information resources to their member institutions and program areas. These data are vital for counseling and guidance purposes, admission of students, student financial aid programs, and related activities. In addition, different administrative functions (such as graduate schools, registrars, institutional research units, and business offices) have their own, extremely useful, representative associations. Likewise, most academic fields and their constantly increasing subdivisions or spin-offs have set up specialized groups. Prime examples are engineering and the allied health professions, both with dozens of separate associations. Many of these academic organizations affect institutions and their program planning in direct ways. In particular, the associations that set up detailed criteria for membership in the association often directly influence allocation of resources. Of the several-thousand-member organizations in this category, sixty to seventy of them, from architecture to veterinary medicine, probably exert the greatest influence, since those programs or academic units admitted to membership are considered accredited. (The following section provides more detail on this group.) A sampling of these organizations illustrates their services, emphasizes their significance, and shows in a limited way their potential impact.

The American Council on Education (ACE) includes separate institutions and other associations, with approximately 1,600 institutional members, representing more than 70 percent of all college and university enrollments in the United States. (There are an additional 200 or so noninstitutional members.) Since the council's establishment in 1918, its work has changed from emphasis on "consensus building," its primary charge for the first fifty years, to initiating action to improve higher education. Its special offices and centers indicate its thrusts: Office of Women in Higher Education, Center for Adult Learning and Educational Credentials, Office of Minorities in Higher Education, Business/Higher Education Forum, Center for Leadership Development, International Initiatives, Division of Policy Analysis and Research, Division of Governmental Relations, Washington Higher Education Secretariat, Labor/Higher Education Council, Health Resource Center (a national clearinghouse on postsecondary education for individuals with disabilities), and numerous other special programs.

The publication program of the ACE provides major documents on the field of higher education, such as the annual editions of *American Universities and Colleges*. It also prepares and distributes such important guidebooks as the *Guide to the Evaluation of Educational Experiences in the Armed Services*. This guide is updated periodically and serves as a bible for most registrars' offices. A comparable ACE publication is *The National Guide to Credit Recommendations for Non-Collegiate Courses*. The extensive service and publications program includes reports from the policy analysis service and many special studies on current critical issues in higher education.

As the twenty-first century arrives, the leadership of the ACE expects to expand efforts in its national network to three additional areas: distance education and expanding use of information technology, institutional accountability, and price/cost issues in higher education. Two special project possibilities have to do with South African universities, perhaps in cooperation with one of the Carnegie foundations, and further work in promoting second-language competency for American citizens.

The Council of Independent Colleges (CIC) began in 1956, as the Council for the Advancement of Small Colleges. In the mid-1990s it had grown to a membership of 400, including more than 320 college and university members, about 50 sponsoring members, and the remainder affiliate members, including state associations of private colleges, regional consortia, and educational offices of religious denominations. The council, from its beginnings, has had a significant program of services to its members. In its early years, some of its member institutions operated without planned budgets or accreditation and with only limited accounting records. Many CIC institutions took advantage of its workshops, seminars, handbooks, and consultants and earned regional accreditation. CIC has secured many millions of dollars to operate programs for its constituency. Many of its special services are supported by useful publications, such as *Academic Workplace Audit, The New Liberal Learning, Technology and the Liberal Arts,* and *International Business Curricula in Independent Liberal Arts Colleges and Universities.*

The Association of Governing Boards of Universities and Colleges is a nonprofit association serving more than 32,000 trustees and officials of close to 1,700 colleges and universities or their foundations, from all types of boards—private, public, two-year, four-year, governing, coordinating, and advisory. Its mission is described as "to strengthen the practice of voluntary trusteeship as the best alternative to direct government and political control of higher education." In addition to membership fees, its support comes from several dozen national, personal, private, and corporate foundations. Its extensive program of publications, videotapes, conferences, and seminars is designed to provide trustees and institutional leaders with timely and useful resources in this specialized area. One package of materials, *Fundamentals of Trusteeship,* is designed for the orientation of new trustees. Another specialized service is its Presidential Search Consultation Service, which often serves several dozen institutions a year. Other projects include a major study of multicampus system operation, a compendium called *Strategic Indicators for Higher Education* (a selection of 150 financial and nonfinancial indicators from more than 700 colleges and universities), and the Trustee Information Center, which provides answers to queries on all aspects of lay trusteeship and governance of higher education institutions, based on the most comprehensive governance library in existence.

The American Association of State Colleges and Universities (AASCU) represents nearly four hundred public colleges and universities (more than 90 percent of the total), plus thirty-three coordinating or governing boards for these institutions. Since its beginnings in 1961, the association has been a leading stimulator of all facets of international education. Its many presidential missions to such countries as Egypt, Israel, Greece, Poland, the People's Republic of China, Cuba, Argentina, Taiwan, Malaysia, and Mexico have fostered continuing educational exchange and on-campus programs. It has taken the national leadership in developing cooperative interassociation and interinstitutional programs and networks, such as the Service Members Opportunity Colleges (with many AASCU institutions involved) and the Urban College and University Network. Its Office of Federal Programs monitors current funding programs and priorities and has been instrumental in increasing AASCU institutions' participation in this ever increasing source of funds. Its Office of Governmental Relations and Policy Analysis analyzes pending legislation, prepares testimony on major national issues, monitors state issues affecting public higher education, conducts surveys, studies trends, and keeps institutional officials informed. The Academic Affairs Resource Center and Academic Leadership Academy serve the chief academic officers of the institutions, emphasizing planning, faculty development, opportunities for minorities and women to attain senior administrative positions, leadership training, financial management, legal matters, and innovative educational ideas for new clientele.

An extensive seminar, conference, and publication program supports this alignment of institutional services. Some examples are the annual summer council of presidents, which emphasizes current issues and presidential leadership; regular meetings of the chief academic affairs officials; the annual President's Academy for new campus chief executive officers; and the National Minority Feeder Program, sponsored jointly with the National Association of State Universities and Land-Grant Colleges. Overall, the AASCU has had a profound effect on the institutions that founded it in 1961, and their graduates represent more than one-fourth of all those earning bacca-laureate degrees and one-third of those earning master's degrees in the United States.

These summaries illustrate the significance and impact of this type of voluntary association. Each contributes in varied ways to the diverse needs of their member institutions or to the program units within them. Fundamentally, the organizations are the creatures of their founding and continuing members, and they serve important functions for these institutions. When institutions need assistance in preserving such important features as autonomy of operation or academic freedom for students and faculty, these professional associations are buffers and important sources of support.

Voluntary Accrediting Associations

The voluntary membership organizations in this important group barely existed a century ago.[3] However, the end of the nineteenth century was a confused and uneasy time in higher education, and major changes were under way. Five key factors contributed to the turbulent state of affairs in the period from 1870 to 1910: (1) the final breakdown of the fixed, classical curriculum and the broad expansion of the elective system, (2) the development and legitimation of new academic fields (psychology, education, sociology, American literature), (3) the organization of new, diverse types of institution to meet developing social needs (teachers colleges, junior colleges, land-grant colleges, research universities, specialized professional schools), (4) the expansion of both secondary and postsecondary education and the resultant overlapping, leading to the question, What is a college? and (5) a lack of commonly accepted standards for admission to college and for completing a college degree.

To work on some of these problems, the University of Michigan as early as 1871 sent out faculty members to inspect high schools and admitted graduates of the acceptable and approved high schools on the basis of their diplomas. Shortly thereafter, pressures developed for regional approaches to these problems in order to facilitate uniform college entrance requirements.

In keeping with accepted American practice and custom, groups of educators banded together in various regions to organize private, voluntary membership groups for this purpose. In New England, for example, a group of secondary schoolmasters took the initiative. In the southern states, it was Chancellor Kirkland and the faculty of Vanderbilt University. Six regional associations have developed throughout the United States, starting with the New England Association of Schools and Colleges in 1885. It was followed in 1887 by the Middle States Association of Colleges and Schools, in 1895 by the Southern Association of Colleges and Schools and the North Central Association of Colleges and Schools, in 1917 by the Northwest Association of Schools and Colleges, and in 1923 by the Western Association of Schools and Colleges. Criteria and requirements for institutional membership (which now serve as the basis for institutions being considered accredited) were formally established by these six associations at different times: in 1910 by North Central, with the first list of accredited colleges in 1913; in 1919 by Southern; in 1921 by Northwest and Middle States; in 1949 by Western; and in 1954 by New England. Thus, at the same time that the federal government instituted regulatory commissions to control similar problems (the Interstate Commerce Commission in 1887, the Federal Trade Commission in 1914, and the Federal Power Commission in 1920), these nongovernmental voluntary membership groups sprang up to provide yardsticks for student achievement and institutional operations.

Regional groups dealt in the main with colleges rather than with specialized professional schools or programs. The North Central Association finally determined to admit normal schools and teachers colleges but on a separate list of acceptable institutions. Practitioners and faculty in professional associations gradually set up their own membership associations. These groups established criteria for approving schools and, based on these criteria, made lists of accredited schools and program units. In some cases, only individuals with degrees from an approved school could join the professional association. Later, some membership groups made the approved program unit or school a basis for association membership. In any case, the specialized academic program and its operational unit had to meet exacting criteria, externally imposed, to acquire and retain standing in the field.

The first of the specialized or programmatic discipline-oriented associations was the American Medical Association (AMA) in 1847. However, approving processes for medical schools did not start until the early 1900s. From 1905 to 1907 the Council on Medical Education of the AMA led a movement for rating medical schools. The first ratings in 1905 were a list based on the percentages of failures on licensing examinations by students from each school. This was followed in 1906/7 by a more sophisticated system, based on ten specific areas to be examined and inspections of each school. Of 160 schools inspected, classified, and listed, 32 were in Class C, "unapproved"; 46 were in Class B, "probation"; and 82 were in Class A, "approved." The Council on Medical Education was attacked vigorously for this listing and approving activity. The recently established Carnegie Foundation for the Advancement of Teaching (1905) provided funds for Abraham Flexner and N. P. Colwell to make their famous study (1908–10) of the 155 schools still in existence (5 already had closed). By 1915, only 95 medical schools remained, a 40 percent reduction, and they were again classified by the AMA Council on Medical Education, with 66 approved, 17 on probation, and 12 still unapproved. This voluntary effort led to the ultimate in accountability: the merger and closing of 65 medical schools. In the process, medical education was changed drastically, and the remaining schools completely revised and changed their curricula, a process still continuing to this day. This case provides an excellent example of the work of an external voluntary professional association that, with financial support from a private foundation, took the initiative to protect the public interest. Thus, in some cases intrusions into autonomy can have beneficial results.

The success of the AMA did not go unnoticed. The National Home Study Council (now the Distance Education and Training Council) started in 1926 to do for correspondence education what the AMA had done for medical education. Between 1914 and 1935 many other professional disciplinary and service associations were started in the fields of business, dentistry, law, library science, music, engineering, forestry, and dietetics, plus the medically related fields of podiatry, pharmacy, veterinary medicine, optometry, and nurse anesthesia. From 1935 to 1948 new associations starting up included architecture, art, Bible schools, chemistry, journalism, and theology, plus four more medically related fields (medical technology, medical records, occupational therapy, and physical therapy). Between 1948 and 1975 the number of specialized associations continued to expand rapidly, for programs from social service to graduate psychology and from construction education to funeral direction. Medical care subspecialties also proliferated, particularly in the allied health field, which included more than twenty-five separate groups. After 1975 the expansion slowed greatly, and only a few new specialized associations developed during the following two decades, these few being in developing allied health areas, for nontraditional types of institution that could not obtain "listing" by recognized national associations, or to expand accreditation opportunities in fields in which existing associations were unduly restrictive. For example, the Association of Collegiate Business Schools and Programs (established in 1988 and recognized by the U.S. Department of Education in 1992) met a need for improved articulation and recognition of business programs in community colleges and teaching-oriented colleges and universities, both four-year and graduate. By 1993 it had 500 members, about equally divided between the two types of institution, and an established, ongoing program of accreditation and service to its members.

All of these external professional associations affect institutional operations directly, including curricular patterns, faculty, degrees offered, teaching methods, support staff patterns, and capital outlay decisions. In many cases, priorities in internal judgments result from the outside pressures. Local resource allocations often are heavily influenced by accreditation reports. For example, the law library, a chemistry or engineering laboratory, and teaching loads in business or social work may have been judged substandard by these external private constituents. If teaching loads in English or history also are heavy or physics laboratories are inadequate, will they get the same attention and treatment as specialized program areas with outside pressures? In such cases, these association memberships are not really voluntary, if the institution is placed on probation, is no longer an accredited member, and sanctions are actually applied. Often, students will withdraw from or not consider attending a professional school or college that is not accredited. States often limit professional licenses to practice in a field to graduates of accredited schools. Federal agencies may not allow students from unaccredited institutions to obtain scholarships, loans, or work/study funds. The leverage of a voluntary association in such cases becomes tremendous, and the pressure for accredited status can be extremely powerful.

Presidents of some of the larger institutions, starting in 1924, have attempted to limit the effects of accrediting associations. Through some of the institutionally based associations described in the previous section, they established limited sanctions and attempted to restrict the number of accrediting associations to which they would pay dues and allow on-campus site visits. These efforts to limit association membership and accreditation failed repeatedly to stem the tide. In 1949, a group of university presidents organized the National Com-

mission on Accrediting, a separate voluntary membership association
of their own, designed to cut down on the demands and influence of
existing external associations and to delay or stop the development of
new ones. The number of new ones dropped for a few years, but pressures of new, developing disciplines on campus led, since the 1950s,
to many new organizations of this type.

In 1949, the regional associations also felt the need for a new
cooperative association and set up what became the Federation of
Regional Accrediting Commissions. In 1975 the two organizations,
FRACHE and NCA, agreed to merge, and they became major factors
in the founding of the new Council on Postsecondary Accreditation.
COPA also included four national groups accrediting specialized institutions, plus seven major, institutionally based associations. They,
in turn, endorsed COPA as the central, leading voluntary association
for the establishment of policies and procedures in postsecondary accreditation. After a few years, the large representative board became
unwieldy and was made much smaller. Also, the presidents, through
their various associations, pushed vigorously for more representation. As a result, COPA reorganized further, into three assemblies: the
Assembly of Institutional Accrediting Bodies (six national and eight
regional), the Assembly of Specialized Accrediting Bodies (forty-two
associations), and the Presidents Policy Assembly on Accreditation
(seven national associations of presidents from differing types of institution).

The system for funding COPA required the member associations,
particularly the large regional associations, to collect COPA dues
along with their own dues, which were tied to institutional accreditation. When in 1993 several regional associations decided not to collect
the dues for COPA, it found itself without financial support and dis-
banded on December 31, 1993. One of COPA'a major functions was
the "recognition" and "listing" of approved voluntary accrediting
bodies, and on January 1, 1994, the less-expensive, streamlined Commission on Recognition of Postsecondary Accreditation (CORPA) was
set up by a voluntary founding commission to maintain this phase of
the work. Nine organizations paid sustaining fees to keep this critical
accrediting function alive. They included the American Association
of Community Colleges, the American Association of Dental Schools,
the American Association of State Colleges and Universities, the
American Council on Education, the Association of American Universities, the Association of Collegiate Business Schools and Programs,

the Association of Governing Boards of Universities and Colleges, the National Association of Independent Colleges and Universities, and the National Association of State Universities and Land-Grant Colleges. Later, a tenth was added, the Western Association of Bible Colleges and Christian Schools.

From 1994 through 1996, various alternatives were debated throughout higher education, alternatives designed to continue a more extensive national accrediting presence beyond the efforts of CORPA. Finally, a presidents work group on accreditation, consisting of twenty-five leaders from all types of institution, developed a prospective new association to be called the Council for Higher Education Accreditation (CHEA). After a number of associations voted to approve its plan for operation, in 1995/96, a ballot was sent to 2,990 colleges and universities. Replies were received from 1,574 (52.5%); of these, 1,476 voted to support the new organization (94%). CHEA and CORPA expected to work together, having CHEA assume the listing and recognition obligation, along with the broader national leadership of voluntary accreditation. The funding system of CHEA is similar to the system used for COPA, with some modification, but the accrediting bodies were still asked to collect the money for their own dues, and for CHEA, as a responsibility when they were recognized and listed. The long-term success of CHEA appears to depend on the success of the funding system. At least two of the regionals and many of the associations that make up the Association of Specialized and Professional Accreditors (ASPA) had serious questions about the new organization and its potential. The ASPA Code of Good Practice for a new national service has seven major areas, some of which the brief CHEA proposal did not address. The period from 1997 until the twenty-first century will test the best way for the voluntary sector to conduct a national presence that is supportive of, and supported by, the diverse and independent accrediting bodies of the United States.

In the meantime, new needs lead to additional accrediting bodies developing in special areas. Two recent examples are the American Academy for Liberal Education (AALE) (1993) and the Association of Collegiate Business Schools and Programs (ACBSP) (1988). Both have complete programs of accreditation and have been listed by the U.S. Office of Education as recognized accrediting bodies in their fields. The ACBSP has more than five hundred members after less than a decade and emphasizes teaching quality in the business field, in both community colleges and baccalaureate/graduate institutions.

The AALE is recognized as the first accrediting body for liberal arts institutions and programs, based on its emphasis on teaching, a commitment to undergraduate education, and a core of studies in the arts, sciences, and humanities. These two new, quite different voluntary accrediting bodies graphically illustrate the importance of the voluntary sector in our society and its constant renewal.

The relationship of voluntary accrediting associations to state and federal governments also is a major factor in current considerations of academic freedom, institutional autonomy, and institutional accountability. Of course, the states charter most of the institutions and, thus, establish their missions, general purposes, and degree levels offered. However, the states also license individuals to practice most vocations and professions. In many fields the licensing of individuals is based on graduation from accredited programs. Thus, a form of sanction has developed, and membership in the involved, specialized professional associations, supposedly voluntary, becomes almost obligatory. In the federal area, the listing of institutions by federal government agencies had little or no effect before World War II.

The entrance of the federal government into the funding of higher education on a massive basis since World War II has drastically changed the overall uses of accreditation. Reported abuses of the Servicemen's Readjustment Act of 1944 (GI Bill) led to a series of congressional hearings, which led in turn to major additions related to accreditation in Public Law 550, the Veterans Readjustment Act of 1952. Section 253 of that law empowered the commissioner of education to publish a list of accrediting agencies and associations that could be relied upon to assess the quality of training offered by educational institutions. State approving agencies then used the resulting actions of such accrediting associations or agencies as a basis for approval of the courses specifically accredited. The enormous increase in federal assistance to students attending postsecondary education since 1972 made this federal listing process extremely important. Federal efforts to exert control over institutional processes have been constant for the past twenty-five years, with institutional membership in a listed accrediting association almost obligatory. Default rates on student loans have been blamed on the institutions and accrediting associations, and laws have been passed making the institutions enforce the police power of the government. Since voluntary associations cannot be either forced or allowed to enforce state police powers, Congress established a new state enforcement system, in 1992, called state postsecondary review entities (SPREs). The public outcry against this law led Congress to rescind it in 1994/95 by not funding it. And in 1995 the president's budget contained no request for funds to continue SPREs, effectively eliminating them.

Extensive legal arguments about the resulting powers of the Department of Education still continue. However, greater institutional dependence on eligibility for funding is now based on membership in much less-voluntary accrediting associations. The courts normally have ruled that accreditation by accrediting associations is not quasi-governmental action. Nevertheless, there has grown up an important new concept called the triad, which involves delicate relationships among the federal government and eligibility for funding, the state government and its responsibilities for establishing or chartering institutions and credentialing through certification or licensure, and voluntary membership associations that require accreditation for membership.

Thus these voluntary associations have come to represent a major form of private constituency with direct impact on internal institution activities. The possible sanctions from state licensing of graduates, the loss of eligibility for funds from federal agencies, and problems caused by peer approval or disapproval enhance the importance of these sometimes overlooked educational organizations.

Voluntary Consortia

Formal arrangements for voluntary consortia based on interinstitutional cooperation among and between postsecondary institutions have been in operation for many decades.[4] Claremont Colleges (California) started in 1925 with Pomona College and the Claremont University Center and were joined by Scripps College in 1926. The Atlanta University Center (Georgia), sometimes called the Affiliation, started shortly thereafter, in 1929, and included Morehouse College, Spelman College, and Atlanta University. Over the decades, both of these groups have added additional institutions to their cooperative arrangements and proven that voluntary consortia can be valuable for long periods of time. Some early examples from 1927–29 illustrate the reality of the cooperation between Morehouse and Spelman. In those years, several faculty were jointly appointed to both faculties. Upper-division students could take courses offered by the other college. Also, they operated a joint summer school with Atlanta University. In 1932, a new library was built, and the three libraries were consolidated into a joint library serving all three institutions. Thus, although they remained separate institutions, they sacrificed some autonomy to extend academic offerings and services.

In the years since these early beginnings, hundreds of institutions have developed informal and increasingly formal arrangements for interinstitutional cooperation. In 1966, a national survey conducted by the U.S. Office of Education determined that there were 1,017 consortia operating in the United States and that the evidence indicated that a number of consortia were not reported. The list included all types of consortium, from simple bilateral arrangements dealing with a single area of service to large complex consortia performing many services and contributing in many areas of education. In 1967, the staff of the Kansas City Regional Council for Higher Education, a leading consortium, published the first directory of consortia, with a list of 31 having these exacting criteria: it was a voluntary formal organization, it had three or more member institutions, it had multi-academic programs, it was administered by at least one full-time professional, and it had a required annual contribution or other tangible membership support.

A voluntary national organization grew up, the Council for Interinstitutional Leadership, composed of many of the consortia. It published an updated directory regularly for more than two decades, until 1991; shortly thereafter, it was replaced by the newly established Association for Consortium Leadership. In 1996 the fourteenth edition of the *Consortium Directory* was published by this organization, with offices at the Virginia Tidewater Consortium, in Norfolk, under the leadership of Lawrence Dotolo. This directory listed data from 80 consortia of many diverse types and representing about 1,800 institutional members. A considerable number of the consortia also include business, commercial, public service nonprofit, and public school district associate members. A careful reading of the directory and consortium activities clearly demonstrates the importance of consortia in the cutting-edge innovations in higher education as well as in overall operational efficiency in providing educational services.

The importance of voluntary consortia to concerns regarding institutional autonomy becomes evident with the enumeration of their activities. The recent directory listed several dozen widely differing programs and services being carried on cooperatively, in seven major areas: administrative and business services; enrollment and admissions; academic programs, including continuing education; libraries, information services, and computer services; student services; faculty; and community services, including economic development. Cross-registration between nearby institutions is quite common, as are joint library services, professional development activities, seminars, joint purchasing through group-negotiated contracts, high school and college career advising services, and new technology, joint development projects. Many of the consortia have World Wide Web pages, e-mail, and fax capability and some have teleconferencing capability.

A few brief examples illustrate the diversity of services expedited by the consortium method of organizing. The Intelecom/Southern California consortium of almost 50 community colleges (started in 1970 by 18 of them) has provided course credit via television and cable for 665,000 students. The Ohio College Association, Inc. (with almost 200 members) has published for almost sixty years a booklet to assist high school students with information about admission to Ohio colleges and their programs. It saves its members over $1 million a year through reduced annual premiums for workers compensation. The QuadCities Graduate Study Center in Rock Island, Illinois, operated through Augustana College for Iowa and Illinois, offers local graduate degree programs for thousands of students (with seven accredited public universities and three other accredited independent universities sending professors to provide the classes and dissertation supervision). The New England Cooperative Extension Consortium has set up e-mail contracts for its members, so the fifteen mail groups can use the internet for rapid communication among cooperative extension faculty and staff in the six states.

One of the major leaders in the consortium movement, the Kansas City Regional Council for Higher Education (started in 1962) had an extensive program of diverse services. Many of them terminated in the early 1990s, but its purchasing service was continued and provides significant savings to its members. Two other examples illustrate the nature of a consortium and its program possibilities.

Virginia Tidewater Consortium for Higher Education is one of six regional consortia covering all of Virginia. They were established in 1973 by state law to coordinate off-campus continuing education courses. The Tidewater consortium is an example of what can happen when the leadership of institutions works cooperatively. It now offers a variety of services, including cross-registration of students, faculty exchanges, interlibrary courier services, cooperative degree programs, and faculty and administrative development programs. In addition, it operates the consortium's higher education cable channel, off-campus centers and their continuing education programs, the Equal Opportunity Center, the Beginning Teacher Assistance program for the State Department of Education, and promotion of college courses by television. It also serves as a national office and center of activity for the Association for Consortium Leadership, including publication of the *Consortium Directory*.

The Colleges of Worcester Consortium (in Massachusetts), founded in 1968, has ten members: seven private colleges and universities and three public institutions. They range from a two-year community college through a graduate medical school and a graduate school of veterinary medicine; Clark University is a distinguished research university, and there are four private liberal arts colleges. There are fourteen associate members, with several museums (including Old Sturbridge Village), craft and science centers, a horticultural and an antiquarian society, plus a radio station. Another dozen schools, foundations, and nonprofit organizations participate in the special purchasing group of the basic consortium. The total consortium program of activities includes cross-registration by full-time day students at each of the member institutions.

A master course list is available on the internet and in print at each institution. Courses within a normal load are available at no additional charge, and a free shuttle bus operates among the colleges and associate members locations, all day until 9 P.M. Grades are compatible with the home college grading system and placed on the official transcript. The consortium operates a joint undergraduate certificate program in gerontology and arranges and supervises its intern program. An interlibrary cooperative service is available, which shares the resources of fourteen libraries, with special book shuttle service available. A statewide Educational Opportunity Service is operated for the entire state of Massachusetts, plus a regional Educational Talent Search service, reaching hundreds of high school students yearly. Also provided are information services, professional development workshops, career counseling and career fairs, and support for economic development projects in the region. A special seed grant program supports faculty groups working on interinstitutional academic programs. Another special continuing emphasis is placed on the use of instructional technology in teaching, the professional development of faculty and staff in this area, and a database of examples of use in learning situations in the service region.

The examples above illustrate the move of consortia from being primarily private institutions to development in all three sectors. Although started essentially by the voluntary enterprise sector, the public enterprise sector has moved in, and several consortia now include the profit-seeking sector. A number of states passed laws to facilitate their start-up. The Illinois Higher Education Cooperative Act of 1972 provided some state support for voluntary combinations of private and public institutions. California, Connecticut, Massachusetts, Minnesota, Ohio, Pennsylvania, Virginia, and Texas have used the consortium approach for specific purposes. This trend toward public financing of consortia thus becomes a factor in institutional planning and even regional intrastate planning.

In the past, consortia have been developed to provide for interinstitutional needs both in times of growth and in times of decline. They are uniquely capable of handling the mutual problems of public and private institutions and thus provide a powerful deterrent to further governmental incursions into private and sometimes public institutional operation. At various levels of formality, consortia currently are being used by significant numbers of institutions of all types to adjust to changing curricular and funding necessities. As governmental controls continue to increase and to affect institutional autonomy and academic freedom, voluntary consortia provide another way to plan independently for future operations and program development.

Regional Compacts

Regional compacts, although they are nonprofit, private organizations, are quasi-governmental. Groups of states create them, provide their basic funding, and contract for services through them. They operate much like private organizations and receive considerable funding from other sources, including private foundations. Some of their studies, seminars, workshops, and policy studies directly affect the institutions in their regions.

Soon after World War II three regional interstate compacts developed to meet postsecondary education needs that crossed state lines. Originally, they concentrated on student exchange programs in the medical education field; however, in the past twenty-five to thirty years their areas of service and influence have expanded considerably. Although established, funded, and supported basically by state governors and legislatures, their indirect effects on institutional programs and operations can be significant. Listed in order of establishment, they are the Southern Regional Education Board (1948), the Western Interstate Commission for Higher Education (1953), the New England Board of Higher Education (1955), and the Midwestern Higher Education Commission (1991).

The Southern Regional Education Board (SREB) includes governors, legislators, and other figures, some from higher education, from fourteen states (Alabama, Arkansas, Florida, Georgia, Kentucky, Louisiana, Maryland, Mississippi, North Carolina, South Carolina, Tennessee, Texas, Virginia, and West Virginia). SREB was formed by the political leaders of its member states, and they retain leadership in the organization. At the time it was started, the separate but equal doctrine, determined by the U.S. Supreme Court in *Plessy v. Ferguson,* was in effect. To meet its requirements in the education of medical doctors, these states sent students to Meharry Medical School in Nashville, Tennessee. Its funding was poor, and in the post–World War II era it was considering closing, but through SREB and a new funding principle, black students from member states could be sent there, with states paying the costs of attendance and, thereby, keeping the medical school open. Since that time, the SREB has played a major part in the development of such important areas as equal opportunity for all students in higher education and expanded graduate and professional education. Its research and information program has been vital in state and institutional planning. Its regular legislative work conferences, planned by its Legislative Advisory Council, have been influential in setting policy and funding directions in the region.

The Western Interstate Compact for Higher Education (WICHE) has members from thirteen states: Alaska, Arizona, California, Colorado, Hawaii, Idaho, Montana, Nevada, New Mexico, Oregon, Utah, Washington, and Wyoming. In addition, it has two affiliate states, North Dakota and South Dakota, which participate in some of its programs. Minnesota also participated for a few years, but it became part of the Midwestern Commission when that group formed. WICHE was planned originally to pool educational resources, to help the states plan jointly for the preparation of specialized skilled manpower, and to avoid, where feasible, the duplication of expensive facilities. The student exchange program in the fields of medicine, dentistry, veterinary medicine, and later in dental hygiene, nursing, mental health, and other specialized fields has been a major effort. Regional conferences on critical topics, annual legislative workshops, and research studies and publications also are regularly carried on by WICHE.

One of its developments, the program in higher education management and information systems, created so much demand for participation among the other thirty-seven states that it was spun off to become the National Center for Higher Education Management Systems. The original professional student exchange program has been expanded, and WICHE now coordinates an undergraduate exchange program to take advantage of underused capacity. Also, a regional graduate program provides nonresident instruction at in-state tuition rates in a hundred graduate programs at thirty-six universities in fourteen states. Home-state support for students attending professional programs in sixteen special fields is provided by contracts through WICHE. More than ten thousand professionals, most in health care professions, have received this support while enrolled in one of the contract programs in another WICHE state. Another special program supports efforts to recruit minority students into graduate degree programs and to assist them in becoming college and university faculty members. All told, WICHE programs of this type assist more than eight thousand students a year, making maximum use of regional institution facilities and saving costs for the states involved and for the students who participate.

WICHE also contributes by sponsoring currently needed special projects. In the 1950s it began and operated a program to encourage the education of nurses. Currently, it makes policy analysis and data available, through the internet, on higher education in North America. A comparative research series was published on major policy issues and differences in higher education in Mexico and the United States. WICHE has developed a Western cooperative for educational telecommunications. It has produced quality standards for distance learning (Principles of Good Practice), a purchasing service for electronic equipment and services, and research on actual returns in learning from these investments, plus an attempt to meet the needs of students in rural or underserved areas. In 1996, WICHE helped design the Western Virtual University, as requested by the governors of the WICHE states.

The New England Board of Higher Education (NEBHE) serves six states: Connecticut, Maine, Massachusetts, New Hampshire, Rhode

Island, and Vermont. It administers such programs as the regional student exchange program, the New England Council on Higher Education for Nursing, a library information network, and an academic science information center. It also conducts studies regarding current needs in higher education that cross state lines. Data on higher education in the New England States are collected, analyzed, and published widely for use by all interested groups in the region. One interesting project of NEBHE was its studies of the need for veterinary medicine in the region. Political disputes about its potential location were so great that it did not develop until Tufts University started one in 1978 on the grounds of an abandoned mental hospital in Grafton, Massachusetts. The state of Massachusetts, through student exchange contracts, supported about a hundred students until 1989, when its higher education system was reorganized. Of the NEBHE states, only New Hampshire now assists students, but New Jersey and New Mexico contract for some state students to attend. In this way, an important project of a regional compact (to bring a needed academic program to its area) led to the service being established by a private university. Currently, about six hundred students from many locations apply for admission, and sixty-five to seventy are accepted in each class, for a four-year program leading to the doctoral degree in veterinary medicine. This is an excellent example of the law of unintended consequences in higher education and of the importance of the voluntary enterprise in American higher education.

The Midwestern Higher Education Commission (MHEC) developed many years after the other three were established. Originally, a consortium of the Big Ten universities plus the University of Chicago was developed, at least partially to forestall establishment of a state-originated commission (the Committee on Institutional Cooperation, founded in 1958). However, plans went forward, and between 1978 and 1980 the Minnesota, South Dakota, North Dakota, and Ohio legislatures approved its establishment. To begin operation, six states had to adopt the plan. If established, it would provide for interstate student exchanges at in-state tuition rates, cooperative programs in vocational and higher education, and an areawide approach to gathering and reporting information needed for educational planning. Finally, seven state legislatures approved the Midwestern Regional Education Compact (Illinois, Kansas, Michigan, Minnesota, Missouri, Nebraska, and Ohio), followed by Wisconsin and Indiana. Iowa is still considering membership, and North and South Dakota are considering affiliate membership, along with affiliate membership in some WICHE programs involving student exchange and the Western Cooperative for Educational Telecommunications.

By the late 1990s, MHEC had developed a broad set of service programs, including a student exchange based on enrollment in nonresident capacity on a space-available basis, at reduced tuition rates. Several hundred students participate, saving millions of dollars, while filling marginally enrolled programs in more than a hundred institutions. Several purchasing cooperative programs save millions of dollars in the purchase of software for academic scheduling and resource management, risk management property and liability insurance, distance education and classroom equipment and services, and other volume-sensitive goods. Programs are under way to do research and implement findings about improved representation of minorities on college faculties in the region. This ties in with an academic position network for faculty placement. A joint project with the regional educational laboratory, the Midwestern Technology in Education Cooperative fosters a cost-effective distance learning program for K–12 schools and midwestern colleges and universities. MHEC has a World Wide Web page covering its many programs, and the internet connection provides rapid communication to implement these diverse programs.

The current four interstate compacts cover all but a few of the states of the entire country. Their diversified programs change as the needs of their regions change. The basic costs of their operations are funded by state legislatures from tax revenues, but foundation grants plus federal projects pay for much of the new thrusts of the regional commissions. This provides another excellent example of the flexible way that the mixed society of the United States operates to adapt to changing needs and emphases.

Conclusion

During the first two centuries of American higher education's existence, religious tenets and basic social agreements resulted in a relatively fixed, classically oriented program of studies. However, as the society began to open up, to industrialize and expand, it demanded change in its colleges. When this was slow to occur, new institutions met these needs, and many existing ones closed. Normal schools,

engineering schools, military academies, and universities were copied
from Europe and adapted to American needs between 1830 and 1900.
However, even these were not sufficient to meet democracy's needs.
New types of institution were developed, unique or almost unique to
America. The land-grant colleges of 1862 and 1890, the junior colleges of the early 1900s, the state colleges of the 1930s to 1960s, and
the post–World War II community colleges all represent essentially
new types of institution. Private constituency groups often pressured
state or local governments to establish them. In some cases, private
constituency groups pressured Congress into funding some of them,
including the 1862 land-grant colleges and, particularly, the 1890
land-grant colleges. The critical point, again, is that in the United
States new institutions replace existing ones that do not change.

Private constituencies such as the five types detailed here have a
significant impact on institutional autonomy and academic freedom.
Much of this impact is positive, supportive, and welcome. However,
those that provide funds can affect institutional trends and direction
by determining what types of academic programs or research efforts
are supported. As federal and state funds tighten up even more in
the years ahead, funds from alternate sources will become even more
attractive. Acceptance of grants moves institutions in the direction
dictated by fund sources, and faculties are well advised to consider
this possibility as the "crunch" of the late 1990s becomes greater.

Finally, the real benefits provided to institutions by private organizations must be mentioned again. Many membership organizations
have been created to provide such benefits. In some cases, these benefits have been greater than anyone could have foreseen. Probably
the most dramatic examples have come from private accrediting associations in relation to state political efforts to limit the autonomy
and academic freedom of their public institutions. In 1938 the North
Central Association (NCA) dropped North Dakota Agricultural College from membership because of undue political interference. The
U.S. Court of Appeals upheld the action of the NCA, and the state
government backed away from its prior method of political interference in internal institutional affairs. In the post–World War II period,
sanctions of the Southern Association stopped legislation banning
on-campus speakers in North Carolina and, after 1954, contributed
strongly to the development of open campuses in other states in its
region. As the nation has worked to expand higher education opportunities for minorities in the 1990s, almost every type of association has

participated. And as the society has demanded that higher education become more cost-effective, many of these associations and commissions have adopted systems that have saved large amounts of money, so that academic programs may still be offered to the students they were established to serve.

Private organizations related in some way to postsecondary education clearly continue the great tradition of direct action by voluntary citizen associations. Increasingly, they stand in the middle, between control-oriented federal and state agencies and the private and public institutions. Governments have abandoned the self-denying ordinance that in recent decades kept the state at a distance from the essence of many of its institutions. The nurturance of supportive and helpful private constituencies, therefore, becomes even more critical as higher education enters the twenty-first century.

NOTES

1. For detailed information about foundations, the best overall source is the Foundation Center, 79 Fifth Avenue, New York, NY 10003. Twelve regular publications constitute its core collection. They have offices and reference collections also in Atlanta, San Francisco, Washington, D.C., and Cleveland and cooperating collection centers in numerous libraries in each state. Its two main references are its own annual, *Foundation Directory,* and the *Annual Register of Grant Support* (R. R. Bowker Co., P.O. Box 1001, Summit, NJ 07902-1001).

2. Two major references with extensive information about institutionally based associations are the *Encyclopedia of Associations,* published annually by Gale Research, 835 Penobscot, Detroit, MI 48226, and the regular editions of *American Universities and Colleges,* available from the American Council on Education, One Dupont Circle, Washington, D.C. 20036.

3. Two key sources of historical background information regarding voluntary institutional accreditation are Kenneth E. Young, Charles Chambers, H. R. Kells, and associates, *Understanding Accreditation* (San Francisco: Jossey-Bass, 1983); and Fred F. Harcleroad, *Accreditation: History, Process, and Problems* (Washington, D.C: ERIC Clearinghouse on Higher Education, 1980). Since 1994, the Commission on Recognition of Postsecondary Education has published the *Directory of Recognized Agencies and Supporters of Accreditation,* after the Council on Postsecondary Education stopped operating in 1993. CORPA's address: One Dupont Circle, Washington, D.C. 20036. A somewhat different list of accrediting associations, by the U.S. Department of Education, has been available since it was required in the Veterans Readjust-

ment Assistance Act of 1952. Inclusion on this list is one of several ways that institutions can participate in a number of federal funding programs.

4. The best source of current information on consortia is the *Consortium Directory*, published by the Association for Consortium Leadership, c/o The Virginia Tidewater Consortium, 5215 Hampton Blvd., 129 Health Sciences Building, Norfolk, VA 23529-0293.

Part Three

The Academic Community

Chapter Ten

Harsh Realities

The Professoriate Faces
a New Century

Philip G. Altbach

American higher education finds itself in a period of significant strain. Financial cutbacks, enrollment uncertainties, pressures for accountability, and confusion about academic goals are among the challenges facing American colleges and universities at the end of the twentieth century. The situation is in many ways paradoxical. The American academic model is the most successful in the world, admired internationally for providing access to higher education to a mass clientele as well as some of the best universities in the world. Yet, higher education has come under widespread criticism. Some argue that the academic system is wasteful and inefficient and place the professoriate at the heart of the problem.[1] Others urge that higher education reconsider its priorities and place more emphasis on teaching, reasoning that the core function of the university has been underemphasized as the professoriate has focused on research.[2] Again, the professoriate is central to this criticism.

A combination of the restructuring of the American economy and a popular revolt against paying for public services, including education, has contributed to the pervasive fiscal problems that colleges and universities face. Because of demands for lower taxes in the public sector and growing price resistance at private colleges and universities, most observers believe that higher education will not fully recover financially in the foreseeable future. It has been argued that higher education's golden age—the period of strong enrollment growth, increasing research budgets, and general public support—is over.[3] This means that the academic profession, as well as higher education in general, must adjust to new circumstances. This adjustment, which has already begun, would be difficult under any circumstances, but it is all the more troubling to the professoriate, coming directly after the greatest period of growth and prosperity in the history of American higher education.

The American professoriate has been shaped by the social, political, and economic context of higher education. While academe enjoys relatively strong internal autonomy and considerable academic freedom, societal trends and public policy have affected institutions of higher education as well as the national and state policies concerning academe. There are many examples. In the 1860s, the Land-Grant Acts contributed to the expansion of public higher education and an emphasis on both service and research, while after World War II the GI Bill led to the greatest and most sustained period of growth in American higher education. Court decisions on government's role in private higher education, race relations, affirmative action, the scope of unions on campus, and other issues have affected higher education policy. Education is a basic responsibility of the states, and the actions of the various state governments have ranged from support for the "Wisconsin idea" in the nineteenth century to the promulgation of the California "master plan" in the 1960s. In New York and Massachusetts, as elsewhere, state policies in the postwar period had a formative influence on postsecondary education and the professoriate.[4] A recurring theme in this chapter is the tension between the autonomy and internal life of the academic profession and the many external forces for accountability.

Precisely because the university is one of the central institutions of postindustrial society, the professoriate finds itself under pressure from many directions. Increasingly complicated accounting procedures attempt to measure professorial productivity as part of the effort to increase accountability. But there is so far no way to measure accurately the educational outcomes of teaching. Calls for the professoriate to provide social relevance in the 1960s were replaced in the 1980s by student demands for vocationally oriented courses. A deteriorating academic job market raised the standards for the award of tenure and increased the emphasis on research and publication. At the same time, there were demands to devote more time and attention to teaching.

A constant tension exists between the traditional autonomy of the academic profession and external pressures. The processes of academic promotion and hiring remain in professorial hands but with significant changes: affirmative action requirements, tenure quotas in some institutions, the occasional intrusion of the courts into promotion and tenure decisions. The curriculum is still largely a responsibility of the faculty, but the debates over multicultural courses or over number of vocational courses, for example, affect curricular decisions. Governmental agencies influence the curriculum through grants and awards. The states engage in program reviews and approvals and through these procedures have gained some power in areas traditionally in the hands of the faculty.

The academic profession has largely failed to explain its centrality to society and to make the case for traditional academic values. Entrenched power, a complicated governance structure, and the weight of tradition have helped protect academic perquisites in a difficult period. But the professoriate itself has not articulated its own ethos.[5] The rise of academic unions helped to increase salaries during the 1970s but contributed to an increasingly adversarial relationship between the faculty and administrators in some universities.[6]

The unions, with the partial exception of the American Association of University Professors (AAUP), have not defended or articulated the traditional professorial role. Few have effectively argued that the traditional autonomy of the faculty and faculty control over many aspects of academic governance should be maintained. We are in a period of profound change in American higher education, and it is likely that these changes will result in further weakening of the power and autonomy of the professoriate. This chapter considers the interplay of forces that have influenced the changing role of the American academic profession.

A Diverse Profession

The American professoriate is large and highly differentiated, making generalizations difficult. There are more than 526,000 full- and part-time faculty members in America's 3,500 institutions of postsecondary education. Almost 1,400 of these institutions grant baccalaureate or higher degrees, and 213 give the doctoral degree. More than a quarter of the total number of institutions are community colleges. A growing number of faculty are part-time academic staff, numbering at least 200,000 nationwide. They enjoy little or no job security and only tenuous ties with their employing institutions. The proportion of part-time staff has risen in recent years, reflecting fiscal constraints. Faculty are further divided by discipline and department. While one may speak broadly of the American professoriate, the working life and culture of most academics is encapsulated in a disciplinary and institutional framework. Variations among the different sectors within the academic system—research universities, community colleges, liberal arts institutions, and others—also shape the academic profession.[7] Vast differences exist in working styles, outlooks, remuneration, and responsibilities between a senior professor at Harvard and a beginning assistant professor at a community college. Further distinctions reflect field and discipline; the outlook of medical school professors, for example, and that of scholars of medieval philosophy are quite dissimilar.

A half century ago, the academic profession was largely white, male, and Protestant. It has grown increasingly diverse. In recent years, the proportion of women in academe has grown steadily and is now 29 percent of the total, although women are concentrated at the lower academic ranks and suffer some salary discrimination.[8] Yet, it is a fact that the proportion of women in the academic profession has increased only a few percentage points since the 1930s, despite the existence of affirmative action programs. Racial and ethnic minority participation has also grown, and while Asian Americans are well represented in the academic profession, African Americans and Latinos remain proportionately few. African Americans constitute only around 3 percent of the total professoriate, and they are concentrated in the historically black colleges and universities.[9] Racial and ethnic minorities make up about 9 percent of the total academic profession. The substantial discrimination that once existed against Catholics and Jews has been largely overcome, and there has been a modest decline in the middle- and upper-middle-class domination of the academic profession.[10] Despite these demographic changes and expansion in higher education, the academic profession has retained considerable continuity in terms of its overall composition.

Any consideration of the role of the professoriate must take into account demographic, cultural, disciplinary, and other variations in the academic profession. If there ever was a sense of community among professors in the United States, it has long since disappeared. At the same time, the large majority of the professoriate retain a basic commitment to the essential values of the profession—teaching, research, and service—and they retain considerable optimism about the profession.

The Historical Context

The academic profession is conditioned by a complex historical development. Universities have a long historical tradition, dating to medieval Europe, and the professoriate is the most visible repository of this tradition.[11] While national academic systems differ, all stem from common roots in Europe. The model of professorial authority that characterized the medieval University of Paris, the power of the dons at Oxford and Cambridge, and the centrality of the "chairs" in nineteenth-century German universities all contributed to the ideal of the American academic profession. The medieval origins established the self-governing nature of the professorial community and the idea that universities are communities of scholars. The reforms in German higher education in the nineteenth century augmented the authority and prestige of the professoriate, while at the same time linking both the universities and the academic profession to the state.[12] Professors were civil servants, and the universities were expected to contribute to the development of Germany as a modern industrial nation.[13] Research, for the first time, became a key responsibility of universities. The role and status of the academic profession at Oxford and Cambridge in England also had an impact on the American professoriate, since the early American colleges were patterned on the British model, and the United States, for many years, was greatly influenced by intellectual trends from Britain.[14]

These models, plus academic realities in the United States, helped to shape the American academic profession. To understand the contemporary academic profession requires a look at the most crucial period of development, beginning with the rise of land-grant colleges following the Civil War and the establishment of the innovative, research-oriented private universities in the last decade of the nineteenth century.[15] The commitment of the university to public service and to "relevance" meant that many academics became involved with societal issues, with applied aspects of scholarship, and with training for the emerging professions and for skilled occupations involving technology. The contribution of the land-grant colleges to

American agriculture was the first and best-known example. Following the German lead, the new innovative private universities (Johns Hopkins, Chicago, Stanford, and Cornell), followed a little later by such public universities as Michigan, Wisconsin, and California, emphasized research and graduate training. The doctorate soon became a requirement for entry into at least the upper reaches of the academic profession; earlier, top American professors had obtained their doctorates in Germany. The prestige of elite universities gradually came to dominate the academic system, and the ethos of research, graduate training, and professionalism spread throughout much of American academe. As these norms and values gradually permeated the American academic enterprise, they have come to form the base of professorial values.

The hallmark of the post–World War II period has been massive growth in all sectors of American higher education. The profession tripled in numbers, and student numbers expanded just as rapidly. The number of institutions also grew, and many universities added graduate programs. Expansion characterized every sector, from community colleges to research universities. Growth was especially rapid in the decade of the 1960s, a fact that has special relevance for the 1990s, for many academics hired at that time will soon be retiring, creating an unprecedented generational shift in the academic profession. Expansion became the norm, and departments, academic institutions, and individuals based their plans on expectations of continued expansion.

But expansion ended in the early 1970s, as a result of a combination of circumstances, including population shifts, inflation, and government fiscal deficits. Part of the problem in adjusting to conditions of diminished resources is the very fact that the previous period of unusual growth was a temporary phase. It can be argued that the period of postwar growth was an aberration and that the current situation is the more normal.[16] The legacy of this aberrant growth is significant for understanding how the professoriate has reacted to current realities.

Expansion shaped the vision of the academic profession for several decades, just as prolonged stagnation now affects perceptions. Postwar growth introduced other changes, which came to be seen as permanent when, in fact, they were not. The academic job market became a seller's market, in which individual professors were able to sell their services at a premium. Almost every field had a shortage of teachers and researchers.[17] Average academic salaries improved significantly, and the American professor moved from a state of semi-penury into the increasingly affluent middle class.[18] The image of Mr. Chips was replaced by the jet-set professor. University budgets increased, and research-oriented institutions at the top of the academic hierarchy enjoyed unprecedented access to research funds. The space program, the cold war, rapid advances in technology, and a fear in 1958 (after Sputnik) that the United States was "falling behind" in education contributed to greater spending by the federal government for higher education. Expanding enrollments meant that the states also invested more in higher education and that private institutions prospered.

The academic profession benefited substantially. Those obtaining their doctorates found ready employment. Rapid career advancement could be expected, and interinstitutional mobility was fairly easy. This contributed to diminished institutional loyalty and commitment. To retain faculty, colleges and universities lessened teaching loads, and average time spent in the classroom declined. Salaries and fringe benefits increased. Access to research funds from external sources increased greatly, not only in the sciences but also, to a lesser extent, in the social sciences and humanities. The availability of external research funds made academics with such access less dependent on their institutions. Those professors able to obtain significant funds were able to build institutes, centers, and in general to develop "empires" within their institutions.

Rapid expansion also meant unprecedented growth in the profession itself, and this has had lasting implications. An abnormally large cohort of young academics entered the professorial ranks in the 1960s. This large academic generation is now precipitating a variety of problems relating to its size, training, and experience. With the end of expansion, this large group has, in effect, limited entry to new scholars and has created a "bulge" of tenured faculty members who will retire in massive numbers in the 1990s. Many in this cohort participated in the campus turmoil of the 1960s and were affected by it. Some graduated from universities of lower prestige that began to offer doctoral degrees during this period and may not have been fully socialized into the traditional academic values and norms. But this generation expected a continuing improvement in the working conditions of higher education. When these expectations were dashed with the changing circumstances of the 1970s, morale plummeted, and adjustment has been difficult.

The turmoil of the 1960s had an impact on contemporary higher

education and on the consciousness of the professoriate. A number
of factors in the turbulent sixties contributed to emerging problems
for higher education. The very success of the universities in moving
to the center of society meant that they were taken more seriously.
In the heady days of expansion, many in the academic community
thought that higher education could solve the nation's social problems, from providing mobility to minorities to suggesting solutions to
urban blight and deteriorating standards in the public schools. It is
not surprising, in this context, that the colleges and universities became involved in the most traumatic social crises of the period, the
civil rights struggle and the antiwar movement triggered by the Vietnam War. The antiwar movement emerged from the campuses, where
it was most powerful.[19] Student activism came to be seen by many,
including government officials, as a social problem for which the universities were to be blamed. Many saw the professors as contributing
to student militancy.

The campus crisis of the 1960s went deeper than the antiwar movement. The new and much larger generation of students, from more
diverse backgrounds, seemed less committed to traditional academic
values. The faculty turned its attention from undergraduate education, abandoned in loco parentis, and allowed the undergraduate curriculum to fall into disarray. Overcrowded facilities were common.
The overwhelming malaise caused by the Vietnam War, racial unrest, and related social problems produced a powerful sense of discontent. Many faculty members, unable to deal constructively with the
crisis and feeling under attack from students, the public, and government authority, became demoralized. Faculty governance structures
proved unable to bring the diverse interests of the academic community together. This period was one of considerable debate and intellectual liveliness on campus, with faculty taking part in teach-ins and
a small number becoming involved in the antiwar movement. However, the lasting legacy of the 1960s for the professoriate was largely
one of divisiveness and the politicization of the campus.

The Sociological and Organizational Context

Academics are at the same time both professionals and employees
of large bureaucratic organizations. Their self-image as independent
scholars dominating their working environment is increasingly at

odds with the realities of the modern American university.[20] Indeed, the conflict between the traditional autonomy of the scholar and demands for accountability to a variety of internal and external constituencies is one of the central issues of contemporary American higher education. The rules of academic institutions, from stipulations concerning teaching loads to policies on the granting of tenure, govern the working lives of the professoriate. Despite the existence in most institutions of an infrastructures of collegial self-government, academics feel increasingly alienated from their institutions. In a recent survey, two-thirds described faculty morale as fair or poor, and 60 percent had negative feelings about the "sense of community" at their institutions.[21]

Academics continue to exercise considerable autonomy over their basic working conditions, although even here pressures are evident. The classroom remains largely sacrosanct and beyond bureaucratic controls, although recent debates about "political correctness" have had some impact on teaching in a few disciplines, and the emerging technologies may stimulate some changes in teaching styles. Professors retain much autonomy over the use of their time outside the classroom. They choose their own research topics and largely determine what and how much they publish, although research in some fields and on some topics requires substantial funding and therefore depends on external support. There are significant variations based on institutional type, with faculty at community colleges and at nonselective teaching-oriented institutions subject to more constraints on autonomy than professors at prestigious research universities.[22] Non-tenure-track and part-time faculty also have much less autonomy than their tenured colleagues.

As colleges and universities have become increasingly bureaucratized and as demands for accountability have extended to professors, this autonomy has come under attack. The trend toward decreased teaching loads for academics during the 1960s has been reversed, and now more emphasis is placed on teaching and, to some extent, the quality of teaching. Without question, there is now tension between the norm (some would say the myth) of professional autonomy and the pressures for accountability. There is little doubt that the academic profession will be subjected to increased controls as academic institutions seek to survive in an environment of financial difficulties. Professorial myths—of collegial decision making, individual autonomy, and the disinterested pursuit of knowledge—have come into conflict with the realities of complex organizational structures and bureaucracies. Important academic decisions are reviewed by a bewildering assortment of committees and administrators. These levels of authority have become more powerful as arbiters of academic decision making.

The American academic system is enmeshed in a series of complex hierarchies. These hierarchies, framed by discipline, institution, rank, and specialty, help to determine working conditions, prestige, and in many ways, orientation to the profession. As David Riesman pointed out four decades ago, American higher education is a "meandering procession," dominated by the prestigious graduate schools and ebbing downward through other universities, four-year colleges, and finally to the community college system.[23] Most of the profession attempts to follow the norms, and the fads, of the prestigious research-oriented universities. Notable exceptions are the community colleges, which employ one-fourth of American academics, and some of the less selective four-year schools. Generally, prestige is defined by how close an institution, or an individual professor's working life, comes to the norm of publication and research, a cosmopolitan orientation to the discipline and the national profession, rather than to local teaching and institutionally focused norms.[24] Even in periods of fiscal constraint, the hold of the traditional academic models remains strong indeed. Current efforts to emphasize teaching and to ensure greater productivity from the faculty face considerable challenges from the traditional academic hierarchy.

Within institutions, academics are also part of a hierarchical system, with the distinctions between tenured and untenured staff a key to this hierarchy. The dramatic growth of part-time instructors has added another layer at the bottom of the institutional hierarchy.[25] Disciplines and departments are also ranked into hierarchies, with the traditional academic specialties in the arts and sciences along with medicine and, to some extent, law at the top. The hard sciences tend to have more prestige than the social sciences or humanities. Other applied fields, such as education and agriculture, are considerably lower on the scale. These hierarchies are very much part of the realities and perceptions of the academic profession.

Just as the realities of postwar expansion shaped academic organizations and affected salaries, prestige, and working conditions and gave more power to the professoriate over the governance of colleges and universities, current diminished circumstances also bring change. While it is unlikely that the basic structural or organizational realities of American higher education will profoundly change, there has been an increase in the authority of administrators and increased bureaucratic control over working conditions on campus. In general, professors have lost a significant part of their bargaining power, which was rooted in moral authority. As academic institutions adjust to a period of declining resources, there will be subtle organizational shifts that will inevitably work to diminish the perquisites, and the authority, of the academic profession. Universities, as organizations, adjust to changing realities, and these adjustments will work against the professoriate.

Legislation, Regulations, Guidelines, and the Courts

In a number of areas the academic profession has been directly affected by the decisions of external authorities. American higher education has always been subject to external decisions, from the Dartmouth College case in the period immediately following the American Revolution to the Land-Grant Act in the mid-nineteenth century. Actions by the courts and the legislative authority have profoundly affected higher education and the professoriate. In the contemporary period, governmental decisions continue to have an impact on American higher education and the academic profession. The fiscal crisis of higher education has already been discussed. However, academe's problems stem not only from new economic priorities but also from quite deliberate policies by government at both the federal and state levels to deemphasize higher education and research. Other pressing social needs combined with public reluctance to pay higher taxes have worked to restrict higher education budget allocations. Cuts in research funding have been felt by both public and private institutions and their faculties.

Specific governmental policies have also had an impact on the profession. One area of considerable controversy has been affirmative action, the effort to ensure that college and university faculties include women and members of underrepresented minorities, to reflect the national population.[26] A variety of specific regulations have been mandated by federal and state governments relating to hiring, promotion, and other aspects of faculty life to ensure that women and minorities have greater opportunities in the academic profession.

Many professors have opposed these regulations, viewing them as an unwarranted intrusion on academic autonomy. These policies have, nonetheless, had an impact on academic life. Special admissions and remedial programs for underrepresented students have also caused considerable controversy on campus and have been opposed by many faculty. These too are programs that have been implemented by governmental intervention.

The legal system has had a significant influence on the academic profession in the past several decades. The courts have ruled on university hiring and promotion policies as well as on specific personnel cases. While the courts are generally reluctant to interfere in the internal workings of academic institutions, they have reviewed cases of gender or other discrimination, sometimes reversing academic decisions.[27] The U.S. Supreme Court decision that compulsory retirement regulations are unconstitutional has had an impact on the academic profession, as well.

These examples illustrate the significance and pervasiveness of governmental policies on the academic profession. Legislation concerning faculty workloads as well as policies on affirmative action affect the profession. Shifts in public opinion are often reflected in governmental policies on higher education and the professoriate. The courts, through the cases they are called on to decide, also play a role. The cumulative impact of governmental policies, laws, and decisions of all kinds has profoundly influenced the professoriate.[28] In the post–World War II era, as higher education has become more central to society, government has involved itself to a greater extent with higher education, and this trend is likely to continue.

The Realities at the End of the Century

The past decade has been, without question, one of the low points in the postwar history of the American professoriate. The immediate future does not offer the promise of any significant improvement. However, demographic changes and the possibility that the profession will adjust to new circumstances may provide a somewhat more optimistic scenario, although the basic configuration of American higher education is unlikely to change dramatically. There has been deterioration, but it has been within the context of the established system. The following issues are likely to be central in the debates of the coming period.

Teaching, Research, and Service

One of the main debates, the appropriate balance between teaching and research in academe, goes to the heart of the university as an institution and is critical for the academic profession. Many outside academe, and quite a few within, have argued that there should be more emphasis on teaching in the American higher education system. It is agreed that research is overvalued and that, especially considering fiscal constraints and demands for accountability, professors should be more productive.[29] The reward system in academe has produced this imbalance. Critics charge that, outside of the hundred or so major research universities, the quality and relevance of much academic research is questionable. Some have gone further, saying that much academic research is a scam.[30]

The issue of faculty productivity has produced action in several states and on a few campuses. Massachusetts, Nevada, New York, Arizona, and Wisconsin are among the states that have been involved in workload studies. The California State University has compared the teaching loads of its faculty members with professors in other institutions. A few states require annual reports on workloads, and some have mandated minimum teaching loads; Hawaii and Florida, for example, require twelve hours of classroom instruction or the equivalent for faculty in four-year institutions.[31] Academic institutions are also studying workloads.

American professors seem to be working longer, not shorter, hours, and classroom hours have not declined in recent years. In 1992, according to a study by the Carnegie Foundation for the Advancement of Teaching, American professors spent a median 18.7 hours a week in activities relating to teaching (including preparation and student advisement).[32] On average, professors spend 13.1 hours per week in direct instructional activity, with those in research universities spending 11.4 hours and those in other four-year institutions teaching 13.8 per week.[33] Not surprisingly, professors in research universities produce more publications than do their colleagues in other institutions. For example, 61 percent of faculty in research universities reported publishing six or more journal articles in the past three years, compared to 31 percent of faculty working elsewhere.[34]

With the pressure for the professoriate to focus more on teaching and, probably, to spend more time in the classroom, there is likely to be more differentiation among sectors within the academic system, so that academics at the top research universities will teach significantly less than their compeers in comprehensive colleges and universities. Greater stratification between the academic sectors and perhaps less mobility among them are probable outcomes. A shift in thinking has taken place about research and its role. External funding for research has declined in most fields, and competition for resources is intense. There is also an orientation toward more applied research, closer links between industry and universities, and more service to the private sector. These changes will affect the kind of research that is conducted. There may well be less basic research and more small-scale research linked to products.

So far, the professoriate has not fully responded to these externally initiated debates and changes. The profession has sought to adapt to changing patterns in funding and to the more competitive research climate. In the long run, however, these structural changes will transform the research culture and the organization of research. In some ways, academics have moved closer to their clientele through the emphasis on service to external constituencies. The debate about total quality management (TQM) in higher education is, in part, an effort to convince academic institutions and the professoriate to think more directly about student needs, using a model designed to focus attention on the customer.[35]

Demographic Changes and the Decline of Community

The "age bulge," discussed earlier, has meant that the large cohort of academics who entered the profession in the 1960s and 1970s takes up a disproportionate share of jobs, especially when openings are restricted. Part-time faculty make up an increasing segment of the profession, further altering the nature and orientation of the profession.[36] It is much harder for a midcareer academic to find another position if he or she becomes dissatisfied or desires a change in location. The safety valve of job mobility no longer functions as well. While the number of retirements is rising rapidly and many institutions have used early retirement incentives to meet mandated budget cuts, this has not produced significant numbers of full-time academic jobs. This is still a time of diminished expectations.

The academic job market for new entrants has dramatically deteriorated as well, although there are some variations by field and discipline. Relatively few recent Ph.D.s are being hired, and as it has become clear that the academic job market has contracted, enrollments in many fields at the graduate level have declined or leveled off, especially in the traditional arts and sciences disciplines. Bright undergraduates have gravitated to law school or management studies. Perhaps the greatest long-term implication is a missing generation of younger scholars, although there is also a generation of gypsy scholars, who are relegated to part-time teaching, with little chance of a full-time tenure-track position. Further, a generation of fresh ideas has been lost. According to some demographic projections, there will be another shortage of trained doctorates around the turn of the century, although the implications are hard to predict because of the increasing use of part-time and full-time term appointments at many schools.[37]

The size and increased diversity of the academic profession have made a sense of community more difficult.[38] As institutions have grown to include well over a thousand academic staff, with elected senates and other, more bureaucratic, governance arrangements taking the place of the traditional general faculty meeting, a sense of shared academic purpose has become elusive. Even academic departments in larger American universities can number up to fifty. Committees have become ubiquitous, and the sense of participation in a common academic enterprise has declined. Increasing specialization in the disciplines contributed to this trend. Two-thirds of the American professoriate in the Carnegie study judged morale to be fair or poor on campus, and 60 percent felt similarly about the sense of community at their institution.[39]

Tenure, Retrenchment, and Unions

The profession has seen its economic status eroded, after a decade of significant gains in real income during the 1960s. Academic salaries began to decline in terms of purchasing power in the 1970s. There was a leveling off in the 1980s and a modest improvement in the 1990s. During the recession of the late 1970s and early 1980s, faculty members in Massachusetts and California saw actual salary cuts, while many states, including New York and Maryland, froze salaries, sometimes for more than a year. Professional prerogatives seemed less secure, and autonomy was threatened.

Perhaps most significantly, the tenure system came under attack in the 1970s and the 1990s. Some argued that the permanent appointments offered to professors once they had been evaluated and promoted from assistant to associate professor bred sloth among those with tenure, although there was little evidence to back up this claim.[40] Tenure was also criticized because it interfered with the institution's ability to respond to fiscal problems or changes in program needs. Professors could not easily be replaced or fired. Originally intended to protect academic freedom, the tenure system expanded into a means of evaluating assistant professors as well as offering lifetime appointments. As fiscal problems grew and the job market deteriorated, it became more difficult for young assistant professors to be promoted. Tenure quotas were imposed at some institutions, and many raised the standards for awarding tenure. These measures added to the pressures felt by junior staff. The system that was put into place to protect professors was increasingly seen as problematic.

The tenure debates of the 1970s ended without any significant changes and with tenure intact. The renewed discussion in the 1990s, stimulated by many of the same concerns as in the earlier period, will probably result in some significant changes, although the tenure system itself will remain without major alteration.[41] Post-tenure review and other reforms are likely to be implemented. There are also a growing number of academics who are not part of the tenure system, and these full-time, non-tenure-track, staff are likely to increase in number as institutions try to maximize their flexibility.

Retrenchment—the firing of academic staff without regard to tenure—has always been one of the major fears of the professoriate.[42] During the first wave of fiscal crises in the 1970s, a number of universities attempted to solve their financial problems by firing professors, including some with tenure, following programmatic reviews and analyses of enrollment trends. The AAUP, several academic unions, and a number of individual professors sued the universities in the courts, claiming that such retrenchment was against the implied lifetime employment arrangement offered through the tenure system. The courts consistently ruled against the professors, arguing that tenure protects academic freedom but does not prevent firings due to fiscal crisis. Universities that were especially hard hit, such as the City University of New York and the State University of New York, declared fiscal emergencies and fired academic staff, including tenured professors, and closed departments and programs. Many institutions found that the financial savings were not worth the legal challenges, decline in morale, and bad national publicity, and in later crises fewer tenured faculty were terminated. The fact is that tenure in American higher education does not fully protect lifetime employment, although, in general, commitments are honored by colleges and universities.[43] The retrenchments, and discussions and debates about retrenchment, left an imprint on the thinking of the academic profession, contributing to low morale and feelings of alienation.

The growth of academic unions in the 1970s was a direct reaction to the difficulties faced by the professoriate. Most professors turned to unions with some reluctance, and despite accelerating difficulties in the universities, the union movement has not become dominant. Indeed, the growth of unions slowed and even stopped in the late 1980s. In 1980, 682 campuses were represented by academic unions. Of this number, 254 were four-year institutions. Very few research universities are unionized; only one of the members of the prestigious Association of American Universities is unionized, for example. Unions are concentrated in the community college sector and in the public lower and middle tiers of the system.[44] Relatively few private colleges and universities are unionized, in part because the U.S. Supreme Court, in the *Yeshiva* case, made unionization in private institutions quite difficult. The Court ruled that faculty members in private institutions were, by definition, part of "management" and could not be seen as "workers" in the traditional sense.

The growth of academic unions has essentially stopped in the past decade. Legal challenges such as the *Yeshiva* decision and a realization that academic unions were not able to solve the basic problems of higher education have been contributing factors. In addition, while unions brought significant increases in salaries in the first years of contractual arrangements, this advantage ended in later contract periods. In normal periods, many faculty see unions as opposed to the traditional values of academe, such as meritocratic evaluation. Often, unions are voted in following severe campus conflict between faculty and administration. Further, unions have been unable to save faculty from retrenchment or a deterioration in working conditions. Both public university systems in New York are unionized, but both have been hard hit by fiscal problems, and faculty unions have not shielded staff from retrenchment, salary freezes, and the like. Neither the rhetoric of the AAUP nor the trade union tactics of the American Federation of Teachers has kept academic institutions and state legislatures from cutting budgets, increasing workloads, or firing professors. Unions, however, were part of an effort in the 1970s to stop the erosion of faculty advantages. Unions were also an expression of the attempt by professors in institutions with only limited autonomy and weak faculty governance structures to assert faculty power. In both of these areas, unions had only limited success.

Accountability and Autonomy

The academic profession has traditionally enjoyed a high degree of autonomy, particularly in the classroom and research. While most academics are only dimly aware of it, the move toward accountability has begun to affect their professional lives. This trend will intensify, not only due to fiscal constraints but because all public institutions have come under greater scrutiny. Institutions, often impelled (in the case of public universities) by state budget offices, require an increasing amount of data concerning faculty work, research productivity, expenditure of funds for ancillary support, and other aspects of academic life. What is more, criteria for student/faculty ratios, levels of financial support for postsecondary education, and the productivity of academic staff have been established. New sources of data permit fiscal authorities to monitor how institutions meet established criteria so that adjustments in budgets can be quickly implemented. While most of these measures of accountability are only indirectly felt by most academics, they nonetheless have a considerable impact on the operation of universities and colleges, since resources are allocated on the basis of closely measured formulas. The basic outputs of academic institutions—quality of teaching and quality and impact of research—cannot be calculated through these efforts at accountability. Indeed, even the definitions of teaching quality and research productivity remain elusive.

If autonomy is the opposite side of the accountability coin, then one would expect academic autonomy to have significantly declined. But, at least on the surface, this has not occurred. Basic decisions concerning the curriculum, course and degree requirements, the process of teaching and learning, and indeed all of the matters traditionally the domain of the faculty have remained in the hands of departments and other parts of the faculty governance structure. Most academics retain the sense of autonomy that has characterized higher education for a century. This is especially the case in top-tier institutions. There have been few efforts to dismantle the basic structure of academic work in ways that would destroy the traditional arrangements.

Yet, there is change taking place at the margins that will con-

tinue to shift the balance increasingly from autonomy to accountability and erode the base of faculty power. Decisions concerning class
size, the future of low-enrollment fields, the overall academic direction of the institution, and other issues have been shifted from the
faculty to the administration or even to systemwide agencies. Academic planning, traditionally far removed from the individual professor and seldom impinging on the academic career, has become more
of a reality as institutions seek to streamline their operations and
worry more about external measures of productivity.

Academic Freedom

American professors at present enjoy a fairly high degree of academic
freedom, although just half of the professoriate agrees that there are
"no political or ideological restrictions on what a scholar may publish."[45] There are few demands for ensuring the political or intellectual conformity of professors, and the concept of academic freedom
seems well entrenched. The AAUP has noted very few cases in which
institutions have sought to violate the academic freedom of their staff.
There has been virtually no governmental pressure to limit academic
freedom. The tensions of the McCarthy era seem far removed from
the current period.[46] The fact that the past decade or more has not
experienced the major ideological and political unrest and activism
that characterized some earlier periods, such as the Vietnam War era,
certainly has contributed to the calm on campus; however, even during the Vietnam War, academic freedom remained relatively secure.
This record was, however, not entirely spotless. A number of junior
faculty were denied tenure during this period because of their political views.[47]

Nevertheless, academic freedom remains a contentious issue. One
of the most visible academic debates of the 1980s and 1990s relates to
political correctness, an unfortunate shorthand term for a variety of
disputes concerning the nature and organization of the undergraduate curriculum, interpretations of American culture, the perspectives
of some disciplines in the humanities and social sciences, and what
some conservatives claim is the infusion of ideology into academe.
Dinesh D'Souza, a conservative writer, argues in his 1991 book, *Illiberal Education,* that American higher education is being taken over
by left-wing ideologists seeking to transform the curriculum through
the infusion of multicultural approaches and the destruction of the

traditional focus on Western values and civilization.[48] Conservative critics, including then Secretary of Education William Bennett, took up the call, and a major national discussion ensued.[49] Some conservatives claim that the academic freedom of some conservative faculty is being violated, although there is no evidence that this is the case. The debate, however, has affected the thinking about the curriculum and the role of multiculturalism on campus. While it has not affected academic freedom directly, the politics of race, gender, and ethnicity has left a significant mark on academic life.[50] These social issues have entered into discussions of the curriculum, and some faculty have claimed that they have inappropriately influenced decision making. There have also been incidents of racial or gender-based intolerance on some campuses.

Most would say that academic freedom is quite free from structural restraints and that external authorities, including both government and college and university trustees, have been overwhelmingly supportive of academic freedom during the past several decades. Contemporary concerns come from public debate about political correctness and from the resulting campus acrimony. Recently outlawed restrictions on student expression may also have added to professorial concern. In addition, some argue that corporate intrusions on the funding of research and the uses that can be made of research conducted by faculty may negatively affect academic freedom.

Students

The two central parts of any college or university are students and faculty. These two groups are not often linked in analyses of higher education, although students have profoundly affected the academic profession throughout the history of American higher education. Before the rise of the research university at the end of the nineteenth century, American higher education was student oriented and interaction between faculty and students was substantial. Even in the postwar period, most colleges remained oriented to teaching, although with the decline of in loco parentis in the 1960s, faculty became less centrally involved in the lives of students.[51] Students affect faculty in many ways. Increases in student numbers had the result of expanding the professoriate, and changes in patterns of enrollments also affected the academic profession. Student demands for relevance in the 1960s had implications for the faculty, as did the later vocationalism of student interests. American higher education has traditionally responded to changing student curricular interests by expanding fields and departments or by cutting offerings in unpopular areas. Student consumerism is a central part of the ethos of American higher education.[52]

Student interests have also had some impact on academic policy and governance. In the 1960s, students demanded participation in academic governance, and many colleges and universities opened committees and other structures to them. These changes were short-lived, but the student demands aroused considerable debate and tension on campus.[53] Recently, students have shown little interest in participating in governance and have been only minimally involved in political activism, on campus or off, although there has been a recent increase in student voluntarism for social causes. Student interests and attitudes affect the classroom and enrollments in different fields of study. Students are themselves influenced by societal trends, government policies concerning the financial aspects of higher education, perceptions of the employment market, and many other factors. These student perceptions are brought to the campus and are translated into attitudes, choices, and orientations to higher education. Student opinions about the faculty and the academic enterprise have a significant influence on institutional culture and morale.[54]

Conclusion

The analysis presented in this chapter is not optimistic. The academic profession has been under considerable pressure, and the basic conditions of academic work in America have deteriorated. Some of the gains made during the period of postwar expansion have been lost. The golden age of the American university is probably over. The basic fact is, however, that the essential structure of American higher education remains unaltered, and it is unlikely to change fundamentally. Despite the likely overall stability of the American academic system, considerable change is taking place, and much of this will adversely affect the academic profession. The professoriate stands at the center of any academic institution and is, in a way, buffered from direct interaction with many of higher education's external constituencies. Academics do not generally deal with trustees, legislators, or parents. Their concerns are with their own teaching and research and with their immediate academic surroundings, such as the department. Yet, external constituencies and realities increasingly affect academic life.

It is possible to summarize some of the basic trends that have been discussed in this analysis, factors likely to continue to affect the academic profession in the coming period.

—Increased competition for federal research funds made research funds more difficult to obtain in most fields.[55] Governmental commitment to basic research declined as well, and funding for the social sciences and humanities fell. With the end of the cold war, the emphasis on military research has diminished, but there are few signs of other fields benefiting from the peace dividend.

—Financial difficulties for scholarly publishers and cutbacks in budgets for academic libraries reduced opportunities for publishing scholarly work, thereby placing added stress on younger scholars, in particular, and on the entire knowledge system in academe. Library cutbacks also place restrictions on access to knowledge.

—Changes in student curricular choices have been significant in the past two decades: from the social sciences in the 1960s, to business, engineering, and law in the 1980s, and currently, to a limited extent, back to the social sciences. Declines in enrollments in the traditional arts and sciences at the graduate level have also been notable.

—Demands for budgetary and programmatic accountability from government have affected higher education at every level.

—In this climate of increased accountability, academic administrators have gained power over their institutions and, inevitably, over the professoriate.

—Economic problems in society have caused major financial problems for higher education, affecting the faculty directly in terms of salaries, perquisites, and teaching loads. The financial future of higher education, regardless of broader economic trends, is not favorable in the medium term.

—A decline in public esteem and support for higher education, triggered first by the unrest of the 1960s and enhanced by widespread questioning of the academic benefits of a college degree, has caused additional stress for the professoriate. There is a tendency to see an academic degree as a private good rather than a public good, so individuals and families rather than the state should pay for higher education.

—The shrinking academic employment market has meant that fewer younger scholars have been able to enter the profession and has limited the mobility of those currently in the profession. The increased use of part-time faculty has further restricted growth.

Given these factors, it is surprising that the basic working conditions of the American professoriate have remained relatively stable. The structure of postsecondary education remains essentially unchanged, but there have been important qualitative changes, generally in a negative direction from the perspective of the professoriate. Academic freedom and the tenure system remain largely intact, but there have been increased demands for accountability. Academics retain basic control over the curriculum, and most institutions continue to be based on the department, which remains strongly influenced by the professoriate. Institutional governance, although increasingly influenced by administrators, remains unchanged.

The period of expansion and professorial power of the middle years of the century will not return. How, then, can academics face the challenges of the coming period? At one level, the academic profession needs to represent itself effectively to external constituencies. If academic unions could more effectively assimilate traditional academic norms, they might have the potential of representing the academic profession. The traditional academic governance structures are the most logical agencies to take responsibility for presenting the case for the academic profession to a wider audience, both to the public and to political leaders, probably in cooperation with university administrators.

The professoriate reacted to the challenges of the postwar period. It was glad to accept more responsibilities, move into research, and seek funding from external agencies. It relinquished much of its responsibility to students (at least in the research-oriented universities) as research became the dominating academic value. The curriculum lost its coherence in the rush toward specialization. Now, it is necessary to reestablish a sense of academic mission that emphasizes teaching and the curriculum. To a certain extent, this has occurred on many campuses, with the rebuilding of the undergraduate general education curriculum and the reestablishment of liberal education as a key curricular goal. The current emphasis on teaching is another important trend that may restore the credibility of the profession.

It is always more difficult to induce changes as a result of conscious planning and concern than it is to react to external circumstances. For much of this century, the professoriate has reacted to conditions.

Now, there are signs that the crisis has stimulated the academic profession to implement positive solutions to difficult problems.

NOTES

I am indebted to Lionel S. Lewis, Patricia Gumport, Robert Berdahl, and Edith S. Hoshino for comments on this essay.

1. See Allan Bloom, *The Closing of the American Mind: How Higher Education has Failed Democracy and Impoverished the Souls of Today's Students* (New York: Simon and Schuster, 1987); Charles J. Sykes, *Profscam: Professors and the Demise of Higher Education* (Washington, D.C.: Regnery, 1988); Martin Anderson, *Imposters in the Temple* (New York: Simon and Schuster, 1992).

2. Ernest L. Boyer, *Scholarship Reconsidered: Priorities of the Professoriate* (Princeton, N.J.: Carnegie Foundation for the Advancement of Teaching, 1990).

3. Harold T. Shapiro, "The Functions and Resources of the American University of the Twenty-First Century," *Minerva* 30 (1992): 163–74.

4. Richard M. Freeland, *Academia's Golden Age: Universities in Massachusetts, 1945–1970* (New York: Oxford University Press, 1992).

5. Edward Shils, "The Academic Ethos under Strain," *Minerva* 13 (1975): 1–37. See also Henry Rosovsky, *The University: An Owner's Manual* (New York: Norton, 1990).

6. Robert Birnbaum, "Unionization and Faculty Compensation, Part II," *Educational Record* 57 (1976): 116–18.

7. Kenneth P. Ruscio, "Many Sectors, Many Professions," in *The Academic Profession: National, Disciplinary, and Institutional Settings,* ed. Burton R. Clark (Berkeley: University of California Press, 1987).

8. Mary M. Dwyer, Arlene A. Flynn, and Patricia S. Inman, "Differential Progress of Women Faculty: Status 1980–1990," in *Higher Education: Handbook of Theory and Research,* vol. 7, ed. John Smart (New York: Agathon, 1991).

9. Martin J. Finkelstein, *The American Academic Profession* (Columbus: Ohio State University Press, 1984), 187–89.

10. Jake Ryan and Charles Sackrey, *Strangers in Paradise: Academics from the Working Class* (Boston: South End, 1984).

11. Charles Homer Haskins, *The Rise of Universities* (Ithaca: Cornell University Press, 1965).

12. Joseph Ben-David and Awraham Zloczower, "Universities and Academic Systems in Modern Societies," *European Journal of Sociology* 3 (1962): 45–84.

13. Fritz K. Ringer, *The Decline of the German Mandarins: The German Academic Community, 1890–1933* (Cambridge: Harvard University Press, 1969).

14. Frederick Rudolph, *The American College and University: A History* (New York: Vintage, 1965).

15. Laurence Veysey, *The Emergence of the American University* (Chicago: University of Chicago Press, 1965).

16. This theme is developed at greater length in David Henry, *Challenges Past, Challenges Present* (San Francisco: Jossey-Bass, 1975).

17. The academic job market of this period is captured in Theodore Caplow and Reece J. McGee, *The Academic Marketplace* (New York: Basic Books, 1958). Current realities are reflected in Dolores L. Burke, *A New Academic Marketplace* (Westport, Conn.: Greenwood, 1988), a replication of the earlier Caplow and McGee study.

18. See Logan Wilson, *American Academics: Then and Now* (New York: Oxford University Press, 1979).

19. Seymour Martin Lipset, *Rebellion in the University* (New Brunswick, N.J.: Transaction, 1993).

20. Burton R. Clark, *The Academic Life* (Princeton, N.J.: Carnegie Foundation for the Advancement of Teaching, 1987). For a structural discussion of American higher education, see Talcott Parsons and Gerald Platt, *The American University* (Cambridge: Harvard University Press, 1973).

21. These figures come from a survey of the views of the American academic profession undertaken by the Carnegie Foundation for the Advancement of Teaching in 1992. See J. Eugene Haas, "The American Academic Profession," in *The International Academic Profession: Portraits of Fourteen Countries,* ed. Philip G. Altbach (Princeton, N.J.: Carnegie Foundation for the Advancement of Teaching, 1997).

22. See James S. Fairweather, *Faculty Work and Public Trust: Restoring the Value of Teaching and Public Service in American Academic Life* (Boston: Allyn and Bacon, 1996); Robert T. Blackburn and Janet H. Lawrence, *Faculty at Work: Motivation, Expectation, Satisfaction* (Baltimore: Johns Hopkins University Press, 1995).

23. David Riesman, *Constraint and Variety in American Education* (Garden City, N.Y.: Doubleday, 1958), 25–65.

24. Alvin Gouldner, "Cosmopolitans and Locals: Toward an Analysis of Latent Social Roles, 1 and 2," *Administrative Science Quarterly* 2 (1957, 1958): 281–303 and 445–67.

25. Judith M. Gappa and David W. Leslie, *The Invisible Faculty: Improving the Status of Part-Timers in Higher Education* (San Francisco: Jossey-Bass, 1993).

26. See, for example, Valora Washington and William Harvey, *Affirmative Rhetoric, Negative Action: African-American and Hispanic Faculty at Pre-*

dominantly White Institutions (Washington, D.C.: George Washington University, School of Education, 1989).

27. William A. Kaplin and Barbara A. Lee, *The Law of Higher Education: A Comprehensive Guide to Legal Implications of Administrative Decision Making* (San Francisco: Jossey-Bass, 1995).

28. Edward R. Hines and L. S. Hartmark, *The Politics of Higher Education* (Washington, D.C.: American Association for Higher Education, 1980).

29. The most influential consideration of this topic is Boyer, *Scholarship Reconsidered*. See also William F. Massy and Robert Zemsky, *Faculty Discretionary Time: Departments and the Academic Ratchet* (Philadelphia: Pew Higher Education Research Program, 1992).

30. Sykes, *Profscam*. See also Page Smith, *Killing the Spirit: Higher Education in America* (New York: Viking, 1990). Both of these volumes received widespread attention in the popular media and sold well.

31. Arthur Levine and Jana Nidiffer, "Faculty Productivity: A Re-Examination of Current Attitudes and Actions," Institute of Educational Management, Harvard Graduate School of Education, 1993.

32. See Ernest L. Boyer, Philip G. Altbach, and Mary Jean Whitelaw, *The Academic Profession: An International Perspective* (Princeton, N.J.: Carnegie Foundation for the Advancement of Teaching, 1994). Academics in other countries report that they teach similar amounts: Germany, 16.4 hours per week; Japan, 19.4; Sweden, 15.9; England, 21.3.

33. Haas, "The American Academic Profession," 351.

34. Ibid.

35. D. Seymour, "TQM: Focus on Performance, Not Resources," *Educational Record* 74 (1993): 6–14.

36. Elaine El-Khawas, *Campus Trends, 1991* (Washington, D.C.: American Council on Education, 1991), 7.

37. William G. Bowen and Julie Ann Sosa, *Prospects for Faculty in the Arts and Sciences* (Princeton: Princeton University Press, 1989). Demographic projections, however, must be carefully evaluated because they have frequently been wrong.

38. Carnegie Foundation for the Advancement of Teaching, *Campus Life: In Search of Community* (Princeton, N.J.: Carnegie Foundation for the Advancement of Teaching, 1990). See also Irving J. Spitzberg Jr. and Virginia V. Thorndike, *Creating Community on College Campuses* (Albany: State University of New York Press, 1992).

39. Haas, "The American Academic Profession."

40. Bardwell Smith et al., eds., *The Tenure Debate* (San Francisco: Jossey-Bass, 1973). For a more recent attack on tenure, see Anderson, *Imposters in the Temple*.

41. Matthew W. Finken, ed., *The Case for Tenure* (Ithaca: Cornell University Press, 1996). See also Cathy A. Trower, *Tenure Snapshot* (Washington, D.C.: American Association for Higher Education, 1996).

42. See Marjorie C. Mix, *Tenure and Termination in Financial Exigency* (Washington, D.C.: American Association for Higher Education, 1978).

43. Sheila Slaughter, "Retrenchment in the 1980s: The Politics of Prestige and Gender," *Journal of Higher Education* 64 (1993): 250–82. See also Patricia Gumport, "The Contested Terrain of Academic Program Reduction," *Journal of Higher Education* 64 (1993): 283–311.

44. For example, in the sixty-four-campus State University of New York system, which is unionized, there is a bifurcation between the four research-oriented university centers, which have been reluctant to unionize, and the fourteen four-year colleges, which favor the union. Since the four-year college faculty are in the majority, the union has prevailed.

45. Boyer, Altbach, and Whitelaw, *The International Academic Profession*, 101. The United States falls at the lower end on this question, with scholars in Russia, Sweden, Mexico, Germany, Japan, and other countries feeling more positive about the freedom to publish.

46. See Noam Chomsky et al., *The Cold War and the University* (New York: New Press, 1997), for a general discussion of the impact of the cold war period on American higher education.

47. Joseph Fashing and Stephen F. Deutsch, *Academics in Retreat* (Albuquerque: University of New Mexico Press, 1971).

48. Dinesh D'Souza, *Illiberal Education: The Politics of Race and Sex on Campus* (New York: Free Press, 1991).

49. Among the numerous books on the topic, see Paul Berman, ed., *Debating P.C.: The Controversy over Political Correctness on College Campuses* (New York: Dell, 1992); Patricia Aufderheide, ed., *Beyond PC: Towards a Politics of Understanding* (Saint Paul, Minn.: Graywolf, 1992); Francis J. Beckwith and Michael E. Bauman, eds., *Are You Politically Correct? Debating America's Cultural Standards* (Buffalo: Prometheus, 1993).

50. Philip G. Altbach and Kofi Lomotey, eds., *The Racial Crisis in American Higher Education* (Albany: State University of New York Press, 1991).

51. Helen Leflowitz Horowitz, *Campus Life: Undergraduate Cultures from the End of the Eighteenth Century to the Present* (Chicago: University of Chicago Press, 1987).

52. Arthur Levine, *When Dreams and Heroes Died: A Portrait of Today's College Student* (San Francisco: Jossey-Bass, 1980).

53. Alexander W. Astin et al., *The Power of Protest* (San Francisco: Jossey-Bass, 1975).

54. Alexander W. Astin, *What Matters in College: Four Critical Years Revisited* (San Francisco: Jossey-Bass, 1993).

55. See Roger L. Geiger, *Research and Relevant Knowledge: American Research Universities since World War II* (New York: Oxford University Press, 1993).

Chapter Eleven

Students, Colleges, and Society

Considering the Interconnections

Eric L. Dey and Sylvia Hurtado

The student role within American higher education and society is complex and requires a new epistemology, or way of thinking about that role, which enhances our understanding. Although college students have received a tremendous amount of attention in the popular and scholarly literature, this attention has largely drawn from perspectives that tend to limit our ability to understand the important interconnections between students, colleges, and society. Over the last three decades, both our society and the nature of our institutions have undergone tremendous changes that call for an understanding of these interconnections in order to improve undergraduate education.

As social institutions, colleges and universities are one element of a larger set of social systems that compose society. Simultaneously, within colleges and universities there exist interconnected social systems composed of groups of students, faculty, and other constituents. It is convenient to think of such systems as separate and discrete entities, but it is perhaps more accurate to acknowledge that these systemic boundaries are permeable and that changes in the social system that is the student body of a college are related to changes in other aspects of the institution and the larger social context. Our goal in this chapter, then, is to review these perspectives and consider recent changes among undergraduates from a perspective that takes into account the challenges posed by recent changes in students' characteristics, attitudes and preferences, and behaviors.

We begin by explaining some of the traditional perspectives that both administrators and researchers adopt in their approach to understanding students in college. Next, we introduce the notion of a dynamic occurring between students, the institutions that both are influenced by students and attempt to shape their development, and changes in the larger social context in American society. This is accomplished through the examination of trend data on generations of college students across three decades. In illustrating these trends, we raise important questions about our assumptions regarding views of college students, the extent to which institutions adapt to changes in student characteristics and activities, and the impact of college during these eras. We conclude with a call for a more dynamic, ecological perspective to understand the interconnections among students, institutions, and society.

Traditional Perspectives

Undergraduates have traditionally been viewed by the ways in which their background attributes—character, preparation, gender, and race—contribute to and help describe the culture and status of individual campuses and larger systems of higher education institutions. Burton Clark, for example, has noted that "students are important to the character of their institution" and that "the student body becomes a major force in defining the institution."[1] Selective admissions policies are often used to select students not only on the basis of academic criteria but on the basis of character and the student's potential to contribute to the college in any number of ways. In addition, students and their perceived academic quality are often seen as an organizational resource and as a measure of institutional quality.[2] More recently, it has become popular to think of undergraduates as the recipient of collegiate influences that produce certain psychological, social, and economic outcomes for individuals as well as for the larger society. This perspective has been popularized by the assessment movement and scholarly interest in questions of college impact; from such a perspective, high-quality programs and institutions are those that bring about the largest growth in student knowledge and personal development.[3]

In addition to these main perspectives, it is also important to consider the ways in which students influence colleges and universities.

This view, which acknowledges students as sources of institutional change, has received much less attention in the research literature.[4] The most visible source of student-led change is protest and direct action, which is reinforced by the observation that an "inactive student body is a much more curious phenomenon than one which is involved to some degree in activism."[5] Historically, student activists have tended to pursue agendas focused on broad social and political concerns, although relatively recent examples of activism include student efforts to institutionalize ethnic studies and multicultural centers, prevent tuition increases, and urge institutions to develop proactive responses to racist and sexist situations on campus.[6] Of course, not all student-led change comes about as a direct result of student protest or other forms of political action. In fact, a tremendous amount of such change develops as a result of natural institutional responses to changing student needs and preferences.

An Ecological Perspective

Although each of these three views is useful in helping us understand different aspects of the role of students within higher education, they can also serve to artificially restrict the ways in which we view students. A more complete view is one in which the relationship between students and the college environment is seen as both reciprocal and dynamic. Such an orientation has been described as an ecological perspective and portrays students as actively shaping their interpersonal environments and, by extension, their institutions and society, with these environments simultaneously providing the potential for transforming the individual.[7]

The ecological perspective is based on Urie Bronfenbrenner's observations about the limitations inherent in the study of human development using traditional perspectives. Of particular concern to Bronfenbrenner was the lack of recognition paid in the research literature to the process of "progressive accommodation between a growing human organism and its immediate environment."[8] Although the importance of the interaction between individuals and environments in fostering human development has long been recognized, psychological research has focused almost exclusively on aspects of the individual, to the neglect of the environment and its influence.

Research on students in higher education, in contrast, has long been concerned with environmental influences, yet the conception of the environment is similar to the traditional psychological perspectives described by Bronfenbrenner. In short, the environment is conceptualized as a "static structure that makes no allowance for the evolving processes of interaction." [9] Such a conception ignores the important processes of personal choice and organizational change that have been described as dynamic stability, or "the process by which the individual constructs circumstances which help maintain prior orientations and which in turn feed back on the person so as to maintain stability over time. The person is thus not only the recipient of influences from the environment; she is also an active agent in shaping that environment." [10]

To explore an ecological perspective of college students and the dynamic relationship between students and institutions, we discuss two important social and educational trends that have helped shape American higher education over the past three decades: changes in the demography of higher education and entering students' educational plans and preferences. We also consider the changes in the experiences of students during college as a third group of data-based observations. In examining these trends, we hope to show the utility of adopting an ecological perspective by highlighting patterns of institutional change related to these student trends. The interplay among students, institutions, and society is both subtle and complex, in which direct cause-and-effect relationships are difficult to detect. We hope to illustrate this perspective by linking what we believe to be interrelated trends. Although our preference would be to provide a more definitive analysis, we are unaware of data resources that would allow us to do so. Our goal here is to encourage others to consider this perspective, since it opens up new possibilities for studying students and higher education institutions and the processes that foster individual, institutional, and social change.

The data on entering college students come primarily from the Cooperative Institutional Research Program (CIRP), coordinated by the Higher Education Research Institute at the University of California, Los Angeles. The CIRP data are based on responses from an annual survey of some 250,000 students entering about six hundred colleges and universities nationwide. [11] Given the large sample sizes we are dealing with, any differences large enough to be interesting are going to be statistically significant. Since this is the case, we do not show formal statistical tests. Furthermore, the CIRP focuses primarily on what are considered traditional American students, so the patterns discussed are likely to understate the extent to which changes have occurred in the general college population. Data on the changing pattern of in-college experiences of students are based on longitudinal surveys of college students who participated in the CIRP freshman surveys and who were followed up several years later.[12]

The Changing Demography of Higher Education

Despite the many changes that have occurred in access to and enrollment in American higher education over the past several decades, we suspect that the traditional image of college students is surprisingly persistent. One reason that traditional images are common is that we often think of specific generations of college students when trying to describe their attributes. Unfortunately, truth and fiction are intertwined in the stereotypes that become attached to each generation. At the same time, some of these generational stereotypes do describe groups of students at particular institutions. To be sure, some institutions continue to seek and enroll students who fit a traditional college student image, while others have taken on more diverse clienteles in order to better serve changing state and local populations. This suggests that there have been changes not only in the type of student now attending college but in institutional mission and policy, as well, that differentiate institutions across the higher education system.

American higher education enrollments have grown considerably despite predictions to the contrary based on the declining number of college-age students during the 1980s. Between 1975 and 1994, fall enrollment in higher education institutions grew more that 25 percent, increasing from 11.2 to 14.3 million students.[13] The 1994 figures represent the second year of small declines in fall enrollments, dropping from an all-time high of 14.4 million in 1992. Much of the growth over the last several decades has been due to increased access by nontraditional students. Adults over the age of twenty-five have been a fast-growing group and currently represent about 44 percent of students in higher education.[14] There has also been a shift toward increased part-time enrollment in higher education, with part-time students now representing about 43 percent of enrollment.

In addition to the changes brought about by increased numbers

Table 11.1

Demographic Characteristics of Entering College Students, 1961–1994 (%)

Characteristic	1961	1974	1984	1994
Gender				
Women	44	48	52	56
Men	56	52	48	44
Age distribution				
18 or younger	—	78	76	68
19 or older	—	22	24	32
Racial/ethnic background				
White/Caucasian	97	89	86	82
African American/black	2	7	10	10
American Indian	Z	1	1	2
Asian American/Oriental	1	1	2	4
Mexican American/Chicano	—	2	1	2
Puerto Rican	—	1	1	1
Other	Z	2	2	3

Source: Alexander W. Astin and Robert J. Panos, *Educational and Vocational Development of College Students* (Washington, D.C.: American Council on Education, 1969); Eric L. Dey, Alexander W. Astin, and William S. Korn, *The American Freshman: Twenty-five Year Trends* (Los Angeles: University of California, Los Angeles, Higher Education Research Institute, 1991); Linda J. Sax, Alexander W. Astin, William S. Korn, and Kit M. Mahoney, *The American Freshman: National Norms for Fall 1995* (Los Angeles: University of California, Los Angeles, Higher Education Research Institute, 1995).

Note: Racial/ethnic labels vary between survey years. Racial/ethnic percentages may total more than 100 after 1974 due to multiple responses given by individual students. Z indicates less than 0.5 percent; — indicates comparable data not available.

of nontraditional students, striking changes in the general composition of college entrants demand a reconception of the traditional college student. Table 11.1 shows the changing demographics of first-time, full-time students drawn from the CIRP data. A typical American college student in the 1990s is likely to be female: women constituted 56 percent of first-year students pursuing a baccalaureate degree in 1994, compared to 44 percent in 1961. The proportion of older students attending college as first-time entering students has also increased over time. These changes in the traditional college-going population indicate that child care services, reentry services, women's centers, women's studies, and the incorporation of gender-related issues in the classroom will continue to be salient for increasing proportions of campus communities.

Table 11.1 also shows that the proportion of white students has steadily declined, while the representation of all other ethnic minority groups has increased among first-time entrants to four-year colleges. Increased access, coupled with the growing representation of minorities within college-age cohorts, has changed the ethnic composition on many campuses. As a result, campuses will need to continue restructuring to become multicultural environments. What is not evident from table 11.1, however, is that while all racial and ethnic groups have recorded enrollment gains, participation rates are not necessarily equitable. Federal enrollment statistics show that between 1993 and 1994, participation rates of whites and African Americans increased slightly, while those of Hispanics decreased slightly. This is consistent with earlier research showing a declining participation rate among Hispanics.[15]

These changing characteristics of America's college students are the result of a combination of demographic growth, changing social views, government policies, and institutional initiatives to recruit students from all potential college populations. Some institutions, for example, have altered their missions and strengthened their commitment to serve special populations. Such changes would have been impossible without the equity reform movements that brought about changes in the nation's collective consciousness as well as tangible federal assistance in the form of financial aid policies. We have also witnessed the development and strengthening of types of specialized institutions. Over the past two decades, more than two dozen tribal colleges were established and have steadily increased their enrollments, and women's colleges and historically black institutions have strengthened their position in terms of attaining a stable and increasing student enrollment in the last ten years. In addition, an increasing number of institutions are expected to become Hispanic-serving toward the end of this decade (defined as institutions that have a minimum Hispanic enrollment of 25 percent).[16] In each case, student characteristics have given further definition to the institution's mission. Aside from these special types of institution, traditional institutions respond to the new student populations by creating new services and incorporating new perspectives in the curriculum and extracurricular programming.[17]

While these changes may appear to have occurred rapidly, creating multicultural environments continues to come about slowly for those who confront institutional resistance. A college's historical legacy of exclusion of specific groups may, for example, continue to influence seemingly neutral institutional policies. Generating a commitment to institutional transformation among administrators and faculty who refuse to examine their own attitudes and practices that affect stu- dents remains one of the greatest challenges, made harder by political attacks on and misunderstandings of policies designed to ameliorate past injustices.[18] In short, ideologies at the individual, institutional, and social levels continue to present barriers to recognizing and meet- ing the needs of today's college student.

Student Values and Politics

Along with the changing demographics of higher education, there has been a shift in the values and ideologies of students compared to those held by students in the recent past. One area in which this has oc- curred most visibly is in student politics. Following on the heels of the volatile, activist 1960s, there is the perception that recent generations of students are more conservative, apathetic, and politically inactive. This perception is true, however, only if we think about student politi- cal preferences in traditional ways. From an institutional perspective, the sociopolitical character of students is important for several rea- sons. To begin with, an accumulation of research evidence concerns the influence that student peers have upon one another.[19] Thus, when the attitudes and values within college peer environments change, the impact of college *regardless of institutional intentions* is altered. In addition, the educational process requires common ground between students and faculty. If students and faculty find few points of agree- ment on attitudes and values, these ideological differences increase the potential for conflicts between students and faculty.

How have the political preferences of students changed? As we can see in the data from entering college students shown in table 11.2, there has been an interesting pattern of change in the way that stu- dents characterize themselves politically. For example, the percent- age of students who classified themselves as liberal declined by nearly one-half between the early 1970s and the early 1980s. While the de- cline was sharp, it stabilized and actually rebounded somewhat dur- ing the 1980s, a time period in which we might have expected to see the strongest conservative influences, given events occurring on the national political scene.

Table 11.2

Political Self-Characterization and Attitudes of Entering College Students (%)

	1970–72	1980–82	1990–92
Political self-characterization			
Liberal	37	21	26
Middle of the road	47	60	54
Conservative	17	19	21
Conservatives/liberals	46/100	94/100	80/100
Political and social attitudes			
Federal government is not doing enough to control environmental pollution	90	79	87
Federal military spending should be increased		39	24
Busing is OK if it helps to achieve racial balance in the schools		45	55
Wealthy people should pay a larger share of taxes than they do now	73	71	72
A national health care plan is needed to cover everybody's medical costs		57	76
Abortion should be legal		54	64
The activities of married women are best confined to the home and family	42	26	26
Marijuana should be legalized	41	34	21
Capital punishment should be abolished	57	31	21
There is too much concern in the courts for the rights of criminals	50	68	66

Source: Eric L. Dey, Alexander W. Astin, and William S. Korn, *The American Freshman: Twenty-five Year Trends* (Los Angeles: University of California, Los Angeles, Higher Education Research Institute, 1991).

Another interesting trend is that the declining number of student liberals seems to have been accompanied mainly by increases in the number of political moderates. Indeed, the number of students who said they were in the "middle of the road" jumped by about one-quarter in the 1970s, while the number of self-proclaimed conservatives increased a scant two percentage points. This may suggest that the issues associated with the 1960s political and social movements are now seen as relatively mainstream issues and are no longer "liberal" causes. It also seems to reflect political trends within the larger society, with politicians of nearly all ideological persuasions concertedly trying to appear moderate while simultaneously painting all others as being outside of the political mainstream.

Taken together, these trends reveal that there has been a tremendous shift in the balance of liberals and conservatives on campus: whereas there were two liberals for every conservative during the early 1970s, by the early 1980s the number of liberals and conservatives were roughly equal. Although this ratio has shifted back somewhat to favor the politically liberal, the ratio of liberals to conservatives is much closer to one-to-one than it was two decades ago. This may help explain the relatively increased effectiveness of conservative political agendas on college campuses and may portend a continuation of the polarized campus politics that has become evident in recent years.

Another way to look at the political preferences of students is to consider the changing patterns of attitudes that entering students have toward a variety of political and social values. Table 11.2 shows a complex set of trends among attitudes that would traditionally be classified as both conservative and liberal. For example, there has been a movement toward the liberal position in areas such as military spending, school busing, national health care, abortion rights, and women's rights, with entering students maintaining a relatively liberal stance toward the environment and taxation. At the same time, students have clearly become more conservative on issues related to crime and drugs: the number of students who believed capital punishment should be abolished dropped by nearly two-thirds since the early 1970s, while the percentage of students who supported the legalization of marijuana dropped by one-half over the same period.

It is important to consider what distinct role, if any, the larger social context plays in determining student views during the college years.[20] The data in table 11.3 show that the attitude changes of students during college are remarkably consistent with trends observed across cohorts of young adults. This can be seen by comparing the 1985 and 1989 attitudes of those students who entered college in 1985 with those of a cohort of college freshmen as measured by the CIRP and those of young adult respondents (noninstitutionalized eighteen- to twenty-three-year olds) to the General Social Survey. For example, the change during college on the political identification item for those students who entered in 1985 is toward increased polarization (a 9% drop in the middle-of-the-road category, with these respondents moving about equally to liberal and conservative positions). The same pattern is evident for the different cohorts of CIRP and GSS respondents. The results in table 11.3 also point to the sharpest increases in

Table 11.3

College Student and Young Adult Opinions on Social Problems, 1985 and 1989 (%)

Social Problem	Student Attitudes During College			CIRP Freshman Survey Respondents			General Social Survey Young Adult Respondents		
	1985	1989	Δ	1985	1989	Δ	1985	1989	Δ
Political ID (Political leaning)									
Far right (extremely conservative)	1	1	0	1	2	1	1	3	+2
Conservative	22	27	+5	20	21	+1	23	26	+3
Middle of the road (moderate)	50	41	−9	57	54	−3	47	38	−9
Liberal	25	29	+4	21	22	+1	28	30	+2
Far left (extremely liberal)	2	3	+1	2	2	0	2	4	+2
Attitude toward capital punishment									
The death penalty should be abolished. (Do you favor or oppose the death penalty for persons convicted of murder?) Strongly disagree or disagree (Favor)	72	73	+1	73	79	+6	73	72	−1
Attitudes toward government's role in providing health care									
A national health care plan is needed to cover everybody's health care costs. (Favor government help to cover medical costs?) Strongly agree or agree (Yes)	56	66	+10	61	76	+15	53	63	+10
Attitudes toward abortion rights									
Abortion should be legal. (Possible to obtain a legal abortion for any reason?) Strongly agree or agree (Yes)	59	74	+15	55	65	+10	35	45	+10

Source: Eric L. Dey, Alexander W. Astin, and William S. Korn, *The American Freshman: Twenty-five Year Trends* (Los Angeles: University of California, Los Angeles, Higher Education Research Institute, 1991); James A. Davis and Tom W. Smith, *The NORC General Social Survey: A User's Guide* (Newbury Park, Calif.: Sage, 1992); F. W. Wood, *An American Profile: Opinions and Behavior, 1972–1989* (Detroit: Gale Research, 1990).

Note: Wording in parentheses was used in GSS. Δ indicates raw percentage difference.

liberal views toward national health and abortion rights; the social trend shows the same pattern. The degree to which these social trends are consistent with changes during college is important in that it demonstrates the webbed nature of social and collegiate influences and reminds us that change during college is not synonymous with college impact. Although some of the observed changes may well be due to college impact or maturation effects, the consistency of results across college and noncollege cohorts suggests that students are not immune to larger social and political forces.

Since these attitudes seem to reflect changing political views on the national political landscape, they also affect the issues that students choose to pursue within the campus political environment. But will today's student pursue these and other issues, or are they politically apathetic, as the common wisdom has it? The data from entering college students are complex in this area, as well. For example, the number of students who worked in political campaigns declined by about two-fifths between the late 1960s and late 1970s, while the number who reported having frequent discussions about politics declined by about one-third between the late 1960s and late 1980s and reached an all-time low of 15 percent in 1995. The 1995 survey results also show that "keeping up to date with political affairs" as an important life goal dropped to an all-time low of 29 percent, compared with 42 percent in 1990 and 58 percent in 1966. These figures clearly suggest that students are not politically active in traditional ways, while other information suggests that students may simply be disillusioned with and alienated from traditional politics.[21]

Educational Plans and Preferences

In addition to the changing composition of students, there have been changes in student plans and preferences for college. Some of these patterns appear to be related to student experiences in high school and to larger economic forces, and others seem more closely related to social forces like changing views about the role of women in American society. First, we consider the issue of student academic experiences during high school and how this appears to relate to their expectations for the college experience.

The data in table 11.4 show that college students who earned A grades in high school essentially doubled between 1966 and 1994, while the percentage earning C or worse grades fell by one-half. The

310   Eric L. Dey and Sylvia Hurtado

Table 11.4
College Freshmen's High School Grades, Various Years (%)

Grade	1966	1975	1984	1994
A or A+	15	18	20	28
B− to B+	54	60	58	57
C+ or less	31	21	22	16

Source: This and the following three tables are based on data from Eric L. Dey, Alexander W. Astin, and William S. Korn, *The American Freshman: Twenty-five Year Trends* (Los Angeles: University of California, Los Angeles, Higher Education Research Institute, 1991); Alexander W. Astin, Eric L. Dey, William S. Korn, and Ellyne R. Riggs, *The American Freshman: National Norms for Fall 1991* (Los Angeles: University of California, Los Angeles, Higher Education Research Institute, 1991): Alexander W. Astin, William S. Korn, and Ellyne R. Riggs, *The American Freshman: National Norms for Fall 1993* (Los Angeles: University of California, Los Angeles, Higher Education Research Institute, 1993); Linda J. Sax, Alexander W. Astin, William S. Korn, and Kit M. Mahoney, *The American Freshman: National Norms for Fall 1995* (Los Angeles: University of California, Los Angeles, Higher Education Research Institute, 1995).

Table 11.5
College Freshmen's Expectations Regarding College Success, Various Years (%)

Expectation	1973	1983	1994
Make at least a B average	35	41	46
Graduate with honors	9	12	16
Be elected to an academic honor society	5	7	9
Fail at least one course	2	1	1
Get tutoring help	7[a]	9	16[b]

Source: See table 11.4.

   a. 1975
   b. 1992

relatively high level of student academic success before college appears to have influenced the expectations students had for college. The CIRP data show strong increases between 1973 and 1994 in the percentage of entering students who expected to earn at least a B average in college, to graduate with honors, and to be elected to an academic honor society (table 11.5). Over the same period, the percentage of students expecting to fail one or more courses dropped by half. These patterns might suggest that students today are better prepared than those entering college two decades ago, but students also reported that they were in need of additional academic support

Table 11.6
College Freshmen's Expectations Regarding Remedial Work, by Subject,
Various Years (%)

Subject	1982	1984	1993
English	11	11	12
Reading	4	5	5
Mathematics	22	27	29
Social studies	2	3	4
Science	9	10	11
Foreign language	7	10	11

Source: See table 11.4.

Table 11.7
College Freshmen's High School Preparation, by Subject, Various Years (%)

Subject	1984	1988	1994
English (4 years)	93	95	96
Mathematics (3 years)	85	92	92
Foreign language (2 years)	66	79	81
Physical science (2 years)	52	50	47
Biological science (2 years)	34	35	36

Source: See table 11.4.

services. For example, the percentage of students who believed that there was a "very good chance" that they would get tutoring help in specific courses during college more than doubled between 1975 and 1992. Similarly, the percentage of students who expected to get special tutoring or remediation in mathematics, science, and foreign language increased between 1984 and 1993 (table 11.6). What makes this interesting is that, over approximately the same period, students were likely to meet the recommended levels of preparation in many of these fields (table 11.7). For example, more than 92 percent of students who entered college in 1994 had at least three years of math during high school, while three out of every ten students in 1993 expected to need special tutoring or remediation in math.

Taken together, these trends suggest that there has been a redefinition of the relationship between academic course work at the high school level and skills related to those courses. This puts tremendous pressure on college and university faculty to work with stu-

312 Eric L. Dey and Sylvia Hurtado

Table 11.8

Undergraduate Major Preferences, Entering College Students, Various Years (%)

College Major	1966	1972	1980	1987	1993
Biological sciences	4	4	4	4	6
Business	14	16	24	27	16
Education	11	7	8	9	10
Engineering	10	7	12	9	9
English	4	2	1	1	1
Health professions	5	11	9	7	16
History or political science	7	4	3	3	3
Humanities	5	4	2	3	2
Fine arts	8	9	5	5	4
Mathematics or statistics	5	2	1	1	1
Physical sciences	3	2	2	2	2
Social sciences		8	5	6	7
Undecided	2	5	5	7	7

Source: Eric L. Dey, Alexander W. Astin, and William S. Korn, *The American Freshman: Twenty-five Year Trends* (Los Angeles: University of California, Los Angeles, Higher Education Research Institute, 1991); Alexander W. Astin, William S. Korn, and Ellyne R. Riggs, *The American Freshman: National Norms for Fall 1993* (Los Angeles: University of California, Los Angeles, Higher Education Research Institute, 1993).

dents who have been academically successful in high school, who met or exceeded recommended levels of high school study, but who may, nevertheless, be underprepared for college-level work as traditionally defined.

The changing pattern of students' preference for undergraduate major when they enter college is an important consideration, since beyond all of the educational philosophy that goes into designing a curriculum, a college's ability to maintain its curricular focus is necessarily dependent upon its ability to enroll students in the courses it offers. Interest in majoring in the humanities, the fine and performing arts, and the social sciences has been declining consistently over the past three decades (table 11.8). Interest in majoring in English, for example, dropped by three-quarters between 1966 and 1993; interest in majoring in biological or physical sciences has remained somewhat stable since the 1960s, while interest in mathematics and statistics has experienced a large decline. Although the relatively new and developing field of computer science may have captured some of the students who otherwise might have majored in mathematics or statistics, this sharp decline in the number of students who enter college with an interest in math and statistics is alarming.

The greatest change in popularity is associated with the field of business. After a period of relative stability, the percentage of students interested in business majors increased sharply during the late 1970s and 1980s. During the past few years, however, interest in business has stopped its climb and is currently in steep decline, with student interest now equal to that registered in the mid-1960s. The cause for this turnaround is not clear. It may be that competition for jobs has increased or that students are disillusioned with the field of business because of scandals such as insider trading, stock fraud, and the savings and loan debacle of the 1980s. While the explanation for these trends may not be clear, one thing is clear: institutions that expanded their business programs to take advantage of growth in student interest may have too many faculty in the field of business relative to student demand. This problem may be especially troublesome for the many small liberal arts colleges that avoided closure during the 1980s by moving away from a traditional liberal arts program to incorporate business education into the curriculum.[22]

While interest in business is in steep decline, interest in the health professions has been increasing. This surge of interest may reflect a search for majors that will lead to profitable and stable careers, since business has apparently lost its attraction. But education for the health professions, which is largely based in the sciences, is more expensive than that associated with business. Moreover, it is impossible to predict how long this trend will last.

Beyond the pronounced changes in the major field choices of students generally are the changing educational preferences of women. Table 11.9 shows the ratio of women students interested in degrees and fields of study, compared with male students interested in the same option. The changes over the two decades show the effectiveness of the women's movement in changing the way women (and to a lesser extent, men) think about certain degrees and careers. For example, with respect to postgraduate degree aspirations upon entry into college, women have essentially reached a point of parity with men. Indeed, aspiration for law and medical degrees among women now slightly exceeds that of men.

In the undergraduate fields in which women were most underrepresented in 1972—engineering, history and political science, biological sciences, and the physical sciences—a pattern has emerged of

Table 11.9
Undergraduate and Graduate Degree and Major Preferences, Entering
Female College Students, Various Years (number per 100 male students)

College Degree and Major	1972	1982	1992
Postgraduate degree aspiration			
Law	32	81	106
Medical	44	90	103
Doctoral	64	86	99
Undergraduate major field preferences			
Biological sciences	64	103	102
Business	80	115	91
Education	329	375	286
Engineering	3	16	16
English	278	167	167
Health professions (nursing, premed, etc.)	550	331	239
History and political science	54	69	83
Humanities	204	163	121
Fine arts (applied and performing)	124	102	60
Mathematics or statistics	100	117	71
Physical sciences	27	38	54
Social sciences	227	275	247

Source: Eric L. Dey, Alexander W. Astin, and William S. Korn, *The American Freshman: Twenty-five Year Trends* (Los Angeles: University of California, Los Angeles Higher Education Research Institute, 1991). Eric L. Dey, Alexander W. Astin, William S. Korn, and Ellyne R. Riggs, *The American Freshman: National Norms for Fall 1992* (Los Angeles: University of California, Los Angeles Higher Education Research Institute, 1992).

progress toward parity. Engineering, for example, had the smallest representation of women in 1972, and this fact remained true two decades later. Despite a fivefold jump in interest in this field between 1972 and 1982, there has been no real change since that time. There may still be strong institutional barriers—such as heavy mathematical course requirements without a realistic possibility of remediation and a male-dominated climate that is unwelcoming for women—that prevent interest levels from moving beyond this plateau. The other science fields with an early underrepresentation of women have fared differently: women's interest in the biological sciences moved quickly to a position of parity, while the physical sciences still have a long way to go despite a doubling of interest between 1972 and 1992. History and political science have also made progress in attracting the interest of women but still remain far below a point of parity. Education shows a declining rate of interest among women, despite being strongly dominated by women. The health professions, which include the large, female-dominated field of nursing, now attracts the interest of fewer women relative to men. In English, the humanities, and the fine arts, there has been a lessening of interest among women, with the decline so sharp in the fine arts that women are now underrepresented. Women are now also underrepresented in the field of business, after reaching and exceeding a position of parity in the 1980s.

These changes will continue to have an impact on institutions as they attempt to balance their traditional educational missions and curricula with the changing interests of students. This is especially true of the changing patterns of interest among women and members of other underrepresented groups, as such trends bring with them pressure to remove inequities and achievement barriers for these groups. In addition to influencing institutional policy and practice, these shifts in student interest are also linked to larger social and economic forces (such as the projected job market) and have direct implications for the nation's talent pool. The continued advancement of all fields of practice or inquiry is determined in good part by the pool of student talent in each field and in part by higher education's ability to meet social and economic needs.

College Experiences

As one might expect, given the many changes described, there have been changes in the nature of the college student experience. Table 11.10 shows changes in student academic performance, activities, and student satisfaction during college from the late 1960s to the beginning of the 1990s. Perhaps one of the most striking changes has been the shift toward high grades. This may indicate that performance and academic success in college have been redefined, creating grade inflation, or it may reflect the fact that students have become more grade conscious and may be more likely to contest their grades. However, the trend may also be fueled by external pressures, as maintaining good college grades has become more closely linked to such economic considerations as the receipt of financial aid, auto insurance discounts, and access to graduate schools and jobs after college. And while more students make high grades, fewer students graduate with honors.

Table 11.10
Student's College Experiences, 1966–1970 and 1987–1991 (%)

Experience	1966–1970	1987–1991
Undergraduate grade point average		
A or A+	1	6
A– or B+	5	27
B	21	36
B– or C+	35	24
C	26	7
C– or less	13	2
Activities since entering college		
Joined a fraternity or sorority	20	21
Graduated with honors	14	12
Frequent activities during student's last year of college		
Drank wine or liquor	12	22
Drank beer	30	38
Stayed up all night	8	14
Participated in an organized demonstration/protest[a]	19	18
Attended a religious service	33	25
Smoked cigarettes	27	12
Percentage of students who were satisfied with:		
Overall quality of instruction	92	90
Opportunity to discuss coursework with professors outside of class	84	88
Lab facilities	90	88
Library	83	83
Overall satisfaction	74	87

Source: Unpublished tabulations, Higher Education Research Institute, UCLA.

a. Includes students marking "frequently" or "occasionally."

Despite the changing political views of students and the persistent (and somewhat contradictory) images of the typical college student as an activist or a member of a fraternity or sorority, we find very little change in the proportion of students who have participated in either of these activities since the 1960s. This suggests that these two activities are relatively generation free, since a roughly stable proportion of students have participated. But despite the apparent constancy in the proportion of students involved in these activities, different generations of students become associated with these images due to larger social and political contexts. For example, even though a minority of students participated in demonstrations in the late 1960s, the general perception of students during this era is that most did.

In terms of health and social behavior, students of the 1990s are less likely to report frequent smoking, due in part to increased health awareness and related restrictions on smoking in school, at work, and in places of entertainment. However, a higher proportion of students in 1987–91 reported that they drank wine, liquor, or beer in college than in 1966–70. While most of the students surveyed would have met drinking-age requirements by their fourth year of college, it would be difficult to restrict their associations with other students who are under the age limit. This shift in student behavior makes it extremely problematic for colleges to monitor and comply with legislation raising the drinking age. Colleges continue to provide opportunities for alcohol-free activities, but providing alternatives for healthy social lives will remain one of the continuing challenges for student affairs staffs on campus.

Student satisfaction and retention are closely related to college impact and institutional accountability, and the data show that student satisfaction with the college experience has remained generally high over time, with only small changes in specific areas of satisfaction. Although students are somewhat less satisfied with laboratory facilities and the quality of instruction on campus, in the early 1990s they were more satisfied with opportunities to discuss course work with professors outside of class.

Overall satisfaction remains high even though student retention has dropped over the years. Table 11.11 shows the proportion of three undergraduate student cohorts that stayed at the college they originally entered, using two retention measures. A decreasing proportion of students have obtained a degree in four years, but the proportion persisting through four years has remained relatively stable, suggesting that later cohorts are taking longer to graduate than earlier cohorts. There is perhaps no single explanation for why students are taking longer to graduate. Students now face additional financial pressures; financial aid has shifted from grants to loans, and to avoid excessive debt, more students are working and attending college part-time.[23] In addition, anecdotal evidence suggests that some students are finding it difficult to enroll in required courses at many large institutions, while others may be delaying their completion by taking advantage of programs for study abroad or other opportunities that

Table 11.11

Graduation Rates, 1966–1991 (%)

Undergraduate Cohort	Obtained Bachelor's Degree	Obtained Bachelor's Degree or Completed Four Years
1966–70	47	59
1978–82	43	56
1987–91	40	56

Source: Alexander W. Astin, *Predicting Academic Performance in College* (New York: Free Press, 1971); Kenneth C. Green, Alexander W. Astin, William S. Korn, and Patricia McNamara, *The American College Student, 1982: National Norms for 1978 and 1980 College Freshmen* (Los Angeles: University of California, Los Angeles Higher Education Research Institute, 1983); unpublished tabulations, Higher Education Research Institute.

broaden their experiences but that also lengthen the amount of time it takes to earn a degree.

Student retention will remain an important area of institutional accountability, and we can expect that more institutions will begin to follow closely the progress of students and make efforts to improve their college experiences. Trends in student graduation rates have redefined *persistence* such that it must be monitored from year to year and over a longer time span. Administrators, legislators, and the general public are becoming increasingly concerned about institutional retention rates, and new federal regulations require that institutions report these rates.

Students, Colleges, and Society

Changes in the composition and nature of American undergraduates and a recognition of the interconnections between students, institutions, and society force us to reconceptualize our thinking about college students. Specifically, the trends across generations of college students encourage a more complex view of the role of students in American higher education. Educational programs are intended to influence those who participate in them. However, the reverse is also true: many institutions change their recruitment strategies, services, and curricula as the constituencies they serve change. The value of an ecological perspective is underscored by the changing demography of higher education, trends in student political preferences and academic interests, and significant changes in aspects of the college experience. Service to special populations has become a central mission of some colleges, while changes in the type of student attending traditional four-year institutions reflect new needs and create new demands for institutional change. In contrast to student protests and political action, a tremendous amount of student-led change arises as the result of natural institutional efforts to serve student needs. Although many of these changes represent responses to recognized problems and come about with pressure from external constituencies (parents, alumni, taxpayers, legislators, peer institutions), they represent an attempt on the part of institutions to improve the educational process for students.

Attempts by students to change institutions through protest and other forms of direct action tend to receive the most attention. But students can also resist attempts to be changed by institutions, and administrators may find it particularly problematic to change students' social habits at institutions with strong student cultures. For example, student drinking has increased, even though new national policies designed to decrease alcohol use have been implemented by the colleges. Institutional efforts designed to eliminate fraternities' hazing and racist or sexist games have also been met with varied success. The roots of this resistance may be based both in politics and in the youth culture, so institutional rules and regulations, regardless of student input in their formation, cannot change student behavior. Thus, students and student culture may instigate change or create resistance within institutions.

Many problematic areas for institutions are caused by students following their own preferences. Perhaps the most troubling information presented in this chapter has to do with the future talent pool in specific fields. How can institutions influence students to pursue careers that will be vital in the future? At some level, students are attuned to the job market, but their goals may not be synchronized with a changing economic future: by the time students graduate from college with specific training, the availability of jobs in their intended fields may have disappeared. The increasing rapidity with which economies change suggests that the length of an undergraduate education will plague students seeking careers in fields with an unstable pattern of job growth.

A complete view of the relationship between students, colleges, and society is both reciprocal and dynamic. Adopting this ecological perspective requires that we rethink the nature of students' role in relation to institutions and the wider society. Students have proactively and subtly induced institutional and social change throughout history and will continue to do so in the future. These changes, in turn, have altered the nature of the student experience and the impact college has on students. Those interested in higher education must recognize and acknowledge these interconnections and begin to view the role of college students in more complex ways.

NOTES

1. Burton R. Clark, *The Distinctive College* (Chicago: Aldine, 1970), 253.

2. Robert Klitgaard, *Choosing Elites* (New York: Harper and Row, 1985); Alexander W. Astin, *Achieving Educational Excellence* (San Francisco: Jossey-Bass, 1985).

3. T. Dary Erwin, *Assessing Student Learning and Development: A Guide to the Principles, Goals, and Methods of Determining Outcomes* (San Francisco: Jossey-Bass, 1991); Ernest T. Pascarella and Patrick T. Terenzini, *How College Affects Students* (San Francisco: Jossey-Bass, 1991); Maryann Jacobi, Alexander W. Astin, and Frank Ayala Jr., *College Student Outcomes Assessment: A Talent Development Perspective* (Washington, D.C.: Association for the Study of Higher Education, 1987); Astin, *Achieving Educational Excellence.*

4. Philip G. Altbach, "Students: Interests, Culture, and Activism," in *Higher Learning in America, 1980–2000,* ed. Arthur Levine (Baltimore: Johns Hopkins University Press, 1993).

5. Seymour M. Lipset, *Rebellion in the University* (New York: Little, Brown, 1971), 263.

6. Altbach, "Students"; Tony Vellela, *New Voices: Student Activism in the '80s and '90s* (Boston: South End, 1988).

7. Duane F. Alwin, Ronald L. Cohen, and Theodore M. Newcomb, *Political Attitudes over the Life Span: The Bennington Women after Fifty Years* (Madison: University of Wisconsin Press, 1991); Urie Bronfenbrenner, *The Ecology of Human Development: Experiments by Nature and Design* (Cambridge: Harvard University Press, 1979).

8. Bronfenbrenner, *Ecology of Human Development,* 13.

9. Ibid., 17.

10. Jeylan T. Mortimer, Michael D. Finch, and Donald Kumka, *Work, Family, and Personality: Transition to Adulthood* (Norwood, N.J.: Ablex, 1986), cited in Alwin, Cohen, and Newcomb, *Political Attitudes,* 252.

11. Alexander W. Astin, William S. Korn, and Ellyne R. Riggs, *The Ameri-*

can *Freshman: National Norms for Fall 1993* (Los Angeles: University of
California, Los Angeles, Higher Education Research Institute, 1993); Eric L.
Dey, Alexander W. Astin, and William S. Korn, *The American Freshman:
Twenty-five-Year Trends* (Los Angeles: University of California, Los Angeles,
Higher Education Research Institute, 1991).

12. Alexander W. Astin and Robert J. Panos, *The Educational and Voca-
tional Development of College Students* (Washington, D.C.: American Council
on Education, 1969); Kenneth C. Green, Alexander W. Astin, William S. Korn,
and Patricia McNamara, *The American College Student, 1982: National
Norms for 1978 and 1980 College Freshmen* (Los Angeles: University of
California, Los Angeles, Higher Education Research Institute, 1983); *The
American College Student, 1991: National Norms for 1987 and 1989 College
Freshmen* (Los Angeles: University of California, Los Angeles, Higher Edu-
cation Research Institute, 1991).

13. Martha L. Hollins, Samuel F. Barbett, Rosalind A. Korb, and Frank B.
Morgan, *Enrollment in Higher Education: Fall 1986 through Fall 1994*
(Washington, D.C.: National Center for Education Statistics, 1996).

14. National Center for Education Statistics, *Digest of Education Statistics, 1996* (Washington, D.C.: NCES, 1996), table 171.

15. National Center for Education Statistics, *Digest of Education Statistics, 1995* (Washington, D.C.: NCES, 1995), table 180; Deborah Carter and
Reginald Wilson, *Minorities in Higher Education: Tenth Annual Status Report* (Washington, D.C.: American Council on Education, Office of Minority
Concerns, 1992).

16. Ellen M. O'Brien, *American Indians in Higher Education* (Washington, D.C.: American Council on Education, 1992); Judith G. Touchton and
Linda Davis, *Factbook on Women in Higher Education* (New York: ACE/Mac-
millan, 1991); see also Carter and Wilson, *Minorities in Education;* Hispanic Association of Colleges and Universities, *Annual Report* (San Antonio:
HACU, 1990).

17. Carol Pearson, Donna L. Shavlik, and Judith G. Touchton, eds., *Edu-
cating the Majority: Women Challenge Tradition in Higher Education* (New
York: ACE/MacMillan, 1989); Daryl G. Smith, *The Challenge of Diversity: In-
volvement or Alienation in the Academy* (Washington, D.C.: Association for
the Study of Higher Education, 1989). Margaret L. Andersen, "Changing the
Curriculum in Higher Education," in *Reconstructing the Academy: Women's
Education and Women's Studies,* ed. Elizabeth Minnich, Jean O'Barr, and
Rachel Rosenfeld (Chicago: University of Chicago, 1988).

18. Sylvia Hurtado, "The Institutional Climate for Talented Latino Students," *Research in Higher Education* 35 (1994): 21–41; Susan Hardy Aiken,
Karen Anderson, Myra Dinnerstein, Judy Lensink, and Patricia MacCor-
quodale, "Trying Transformations: Curriculum Integration and the Problem of Resistance," in *Reconstructing the Academy: Women's Education and*

Women's Studies, ed. Elizabeth Minnich, Jean O'Barr, and Rachel Rosenfeld (Chicago: University of Chicago Press, 1988); Sylvia Hurtado and Christine G. Navia, "Reconciling College Access and the Affirmative Action Debate," in *Affirmative Action's Testament of Hope,* ed. Mildred Garcia (Albany: State University of New York Press, 1997).

19. Alexander W. Astin, *What Matters in College: Four Critical Years Revisited* (San Francisco: Jossey-Bass, 1993); see also Pascarella and Terenzini, *How College Affects Students.*

20. Eric L. Dey, "Undergraduate Political Attitudes: An Examination of Peer, Faculty, and Social Influences," *Research in Higher Education* 37 (1996): 535–54.

21. Linda J. Sax, Alexander W. Astin, William S. Korn, and Kit M. Mahoney, *The American Freshman: National Norms for Fall 1995* (Los Angeles: University of California, Los Angeles, Higher Education Research Institute, 1995); Paul R. Loeb, *Generation at the Crossroads* (New Brunswick: Rutgers University Press, 1994).

22. David W. Breneman, "Liberal Arts Colleges: What Price Survival?" in *Higher Learning in America, 1980–2000,* ed. Arthur Levine (Baltimore: Johns Hopkins University Press, 1993).

23. College Board, *Trends in Student Aid: 1980 to 1989* (New York: College Board, 1989); Alexander W. Astin, Eric L. Dey, William S. Korn, and Ellyne R. Riggs, *The American Freshman: National Norms for Fall 1991* (Los Angeles: University of California, Los Angeles, Higher Education Research Institute, 1991).

Chapter Twelve

The Dilemma of Presidential Leadership

Robert Birnbaum

If any man wishes to be humbled and mortified, let him become president of Harvard College (plaintive cry of Harvard president Edward Holyoke on his deathbed in 1769).

—F. S. Horn

Every decade, about five thousand persons serve as college or university presidents. Over a term of office averaging less than seven years, the president is expected to serve simultaneously as the chief administrator of a large and complex bureaucracy, as the convening colleague of a professional community, as a symbolic elder in a campus culture of shared values and symbols, and (in some institutions) as a public official accountable to a public board and responsive to the demands of other governmental agencies. Balancing the conflicting expectations of these roles has always been difficult; changing demographic trends, fiscal constraints, and unrealistic public expectations now make it virtually impossible for most presidents to provide the leadership that is expected.

The college presidency may not be the second oldest profession in America, but the role has existed in this country from the time of the founding of Harvard in 1636, a century and half before there was a nation. From the colonial period until the Civil War, institutions were for the most part small, simply structured, and controlled by their lay boards of trustees, leading to a weak presidency. The president's role even in those days was a demanding one and included teaching, preaching, fund raising, record keeping, and (most especially) student discipline, but in a simpler world of certain knowledge and accepted authority most presidents were able to perform effectively the tasks expected of them.

The period between the Civil War and World War I was one of expansion and transformation in higher education. New and more complex institutions were created as research and public service were added to the traditional teaching mission. The late nineteenth and early twentieth centuries were times of the "great men," presidents who often wielded unchecked authority to create great institutions. Trustee boards were increasingly composed of businessmen who embraced the developing concepts of scientific management. Viewing the college as comparable to a business firm, faculty were considered to be employees hired to do as they were told, and the president, in Thorstein Veblen's caustic term, was the "Captain of Erudition," responsible for increasing enrollment, capital, and reputation, while controlling costs.[1]

The job was clearly becoming more difficult, and observers of that day could note that "the duties imposed upon the modern university president are so multifarious that it is becoming exceedingly difficult to find a man capable of filling the position in the larger institutions."[2] But although the role had become more complex, it was still one possible to fulfill; presidents had the power, and if they wished (and many did) they could administer following the precept attributed to Benjamin Jowett, the head of Balliol College, Oxford: "Never retract. Never explain. Get the thing done and let them howl!"

As institutions became more comprehensive and involved in scholarship, the faculty became more specialized, more professionalized, and less tolerant of administrative controls. Increasingly until World War II, and then with accelerating force during the 1950s and 1960s, faculty claimed for themselves the right not only to make decisions concerning the major educational activities of the institution but also to participate fully in setting institutional policy and to have a voice in its management. The growing power of the faculty, a change significant enough to justify referring to it as the "academic revolution,"[3] was one of the forces that led postwar presidents to claim that "the fundamental difficulty with the office of university president arises out of the current system of controlling modern universities. . . . He has vast responsibilities for all phases of the life and welfare of the university, but he has no power."[4]

Presidential discretion was increasingly limited not only by forces within the academy but by those outside as well. In particular, federal and state agencies were exerting influence over matters that had previously been considered internal institutional prerogatives. The loss of effective presidential authority, related internally to changes in organizational complexity and patterns of influence and externally to increased environmental constraints, helped to transform the role from a difficult job to an impossible one.

This claim must be accompanied by a caveat. There are more than 3,500 colleges and universities, most (but not all) headed by a chief executive officer with the title of president (or, less frequently, chancellor). The composite public image of a small number of the more visible institutions tends to obscure their great diversity in size, wealth, program level, complexity, student selectivity, faculty preparation, and public or private sponsorship—all factors that affect presidential authority and therefore the extent to which presidents can be effective. The historical generalizations that have already been made, and the analyses that follow, must therefore be applied with caution. In discussing the presidential role, this chapter focuses primarily upon institutions with at least moderate enrollments, multiple missions, and comprehensive programs. Such institutions enroll most of the students in higher education, but they probably represent less than half of the total number of the nation's colleges and universities.

The Presidential Role

There is no standard definition of the presidency nor description of the expectations placed on the performance of its incumbents. Presidents traditionally have no stated term of office but serve "at the pleasure" of a public or private board of lay trustees. Institutional statutes or bylaws commonly identify the president as the chief executive and administrative officer of the board as well as the chief academic officer of the faculty, and they delegate to the president all powers necessary to perform these functions. Statements of such sweeping authority may appear to the uninitiated to offer almost unlimited control over administrative and programmatic initiatives, but the reality of presidential influence is quite different. As one president has commented, "regardless of what may appear in the charter and bylaws, the authority of the president, his real leadership, depends on the willingness of the campus to accept him as a leader. If it will not, well there are other ways for him to earn a living."[5]

There are many ways of looking at the components of the presidential role. One typical listing identifies and describes responsibilities inside and outside the institution. Inside, the president is responsible for managing the finances of the institution and its budget, long-range institutional planning, coordination of the academic program, and the maintenance of appropriate standards of quality, personnel policies, and student affairs. Outside, the president solicits support from donors, represents the institution to legislative and other external audiences, deals with alumni and athletics, protects academic freedom, and makes public pronouncements on educational issues.[6]

From a more analytical perspective, presidential tasks can be seen as comprising administrative, political, and entrepreneurial components.[7] As administrator, the president carries out the policies of the trustees, supervises subordinates, allocates resources, establishes systems of accountability, and performs functions similar to those found in any complex organization. As politician, the president must be responsive to the needs of various constituencies whose support is critical to the maintenance of his or her position. The interests of groups and subgroups of faculty, students, alumni, and others whose actions may constrain presidential discretion must be considered and courted, and the president must often form coalitions and propose compromises that will permit peace with progress. As entrepreneur, the president is expected to develop and exploit markets that offer necessary resources for the institution. Fund-raising is perhaps the most visible component of this role, but communication with legislators in the state house or in Washington, securing grants, developing marketing plans, and managing institutional relations programs are important and time-consuming activities as well.

There may be agreement on the components of the role, but there is no model of the presidency that identifies priorities between them. Presidential activities are to a great extent contingent on the characteristics of their institutions, the inexorable ebb and flow of the academic calendar, the emerging exigencies of the environment, and their own personal interests. Some presidents spend a majority of their time in fund-raising, public representation, and related resource acquisition activities. The typical president spends little time on academic matters.

The pace, intensity, and comprehensiveness of the presidency are in many ways comparable to those of managers and executives in other settings.[8] But there is a fundamental difference. On a college campus the exercise of authority in governance is not solely an administrative prerogative but, rather, a shared responsibility and joint effort that properly involves all important campus constituencies, with particular emphasis given to the participation of the faculty. The influential "Joint Statement on Government of Colleges and Universities," for example, gives to the faculty the "primary responsibility" for "curriculum, subject matter and methods of instruction, research, faculty status, and those aspects of student life which relate to the educational process." In such matters, the president is expected to "concur with the faculty judgment except in rare instances and for compelling reasons which should be stated in detail." If, as it is generally agreed, the central questions that define the essential nature of a college or university are "Who should teach?" "What should be taught?" and "Who shall be taught?" the normative precepts of the joint statement reserve these matters for the direct control of the faculty and not for either the president or the trustees.[9]

The joint statement codified what had been true for many years at academically strong campuses and what was evolving as good practice at many others. In doing so, it highlighted the basic managerial dilemma of the president; essential questions of institutional "production" or service, which would be considered matters of managerial prerogative in other settings, were in colleges and universities to be decided by the faculty, who were "employees." In a business firm, the president or CEO is solely accountable to a board of directors. In higher education, the president functions between two layers of organizational operations—the trustees and the faculty—and is accountable to both. Conflict between constituent groups is common in many organizations, but its importance and consequences for the college president may be unique. In a business firm, presidential tenure is the sole prerogative of the board of directors. Within many colleges or universities, however, faculty (and often other groups as well) assert the right to participate in presidential selection and evaluation. And, as many presidents have discovered, a faculty vote of no confidence often has the same power to end a presidential career as does a formal vote by the trustees.

The Impossible Job

There is no educational, social, or political consensus on exactly what
higher education should be doing, what constituencies it should serve,
and how it should serve them. At different times and on different campuses, emphasis has been given to transmitting values, to discovering
knowledge, or to improving society. Some of the manifest purposes
of higher education—the education and development of individual
students, transmitting the culture and advancing society in general,
providing for educational justice and social mobility, supporting intellectual and artistic creativity, and evaluating society so that it can
become self-renewing[10]—enjoy general support as principles but become contentious as people attempt to describe how such vague ideals
should best be implemented.

   In addition to these obvious aims, colleges and universities have
latent purposes as well. Among other things, they serve a custodial
function by removing from parents the burden of controlling the behavior of young adults; they serve as a means of certifying to employers that graduates possess diligence and at least a modicum of
intelligence; they socialize students and help them develop networks
that will prove useful later in life; and they perpetuate the existing
social order. These latter functions often conflict with the avowed purposes of colleges and universities, and although less often discussed,
they are nonetheless important.

   Goals of access, quality, and diversity, which are in conflict and
which call for quite different institutional structures and responses,
appear and then wane on the public policy agenda in cycles; the essential educational missions of teaching, research, and service compete
for resources; and there is no rational way to assess the legitimacy of
the competing and incompatible demands of many internal and external groups. Internally, faculty and administrators may disagree on appropriate levels of workload or salary, students and faculty may be in
conflict about degree requirements or the academic calendar, alumni
and trustees may debate the virtues of tradition and change, and students may disagree with administrative perspectives on investments
or on campus recruitment by intelligence agencies. Externally, institutions may find themselves arguing with local governments over
the cost and availability of civic services, with environmental groups
about waste disposal, with neighboring institutions offering compet-

ing programs, or with industries asking that curricula be developed to meet their needs.

Virtually all of these demands have some merit, and few can be dismissed out of hand. Yet there is no accepted criterion presidents can employ to judge the benefits of one course of action over another, and little assurance that they could implement their preferences even if they could specify them. Presidential authority is limited, complete understanding of the scope and complexity of the enterprise exceeds human cognitive capability, and unforeseen changes in demographic, political, and economic conditions often overwhelm campus plans. Presidents fortunate enough to preside during good times may reap the benefits of a munificent environment over which they have had no control, and even the incompetent may appear heroic; presidents during times of depression or social ferment may reap a whirlwind they did not sow.

The following sections consider four of the factors that limit presidential leadership: the constraints on presidential discretion, the unique characteristics of academic organizations, the problems of assessing effectiveness, and the limitations of the presidential role itself.

Constraints on Presidential Discretion

Many factors increasingly limit presidential leadership.[11] Some of these result from interactions with other organizations, others arise within the institutions themselves. Environmental constraints more federal and state controls; involvement by the courts in academic decision making; layers of governance, particularly in institutions that are part of statewide systems; few opportunities for growth and, consequently, for changes accompanying growth; questions about the mission of higher education; concerns about costs; issues of accountability; lack of acceptance of authority, in general; and fewer potential applicants and, therefore, greater responsiveness to the student market. Within institutions, constraints to leadership arise due to involvement by faculties in academic and personnel decisions; faculty collective bargaining; goal ambiguity; fractionation of the campus into interest groups, leading to a lack of consensus and community; greater involvement by trustees into campus operations; and increased bureaucracy and specialization among campus administrators.

Statewide coordinating or governing boards in almost all states exercise increasing influence over matters reserved in the past to the campus, including such critical issues as faculty personnel policies and review of academic programs. Other state executive or legislative agencies have become involved in facility reviews, administrative operations, budgeting, and planning. Although these intrusions focus on public institutions, they may also, directly or indirectly, affect private institutions. As the locus of influence moves from the campus to the state, public sector presidents may find themselves becoming like middle managers in public agencies rather than campus leaders.

As patterns of authority become confused, particularly in larger and more complex institutions, schools or departments become the locus of educational decision making. The institution may become an academic holding company for a federation of quasi-autonomous subunits. Unable to influence the larger institution, faculty may retreat into the small subunit for which they feel affinity and from which they can defend their influence and status, and presidential influence over their activities decreases still further.

In addition to these political and structural constraints, presidential influence is severely limited by both the paucity of resources available and the short-term difficulties in internally reallocating those resources that exist. Some intangible campus resources, such as institutional prestige and attractiveness to students and potential donors, are tied into a network of external relationships that are virtually impossible to change in the short run and difficult to change even over long periods of time. Internally, on most campuses the personnel complement is largely fixed through tenure and contractual provisions, program change is constrained by faculty interests and structures as well as by facility limitations, and yearly planning begins with the largest share of the budget precommitted.

Unique Organizational Factors

The administration of colleges and universities presents "a unique dualism in organizational structure,"[12] with two structures existing in parallel. One is the conventional bureaucratic hierarchy responsive to the will of the trustees; the other is the structure through which faculty make decisions regarding those aspects of the institution over which they have professional jurisdiction. Trustees, who hold all legal authority, are primarily business executives who are more likely than the faculty to see the organization as comparable to a business firm in its structure and authority pattern and to support top-down management. The president, viewed as their CEO, is expected to carry out their wishes and to be accountable for faculty performance. The faculty, on the other hand, expect to exercise primary authority over educational processes, and trustee or presidential intrusion into academic affairs is likely to be viewed as illegitimate.

The problems caused by dual control are exacerbated by the conflicting nature of administrative and professional authority. In most organizations, major goals activities are subject to the bureaucratic authority of administrators, which arises from their position within the hierarchy and their legal right to give directives. The professional authority of faculty members, on the other hand, comes from their expertise and training.[13] Administrative and professional authority are not only different but also mutually inconsistent, driven by incompatible systems of authority. The president is imbedded in both authority systems, and therefore is continually subject to incompatible demands and behavioral expectations.[14] As the leader of a bureaucracy, the president is expected to establish goals, decide how they are to be achieved, scientifically organize the work of subordinates, plan, and monitor organizational functioning. As the head of a professional and collegial body, the president is expected to be the first among equals and to move the group toward consensus by listening, proposing, mediating, persuading, and influencing through information sharing and appeals to reason. The use of legal authority or status differentials, which is an important means of gaining influence in one system, is illegitimate and unacceptable in the other.

Problems of Assessing Effectiveness

The particular organizational complexities of colleges and universities, exacerbated by the conflicting demands of their environments and the difficulty of understanding exactly how they function, has led to their identification as "organized anarchies."[15] An organized anarchy exhibits three characteristics: problematic goals, an unclear technology, and fluid participation in decision-making processes.

The concept of organized anarchy suggests that colleges and universities often make choices through a process of "garbage-can decision making."[16] Problems, solutions, and participants form steady streams, flowing through the organization as if they were poured into a large can. When one participant tries to make a decision, others

in the can may become attached to it because they are contempora-
neous, even though they may not appear to be logically connected.
For example, a presidential decision to build a faculty parking lot on
some unused campus land would appear to be easily made if there
were enough data on parking needs and available resources to perform a cost/benefit analysis. But such apparently simple decisions become incredibly complex as elements seen by the decision maker as
extraneous (that is, "garbage") become attached to it. The biology department may argue that the lot will destroy adjacent trees and use
the incident to press its continuing proposal for an institutional environmental master plan; a candidate for student government office
may use the lot as a symbol of administration indifference to student
needs and ask for student membership on the board of trustees; and
a faculty member may link the cost to recent cuts in library budgets
and use the incident as a forum for discussing educational priorities.
Since "garbage" is in the eye of the beholder, it is possible for almost
any two issues to be seen by someone on campus as connected and for
any problem to become coupled to any decision. Making a decision on
the parking lot may be impossible unless some way can be found of
severing its connection to environmental plans, student trustees, and
educational priorities.

Institutional outcomes may be a result of only modestly interdependent activities and are often neither planned nor predictable. For
example, a campus may receive a federal research grant because
a president gave additional resources to a department, because a
grant proposal by chance was assigned to one reviewer rather than
another, or because the granting agency was obliged to seek a geographic distribution in its awards. People in different parts of the
organization may have access to information making any of these
or other explanations plausible. Such ambiguity inhibits the making
of valid inferences about cause and effect, and presidential learning
becomes exceptionally difficult. Presidents may spend more time in
sense making[17] and in engaging in activities that verify or enhance
their status, than in decision making. The decoupling of choices and
outcomes makes symbolic behavior particularly important.

The ambiguities of institutional life are intensified by the absence
in colleges and universities of accepted and valid indicators of effectiveness. There are different definitions of effectiveness, all of which
are difficult to measure; different audiences use different criteria to
make the assessment; and achievement of effectiveness in one area

of institutional functioning may inhibit or prevent it in another.[18] Without measures of organizational effectiveness, it becomes difficult for presidents — or others — to objectively assess presidential effectiveness. As a consequence, institutional outcomes in general, and perceptions of presidential success or failure in particular, may be "largely a matter of luck. . . . The president is always in a war, and whether he wins or loses bears only a marginal relation to his foresight, his wisdom, his charm, his blood pressure."[19] In the final analysis, "the effects that presidents can have on their campuses are confounded by the actions of other institutional leaders, changes in the environment, and internal organizational processes such as culture and history that are difficult to change. Presidents are major participants in institutional events that have important organizational consequences . . . but in many ways they follow common scripts and play roles that are independent of their own personal characteristics."[20]

Limitations of the Presidential Role

Much of the literature on the presidential role comes from presidents themselves. There is a tendency by some to celebrate their own accomplishments, but there is often a strong undercurrent of despair or anger along with resignation to the fact that, in the long run, their success or failure may be due more to the vagaries of luck and history than to their own dedication and skill. Presidents are subject to role overload and role ambiguity, as they respond both to their own personal interpretations of their roles and to the legitimate demands of many groups.

One consequence of multiple and conflicting roles is that any actions by a president are likely to be criticized by someone. The pace, the unrelenting pressure, and the marginal membership of presidents in conflicting groups affect their health, both physical and mental. Every decision will have its personal costs. And private time for family or recreation will be scarce.

The popular view of the role may identify the president as a larger-than-life, heroic leader, whose wise decisions and forceful administration solve problems and advance the institution's fortunes. But in fact, presidential decisions may have little effect on disparate organizational subsystems; changes in the environment may often overpower any internal changes; and administrative structures and processes of organization and control are relatively weak vis-à-vis the autonomy of professional participants. A president can attend to only a small number of matters, but there is no way of knowing beforehand (or often even afterward, for that matter) whether these are the most important matters. These problems led Michael Cohen and James March to call the presidency an illusion: "Important aspects of the role seem to disappear on close examination. Compared to the heroic expectations he and others might have, the president has modest control over the events of college life. The contributions he makes can easily be swamped by outside events or the diffuse quality of university decision making."[21] These limits on influence and the ambiguities of purpose, power, experience, and success make it difficult for presidents to learn what works.

If the institution has ambiguous and multiple purposes and lacks a sense of shared direction, how can presidents justify their actions or know if they have been successful? If influence is dispersed throughout the institution and decentralized, how can presidents know how much power they have or what they can or cannot do? If what happens on a campus depends as much on the actions of others and on environmental pressures as it does on presidential behavior, what can presidents accurately learn from their experiences? And if presidents have confirmed their success earlier in their careers because they have been promoted, how can they assess their present success when promotion is no longer possible?

Behavioral and Cognitive Strategies

Survival requires the development of coping mechanisms that help the organization and the people within it make sense of the ambiguities of their daily lives. Colleges and universities have evolved ways of responding to the difficulties caused by their complex environmental relationships, inchoate influence patterns, and inability to rationalize their technology. For example, institutions meet the conflicting demands of interest groups by decentralizing and permitting subunits to operate in a quasi-autonomous fashion. Subunits can then meet specific needs, but the cost is high: presidential authority is diminished, it becomes almost impossible to coordinate activities, and maintaining a sense of coherence and common purpose is extremely difficult.

Institutions may attempt to cope with the difficulty of assessing effectiveness by publicly focusing attention on inputs (such as percentage of faculty with the doctorate) rather than outputs (how much a student has learned) and by actively discouraging inspection and relying instead upon established reputation, tradition, and goodwill to justify continued political and fiscal support. Presidents are expected to provide leadership, direction, coherence, and progress in an organization with conflicting authority structures, multiple social systems, and contested goals.

A national commission on the presidency found that "our colleges and universities are in desperate need of leadership" and noted that the presidency is weaker and less attractive to persons of talent now than in the past.[22] The commission found that a quarter of all presidents were dissatisfied, some despairingly so, and that the turnover rate among presidents was about 30 percent every two years. Presidents were acutely aware of limitations in performing their roles.

External observers who criticize higher education leadership and the conduct of the presidency have offered suggestions meant to make the job more doable. One common proposal suggests strengthening the presidency through the selecting of better presidents. It assumes (although without supporting data) that today's presidents do not have the same characteristics of courage and decisiveness as presidents of the past. The obvious solution is for presidential search committees to seek stronger and more decisive candidates. Alternatively, it has been suggested that the presidency could be strengthened by increasing the legal authority of the position and curtailing the influence of other groups. If one of the causes of presidential weakness is the anarchical nature of the organization, then a possible solution is to increase the use of rational processes, rather than political or symbolic processes, in decision making. But the many attempts to do so through the imposition of management systems, personnel policies that increase administrative discretion to reduce staff size, or formulas for budget allocations have by and large not had the desired and expected effects. In many cases, processes set up to respond to problems have only exacerbated them.

It has also been suggested that presidential effectiveness might be improved if trustee boards provided more support to their presidents, giving them leadership positions on the board, encouraging faculty support for them, resisting attempts to involve boards in administration, and using presidents as their sole conduit into the administrative structure.[23] The frantic pace of presidential life has also been identified as a major constraint upon presidential effectiveness, and it has been suggested that providing presidents with more personal assistance would free their time for contemplation and long-term planning. This suggestion almost always overlooks the likelihood that presidents do not become busy people but rather that busy people become presidents. Presidents complain about lack of time for contemplation, but there is no reason to believe that if they had more free time they would use it for that purpose.

There is no dearth of advice about how to be a successful president. Some authorities suggest that presidents remain distant, others that they be intimately involved with constituents; that they focus on resource acquisition or that they focus on academic matters; that they stress accountability or that they foster creativity; that they set goals or that they help others achieve their own goals. The proposals are inconsistent, and their behavioral implications are unclear. Nevertheless, the following section suggests some presidential administrative strategies that might increase their effectiveness and improve their institutions.[24] It also examines some of the cognitive and symbolic strategies that permit presidents and institutions to cope with the discrepancies between authority and responsibility, expectations and achievement. Finally, it considers the possibility that, because of certain characteristics of colleges and universities, a weak presidency may have an important organizational function.

Successful Administrative Strategies

Successful presidents are likely to be realists rather than idealists. They accept a decentralized structure, conflicting authority systems, and loose coupling as inherent organizational characteristics and try to work within these constraints. They know that essential institutional functions are likely to continue to operate, even in the absence of presidential direction, because of ongoing administrative systems and the largely autonomous activities of professional faculties. In many ways, the organization works as a cybernetic system in which negative feedback serves to activate processes that maintain the institution's current level of functioning.[25] Presidents appreciate that some of their energy will be occupied with the day-to-day activities of monitoring these processes and with identifying and attending to institutional weaknesses and problems.

However, presidents also recognize that they can have an impact on the institution if they focus on a few limited objectives or programs and devote extraordinary energy to them. Presidents can be effective even in areas such as curriculum, in which administrative influence is traditionally weak, if they are willing to accept the inevitable cost of other opportunities forgone. Presidents who try to do too many things, either on their own initiative or in response to perceived environmental demands, often end up accomplishing none of them.

Effective presidents understand the culture of their institution and the symbolic aspects of their positions. Recognizing that their effectiveness as leaders depends upon the willingness of highly trained professionals to be followers, they avoid actions that would violate cultural and academic norms and thereby diminish their own status. Effective presidents spend a great deal of time in understanding their institutional culture. They go out of their way to walk around their campuses to see and be seen, to confer with other formal and informal campus leaders for opinions and advice, to learn institutional histories, and to understand the expectations others have of presidential behavior. They also recognize that as a symbolic leader they must consistently articulate the core values of the institution and relate them to all aspects of institutional life in order to sustain and reinvigorate the myths that create a common reality. Management skills may be a necessary, but usually not a sufficient, concomitant of presidential success. For example, Ellen Chaffee has suggested that presidents who focus on resource acquisition strategies alone to resolve fiscal crises are not as successful as those who combine them with interpretative strategies that change campus perceptions and attitudes.[26]

Since centralized control cannot be achieved in complex, nonlinear, social systems, effective presidents realize that prevention of error is not possible. They therefore emphasize the design of systems to detect error and to make institutional processes self-correcting. They support the collection, analysis, and public dissemination of data on aspects of institutional functioning, data that permit interest groups to monitor the institution. Organizational stability is increased as institutional components pay attention to different aspects of the environment and serve as controls and checks on each other's activities. The effectiveness of a free flow of information is increased when presidents support and publicly articulate the value of open communication and a will to tolerate and encourage, rather than to punish, disagreement.

Effective presidents recognize that the inherent specialization and

fractionation essential to the maintenance of quality and responsiveness must be coordinated unobtrusively in order to avoid alienation.
They do this in part by establishing formal opportunities for interaction, and they emphasize forums such as senates, cabinets, retreats,
and task forces that bring together persons representing different
constituencies and different institutional levels. Senate presidents
who sit on administrative councils, deans who attend senate meetings, and students, faculty, and administrators who serve on joint
committees interact in ways that make their perceptions and interests more consistent.

Presidential effectiveness is based as much upon influence as upon
authority, and influence in an academic institution depends upon mutual and reciprocal processes of social exchange. Effective presidents
influence others by allowing themselves to be influenced. This requires that presidents listen carefully, which might be difficult for
presidents who believe that the proper role of leaders is to tell others
what to do.

Cognitive and Symbolic Strategies

Individuals typically become presidents after successful performance
in a series of related positions of increasing responsibility. One reason
for considering the presidency an impossible job is the extensive criticism by reputable sources directed at the presumably failing efforts
of so many previously accomplished people. Presidents rely upon unconscious cognitive strategies to reconcile this discrepancy between
past achievement and present criticism. They see themselves as successful even as others see them as failing.

Presidents talk easily about the deficiencies of their confreres, but
when asked about their own performance, self-assessments are almost uniformly positive. In one study, presidents rated the quality of
their own "institutional leadership" as seventy-seven on a hundred-
point scale, while they rated that of the "average president" as sixty-
six and their predecessor as only fifty-two.[27] They also indicated that
the quality of their own campus had improved on each of seven dimensions since they became president, a finding contradicted by a host of
recent reports critical of American higher education. Presidents build
schemas of effectiveness based upon previous career success; when
they encounter ambiguous situations, they are likely to anticipate,
and therefore to observe, successful outcomes and to attribute these

to their own efforts. When presidents were asked to identify a recent event that had positive outcomes on their campus, for example, 74 percent indicated that they had initiated it. But when asked to identify an event with a negative outcome, only 14 percent accepted responsibility. There seems to be evidence of a success bias that leads these successful people to believe that they have been responsible for successful outcomes, and that permits them to disassociate themselves from failure. In a recent study of the performance of thirty-two college presidents, all but one considered themselves successful, even though a quarter of them had lost sufficient constituent support to be identified by the researcher as having been a failure at the job.[28]

Academic presidents occupy a prestigious position in American life. They are major figures in their communities, sought after as speakers for local functions, and interviewed by the media. They are at the core of impressive academic ceremonies, they have the highest salaries and most significant perquisites a campus has to offer, and they are surrounded by respectful aides and by associates with vested interests in maintaining a successful presidency.

The Latent Organizational Functions of Impossibility

It may be so vital for symbolic reasons for organizational members to believe that their leaders are important that both leaders and followers may cope with the reality of weak presidential influence by constructing an illusion of their power. We have developed highly romanticized, heroic views of leadership—what leaders do, what they are able to accomplish, and the general effects they have upon our lives. It amounts to what might be considered a faith in the potential if not in the actual efficacy of those individuals.[29]

In many situations, presidential leadership may not be real but, rather, a social attribution, a result of the tendency of campus constituents to assign to a president the responsibility for unusual institutional outcomes because the president fills a role identified as a leader, because presidents are visible and prominent, because presidents spend a great deal of time doing leaderlike things (such as engaging in ceremonial and symbolic activities), and because we all have the need to believe in the effectiveness of individual control. Leaders are people believed by followers to have caused events. "Successful leaders," says Jeffrey Pfeffer, "are those who can separate themselves from organizational failures and associate themselves with organizational successes." [30]

In organizations with clear goals, understood technologies, and hierarchical power structures, illusionary leadership may be dysfunctional. In such institutions, increasing the authority of competent leaders would reduce the extent to which their job might be thought of as impossible and would thereby increase organizational effectiveness. But when these organizational characteristics are not present, it is highly questionable whether increasing presidential power would yield positive outcomes. It may even be that the very factors responsible for the impossibility of the presidential role are also important components of organizational effectiveness and that action taken to strengthen the one would weaken the other. Higher education may be effective not despite its arational characteristics but because of them.

While presidents may rail against the frustrations of their job, they assumed their positions aware of the constraints they would face. Some may have had egocentric motives, but for most a natural interest in power, money, and prestige is strongly tempered by a dedication to the enduring values of education and a commitment to serve the interests of their institutions. If the presidency had greater authority than it does, it might attract to it a different kind of person, one perhaps less committed to the concept of leader as institutional servant and more to the concept of leader as institutional master. It might be that if presidents had greater authority they might enjoy it more, but in Harold Stoke's thoughtful aphorism, "those who enjoy it are not very successful, and those who are successful are not very happy. . . . Those who enjoy exercising power shouldn't have it, and those who should exercise it are not likely to enjoy it." [31]

The collegial traditions of higher education suggest that presidential vacancies are filled by faculty who are selected by their colleagues, serve them in leadership roles for limited terms, and then return to their first love—teaching and research. While this may be more a fond fantasy than an established fact, it reflects the normative sense among many academics that, while college teaching may be a profession, high administrative office is only one of several temporary roles within it. The critical difference is between seeing the presidency as a profession and seeing it as a role. Incumbents who view the presidency as a profession are likely to see the maintenance of their position as a major objective. Such presidents "simplify their task by making only one calculation—calculating what is contributory to the welfare of the president, given the incentives to do so in the presence of job insecurity on the one hand and the impossibility of a precise definition of the institution's general welfare on the other." [32] In contrast, incumbents who see the presidency as a role can give primary attention to the needs of the institution rather than of themselves. This makes it possible for them to accept that, sometimes, the greatest service a president can perform is to leave office, because "the survival of the president is not the goal. The leader is temporary and, if necessary, expendable in service to the potential value of the institution." [33] Presidents who view their obligations as part of a role are able to enjoy the roller coaster of the presidency during its initial phases and then leave without regret. They are able to see themselves as an important but replaceable component in a large, cybernetic organization, and they are able to "cope by perceiving exit as a symbolic, political act of a pluralistic democratic organization, not as a threat to managerial competence." [34]

Some presidents never come to terms with the impossible nature of their jobs. Frustrated in their attempts to have the influence they desire, they may eventually find solace in cognitive distortions that lead them to see what they wish to see. Others may follow the route of the zealot, redoubling their efforts as they lose sight of their goals. One consequence of these behaviors is to create self-fulfilling prophesies: aggressive administrative action leads to resistance, which in turn becomes the justification for still more assertive presidential behavior. Other presidents make peace with their positions by bringing to it an understanding of the peculiar nature of their organizations and of their roles within them. Their goal is a peaceful balance of institutional interests within which they can make marginal improvements in a limited number of areas. They reconcile themselves to the possibility of future failure by acknowledging the role played by uncontrollable external sources, recognizing that some of what happens to them—both good and bad—may be a product of luck. Presidential roles may be as much a product of social attributions as a set of desirable behaviors. By creating a role that we declare will provide leadership to an organization, we construct the attribution that organizational effects are due to the leader's behavior. This allows us to simplify and make sense of complex organizational processes that would otherwise be impossible to comprehend.[35] It is perhaps as sensible to say that successful organizational events cause effective presidents as it is to say that effective presidents cause successful events.

One of the reasons that colleges and universities have been so successful is that, as their environments have become more complex, they have created decentralized, flexible, and only moderately interdependent structures, which have been effective in responding to environmental change. This may make coordination by the president exceptionally difficult, but the same forces that limit presidential authority may also make these organizations exceptionally adaptable and stable. The paradox of an institution that gives precedence to professional, rather than administrative, authority is that management weakness may be a significant source of organizational strength.

Calls for strengthening the presidency abound, but they are commonly grounded in a view of presidential power based more on hope than on experience. The report of a recent five-year study of academic leadership reached a conclusion about the importance of presidents that, if less heroic than the views of many, may be more realistic:

> Presidents may be important in some situations, but the performance of colleges may usually be less dependent upon presidential leadership than most of us care to believe. Most college presidents do the right things, and do things right most of the time. It is possible that college leaders can become marginally more effective. But those who seek major changes in the ways presidents behave, or believe that such changes will make major differences on our campuses, are likely to be disappointed. . . . Good presidents come to their positions with useful competencies, integrity, faith in their colleagues, and a firm belief that by listening carefully and working together they can all do well. In a turbulent and uncertain world, what happens after that is as much in the laps of the gods as in the hands of the president.[36]

NOTES

This chapter is a revised version of Robert Birnbaum, "Responsibility without Authority: The Impossible Job of the College President," in *Higher Education: Handbook of Theory and Research,* ed. John C. Smart, vol. 5 (New York: Agathon, 1989).

1. Thorstein Veblen, *The Higher Learning in America* (New York: Sagamore, 1957 [1918]).

2. Edwin E. Slosson, "Universities, American Endowed" in *Cyclopedia of Education,* ed. P. Monroe, vol. 5 (New York: Macmillan, 1913).

3. Christopher Jencks and David Riesman, *The Academic Revolution* (New York: Doubleday, 1968).

4. Homer P. Rainey, "How Shall We Control Our Universities? Why College Presidents Leave Their Jobs," *Journal of Higher Education* 31 (1960): 376–83.

5. Frederick F. Ness, *An Uncertain Glory* (San Francisco: Jossey-Bass, 1971).

6. Nicholas J. Demerath, Richard W. Stephens, and R. Robb Taylor, *Power, Presidents, and Professors* (New York: Basic Books, 1967).

7. Michael D. Cohen and James D. March, *Leadership and Ambiguity: The American College President* (New York: McGraw-Hill, 1974).

8. Henry Mintzberg, *The Nature of Managerial Work* (New York: Harper and Row, 1973).

9. American Association of University Professors, "Joint Statement on Government of Colleges and Universities," in *Policy Documents and Reports* (Washington, D.C.: AAUP, 1984 [1966]).

10. Carnegie Commission, *The Purposes and Performance of Higher Education in the United States* (New York: McGraw-Hill, 1973).

11. Commission on Strengthening Presidential Leadership, *Presidents Make a Difference: Strengthening Leadership in Colleges and Universities* (Washington, D. C.: Association of Governing Boards of Colleges and Universities, 1984).

12. John J. Corson, *Governance of Colleges and Universities* (New York: McGraw-Hill, 1960), 43.

13. Peter M. Blau, *The Organization of Academic Work* (New York: Wiley, 1973).

14. J. Victor Baldridge, David V. Curtis, George P. Ecker, and Gary L. Riley, *Policy Making and Effective Leadership: A National Study of Academic Management* (San Francisco: Jossey-Bass, 1978); Robert Birnbaum, *How Colleges Work: Patterns of Organization, Management, and Leadership in Higher Education* (San Francisco: Jossey-Bass, 1988).

15. Cohen and March, *Leadership and Ambiguity.*

16. Michael D. Cohen, James D. March, and Johan P. Olsen, "Garbage Can Model of Organizational Choice," *Administrative Science Quarterly* 17 (1972): 1–25.

17. Karl E. Weick, *The Social Psychology of Organizing* (Reading, Mass.: Addison-Wesley, 1979).

18. See Kim S. Cameron, "The Effectiveness of Ineffectiveness," in *Research in Organizational Behavior,* ed. Barry M. Staw and L. L. Cummings, vol. 6 (Greenwich, Conn.: JAI, 1984); Kim S. Cameron and David A. Whetten, *Organizational Effectiveness* (New York: Academic, 1983); Kim S. Cameron,

"Measuring Organizational Effectiveness in Institutions of Higher Education," *Administrative Science Quarterly* 23 (1978): 604–32.

19. Ness, *Uncertain Glory,* 8.

20. Robert Birnbaum, *How Academic Leadership Works: Understanding Success and Failure in the College Presidency* (San Francisco, Jossey-Bass, 1992), 166.

21. Cohen and March, *Leadership and Ambiguity,* 2.

22. Commission on Strengthening Presidential Leadership, *Presidents Make a Difference,* xii.

23. Ibid.

24. Support for these strategies can be found in the several reports of the Institutional Leadership Project, a five-year longitudinal study of presidential, administrative, faculty, and trustee leaders at thirty-two colleges and universities. A list of these reports can be found in Birnbaum, *How Academic Leadership Works,* 231–35.

25. Birnbaum, *How Colleges Work.*

26. Ellen E. Chaffee, "Successful Strategic Management in Small Private Colleges," *Journal of Higher Education* 55 (1984): 212–41.

27. Robert Birnbaum, "Leadership and Learning: The College President as Intuitive Scientist," *Review of Higher Education* 9 (1986): 381–95.

28. Birnbaum, *How Academic Leadership Works.*

29. James R. Meindl, Sanford B. Ehrlich, and Janet M. Dukerich, "The Romance of Leadership," *Administrative Science Quarterly* 30 (1985): 78–102.

30. Jeffrey Pfeffer, "The Ambiguity of Leadership," *Academy of Management Review* 2 (1977): 104–19.

31. Harold W. Stoke, *The American College President* (New York: Harper and Row, 1959).

32. Clark Kerr, and Marian L. Gade, *The Many Lives of the Academic President* (Washington, D.C.: Association of Governing Boards of Universities and Colleges, 1986).

33. Joseph F. Kauffman, *At the Pleasure of the Board* (Washington, D.C.: American Council on Education, 1980), 14.

34. Donald E. Walker, "Goodbye, Mr. President, and Good Luck!" *Educational Record* (Winter 1977): 57.

35. Pfeffer, *Ambiguity of Leadership;* Meindl, Ehrlich, and Dukerich, *Romance of Leadership.*

36. Birnbaum, *How Academic Leadership Works,* 196.

Part Four

Central Issues for the Twenty-first Century

Chapter Thirteen

Financing Higher Education
Who Should Pay?

D. Bruce Johnstone

The funding of higher education is a large and complex topic. It is complex in part because of its multiple sources of revenue and its multiple outputs, or products, which are only loosely connected to these different revenue sources. Furthermore, these revenue and expenditure patterns vary significantly by type of institution (university, four-year college, two-year college), mode of governance (public or private), and state. Within the private sector, expenditure levels as well as patterns of pricing and price discounting vary greatly according to institutional wealth and the depth, demographics, and family affluence of the applicant pool. In the public sector, these patterns also vary according to state funding levels, tuition policies, and enrollment limits set by state governments or public multicampus governing boards.

The topic is large because finance underlies much of the three overarching themes of contemporary higher education policy: *quality,* and the relationship between funding and quality in any of its several dimensions; *access,* or the search for social equity in who benefits from, and who pays for, higher education; and *efficiency,* or the search for a cost-effective relationship between revenues (particularly those that come from students, parents, and taxpayers) and outputs (whether measured in enrollments, graduates, student learning, or the scholarly activity of the faculty).

Within these broad themes lie public and institutional policy ques-

tions that are informed, if not answered, by economic and financial
perspectives. How, if at all, can costs—especially to the taxpayer and
the student—be lowered without damage to academic quality or to
principles of access and participation? What are appropriate ratios
of students to faculty and to professional and administrative staff
at various kinds of institutions? What are reasonable conceptions
and expectations of higher educational productivity? How can institutional aid, or price discounting, be used to maximize net tuition revenue in the private sector? Are taxpayer dollars in the public sector
best used to hold down tuition, or should they go toward expanding
need-based aid, with public tuitions raised closer to the full average
costs of undergraduate instruction? Are public aid dollars best used
for grants and loan subsidies? What of public aid based on academic
promise and performance rather than family need? And what is the
appropriate response by institutions and governments to the pervasive condition of austerity in higher education, whether brought on by
declining enrollments, declining state assistance, or runaway costs?[1]

Although this chapter concentrates on American higher education,
the financial principles and problems are much the same worldwide.[2]
Our understanding of the particular financial conditions and problems of American higher education can be sharpened by noting what
is peculiar to the financing of the American university: the sheer size,
and consequent accessibility, or what the Europeans call "massifica-
tion"; the large private sector, which includes the most and the least
prestigious institutions; and the great reliance on nongovernmental
revenue—mainly tuition but also private gifts and return on endowments.

Who pays and who should pay? Students and parents? Taxpayers?
Philanthropists? How much higher education? At what cost or level of
efficiency? These questions can be adequately addressed only within
the broader context of American society in the late 1990s.

The Economic, Social, and Political Context

Higher education is recognized both as an engine of economic growth
and as a gatekeeper to individual positions of high remuneration and
status. Advanced education—particularly in high technology, information processing, and sophisticated management and analysis—is
thought to be essential to maintaining America's economic position

in the increasingly competitive global economy. It follows that most jobs of high remuneration and status will require an advanced degree, probably beyond the baccalaureate, and it further follows that the lack of postsecondary education creates a likelihood of marginal income and status. These propositions, however, do not mean that advanced education necessarily makes individuals more productive or that all recipients of advanced education will find remunerative, high-status employment. Higher education can make individuals more productive; but it can also simply screen, or select, for the kinds of intellectual, social, and personal characteristics required for the high-remuneration, high-status jobs that may be available. In short, higher education is essential for most good jobs, and the absence of education beyond high school will be an increasingly formidable barrier to obtaining them; but the mere possession of an advanced degree will guarantee neither good, nor lasting, employment.

American society is being increasingly polarized by class, race, and ethnicity. More and more children grow up in poverty, both rural and urban. The dilemma presented by higher education's gatekeeper function is that access to, and especially success in, college and university remains highly correlated with socioeconomic class. This correlation has not significantly diminished in recent years, even though American higher education is more accessible than the higher education systems of other countries. Thus, with the increasing polarization of income in the 1980s and 1990s, and with the increasing relationship of economic success in life to success in college, there is reason to be alarmed at the degree to which our colleges and universities perpetuate, and even accelerate, the intergenerational transmission of wealth and status.

As to the political context, American society, or at least a voting electorate, is becoming increasingly conservative. Key elements of this conservatism include resistance to the notion of a benign government, to social welfare programs, and to transfer payments from the rich to the poor. Insofar as there is to be a public agenda for education, it is to be advanced through private, or at least market-oriented, mechanisms: charter schools and vouchers for education reform and tuition tax credits and portable need-based aid to increase accessibility to higher education. A third element of this resurgent conservatism is increasing concern over crime and moral laxity, coupled with a diminishing inclination to view social deprivation or racism as an acceptable excuse for "deviant" (i.e., non-middle-class) behavior.

These themes are intertwined, of course. For example, the political inclination to seek private solutions to what used to be viewed as public problems is given impetus by declining public revenues—which, in turn, is a function, at least in part, of the globalization of the economy and the increasing propensity of wealthy individuals to flee to low-tax havens and to move their enterprises to low-wage economies. There are also internal inconsistencies among these themes: for example, increasing dissatisfaction with governmental intrusion contradicts not only the demand for more costly and intrusive accountability but also direct political intervention into matters of curriculum and programs. But these economic, social, and political themes, for all their complexity, provide a context for consideration of the three broad issues of higher education finance:

— *The size of the nation's higher educational enterprise.* How much publicly supported higher education does the nation need, or will it choose to afford, measured either in total expenditures or as a percentage of the nation's gross domestic product?
— *The efficiency and productivity of this enterprise.* What should higher education (particularly public) cost per unit, whether the unit is students enrolled, degrees granted, scholarship produced, service rendered, or combinations thereof?
— *The sources of revenue to support this enterprise.* Who pays for the costs of higher education? Students and parents? Government and taxpayers? Philanthropists?

Size of the Enterprise

The American higher education enterprise is enormous, even when controlling for our great wealth and population. For example:

— Total current-fund expenditures for all institutions of higher education in 1993/94 were $173,350,617,000, of which total education and general expenditures (that is, excluding institutionally provided room and board, other auxiliary enterprises, university hospitals, Pell grants, and certain other expenditures) were $136,024,350,000.[3]
— The total expenditure on higher education, including all institutional current-fund expenditures plus additions to plant value,

or about $200 billion, is about 3 percent of the nation's gross national product.[4] Among the seven highly industrialized countries, the United States is second only to Canada in higher education expenditure as a percentage of gross domestic product, spending more than France, Germany, Italy, Japan, or the United Kingdom.[5] (Per student expenditures, however, are less than those of most other affluent nations.)

— A total of 14,305,658 students, full- and part-time, were enrolled in the fall of 1993.[6] These students included 62 percent of all high school graduates from the immediately preceding year. Thirty-one percent of all young people aged twenty-two to twenty-four and 60 percent of all young people aged eighteen to nineteen were in some postsecondary institution in 1994. Finally, 22 percent of all persons over the age of twenty-five claimed in 1994 to have completed at least four years of college.[7]

— These students were enrolled in 3,688 colleges and universities, including 1,641 public and 2,047 private institutions, enrolling 11,184,080 and 3,116,570 students, respectively. In addition, some 1,027,713 students were enrolled in 6,737 noncollegiate postsecondary (mainly short-term vocational) institutions, more than 5,000 of them proprietary.[8]

By these and other measures, it is clear that America has chosen to support a large, accessible (both in cost and in admission standards), and highly diverse system (some would say a "nonsystem") of higher education. These "choices" are made in the form of literally millions of decisions by parents and students to pay the costs of college, thereby giving expression to the value they place on higher education for themselves or for their children, and by even more citizens and elected officials, mainly at the state level, who spend tax funds to maintain public colleges and universities, to provide assistance, mostly via student aid, to private colleges and universities, and finally, to support an academic research enterprise that is far and away the largest and most productive in the world.

As the nation approaches the millennium, four forces will expand this already large enterprise. The first is an expansion of the eighteen-to-twenty-four-year-old age cohort. Between 1996 and the year 2006, this traditional college-going age cohort will increase by about 16 percent. The middle-age cohort will continue to decline as the low birth rates of the 1960s and 1970s work their way through, resulting in a possible decline in nontraditional enrollments. Projections of enrollment growth between 1996 and 2006 by the National Center for Education Statistics range from a high of 27 percent to a low of 4 percent, with a middle estimate of 14 percent, or a projected enrollment growth for the decade of just under 2 million students.[9] This growth will occur unevenly, concentrated mainly in the high-growth states of the West, Southwest, and South. Probably nowhere is there such anxiety over a state's ability to accommodate a projected explosion of student enrollments as in California, where experts are forecasting "tidal wave II," during which the colleges and universities of California may need to accommodate at least 450,000 additional students over the next decade, at a projected additional cost in 1995/96 dollars of $5.2 billion annually—if California is to maintain its historic accessibility to publicly supported higher education.[10]

A second force for more higher education is an expansion of participation and completion due to a perception of higher private rates of return and the perceived need for at least some higher education for positions of remuneration and status. If efforts to reduce the current high attrition rates in U.S. colleges prove successful, there will be a significant increase in enrollment even without any expansion of first-time participation.

A third force, related to the above, is the accretion of degree level sought by the average student. This phenomenon is probably a function of the increasing amount and complexity of knowledge, the increasing educational demands of the productive economy (whether for actual skills, or simply for higher education's screening function), and the tendency of most professions to enhance their status by requiring ever more education prior to entry and perhaps more continuing education to maintain current licensure.

A fourth force, identified more through conjecture than hard evidence, is the incentive for enhancement that seems to be built into the traditions of the academy. William Massy and Robert Zemsky identify this force as "the ratchet." [11] It manifests in a perpetual dissatisfaction on the part of professors, staff, and administrators with the status quo and in a determination to do more and better: to teach new materials, to advise students more effectively, to perform more sophisticated (and usually more costly) research, and generally to advance in the highly competitive pecking order of individual and institutional scholarly prestige, without regard to whether more and better is either cost-effective or demanded by those who must pay the bills.

The Efficiency and Productivity of the Enterprise

Another issue within the financing of higher education is the efficiency with which all of these resources are employed in the higher educational enterprise and their productivity. Productivity and efficiency look at both costs, or expenditures, and at benefits, or outputs. These concepts deal with costs *per:* whether per student (which, of course, is not really an output but which has the advantage of being easily and unambiguously measured), or per unit of research, or per unit of learning (however measured), or per learning added by the institution. Because the real outputs of the university (the discovery, transmission, and promulgation of knowledge) are both multiple and difficult to measure, and because revenue, at least for the support of instructional expenditures, follows student enrollment in both the public and the private sectors, the cost per student inevitably and overwhelmingly dominates approaches to questions of productivity and efficiency. But we ought never to forget that enrollment, however measured—and however sensitive to fields of study, levels of education, or methods of instruction—is still merely a proxy for the hard-to-measure real output, which is student learning.

Variation in Unit Costs

In the production of goods, there are usually multiple ways of combining productive inputs—mainly different combinations of labor, capital, materials, and managerial effectiveness—to produce a unit of output. The most efficient combination of inputs is determined by the alternative manufacturing technologies and the relative costs of the inputs. Given a set of input costs and a set of technologies for combining inputs into desired outputs, there is an unambiguous most efficient way: that is, a lowest cost per unit. The efficiency, then, of any alternative producer or production process can be measured by how that producer or that process compares to that most efficient way.

Higher education is not as fortunate as these goods-producing enterprises. The technology of university production (of learning and scholarship) is unclear and highly idiosyncratic to the institution, the department, and the individual professor. We do know that per student costs vary greatly. Thus, higher education is generally assumed to be more costly at research universities than at undergraduate colleges due to the higher salaries, lower teaching loads, and more extensive academic support (e.g., libraries and computer facilities) accorded the faculty of the research university. However, the direct instructional costs (especially at the margin) of at least freshmen and sophomores at a typical public research university can be rather low due to the prevalence of low-cost teaching assistants and very large lecture courses—in contrast to the typical public four-year college, where most instruction is carried out by regular faculty in moderate-sized classes, albeit with heavier average teaching loads. In the end, it is probably appropriate to claim that per student costs at a research university are higher than at a four-year college; but it must not be forgotten that this is so at least partly because of certain assumptions and cost allocations that, while reasonable, are nonetheless judgmental and sometimes questionable.

Among like institutions, most interinstitutional variation in per student costs can be attributed to differences either in the amenities provided to the students (recreational and cultural facilities, for example, or academic and student services support staff) or in the costs of faculty. Differential faculty costs, in turn, reflect differences not only in salary (which are low for part-time faculty, who provide much of the teaching at low-cost colleges, and high for the full-time senior professoriate at prestigious private colleges) but also in that other major faculty expense, time (which translates into light teaching loads at wealthy colleges and heavy teaching loads at low-cost "access" colleges).

Howard Bowen, in his classic 1980 study of higher education costs, found great variation in costs among seemingly similar institutions with seemingly similar outcomes.[12] Among a sample of research and doctoral-granting universities arranged from lowest to highest in per student expenditures, the average university in the third quartile spent twice as much per student as the average in the second quartile, and the highest-spending university in the sample spent almost seven and one-half times as much as the first quartile average. Variation among colleges was less, but the colleges in the third quartile of per student costs still spent about 50 percent more than the colleges in the second quartile. More recent data on current-fund expenditures on instruction shows per student spending of $7,573 at universities, $4,788 at "other four-year," and $2,727 at two-year colleges.[13]

This great spread in unit costs is seen by some as profligacy on the part of the highest-cost institutions. Bowen accounts for such variation with his revenue theory of costs, which states that institutions raise all the money they can (which, in the case of highly endowed institutions with wealthy alumni that continue to attract children of affluent families, is a very large amount indeed), and spend all that they raise, purposefully and honorably, even though the amounts spent do not emerge from any discernible production function, as such, as in the industrial manufacture of goods.[14]

But even if the "cost" we use to calculate the cost per student at Harvard were to mean the same thing as the "cost" in per student costs at, say, neighboring Wheelock College or at UMass, Boston, we still cannot say unambiguously that Wheelock and UMass, Boston, are more efficient or more productive than Harvard. They may be cheaper per student, to be sure, but whether they are more efficient requires a measure of output that we do not have and that we probably could not agree upon. And if Harvard were to contest its possible characterization as "inefficient" or "unproductive," it would point to the extraordinary knowledge and competence of its graduates, or to the lifetime of added benefits that Harvard presumably helped to produce, or the value to the society (uncaptured by private lifetime income streams) that Harvard "created".

In short, without better agreement on the proper outputs of higher education, not to mention how to weigh and how to measure them, we are left with cost per full-time equivalent student, as best as we can measure it, as an index of productivity—and as something that should presumably get lower (or cheaper) in response to the demands of students, parents, and taxpayers that higher education become less costly.

Inflation in Unit Costs

Actually, the problem of unit costs and efficiency (or inefficiency) in higher education is less a function of unit costs, per se, and more a function of the seemingly inexorable increase of such costs and of the resulting tuition increases at rates considerably in excess of the rate of inflation. This is the "cost disease" described by William Baumol as characteristic of the so-called productivity-immune sectors of the economy, which are generally labor-intensive, with few opportunities for substitution of capital or new production technologies for labor (live theater, symphony orchestras, social welfare agencies, and education).[15] Unit costs in such enterprises track their increases in compensation. Because workers in such enterprises (e.g., faculty) typically get the same wage and salary increases as those in the productivity-sensitive, goods-producing sectors of the economy, in which constant infusions of capital and technology produce real productivity gains and allow unit cost increases to be less than compensation increases, the unit costs in productivity-immune sectors will inevitably exceed those in goods-producing sectors. Thus, unit-cost increases in higher education will be "above average." And since the rate of inflation is nothing more than a weighted average of many price increases, it is inevitable that unit costs—and thus tuitions—in higher education will rise in normal years faster than the rate of inflation.

This is the normal, or default, condition in higher education: unit costs increase slightly in excess of the prevailing rate of inflation and tuition increases even more, substantially exceeding the prevailing rate of inflation, resulting in the following:

—State governments shift the cost burden from taxpayers to students and families through very high percentage tuition increases in the public sector.
—Private colleges put more of their marginal tuition dollar back into student aid, thus requiring even larger tuition increases to keep up with rising costs.
—Faculty compensation increases exceed compensation increases generally prevailing in the economy.
—Higher education becomes "input rich" in the form, say, of more technology per student, higher faculty and staff to student ratios, or more costly physical plant per student.

All of these factors have been at work for the past decade or more, resulting in very substantial tuition increases in both the private and the public sectors. From 1975 to 1995, tuitions rose at private universities by 105 percent, at private colleges by 108 percent, at public universities by 115 percent, and at public two-year colleges by 228 percent (table 13.1).[16] The very high rates of tuition increase in the priciest private colleges are the result of an enrichment of the amenities, a lowering of faculty/student and staff/student ratios, and the increase in institutionally provided financial aid (i.e., a lowering of the net revenue yield from a dollar of tuition increase). Rising tuitions in the public sector is overwhelmingly caused by the withdrawal of state tax revenue and a shift in relative cost burden from the taxpayer to students and parents.

Table 13.1
Annual Tuition, Private and Public Colleges, 1974/75–1994/95 ($)

Year	Private Institutions		Public Institutions	
	University	College	University	Two-Year
1974/75	2,614	1,954	599	277
1979/80	3,811	3,020	840	355
1984/85	6,843	5,135	1,386	584
1989/90	10,348	7,778	2,035	756
1994/95	14,510	10,698	2,982	1,914
% increase 1990–95	40	86	47	153
% increase 1985–95	24	108	115	228

Source: National Center for Education Statistics, *Digest of Education Statistics, 1995* (Washington, D.C.: U.S. Department of Education, 1995), table 306.

Diverging Trajectories of Costs and Revenues

The natural trajectory of unit costs in higher education, as described above, is steeply upward, at rates in excess of prevailing rates of inflation. The corresponding rate of increase of anticipated revenues is substantially flatter, being dampened by the following:

— Price resistance from upper-middle-class parents, apparently less willing to accept tuition increases that are considerably in excess of inflation and that take increasing portions of family income.[17]
— Price resistance from older students and from graduate and advanced professional students facing mounting debt loads.[18]
— Decreasing support from governors and state legislatures faced with other compelling public needs, decreasing federal financial assistance, and restive or angry state taxpayers.
— Increasing costs of "big science" without concomitant increases in federal research support.
— Decreasing support for academic health centers, caught between cost-cutting insurers and low-cost alternative providers.

The resulting scenario is frightening, especially for high-cost research universities and for public colleges and universities that face declining state tax revenues and increasing enrollment without the benefit of substantial endowments, wealthy alumni, internationally eminent scientists, or deep and affluent applicant pools. Some institutions have turned their fortunes around through vigorous cost cutting, restructuring, and moving into a narrow market niche, but the late 1990s will be a period of great uncertainty and continuing financial stress for most colleges and universities.[19]

Sources of Revenue for the Enterprise

The financing of higher education poses the question of how the costs should be apportioned among four parties: parents, students, taxpayers, and philanthropists.[20] Parents would finance their children's education from current income, savings, or future income via increased indebtedness. Students would finance their own education from savings, summer earnings, term-time earnings, and future earnings via loans or graduate tax obligations. Taxpayers at the federal, state, and local levels would finance students' education through taxes on income, sales, property, assets, business or manufacturing taxes (via the higher prices of the goods or services so taxed) or through the indirect "tax" of inflation brought about by public deficit spending. And philanthropists would finance students' education either through endowments or current giving.

The sharing and shifting of the costs among these parties is a zero-sum game, in which a lessening of the burden upon, or revenue from, one party must be compensated either by a reduction of underlying costs or by a shift of the burden to another party. Thus, if state taxpayers' share of higher education costs is to be lessened, that reduced share must either lead to reduced institutional costs or be shifted, probably to students and parents via higher tuition. But if parents cannot pay or have enough political power to limit, by statute or regulation, a higher parental contribution (as happened when voter pressure forced Congress to eliminate home equity from the assets considered in determining "need" for awarding federal Pell grants), the burden would shift to students, principally through higher debt loads. This scenario—lower taxpayer contributions, reduced institutional budgets, higher tuitions, level parental contributions, and much higher debt burdens—is exactly what has happened in the last decade or two.

The policy questions sharpened by the cost-sharing perspective are as follows:

—What is the appropriate amount that should be expected from parents to cover the higher educational costs of their children? Is this

share to be a function only of current income, to be met by family
belt tightening? Or are parents also expected to have saved from
the past or to borrow against the future? Are assets to be figured
in the calculation of need? How long should parental financial responsibility continue: through undergraduate years only, or until
the age of, say, twenty-four or twenty-five? And what is the expected contribution from a noncustodial parent?

—With regard to student share, are there any limits to the hours of
term-time work compatible with full-time study? Are there any
limits to the amount of indebtedness that students should be allowed to incur in pursuit of their education? Should this limit
be a function of likely completion of studies or of the anticipated
earning power of the intended occupation or profession? Would
this deferred payment obligation be best handled via a conventional mortgage-type loan, an income-contingent obligation, or a
graduate tax obligation (assuming that the present value of the
repayment stream under all options would yield the same repayments, at least over a cohort of borrowers)?

—Should public (taxpayer) financial support be linked to governmental ownership and ultimate control, as in the support of public
higher education? Or should taxpayers support certain costs di-
vorced from control, such as vouchers (e.g., Pell grants), which
support both public and private—and even proprietary—sectors
of higher education? Should taxpayer support per student continue to be a function mainly of family income and sector costs
(e.g., public research universities as opposed to public community
colleges)? Or should the government, through the financial aid
system, differentiate among students by their academic potential
or attempt to influence their choice of academic field or intended
occupation?

There has been a considerable increase in education costs borne by
students and parents, mainly through higher tuitions, especially in
the 1980s for private institutions and in the 1990s for public institutions (table 13.1). However, before drawing conclusions about either
the relative shares borne by students, parents, and taxpayers or the
impact of these increasing costs, we need to adjust for the impact of
inflation, for increases in family incomes, and for the effects of financial assistance. Table 13.2 shows the cost of higher education in the
percentage it took (after financial aid) of family incomes at selected
levels.

Table 13.2
Tuition, Room, and Board as Percentage of Family Income, by Income Percentile,
Public and Private Colleges, 1979–1994 (constant 1975 $)

	Public Institutions			Private Institutions		
Year	25th Percentile	50th Percentile	75th Percentile	25th Percentile	50th Percentile	75th Percentile
1979	15.1	9.1	6.3	34.3	20.7	14.4
1984	20.5	11.7	7.7	49.3	28.1	18.5
1989	21.4	12.0	7.9	57.1	32.1	21.2
1994	26.2	14.2	9.1	71.3	38.7	24.8
% increase 1979–94	74	56	44	108	87	72

Source: National Center for Education Statistics, *The Condition of Education, 1996* (Washington, D.C.: U.S. Office of Education, 1996), 62.

Tables 13.3 and 13.4 show how the expenses of private and public institutions, both high cost and low cost, are met through combinations of family contributions, federal and state aid, loans, and institutional (philanthropic) grants for high-, middle-, and low-income families.

Some observations from tables 13.3 and 13.4:

—The costs of college borne by the student and parent are high but are very high only for relatively affluent families at high-cost private institutions.
—Meeting the high costs at expensive private colleges and universities without substantial parental contributions requires both very high institutional, or philanthropic, support as well as very substantial student indebtedness.
—The key to financial accessibility lies less in level of tuition, or even in expected parental contribution, than in students' willingness to incur substantial indebtedness. Total student debt for four or more years of undergraduate education, plus three or more years of graduate or advanced professional school, can easily reach $50,000 to $100,000 or more, presenting the student with a repayment obligation that can either discourage advanced higher education altogether or distort career and other life choices.
—High-cost public institutions (high tuition plus residency) require substantial indebtedness, considerably diminishing the price advantage over high-cost private institutions.

Table 13.3

Student Budgets at Private Institutions, Sources of Support, by Family Income ($)

Source of Support	High Cost Institution			Low-Cost Institution		
	Low-Income Family	Middle-Income Family	High-Income Family	Low-Income Family	Middle-Income Family	High-Income Family
Parental contribution	0	3,000	25,500	0	2,000	16,500
Federal grants	4,000	0	0	4,000	0	0
State grants[a]	3,000	1,500	0	3,000	1,500	0
Institutional grants	13,500	16,000	0	4,000	6,500	0
Student summer savings	1,500	1,500	1,500	1,500	1,500	1,500
Student term-time earnings	2,000	2,000	0	2,500	2,500	0
Student loans	5,000	5,000	2,000	3,000	4,000	0
Total from taxpayer[b]	8,365	2,865	546	7,819	2,592	0
Total from parents[c]	0	3,000	25,500	0	2,000	16,500
Total from student[d]	7,135	7,135	2,954	6,181	6,908	1,500
Total from philanthropists[e]	13,500	16,000	0	4,000	6,500	0

Note: Low income, $12,000; middle income, $38,752; high income $100,000. Most high-cost private colleges use the College Scholarship Service or a similar system, which yields a higher family contribution. Many systems use the concept *family contribution*, which includes the summer savings assumption.

a. State need-based grant assumes approximately 75% of New York State Tuition Assistance Program (the most generous in the nation).

b. Total from taxpayer is sum of federal and state grants plus the present value of loan subsidies.

c. Total from parents is the expected family contribution minus assumed summer savings from the student.

d. Total from student is the sum of term-time earnings, summer savings, and the present discounted value of expected loan repayments.

e. Total from philanthropists represent all institutional grants.

From time to time, a proposal is made that direct public funding of state colleges and universities, at least for the support of instruction, be drastically reduced or eliminated altogether, with tuitions raised to full or near full cost, eliminating or greatly reducing what the proponents of this view call the "subsidy" to the students and families of students attending public colleges and universities. In place of direct state revenue, which currently supports from 60 to 90 percent of public four-year undergraduate instructional costs, proponents of the high-tuition, high-aid model would substitute a much expanded program of need-based grants, which would diminish as parental or student incomes rose. The grants would phase out entirely for fami-

Table 13.4
Student Budgets at Public Institutions, Sources of Support, by Family
Income ($)

Source of Support	High-Cost Institution ($12,000)			Low-Cost Institution ($6,000)		
	Low-Income Family	Middle-Income Family	High-Income Family	Low-Income Family	Middle-Income Family	High-Income Family
Parental contribution	0	2,500	8,500	0	2,000	4,000
Federal grants	3,000	0	0	2,340	0	0
State grants	2,000	750	0	1,160	250	0
Institutional grants	0	0	0	0	0	0
Student summer savings	1,500	1,500	750	500	1,500	1,000
Student term-time earnings	2,000	2,500	750	1,000	1,250	1,000
Student loans	3,500	4,750	2,000	1,000	1,000	0
Total from taxpayer	5,955	2,050	545	3,775	525	0
Total from parents	0	2,500	8,500	0	2,000	4,000
Total from student	6,045	7,450	2,955	2,225	3,475	2,000
Total from philanthropists	0	0	0	0	0	0

Note: See table 13.3.

lies and students whose income was deemed sufficient to pay the full cost of tuition in addition to other expenses.[21]

The high-tuition, high-aid model is based on claims of efficiency and equity. The efficiency claim begins with the tenet of public finance theory that any public subsidy of a good or a service that consumers are likely to purchase anyway, in the absence or diminution of the subsidy, is an inefficient use of public tax dollars. The tax dollars released, if public sector tuitions were allowed to rise, would supposedly go toward public needs of greater priority: more need-based student aid, health care, public infrastructure, tax cuts, or public deficit reduction. And if the demand for public higher education should decline as a result of lower subsidies and higher prices, this too might be a move in the direction of a more efficient use of the nation's resources. Subsidies can generate overproduction of a good or service, and a higher priced public higher education might discourage ambivalent, ill-prepared students whom advocates of high tuition and high aid assume are taking up space and wasting precious resources in our public colleges and universities.

A corollary of the efficiency claim is that there exists, at least in some states, underutilized capacity in the private higher education sector that could be filled at relatively low marginal cost. A shift of tax dollars from the direct support of public colleges and universities to need-based student aid, portable to the private sector, would presumably shift enrollments there and enable the socially optimal level of enrollments to be supported more in the private sector but at a lower additional net cost to the taxpayer.

The equity argument in favor of high tuition, high aid is based on two assumptions: first, that public higher education is actually partaken of disproportionately by students from upper-middle-income and affluent families; and second, that the state taxes used to support public higher education tend to be proportionate or even regressive and thus are paid by many lower-middle-income and poor families, who are unlikely to benefit. Thus, the high-tuition, high-aid model of public higher education finance is claimed to be more equitable than across-the-board low tuition because it targets all public subsidy only on the needy and imposes full costs on students or families affluent enough to pay.

The case against the high-tuition, high-aid model rests partly on the oversimplification and political naïveté of the case made on its behalf, summarized above, and partly on the case to be made for the very existence of a public higher education sector. The case against high tuition, high aid may be summarized by four points.

First, a "sticker price" of $15,000 to $18,000 for a full-time year at a public college or university would almost certainly discourage many from aspiring to higher education, even with the prospect of financial aid or a lower tuition for those in need.[22] The total costs to students and parents of a year of full-time study at a public four-year college or university, as shown in table 13.3, make even public higher education today a relatively heavy financial burden for most families and for nearly all independent students. This fact alone does not fully negate the more theoretical arguments of efficiency and equity presented on behalf of full-cost or near-full-cost pricing for public higher education, as summarized above. But even with financial aid, costs at a public college might seem daunting to many students and their parents, especially to students from disadvantaged and nonwhite families.

Second, a high-tuition, high-aid policy would lessen the quality of public colleges and universities. The purpose of high-tuition, high-aid plans is to reduce state tax revenues currently going to public colleges and universities, even though some proponents claim that this revenue loss would be made up by increased revenue from the much higher tuitions paid by the more well-to-do. Private sector proponents of high tuition, high aid, however, make no secret of their aim to shift enrollments and tuition dollars of middle- and upper-middle-income students (or at least the most attractive and able ones) from the public sector to the private sector. With little or no price advantage left in the public sector; with the resource advantage of large endowments, wealthy alumni, and the tradition of philanthropic support in the private sector; with the patina of elitism and selectivity associated with private colleges and universities (especially in the Northeast); and with greater constraints and burdens remaining on the public sector, many of the nation's 1,600 public colleges and universities would become places for students whom the private colleges, now priced the same as public colleges, do not accept. Such an erosion in the relative status and quality of public colleges and universities does not seem to be in the nation's public interest.

Third, high tuition does not guarantee high aid. Governors, legislators, and voters, continually pressed by public needs exceeding available resources, are likely to support that part of the public sector in which they perceive that they or their children have a stake. They are much less likely to maintain the financial aid, or "tuition discount," portion of the public higher educational budget when it is devoted almost exclusively to the poor. The not unlikely consequences of a policy of high tuition, high aid, rather than the purported enhancements of efficiency and equity, are higher tuition, lower taxes, inadequate aid, diminished access, and deteriorating public colleges and universities.

Fourth and fundamentally, the high-tuition, high-aid model is a denial of the appropriateness of higher education as a public good. The nation's public colleges and universities have been built and supported over the last century and a half not merely to provide a subsidized education to those who might not otherwise have an opportunity for higher education. Rather, voters and elected officials wanted public colleges and universities that would attract and hold the best and brightest students and scholars, serve society, aid the economy, and be a signal of the state's culture. The high-tuition, high-aid model essentially denies most of these public purposes to public higher education and substitutes only a public subsidy for those who are too poor to afford what would become an otherwise unsubsidized, expensive, and essentially privatized product. States need to consider whether these continue to be important reasons for supporting public higher education or whether they mainly want to get needy students into some college, in which case high tuition, high aid is almost certainly, as public finance theory correctly states, less expensive to the taxpayer.

Summary and Conclusions

The financial fortunes of American colleges and universities vary greatly by institution. Those relatively few private institutions with large endowments, traditions of generous alumni giving, and deep and affluent student applicant pools will experience continuing cost pressures but will be able to increase revenues commensurably and continue to prosper. Some public institutions similarly situated with deep and affluent applicant pools, with established traditions of philanthropic support, and with research strengths in areas of continuing public investment (e.g., biomedical and applied sciences) will prosper. Some less-well-endowed private institutions will seize a specialized market niche, either vocational (e.g., health-related professions) or cultural/ideological (e.g., conservative Christian) and, with good management and low faculty costs, will also prosper. Most private colleges and universities, however, will feel a fierce revenue squeeze, primarily driven by the lack of growth in the number of upper-middle-class parents able or willing to pay the high tuitions and in the number of students willing to take on increasing levels of indebtedness. And most public colleges and universities will continue to experience flat or declining state tax support, forcing even higher tuition, more program closures, and an increasing reliance on part-time and adjunct faculty.

As more and more colleges and universities exhaust the available cost-side measures for increasing productivity, interest is turning to increasing productivity by enhancing higher education's output, or learning.[23] Expressed another way, the major remaining productivity problem in higher education may not lie in excessive costs but in insufficient learning—a function of such features as redundant learning; aimless academic exploration; the unavailability of courses at the right time; excessive nonlearning time in the academic day, week, and year; insufficient use of self-paced learning; and insufficient realization of the potential of collegiate-level learning during the high school years. Enhancing the productivity of learning, then, would reduce vacation time and other time spent in other-than-learning activities; provide better advising and other incentives to lessen aimless curricular exploration; enhance opportunities for self-paced learning, perhaps through the aid of instructional technology; minimize curricular redundancy; and maximize the potential of college-level learning during the high school years.

Technology in the form of personal computers, new instructional software, the internet, and instructional videocassettes, will profoundly affect the way faculty and advanced students conduct research, and it will enrich some teaching. However—aside from some pockets of distance learning and users of a virtual university, generally limited to nontraditional and technologically inclined students—technology will mainly enable more and better, not cheaper, learning.

The shift in burden from parents and taxpayers to students, paid for with more part-time (and even more full-time) work and much more debt, will continue, but there is reason to believe that the long-expected price resistance is happening. Marketing will become even more frenzied, and so will governmental efforts to "solve the problem" without spending any taxpayer revenue: tuition prepayment, tax-exempt savings plans, non-need-based price discounting, income-contingent repayment plans, and the like.

State higher education budgets will be smaller, but this reduction will be accompanied by greater flexibility and performance criteria, such as premiums to institutions that improve retention and completion rates. Most institutions have been shaping their missions for years to adjust to more low-income, minority, older, part-time, and place-bound students; greater applied and vocational interest among most students; and less revenue and the need to trim or eliminate that which is neither excellent nor popular nor central to the institution. In short, much of the vaunted restructuring that management consultants and many observers and analysts of higher education have been calling for as a solution to the financial dilemma of U.S. colleges and universities is probably not a solution at all, for the simple reason that it has been going on for years. Most of the smaller and comprehensive colleges have reallocated resources and altered their programs and faculty profiles dramatically; many have changed mission altogether. Many of those that have not are either rich or private or both and have no need to change dramatically (at least no need that can be called a public policy issue).

The largest class of institution for which this is not necessarily the case are those universities, largely regional and with minimal or uneven scholarly reputations, that continue to pursue the research university model but that are unlikely to penetrate the top ranks, measured by the scholarly prestige of their faculty or their graduate programs. Here, pressures to control costs are likely to focus on an increasing separation of funding for instruction and research, much as has occurred in the United Kingdom. If these measures are successful, the result could be less indirect public subsidization of faculty scholarship, a widening difference in faculty workloads, and a reduced administration overhead on competitive research grants.

Although American higher education does more than the systems of any other nation to provide postsecondary opportunities to those from low socioeconomic backgrounds, the larger American society is becoming not only more unequal but also more predictable in intergenerational transmission of higher educational attainment. In other words, the children of well-educated, well-off parents generally achieve and persist in college, and those of the very poor, unless they are very bright and very lucky, generally do not. The likely continuation of sharply rising public tuitions, political attacks against remedial courses, elimination of affirmative action considerations in admissions and financial aid, and the conservative assault against curricula acknowledging multicultural values will likely accentuate this pattern.

NOTES

1. The prevailing condition of austerity in higher education is described in David W. Breneman, *Liberal Arts Colleges: Thriving, Surviving, or Endangered?* (Washington, D.C.: Brookings, 1994); Carol S. Hollins, *Containing Costs and Improving Productivity in Higher Education* (San Francisco: Jossey-Bass, 1992); D. Bruce Johnstone, *Working Papers in a Time of Fiscal Crisis* (Albany: State University of New York, 1992); William B. Simpson, *Managing with Scarce Resources* (San Francisco: Jossey-Bass, 1993).

2. D. Bruce Johnstone, "The Costs of Higher Education: Worldwide Issues and Trends for the 1990s," in *The Funding of Higher Education: International Perspectives,* ed. Philip G. Altbach and D. Bruce Johnstone (New York: Garland, 1993). For a perspective on the austerity of higher education in developing countries and the similarity with the United States and Europe in both analyses and policy solutions, see Adrian Ziderman and Douglas Albrecht, *Financing Universities in Developing Countries* (Washington, D.C.: Falmer, 1995).

3. National Center for Education Statistics, *Current Funds Revenues and Expenditures of Institutions of Higher Education: Fiscal Years 1986 through 1994* (Washington, D.C.: U.S. Department of Education, 1996), table 2.

4. National Center for Education Statistics, *Digest of Education Statistics, 1995* (Washington, D.C.: U.S. Department of Education, 1995), table 30.

5. National Center for Education Statistics, *The Condition of Education, 1996* (Washington, D.C.: U.S. Department of Education, 1996), 162.

6. National Center for Education Statistics, *Digest of Education Statistics, 1995,* table 165.

7. National Center for Education Statistics, *Condition of Education, 1996,* indicator 7; National Center for Education Statistics, *Digest of Education Statistics, 1995,* tables 8, 6.

8. National Center for Education Statistics, *Digest of Education Statistics, 1995,* tables 165, 233, 350.

9. National Center for Education Statistics, *Projections of Education Statistics to 2006* (Washington, D.C.: U.S. Department of Education, 1996), chap. 2.

10. *The Challenge of the Century* (Sacramento: California Postsecondary Education Commission, 1995). The privately financed California Policy Center sets the number at 488,000; see *Shared Responsibility: Strategies to Enhance Quality and Opportunity in California Higher Education* (San Jose: California Higher Education Policy Center, 1996).

11. William F. Massy and Robert Zemsky, "The Lattice and the Ratchet," *Policy Perspectives* 2 (1990). See also, Robert Zemsky and William F. Massy, "Toward an Understanding of Our Current Predicaments," *Change,* Nov./ Dec. 1995.

12. Howard R. Bowen, *The Costs of Higher Education* (San Francisco: Jossey-Bass, 1980), 116–19.

13. National Center for Education Statistics, *Digest of Education Statistics, 1995,* table 343.

14. Bowen, *Costs of Higher Education,* 19–26.

15. William J. Baumol and William G. Bowen, *Performing Arts: The Economic Dilemma* (New York: Twentieth Century Fund, 1966); William G. Bowen, *The Economics of the Major Private Universities* (Berkeley, Calif.: Carnegie Commission on the Future of Higher Education, 1968).

16. For accounts of recent tuition increases, see Arthur Hauptman, *The College Tuition Spiral* (Washington, D.C.: College Board and American Council on Education, 1990); Carol Francis, *What Factors Affect College Tuition?* (Washington, D.C.: American Association of State Colleges and Universities, 1990); Michael S. McPherson, Morton Owen Shapiro, and Gordon C. Winston, *Paying the Piper: Productivity, Incentives, and Financing in U.S. Higher Education* (Ann Arbor: University of Michigan Press, 1993); Michael Mumper,

Removing College Price Barriers: What Government Has Done and Why It Hasn't Worked (Albany: State University of New York Press, 1996).

17. "$1000 a Week: The Scary Cost of College," *Newsweek,* Apr. 29, 1996.

18. National Center for Education Statistics, *Student Financing of Graduate and First-Professional Education, Contractor Report* (Washington, D.C.: U.S. Department of Education, 1993).

19. David Leslie and E. K Fretwell, *Wise Moves in Hard Times: Creating and Managing Resilient Colleges and Universities* (San Francisco: Jossey-Bass, 1996). See also David W. Breneman, *Higher Education on a Collision Course with New Realities* (Washington, D.C.: Association of Governing Boards, 1994). Reprinted with permission by American Student Assistance.

20. Some consider "business" a possible fifth party to bear a share of higher education costs. However, grants from business to higher education can be viewed in one of three ways: (1) as the purchase of a service, whether research or specialized training, in which case the grant should cover the costs of the added service but is not expected to bear a share of the core instructional costs of the college or university; (2) as voluntary contributions coming out of owner profits, in which case they would fall under "philanthropy"; or (3) as contributions considered part of the cost of doing business, included in the price of the products and paid for by the general consumer, like a sales or consumption tax, in which case the incidence, or burden, is indistinguishable from that of other taxes and may be considered to be included, at least conceptually, in the "taxpayer" party. See D. Bruce Johnstone, *Sharing the Costs of Education* (New York: College Board, 1986).

21. The case for high tuition, high aid was popularized in W. Lee Hansen and Burton A Weisbrod, *Benefits, Costs, and Finance of Public Higher Education* (Chicago: Markham, 1969). See also Carnegie Commission on Higher Education, *Higher Education: Who Pays? Who Benefits? Who Should Pay?* (New York: McGraw-Hill, 1973); Frederick J. Fischer, "State Financing of Higher Education: A New Look at an Old Problem," *Change,* Jan./Feb., 1990; and McPherson, Shapiro, and Winston, *Paying the Piper.* The case against draws heavily on D. Bruce Johnstone, *The High-Tuition–High-Aid Model of Public Higher Education Finance: The Case Against* (Albany: State University of New York, for National Association of System Heads, 1993).

22. The figures assume nontuition expenses of $8,000 annually and tuition expenses of $7,000 to $10,000, or approximately 75 percent of undergraduate instructional costs.

23. D. Bruce Johnstone, *Learning Productivity: A New Imperative for American Higher Education* (Albany: State University of New York Press, 1992).

Chapter Fourteen

Technology and Higher Education

Opportunities and Challenges for the New Era

Patricia J. Gumport and Marc Chun

One cannot overestimate the influence of technology on the everyday life of academe.[1] The extensive reach of technology into higher education is captured by briefly recounting the process of writing this chapter. For much of the time that the chapter was being written, we were traveling, and therefore communicated with each other and with the volume editor via phone, voice mail, and e-mail. References and background information were located through computerized searches of the library holdings, by reviewing on-line journals, and via the World Wide Web. Drafts of the chapter flew through phone lines as electronic versions and as faxes. Not only did technology provide access to information we used, but it also shaped the very way in which we collaborated. In other words, both the product and process were heavily influenced by technology.

But despite the many ways technology facilitated this process, there were also numerous incidents of technological difficulties: problems converting files to other software, an inability to access e-mail, and network servers going "down." An irony, of course, is that although we acknowledge the power of technological advancements, the end result is not distributed on CD-ROM or posted on a Web page but is a chapter in a book, a medium that is now considered a low-technology means of disseminating knowledge. Although many of us may take for granted the ways in which technology has altered academic work, such experiences remind us that it is useful to step back and reflect on the nature of these changes.

As we near the turn of the millennium, advancements in information technology and communications technology have made possible approaches to teaching, learning, and research that were previously unimagined. While some advancements have been wholeheartedly embraced as valuable educational innovations, others have been less enthusiastically received. The goal of this chapter is to discuss how technology potentially impacts higher education, while acknowledging its interdependence with a complex array of opportunities and pressures that reside in the higher education system and in the wider societal context. We focus our analysis on five areas: (1) higher education and technology in modern society; (2) a historical perspective on technology and education; (3) contemporary advancements in technology and education; (4) wider policy pressures and legitimacy considerations; and (5) resistance to widespread technological change within higher education.

Technology and Modern Society

In modern society, the educational system has been called upon to engage in teaching, learning, and research in the name of "progress." Toward this end in the United States, federal and state governments have taken an interest in education at all levels, with dramatically different arrangements across the basic levels: while assuming primary responsibility for elementary and secondary education—to the extent that K-12 education is both mandatory and publicly funded—postsecondary education is characterized by more decentralized control at state, campus, and classroom levels. Although the government provides financial support for tuition and research through various funding mechanisms to states, campuses, and students as well as legislates policies (e.g., Title IX, health and safety regulations), there are few constraints on higher education's core academic processes: curriculum, teaching, learning, and classroom practices.

Given this context, higher education institutions have historically been accredited as legitimate providers and well positioned within teaching and research markets. At the same time, however, higher education has long been susceptible to a range of market forces and dynamics, with new providers vying to provide educational opportunities to the post-secondary-education population. A wide range of institutional resources enable students to avail themselves of the many sources and combinations of information and knowledge in a market economy.[2] However, with advancements in technology, especially in the post–World War II era, the strong market position of traditional higher education providers has become more vulnerable to challenges from new providers with potentially farther reaches, such as corporations, proprietary schools, and other for-profit ventures.

Some observers claim that recent advances in technology will revolutionize teaching and learning practices and delivery systems for higher education. Spreading with the speed and heat of a wildfire, the current spate of technology has been branded a panacea for lack of efficiency, access, quality, and other enduring challenges facing higher education. However, as with other movements situated between revolution and trend, technology may in the end drastically disappoint, a victim of unrealistic expectations.

Applications of technology to higher education must be seen in light of broader societal transformations in the past two decades. Technology—specifically, information and telecommunications technology—has already become well entrenched in everyday life, so much so that we often overlook the range of its functions. In the home we find telephone answering machines, videocassette recorders, cable television, and personal computers. In the workplace it is common to see networking among local work groups, computer work stations, and access to the internet for communication and expanded markets. The personal computer has perhaps the greatest impact, having gained a significant presence in the daily lives of many Americans, who comfortably log on, reboot, input, copy, paste, spellcheck, scroll, e-mail, download, search, print, escape, and quit several times a day. The applications for computers seem limitless: they are used for word processing, for e-mail, for accessing the internet, for round-the-clock banking services and shopping, or even for the annual filing of income tax returns. Such technological breakthroughs for the home and office are typically celebrated for the ways in which they make life easier.

Technology is also reshaping the world of higher education. Consider the wide range of technological applications under way at Stanford University in 1997. An aeronautical engineering professor is lecturing to her class on wing design when interactive video enables a classmate from one of several remote company sites to interrupt and explain that his company's wing design practice is now different. Interactive video links students in three locations to a music class; a third of the class is on campus, a third is at San Jose State University, and a third is at Princeton University. Together, the class critiques a classical performance. In another classroom, only a fourth of the students enrolled in the class are present for a physics lecture; the remainder had schedule conflicts and will watch the lecture later, on video, by logging onto the World Wide Web.

In another classroom, students work on problem sets; their notes are incorporated into the original class material, for future access through a device called a Softbook. At a doctoral oral examination, video conferencing connects faculty members present at the exam with two faculty examiners located off campus, one in Boston, the other in London. In another classroom, a course on Shakespeare is taught jointly by faculty at Stanford University and the Massachusetts Institute of Technology. In a mechanical engineering classroom, teams of three students, located in three locations (Stanford University, Tokyo, and New York) design products through e-mail, desktop video conferencing (complete with a shared work space), and overnight package delivery services. Students in a French class use computers to complete their homework, while a voice emulator allows them to listen to lessons. In the main library computer cluster, a student logs on to check her grades for her last quarter's courses, while her friend does a search through biology journals on the World Wide Web. An anthropology professor demonstrates for his students a CD-ROM he developed that provides a virtual reality walk through an archaeological excavation site. Students in an English class, working on a project about World War II, access materials from the Hoover Archives on the Web and, from their computer screens, review photographs, propaganda posters, and recordings of Hitler's speeches. Few faculty and students are aware of the full range of these possibilities. And nationwide, even fewer can afford them.

The information age has arguably brought about a transformation of society, dramatically changing communication, the workplace, science, and entertainment. It has also impacted education, but the nature and scope of such changes are still contested. Many trumpet technology as an educational cure-all that will transform the delivery and nature of educational processes. Others remain skeptical, claiming that systemic educational problems cannot be solved by technology alone, that technology is merely a tool, the successful use of which may entail a paradigmatic shift in the orientation of all involved in teaching and learning. Technology makes transformation possible, but does not guarantee it. This point can be exemplified by taking a historical perspective.

A Historical Perspective

Thomas Edison, speaking seventy-five years ago about motion pictures, said that it was "destined to revolutionize our educational system" and predicted that it would, in a few years, "supplant . . . textbooks." [3] This could easily be a quote from an Apple or Microsoft executive about the future of computers. History demonstrates two certainties with respect to the impact of technology on education: first, prognosticators will herald the radical rebirth or inevitable demise of the educational system; and second, more often than not, their predictions will be wrong. The educational timeline for adoption of technology is dotted with unexpected failures and unexpected successes.

Americans seem to be in love with the idea that any new technology can, in and of itself, fix all problems. Despite the overwhelming multiplicity of problems facing education, many seek the latest gizmo as the technical "fix" that the system requires. The arrival of new technologies for education has often been accompanied by bold predictions for its transformation. Recent claims about the power of high technology to revitalize education are likely to conjure up a collective sense of social déjà vu. The blackboard, for example, was expected to turn education on its ear. Some predicted that television would eliminate illiteracy in America, a 1957 Ford Foundation report foreseeing television as "the greatest opportunity for the advancement of education since the introduction of printing by movable type." [4]

On the other hand, many experts sound the tocsin of doom, predicting that a new technology will bring on the downfall of the educational system. In the fifth century B.C., there was tremendous controversy surrounding the use of written records in teaching. The Stanford University philosopher Patrick Suppes noted that, at the time, many believed that the adoption of written materials would undermine the learning process and diminish the personal relationship between tutor and student. In *Phaedrus,* Socrates predicted that the use of written materials "will create forgetfulness in the learners' souls, because they will not use their memories; they will trust to the external written characters and not remember of themselves. . . . They will appear to be omniscient and will generally know nothing."[5] It was also feared that the printed word would undermine the authority of the scholar because students would have access to another source of knowledge. In addition, some observers were concerned that the shift toward written text and standardized knowledge would lead to impersonal and repetitive action, precluding opportunities for creativity, such as when scribes would amend the manuscripts they were copying. A more recent example of doomsday concern comes from the early 1960s, when instructional television disappointed proponents and users alike. Initial high hopes were accompanied by grave fears; some predicted that classrooms would be staffed primarily by teaching assistants whose sole role would be to keep students quiet.[6]

As we now know, predictions of massive improvement and warnings of unavoidable collapse of the educational system never came to pass. This is not to say that the effects of such technology were not felt on college and university campuses; rather, it suggests that the actual impact did not live up to grandiose expectations. It is nevertheless interesting to consider prominent examples of technology and their subsequent impact on education. The introduction of technology into educational settings has often met with lukewarm support and mixed results, but its slow adoption has had far-reaching impact. Written materials, for example, eventually gained popularity and found widespread use, contrary to the chorus of warnings. Moreover, not only was this technology adopted, but it also brought about other significant and profound changes in teaching and learning. The accumulation of written documents has led to the development of libraries as well as to centralized and organized bodies of knowledge that expanded as scholars developed intellectual networks. These developments occurred in tandem with the growth of the academic profession and the proliferation of academic disciplines, which carved up the academic landscape in the twentieth century.

In some cases, the lag between the development of technology and its adoption can last centuries. The historical record shows instances of some innovations spreading slowly and gaining momentum only later. The technology of mass printing, developed by the mid-1400s, permitted educational documents to be distributed both widely and inexpensively. Suppes noted, however, that, surprisingly, the use of textbooks did not catch on until the end of the eighteenth century.

Another example is formalized testing, which is widely used in the
United States as a means to remove bias in evaluation as well as to
establish standards and measure achievement and skills. Nevertheless, testing had been used centuries before in China for the selection
of mandarins.[7] The impact of some technology will not be realized
until it has an opportunity to spread, in much the same way that
the revolutionary influence of the telephone was not felt until there
was a critical mass of users.[8] When the technology radically alters the
basic structures of the educational process or challenges long-held
assumptions, it is likely to face such opposition. By contrast, when
the technology fits within the basic paradigm, its adoption is often
less controversial; for example, the photocopying machine, which in
essence replaced the mimeograph machine, was integrated into educational settings immediately.

Of course, the adoption of technology has not necessarily led to
actual changes in the educational process. Many misbegotten fads,
each with its own advocates and enthusiasts, eventually fell by the
wayside. The promise held out for radio and filmstrips, for example,
never materialized, and tremendous initial investments were made
in computer systems that were soon outdated. Huge cadres of students learned computer languages that are now obsolete. Moreover,
there is very little evidence of sustained improvements in student
performance as a result of new information technology, either at the
K–12 level or at the postsecondary level. Despite decades of research
and waves of reform, not much has changed in the classroom. In fact,
the book still remains the primary classroom tool and the coming
together of teachers and students the essential means of teaching and
learning.

The current wave of technological advances may mark a new
chapter in the history of higher education. The primary differences
between this technology and those of the past are its extreme flexibility and relative pervasiveness. Today's technologies are extremely
malleable and do not come with an obvious targeted application or
audience; it is entirely possible that some technologies may have
an unlimited number of applications. Contrast the printing press, a
single technology with the explicit purpose of mass-producing books,
to three-dimensional (3D) modeling and its potential in educational
settings: in biochemistry, to examine, build, and manipulate mo-
lecular structures; in archaeology, to map with great precision the
features of a site on another continent so that students can later ex-

amine it in laboratories; in art history, to model the architectural details of an ancient cathedral such that a student can virtually enter it and study it from an unlimited number of vantage points. In each case, the student can see things not necessarily intended by the 3D modeler. In some important educational ways, the model may even be considered better than the real site, because it provides more complete access to more information, which can be retrieved and reviewed without the constraints of place and time.

In addition to its flexibility, the new technology is becoming omnipresent throughout the educational system. Although many of its applications to higher education are still being identified, all levels of the national system of higher education and its participants are currently affected. For example, prospective students and parents can get information about colleges and universities on-line, and in some cases they can apply for admission and financial aid electronically. Course registration now occurs on-line—gone are the days of students standing in long lines in gymnasiums. Students and faculty can search through scholarly citations and electronic databases and even, in some cases, obtain the full text of library documents. Academic support staff order supplies and process reimbursements on-line and use e-mail to communicate with faculty, students, and other staff members. Some academic departments have eliminated secretarial positions, encouraging their faculty members to handle their own scheduling, correspondence, and preparation of course materials and manuscripts. It is also increasingly common for students to check out a video of a lecture from a departmental library, much as they would borrow a book.

Thus, technological advancements have already altered the rhythms of higher education settings, and they have the potential to further transcend constraints of time, place, and participants. Technology circulates so pervasively through modern society that traditional higher education is unlikely to be insulated; as new educational providers that rely on technology enter the market, they will reshape the landscape of higher education. Although history has shown us that the impact of technology is impossible to predict and that the most outspoken advocates and naysayers have often been inaccurate in their prognostications, it is almost certain that there will be some effect. Thus we now turn to a discussion of the potential arenas for impact.

The Arenas of Impact on Higher Education

Contemporary advancements in technology may be characterized as potentially impacting three broad arenas of higher education: the nature of knowledge, the nature of teaching and learning, and the organization of teaching and learning.

The Nature of Knowledge

At the most basic level, technology has affected the nature of knowledge itself. It shapes what counts as knowledge, how knowledge is produced, how people are involved in the production of knowledge, and how academic knowledge is valued.

There is a burgeoning assumption that legitimate knowledge must be capable of being computerized. Knowledge is increasingly created, processed, manipulated, and stored with technology. In addition, the way knowledge is produced in academic settings has been greatly expanded. Computers make feasible complex statistical analyses; laboratory equipment enables the study of subatomic matter and distant galaxies; and x-ray technology allows the examination of images hidden beneath the paint on art masterpieces.

Changes in the nature of knowledge also affect relationships between people and knowledge in higher education. For example, the nature of what it means to be "educated" has shifted: one now must be able to demonstrate computer literacy and to keep up with rapid changes in what constitutes computer literacy. In the era of the internet, access to many forms of knowledge are restricted to those who have the skills and the equipment to access it. Even the daily lives of knowledge producers have changed; for instance, faculty who in the past dictated material to their secretaries to type now create their work on their computers. Computers allow easier revisions in written material compared to the past, when changes required retyping an entire document. They allow easier collaboration between colleagues, who can exchange documents on-line. And they allow new forms of knowledge dissemination, such as electronic journals that can be read on-line and documents from World Wide Web sites.

More generally, however, advances in technology have occurred in tandem with an increased awareness of the knowledge industry, in which higher education participates.[9] New markets for knowledge have ushered in new and complicated issues of intellectual property, as notions of the production and consumption of knowledge have become internalized by faculty and their employing institutions. This orientation has profound implications for conceptualizations of higher education's social functions — principally a shift in the primary emphasis from the development of the individual to an emphasis on the transmission, production, and dissemination of knowledge. Thus, students and faculty are more often seen as knowledge consumers and knowledge producers functioning within market forces. As new technology has opened up new possibilities for the exchange and packaging of information, a proprietary orientation has gained prominence in higher education, given the new markets for research and teaching products. New policies and personnel are required to mediate between individuals and higher education institutions in the ownership and management of academic knowledge.

The Nature of Teaching and Learning

The dominant ideal for teaching and learning in traditional higher education settings presupposes that faculty and students come together in the same place at the same time, communicating principally with the spoken word, and using the very basic technologies of chalk and blackboard and printed materials (i.e., textbooks). The image of the faculty member has been that of "the sage on the stage," a mode of instruction that gives students credit for contact — also known as seat time — whether they are in a lecture, seminar, discussion, or laboratory.[10] Some new technologies have effected essentially first-order changes, making such traditional teaching and learning activities more efficient or expedient without altering the basic premises. Technology thus changes the medium of information exchange without significantly changing the content.

Such first-order changes in higher education classes are common. Technological advancements have provided faculty with a wider range of ways to present and represent information, including slides, filmstrips, motion pictures, and overhead projectors. Other technological advancements — the microphone, computerized scanners for scoring tests, and mimeographing machines to duplicate course materials — have enabled faculty to capitalize on economies of scale. Communication outside of class hours and across distances has been strengthened through the postal service and the telephone. E-mail exchanges dramatically increase the frequency and alter the nature of student/

faculty interaction into "anytime, anywhere" contact. Reports by faculty indicate that e-mail has increased participation by those students who have not been inclined to speak in class discussions.[11]

Some other uses of technology extend the traditional teaching and learning processes, using technology to expand the scope of activity, again without altering the underlying educational model. For example, whereas students have in the past used only the databases available to them on their own campuses, computers have made possible access to databases around the world. This change has also affected the nature of research, expanding access to new information and new forms of information as well as the range of areas for investigation. For the most part, such technological adaptations are simply "bolted" onto old instructional methods.[12]

Computers are a prime example of technology that created first-order change, in which the basic activities of education remain the same. Computerized equipment allows students to be more precise in their work, and word-processing applications make revising drafts of a paper more convenient—just as pocket calculators make mathematical computations easier. Computers have also been widely adopted, although there is variability in campus approaches to implementation. Some colleges and universities require all students to purchase a computer; others supply equipment for the campus community to share. It is not uncommon for students to own personal computers with CD-ROM drives, multimedia software, and access to the World Wide Web, although estimates of computer ownership and usage differ.[13] Although computers have the potential for students to do desktop publishing, computer-aided design, and high-level modeling, some observers claim that they are often used primarily for the most pedestrian uses, such as word processing. Computers also permit a first-order change on a previous second-order revolution: just as the postal service made correspondence courses available, distance learning via the computer renders this enterprise more efficient and far-reaching. All of this, of course, does not alter the traditional teaching and learning paradigm: technology has been used essentially to enhance the fundamental faculty/student classroom interaction.

Technology also brings about transformations of a second-order nature. Such changes require more money and a redesigning of courses to incorporate specific technological applications and, thus, has the potential to alter core educational processes and the very nature of teaching and learning. As technology alters how knowledge is obtained, classified, utilized, and represented, such changes reshape both content and delivery of education.

With respect to content, technology enables teachers to shift the focus and orientation of their courses. By relinquishing the drudgery of technical work to computer models and simulations, faculty no longer need to devote such large proportions of class time to routine work—for example, calculating ANOVAs by hand—and can instead consider additional principles or higher-order concepts. In addition, technology has changed the nature of the laboratory, a pedagogical device once exclusive to the natural sciences. Increasingly, faculty in the social sciences are using laboratories as a means for students to gain hands-on experience with course material, in much the same way that faculty in biology, chemistry, physics, and astronomy have. For example, a professor teaching a course in social stratification might ask students to manipulate census data, giving the students direct experience with statistical patterns of discrimination and allowing them to draw their own conclusions about social patterns. In other words, technology facilitates a shift from passive to active learning. A transformation has taken place; the classroom is no longer faculty centered but is student centered, and academic credit is no longer given for time spent on subject matter coverage to students' learning outcomes and demonstrated competence.

The incorporation of such technologies extends to faculty across the disciplines, as they gain access to resources that may entail a redesign of courses and teaching methods. Faculty enhance the display of information in the classroom: in an art history class, teachers can zoom in on details of paintings; in a literary criticism class, they can show a scene from a play. Computers, no longer seen solely as number crunchers, are conceived of more broadly as symbol crunchers, with the ability to manipulate numbers, words, concepts, and images, to extend communication, and ultimately to enrich teaching and learning relationships.

New technology has transformed the basic building blocks of the teaching and learning process. It has changed the roles of the participants: students have become active rather than passive learners; faculty have become "the guide on the side" rather than "the sage on the stage"; and others, such as software developers, have become participants. It has changed the nature of time: rather than being subject to the regimented schedules characteristic of classroom settings, students use educational software packages at their own pace and at times of their choice and convenience. And it has changed content delivery: syllabi, lectures, course readings, and class notes are placed on-line. Such changes have put the responsibility on students to integrate these information bundles and on faculty to assume a primary role in assisting students through this process.

The Organization of Teaching and Learning

Finally, technology has affected the social organization of teaching and learning through expanding the delivery of higher education. Technology opens up the possibility of rethinking the fundamentals of the higher education setting: the dimensions of roles, time, place, and organizational participants.

First, technology can alter the nature of the participants' roles. As discussed, the shift in higher education may be toward a more learner-centered mode: as students turn to more individualized learning, teachers are called upon to guide students through the information resources rather than being the primary distributors of content. The role of faculty becomes that of helping students learn *how to learn;* for example, faculty may now help students decide which computerized module will best suit their educational needs or how to take greatest advantage of the package. It also changes the nature of the participants, allowing access to people heretofore unable to participate—including both those without the resources to attend and "adult learners" for whom distance learning is more convenient. In addition, the information networks permit contact and interchanges across all conventional bounds of geography—for example, a student can use e-mail to consult with people and resources anywhere in the world.

Second, technology can alter the temporality of education. Computer modules can accommodate individual needs through self-pacing. When students use learning modules, they can review material or move forward to new material, while the professor can expand her monitoring throughout an entire computerized lecture hall—taking on a role more like that of a coach.

Third, technology may alter the geography of education. Technology permits students in traditional education settings to engage in the learning process in nontraditional ways—for example, to watch a "live" simulcast from a satellite classroom, to listen to a presentation in the lecture hall, or to watch a videotape in their residence hall rooms. Distance education also allows students to participate in educational programs without setting foot on campus; such out-of-class communication can be enhanced through e-mail, list servs, and on-line discussions, thus blurring the boundary between in and out of class. Perhaps a more profound shift is to incorporate into a "live" class individuals who are located at remote sites; downlinks may be set up at other campuses, at companies, in community learning centers, or even in high schools. Dramatic progress has been made with the use of two-way video and audio transmission.

Fourth, this upheaval in the assumptions of higher education has resulted in dramatic shifts in the organizational landscape. As new providers of teaching resources challenge the market share of existing colleges and universities, many organizations, especially computer and software companies, have recast themselves as participants in the knowledge business.

The most dramatic case of the changing social organization of teaching and learning is that of virtual higher education. Transcending time and place for new learning opportunities, this alternative to face-to-face education extends prior conceptions of distance education, or distance learning, which once took the form of correspondence courses made possible by the postal service. During the past two decades, a range of additional communications technologies have been used in virtual higher education, including telephone, television by satellite, videotapes, and more recently modems and fiber-optic networks.

The advent of computer interactive digital technology has opened up more possibilities, including new organizations and institutional forms. These forms make possible either collaboration or competition between existing campuses and new providers. Some observers envision multisite learning communities, which will replace the classroom, the faculty, and the campus. Communications technology makes possible both synchronous and asynchronous communication. If communication is synchronous, for example in an on-line discussion, it simulates live interaction. If it is asynchronous, students may go back for review as often as they want to. An illustration of the latter is a simulated dissection of a virtual cadaver, which a student can begin anew until the skills are perfected, unlike plunging into a real cadaver with scalpel and rib spreaders.

Numerous external forces are driving the new-found interest in virtual higher education. A major one is demographic, in particular the emerging needs of adult learners. From the perspective of employers, workers need to update their knowledge and skills in order to adapt to rapid, technological changes in the workplace. At the same time, adults may want intellectual enrichment; since the late 1980s one company (whose advertisement goes, just because "you are not in school anymore doesn't mean you want your mind to turn to mush") annually enrolls five thousand students in its cable channel classes.[14]

Given the present era of resource constraints in higher education, especially for public universities, virtual higher education might enhance the sharing of educational resources when comprehensive field coverage is deemed too costly. For example, if the University of California, Berkeley, has an expert in ancient Greek, a course could be taught for students on other University of California campuses. Similarly, Berkeley could be a receiving site for University of California, Los Angeles, courses in a history or linguistics specialization, if such subject matter specialists are not on the local faculty. Other proposals for virtual higher education involve cooperation with other states. States such as North Dakota and Maine have already developed an extensive interactive video network.

Alternatively, virtual higher education may generate competition and subject existing higher education providers to unprecedented market forces. Virtual private, for-profit ventures are becoming more common. Perhaps the oldest such institution, the University of Phoenix, was founded in 1978 to provide educational programs for working adults, enrolling more than 40,000 students in undergraduate (e.g., in business and health care) and graduate programs (e.g., in business and education). The university has granted more than 370,000 degrees and certificates and thus has a significant market share of part-time students. While the University of Phoenix has a reputation for producing MBAs, the National Technological University has a reputation for engineering education. Founded in 1984, it uses advanced satellite technology to enable working students to be trained as engineers and technology managers.

In 1990 another virtual higher education initiative, the Teaching Company, was launched, with fifteen courses on videotapes and written materials. By 1997, the Teaching Company offered more than a hundred courses, with videotapes of lectures by star faculty from some of the country's most selective universities. In addition, the Teaching Company's newest division, Mirus University, has gained preliminary certification for degree-granting status by the State Council on

Higher Education in Virginia to offer bachelor's and master's of arts degrees in liberal studies.[15] Interestingly, this approach reinstates the faculty as central performer.

Another example of a virtual higher education provider is Magellan University, based in Tucson, Arizona, which in 1995 started promoting its virtual classes, relying on the internet's World Wide Web network. While this university began as a nonprofit organization, its founder is optimistic it will become a viable commercial enterprise and hopes to establish a market niche among the tens of millions of homes and businesses that have networking capabilities.

Perhaps the most visible initiative crossing state lines is the proposed Western Governors University. Endorsed by the Western Governors Association in 1995, planning for the cyberuniversity is proceeding with two aims: to broaden access to technologically delivered educational programming, and to provide certification of competency —that is, learning achieved regardless of source. The goal is to establish a free flow of high-quality educational materials across institutional, state, and other boundaries yet maintain access at in-state tuition rates. According to the implementation plan, the new entity will broker the distribution of services, foster the development of educational materials, and help connect users with providers through student support services. Thirteen governors committed $100,000 each during fiscal year 1997, agreed to assist in obtaining the financial resources required to develop the virtual catalog and management systems, and promised to remove barriers ("regulation, bureaucracy, tradition, and turf")[16] that might prevent the initiative from functioning effectively.

Proponents of Western Governors University see substantial benefits for several constituencies: students will have greater access; employers will be able to assess the skills of new employees and enable current employees to upgrade skills; colleges, universities, and other providers will have an expanded market; and states will better meet the demands emerging from changing demographics and labor force needs. At the same time, however, several concerns have been voiced about quality—that is, ensuring standards—and the possible loss of public funds for existing colleges and universities. It is noteworthy that California's governor, Pete Wilson, decided not to participate in Western Governors University and has, instead, launched a plan for California Virtual University. Reflecting confidence in California's established and accredited colleges and universities, the California plan aims to serve the needs of the state while generating funds within California.

The financing of such virtual ventures along with other virtual universities concerns participants and observers alike. On the one hand, there may be tremendous cost savings, since there will be no buildings, no faculty, and no printed catalog. There will still be personnel costs, but these will be limited.

Many questions remain. Who will underwrite the cost of the technology? Many hardware, software, and teaching video companies are jockeying for position, in hopes of securing big profits. How will learning outcomes be assessed? Some critics claim that competency-based assessment is inappropriate, noting that higher education provides an all-important credentialling function, rather than knowledge acquisition or skill building, per se. From this perspective, a college degree may also demonstrate the ability and willingness to persevere in pursuit of a long-term goal rather than competency in subject matter. A focus on learning outcomes and competency-based testing is criticized by others for missing crucial socialization functions. Even at its best, critics argue, virtual higher education would provide a suboptimal educational experience, the antithesis of Goffman's conception of the "total institution," wherein socialization is most readily achieved in the bounded, residential nature of classical colleges. Of course, with the increase in part-time enrollments and the expanded reach of community college courses, that classical model may end up serving a smaller and smaller proportion of the postsecondary student population, raising challenges for finding socialization alternatives in community-based organizations.

To summarize, technology has affected or is likely to affect many dimensions of higher education, including the nature of knowledge, the nature of teaching and learning, and the organization of teaching and learning. The case of virtual higher education incorporates issues from all three arenas and raises many questions. In the previous two sections of this chapter, we discuss the past, present, and potential future impact of technology on education. We note how some technologies have brought about revolutionary change while others have had little or no impact. Our claim is that such variability in effect is neither the result of chance nor a Darwinian survival of the fittest. Rather, because change is affected by social, political, and economic factors, it is essential to consider the wider policy pressures and opportunities that accompany the discourse about technology. At the same time, it is essential to note that technology is carried forward by individuals who negotiate the policy pressures and who determine the extent to which technology takes hold in higher education.

Policy Pressures and Legitimacy

Scholars have argued that the nature of higher education—its multiple goals and its unclear core technology—leaves it susceptible to policy pressures as well as institutional imperatives for legitimacy. That is, colleges and universities justify their activities—and are therefore seen as "modern" and legitimate—by appealing to culturally approved assumptions.

Improvements in higher education activities are therefore often presented as responses to distinct policy pressures. Given pervasive pressures on higher education to reduce costs, increase access, and improve quality, it is not surprising that campuses are considering technological breakthroughs and their potential applications. The cumulative pressure on colleges and universities to do more with less is a powerful catalyst for the reconsideration of delivery systems, curricula, organizational structures, and mix of technology and personnel.[17] The hope is that technology will be the key to more affordable, accessible, and effective teaching and learning.

At the same time, improvements tend to be constructed through one of three legitimizing frames: efficiency, access, or quality, each of which is cast as advancing societal aims. Notions of efficiency often invoke the metaphors of neoclassical economics, aiming to optimize the delivery of education to students and to maximize students' subsequent contributions to society. Access is often construed as emancipation and social justice, wherein educational opportunities are extended to those who have been excluded from higher education. Quality often includes shades of the previous two but includes a range of supporting rationales.

Higher education has traditionally been a labor-intensive industry. Strategies for cutting costs in higher education often focus on personnel, which historically accounts for approximately 80 percent of campus expenditures. Common sense indicates that less expensive labor might replace more expensive labor and that economies of scale might be achieved by having larger class enrollments. From this perspective, the potential for educational technology to reduce costs by replacing

faculty becomes an even more attractive policy option, given anticipated higher education enrollment increases in many states over the
next two decades. However, while changing the mix of technology
and personnel may result in long-run cost savings, the development
and delivery of technology incurs its own costs, not only to invest in
hardware, software, and networking infrastructures but also to hire
personnel to maintain and support its usage as well as to upgrade the
skills of existing personnel. Even proponents of such investments acknowledge that substituting technology for labor is unlikely to reduce
costs.[18] In addition, given the social and economic returns to higher
education, it is worrisome that the capitalization of technology might
be underwritten by the consumer—the student.

The United States has moved from elite higher education to mass
higher education, and the pressure is now to provide universal higher
education. This means that colleges and universities are increasingly
called upon to provide educational opportunities to those who have
been excluded from the system by virtue of demographic as well as
geographic factors. Moreover, with the social value placed on lifelong
learning, increasing numbers of adult learners are seeking access to
higher education. The question of course, is access to what? If it is access to academic programs at one of the 3,600 accredited colleges and
universities, then logistical challenges can be identified and resolved.
If, on the other hand, it is access to a wider range of learning opportunities in virtual classrooms and virtual universities offered by a range
of providers, the challenges for quality assurance are enormous.

The application of technology has been framed as a way to improve
the quality of teaching and learning, using information technology
and communications technology to enhance student/faculty ratios as
well as student/student and faculty/student interactions. The hope is
also to tailor educational services to a more diverse student population, increasingly characterized by a wide range of cognitive learning styles and academic preparation. Such outcomes are not assured.
In fact, skeptics are concerned that technological applications might
have the opposite of their intended effects and undermine the quality
of teaching and learning. It is possible that e-mail will replace office
hours, videos will replace active participation in class, and students
at remote sites will miss out on some crucial aspects of hands-on,
in-class experiences. Other concerns include the viability of an educational operation without a faculty, the value of a credential from
such an experience, the validity and utility of competency-based cre-

dentials, and whether such students will be—or will be perceived to be—less competitive in the job market and perhaps less socialized as citizens and leaders than their counterparts from traditional colleges and universities.

Although issues of efficiency, access, and quality are often addressed separately in policy arenas, they are interdependent considerations in what constitutes legitimate higher education. For example, the argument that technology makes continuing education and lifelong learning available relies upon a rationale of efficiency as the training of a worker to contend with the changing requirements of the workplace and a rational of access as ensuring participation in a system wherein direct contact with teachers is replaced by machines, content no longer flows directly from teacher to student, and students learn on their own, at their own pace, in their own space. Several legitimizing frames are used to justify this emphasis for the higher education enterprise: some may claim that the underlying goal is to increase efficiency, but its legitimacy is secured by framing the change as increasing access. Jean-François Lyotard cautions that we should be mindful and critical of such rhetorical games, discerning which Trojan horse is being used for which political agenda.[19]

Policy pressures for efficiency, access, and quality are long-standing and complex. However, despite some proponents' claims that the current wave of technological advancement will resolve these policy issues, history has shown that the degree to which a technological change is embraced depends in part on how it is constructed and in part on the social legitimacy it can marshal. While information technology and networking capabilities may enhance communications environments, learning infrastructures, and information infrastructures, they may have unforeseen consequences.

Resistance to Technological Change

Historically, higher education has been slow to adopt change. The university emerged during medieval times, and because it has not changed dramatically since that time, it in many ways reflects the past. The scientific revolution took place for the most part outside of academe, and many academics shunned the industrial revolution. The university's tremendous inertia is the result of a long-standing, well-established system. Despite the tremendous public attention given to technology, to date the majority of the academic profession across the country has not dramatically transformed their teaching methods or redesigned their courses.[20] To do so is time-consuming, as is the development of innovations in courseware. Such activities have not yet been significantly rewarded in promotion and tenure review the way scholarly publications are. Perhaps the disincentives of the current academic reward structure account for the absence of a burgeoning educational technology industry for higher education, in contrast to the K–12 level. From another perspective, even willing faculty members are likely to be unprepared to take on such projects. On some campuses, new positions for information resource specialists have been established to work one-on-one with faculty who want to learn.

Advancements in instructional technology are not likely to spread uniformly across the many types of higher education institutions in the United States. Differences in mission and financial resources among community colleges, liberal arts colleges, and research universities, for example, may guide the decision making about alternative investments.[21] A liberal arts college, for instance, may be able to link all classrooms to the internet but not be able to afford a huge computer laboratory; a community college, trying to maintain expanded access, may decide that it cannot afford *not* to do both. In fact, community colleges over the past few decades have positioned themselves as frequent users of mechanisms for off-campus learning, ranging from correspondence courses, video courses, and audio cassette courses to television courses. State-of-the-art equipment and skills have a relatively short life cycle, becoming obsolete faster than ever before. While the problem of obsolescence is not unique, what is arguably unusual is the enormous cost and risk involved in both adopting and failing to adopt technological innovations. When Harvard University did not immediately adopt computer technology, an observer noted that "they have the financial resources to let everyone else make the mistakes and then buy their way to the forefront when the dust has settled."[22]

Much of the opposition to technological applications to education has been waged against its touted efficiency imperatives, with many critics concerned about the quality of education delivered by the new media. A case in point is statewide interactive video networks. Whether these networks should simply export programs to those whose geography precludes access or whether the networks should themselves become degree-granting electronic campuses has emerged as a topic of great controversy. In Maine, after faculty protests, the chancellor resigned after a vote of no confidence from all seven Maine campuses. Faculty, among the most vocal critics of the Educational Network of Maine, feared that distance education opportunities would "empty their classrooms and rob them of their livelihoods."[23] Yet, the greatest concern focused on matters of quality, which overrode potential gains in efficiency and access; this concern notes that teaching delivered over such networks requires different pedagogical skills than those used in face-to-face classroom interaction. Thus, while the use of technology may indeed make more information available—issues of access and efficiency—the question remains as to whether such uses are desirable for higher education— issues of quality.

Conclusion

Technological applications have the potential to enrich traditional classroom settings and to extend the boundaries for teaching and learning in higher education, and these possible applications prompt us to rethink some fundamental beliefs about the nature of colleges and universities as places, communities, storehouses of knowledge, and sites of learning. They also prompt us to consider the roles of teachers and learners and the optimal conditions for learning. Although they are unlikely to solve higher education's problems of costs or quality, technological advances do have the potential to expand access and to tailor learning to different cognitive styles and levels of preparation. The new library service model, for example, is fundamentally virtual, as it must provide access to information resources, not merely store collections. Such applications also reconceptualize higher education providers as service providers, requiring colleges and universities to rethink delivery systems and to devise strategies to protect and extend their market niches. Thus, the implications for rethinking the what, where, how, who, and when of higher education are limitless.

How will the current wave of information and communication technologies affect the future of higher education? Will technological advances allow universities to provide higher quality education to a larger portion of the populace? Or will they result in a net decrease in educational quality and accentuate the divide between the educational haves and the have-nots? Will they make possible cost savings and productivity increases that will rescue colleges and universities from steadily tightening budgets? Or will they place additional pressure on those budgets, as colleges and universities are forced to keep up technologically without any compensatory reduction in costs or growth in revenues? Or will the advances spell the eventual demise of higher education as we know it?[24]

The only prediction that can be made with real confidence is that technology will have an impact on higher education and that the impact will be far-reaching. To pretend we can see the future is, in this arena, simple hubris. The role that any specific technology will play in higher education cannot be forecast with any accuracy. Consider the very different histories of two recent technologies: multimedia software and the World Wide Web. These developments are similar in that they both bring a range of existing base technologies together into easily usable packages. Multimedia has been around for five years or more. An industry darling, it has been consistently overpromoted and has just as consistently underperformed. In contrast, the World Wide Web exploded from a European physics lab and a midwestern supercomputing center—out of nowhere, from the perspective of the commercial computer industry. These examples illustrate an important point: in the arena of technology, the event horizon beyond which accurate predictions cannot be made is roughly six months. This is partly due to the unpredictability of technological development but more due to the complex social, behavioral, and economic contexts into which new technologies are embedded. Predicting which entertainment technologies will work and which will not, which will appeal and which will not, which will sell and which will not is extremely difficult. Predicting the future of educational technology, embedded as it is in a complex and poorly understood endeavor, is close to impossible.

When considering how technology will affect higher education, we must also keep in mind that there is no single answer. Since differentiation has long been the hallmark of higher education in the United States, technological investments and applications are likely to show great variation across campuses, with dramatically different opportunities available across different populations of students and faculty. Although we advocate proceeding with caution, we also believe that it is not useful to react defensively. The massive technological changes of the new era cannot be resisted; if they are going to happen, they will happen in spite of defenses. Just as one responds to news of an imminent tidal wave, a prudent course may be to position ourselves in order to survive. Others of course may decide that a prudent course of action is to be out in front, determined to embrace and, where possible, shape the impact. In either case, we believe that technological advancements need to be seen as means to several potential ends and not as ends in themselves.

Change in the processes and products of higher education is the result of a complex interplay of wider societal forces. While technology provides opportunities, it also makes for pressures that at times entail contradictory prescriptions for those who are responsible for shepherding the higher education enterprise through turbulent times. Technology is not a magic wand but merely a set of tools. The ultimate challenge may involve not only positioning and investing—keeping in mind social, political and economic considerations—but also nurturing the imagination for harnessing its power and potential.

NOTES

The writing of this chapter was, in part, supported by the Educational Research and Development Center program, agreement number R309A60001, CFDA 84.309A, as administered by the Office of Educational Research and Improvement (OERI), U.S. Department of Education. The findings and opinions expressed herein do not reflect the position or policies of OERI or the U.S. Department of Education. The preparation of this chapter benefited considerably from the first author's conversations with Stanford University Professor John Etchemendy, an innovator and astute observer who provided generous advice and insight into several examples of contemporary technological applications in addition to articulating the wisdom of adopting a cautious yet open stance.

1. Although *technology* has many different meanings, in this chapter we mean the fungible categories of information and communications technology, which includes devices used to collect, transmit, and process information. We begin with the assumption that technological change is a social process: technology not only impacts society, it is also a cultural product subject to larger social structures and social trends.

2. Robert Usher and Richard Edwards, *Postmodernism and Education* (London: Routledge, 1994).

3. Steve Lohr, "When the Alma Mater Ends with '.edu'," *New York Times,* July 7, 1996.

4. Robert Snider, "The Machine in the Classroom," *Phi Delta Kappan* 74 (1992): 316–23.

5. Edward Fiske, "Computers in the Groves of Academe," *New York Times*, May 13, 1984; Snider, "The Machine in the Classroom."

6. Lohr, "When the Alma Mater Ends with '.edu'."

7. William Massy, *Leveraged Learning: Technology's Role in Restructuring Higher Education* (Stanford, Calif.: Stanford Forum for Higher Education Futures, 1995).

8. Fiske, "Computers in the Groves of Academe"; Claude Fischer, "'Touch Someone': The Telephone Industry Discovers Sociability," *Technology and Culture* 29 (1988): 32–61.

9. Jean-François Lyotard, *The Postmodern Condition: A Report on Knowledge* (Manchester: Manchester University Press, 1984). At the same time, academic study of the knowledge industry is gaining visibility. While previously the domain of sociologists of knowledge and science, the endowment of a new chair for a "distinguished professor of knowledge" in the business school of the University of California, Berkeley, signals broader interest in the phenomena. See James Sterngold, "Welcome to Berkeley: Professor Knowledge Is Not an Oxymoron," *New York Times*, June 1, 1997.

10. The role of faculty as coaches describes the shift away from the belief that the faculty member should be the focus of attention and authority.

11. Steven Gilbert, "Making the Most of a Slow Revolution," *Change*, Mar./Apr., 1996.

12. Carol Twigg, "Navigating the Transition," *Educom Review* 29 (1994).

13. For attempts to gauge usage and ownership, see Gilbert, "Making the Most of a Slow Revolution"; Kenneth Green, "The Coming Ubiquity of Information Technology," *Change*, Mar./Apr., 1996; Kenneth Green and Steven Gilbert, "Great Expectations: Content, Communications, Productivity, and the Role of Information Technology in Higher Education," *Change*, Mar./Apr., 1995.

14. See Reid Cushman's excellent article, "From a Distance: Who Needs a Campus When You Have a Downlink," *Lingua Franca* 6 (1996): 53–63, in reference to the Mind Extension University.

15. G. Jacobsen, "Three Entrepreneurial Companies Offer Educational Services," *Success* 44 (1997): 24.

16. Michael Leavitt, governor of Utah, in "The Western Governors University: A Learning Enterprise for the CyberCentury," unpublished manuscript, 1997, available at http://cause-www.colorado.edu/information-resources/ir-library.

17. For a discussion of the changing environmental demands and the emerging restructuring initiatives, see Patricia Gumport and Brian Pusser, "Restructuring the Academic Environment," in *Planning and Management for a Changing Environment*, ed. Marvin Peterson, David Dill, Lisa Mets, and associates (San Francisco: Jossey-Bass, 1997). For an analysis of resource allocation trade offs, see Massy, *Leveraged Learning;* William Massy, "Life

on the Wired Campus," in *The Learning Revolution,* ed. Diana Oblinger and Sean Rush (Washington, D.C.: Anker, forthcoming).

18. William Massy and Robert Zemsky, *Using Information Technology to Enhance Academic Productivity* (Washington, D.C.: EDUCOM, 1995).

19. Lyotard, *The Postmodern Condition;* Robin Usher and Richards Edwards, *Postmodernism and Education* (London: Routledge, 1994).

20. Snider, "The Machine in the Classroom"; Green, "The Coming Ubiquity of Information Technology."

21. Green, "The Coming Ubiquity of Information Technology"; Robert Heterick Jr., ed., "Reengineering Teaching and Learning in Higher Education: Sheltered Groves, Camelot, Windmills, and Malls," CAUSE, Boulder, Colo., 1993).

22. Fiske, "Computers in the Groves of Academe."

23. Cushman, "From a Distance," 56.

24. For a thoughtful perspective on some of these questions, see Gerhard Casper, "Come the Millennium, Where the University?" paper prepared for the annual meeting of the American Educational Research Association, Apr. 1995.

Chapter Fifteen

Graduate Education and Research

Interdependence and Strain

Patricia J. Gumport

Signs of strain are currently evident in American graduate education. Some of these have been reflected in the national media during the past decade: graduate student teaching assistants go on strike at Yale and Berkeley to gain bargaining status as employees; graduate student loan debt climbs to record highs; the Internal Revenue Service subpoenas students' financial records for failure to pay tax on scholarship income; violent demonstrations erupt as University of California, Los Angeles, students wage a hunger strike to gain departmental status for Chicano studies; a doctoral candidate at Washington State is imprisoned after refusing to disclose confidential information about animal rights activities from his research subjects; a former University of South Florida student is imprisoned for "stealing his own intellectual property"; and a bleak national report documents the overproduction and underemployment of Ph.D.s.[1]

How are we to interpret this dizzying spiral of events? Although some may seem to be local aberrations, these news items are not to be dismissed for their lack of representativeness. Rather, they may prompt us to consider some signs of strain in the structural and normative foundations of graduate education. Specific dimensions of strain are evident in the graduate education/research nexus: problematic mechanisms for the financing of graduate education, differential valuing across academic fields of study, variable expectations for the conduct of research, instrumental valuing of research products, and projections for an unfavorable academic labor market upon degree completion. Moreover, when viewed historically, these signs of strain demonstrate that wider social, political, and economic contexts have prominent manifestations in the content and operation of graduate programs. A range of contextual influences generates external demands: state governing boards, government financial aid policies, research funding sources, broad social movements, and the economy, to name a few evidenced in the aforementioned news items.

Such contextual influences on graduate education have potentially far-reaching implications, which warrant careful examination. As a step in that direction, the purpose of this chapter is to show some elements of this dynamic interplay between the graduate education/research nexus and its wider social, political, and economic contexts.[2]

Given space limitations, this chapter focuses on the intersection between doctoral education, academic research, and the federal government, since these interdependent activities reveal the force of contextual influences, and fluctuations in funding patterns serve as a suitable proxy for shifts in dominant societal values.[3]

The thesis developed in this chapter is as follows: although the past century reflects continuity, especially in the structural foundations of graduate education programs, changes in the political and economic contexts of graduate education and academic research have altered the operation of graduate programs. Especially since the early 1970s, signs of strain in the graduate education/research nexus have become more evident as universities have begun to act more like modern research complexes.[4] An underlying theme in this historical development is a tension between, on the one hand, the legacy of academic autonomy that resides in decentralized, departmentally based, graduate programs and, on the other hand, the initiatives of campus officials, outspoken external authorities, and even graduate students, each seeking greater control in the conduct of these academic affairs.

Historical Overview

Among the major transformations in American higher education over the past century is the growth of graduate education. Of the society forces affecting this growth, the federal government has been

the major substantive and symbolic external presence. In the evolving relationship between universities and the federal government,
American graduate education expanded and became intertwined
with complex organizational arrangements for academic research,
research funding, and undergraduate education. The thrust of this
historical overview identifies a paradox of expansion and continuity
in the structural foundations in the midst of qualitative changes in
the nature of social relations.

In a fundamental sense, the historical development reflects much
structural consistency in graduate programs, especially at the doctoral level. Graduate education in the United States has been neither
a unified nor a standardized educational enterprise. By cross-national
standards, this country has the largest, most decentralized, and
highly differentiated set of arrangements for advanced education,
spanning more than 750 campuses, enrolling nearly 2 million students
in graduate and advanced professional degree programs, and granting about 387,000 master's degrees and 41,600 doctorates annually.[5]

Although the content of graduate programs varies across campuses
and disciplines, the decentralized organization, with faculty authority
at the department level, has remained. In addition, the basic model
for doctoral education has been sustained: a few years of prescribed
courses, followed by examinations for advancement to degree can-
didacy, culminating in a dissertation that reflects original research
conducted by the student under the guidance of a faculty committee.
The ideal, dating back to Humboldt, has been for students to engage
in advanced study along with research training.[6] Arrangements for
research training have reflected consistent disciplinary differences:
in the sciences, with its laboratory-intensive research, a graduate
student may work under faculty supervision, with the dissertation
as a piece of a faculty member's research project; in the humanities, with its library-intensive research, a student may work independently, having infrequent contact with faculty supervisors and graduate student peers.

In spite of such structural continuities, the historical development
simultaneously reveals some profound changes in the nature of social
and intellectual relations, especially among graduate students and
faculty. As Nevitt Sanford assessed with critical concern back in 1976:

> The structure of graduate education seems to have changed hardly at
> all since the 1930s. . . . What has changed are the purposes for which

the structure is used and the spirit with which it is managed. The motives of professors and graduate students are less purely intellectual and more professional. . . . The general climate of today is one of competitiveness among universities, between departments in a given university, and between subgroups and individuals within the same department. Students are regarded less as potential intellectual leaders and more as resources to be used in the struggle for a place in the sun.[7]

To the extent that Sanford's characterization may be considered apt today, the research foundations of graduate education need to take center stage in the analysis of how this came about and what the consequences have been. Specifically, changes in the funding patterns for graduate education and university research need to be examined as a critical mediating force in this transformation.[8]

Historically, the financing of graduate education has relied primarily on the sponsorship of university research and secondarily on a variety of loan programs along with state-funded and institutionally funded teaching assistantships. Federal support of academic research has been concentrated in the most visible hundred or so research universities—less than 3 percent of American higher education institutions—which produce about 80 percent of all doctorates and 50 percent of all master's degrees.[9] Such sponsorship of university research has its greatest effect on this sector of dependent campuses and the heavily funded sciences within them, but it also has salience for others throughout the system, even if only by denying them funds.

Federal involvement in graduate education and research can be traced back to the late nineteenth century, when the emergence of the modern research university entailed adapting campus organizational structures to graduate programs and scientific research. As these activities expanded in scale, and as faculty and campus administrators sought more external sponsors, the funding base for both activities became a source and a condition for further organizational changes on campuses and throughout the higher education system. Since the federal government has been a principal source of funds, it has played a pivotal role in these and other more subtle changes in the nature of graduate education. Three changes have been most apparent: an increased specialization of faculty and administrative positions and procedures; greater systemwide stratification along with heightened within-sector competition for fiscal and human resources; and a proliferation of organizational subunits for academic research that reflect the instrumental and increasingly economic agenda of external sponsors.

Nineteenth-Century Beginnings

Graduate education achieved a stable American presence during the last two decades of the nineteenth century, when awarding the Ph.D. became a laudable academic goal. The founding of the Johns Hopkins University in 1876 is often thought of as marking the establishment of graduate education. Johns Hopkins became known as the "proto-type and propagator" of research as a major university function.[10] Coupled with its commitment to scientific research, Johns Hopkins offered merit-based graduate fellowships for full-time study that included state-of-the-art research training.

Both within and immediately surrounding higher education, interest in scientific research had been burgeoning since the mid-nineteenth century. With great frequency, scientists and those seeking advanced study traveled to Germany for the requisite exposure— work in chemistry even into the 1870s required a trip to Germany. On the American front, after initial resistance to the German idea of studying science for its own sake—and after conflicts between self-identified pure and applied scientists—scientific research gradually gained more acceptance, although it took on a distinctive meaning in the American context: American science would be "a collective enterprise like those in business. Modern science needed labor, capital, and management."[11] Proclamations at Johns Hopkins reflected this change in scientific research from "a rare and peculiar opportunity for study and research, eagerly seized by men who had been hungering and thirsting for such a possibility," to an increasingly more prestigious endeavor, proclaimed by Clark University's president as "the very highest vocation of man—research."[12] Science became an increasingly specialized activity that professors could pursue autonomously yet with the security of support, personal advancement, and even prominence within an academic institution.

Following Johns Hopkins' ideal of linking scientific research and graduate education, other graduate schools emerged in the 1890s as parts of larger universities whose undergraduate missions and size offered a broad and stable base of support in endowment funds and tuition. Some were established by the founding of a new university, offering both undergraduate and graduate instruction, such as Stanford University (1891) and the University of Chicago (1892). Others, like Harvard University and Columbia University, added the graduate school onto an established private college. Some state universities—Wisconsin, Michigan, and Illinois—evolved out of land-grant colleges, established with government funds for agriculture and mechanical arts through the Morrill Acts of 1862 and 1890 and the funding of experimental agricultural stations through the Hatch Act of 1887. By 1900, the number of Ph.D.-granting institutions had grown to fourteen and had awarded three hundred doctorates.[13]

In addition to taking on scientific research commitments, Ph.D. programs came to be viewed as an attractive feature for expansion and for advancing an institution's competitive position in the growing higher education system. Based on a desire to confer prestige on their institutions, an increasing number of institutions sought out faculty with research interests and actively sought sponsored-research funds to build laboratories that would attract eminent scientists. Since faculty increasingly wanted to pursue basic research and to train selectively chosen graduate students, institutions were compelled to provide them with opportunities for research and advanced training and, hence, graduate programs across disciplines.

The Principle of Departmental Organization

The widespread adoption of graduate programs within higher education institutions was enhanced by the development of departmental organization that occurred in the last quarter of the nineteenth century. Departments provided a flexible organizational structure for decentralizing and compartmentalizing graduate instruction. While Ph.D. programs were integrated organizationally as a separate level from the liberal education of undergraduate colleges, they were also made parts of departments responsible for undergraduate instruction in a discipline, a linking arrangement that has been remarkably stable and uniform over time and across campuses. The drive to conform to this structure was so strong that Johns Hopkins expanded its organizational structures to offer undergraduate as well as graduate programs.

This organizational arrangement permitted control of undergraduate and graduate programs to reside within the same faculty.[14] Course work as well as research training could be designed appropriately to each discipline and coordinated by each department's faculty. One functional by-product of this arrangement was that graduate programs maintained both faculty and institutional continuity: they allowed faculty to propagate themselves by training their professional successors; and they promoted cohesion, since the responsibility for graduate students kept faculty attentive to their departments. Graduate programs kept research and teaching activities interlocked and the institution functionally integrated—at least at the department level—in spite of increased disciplinary specialization.

Corresponding to established areas of knowledge at the time, departments were able to design research apprenticeships appropriate to the specialized training in each of the disciplines. The specialization of disciplines mirrored by departments represented professors' vocational aspirations, which were especially apparent in the newly established natural and social science departments, whose very existence was justified on the basis of specialized research. As disciplines crystallized into national professional associations, these associations came to serve as visible external referent groups that would give a semblance of standardization across graduate programs: "disciplines and departments had powerful reciprocal effects upon one another" in reinforcing the authority of departments on campus and the professional judgments of faculty nationally.[15] Thus, the emergence of associations further facilitated the growth of Ph.D. programs.

The size and complexity of the graduate education and research enterprise, especially during the 1890s, encouraged coordination and control, which were reflected in the emergent bureaucratic administration on campus. While departments served faculty interests in autonomy in research and instruction, hierarchies of rank within departments and competition across departments served administrative interests in "productive work" as measured by research output. One observer noted, "Clearly it had become a necessity, from the administrator's point of view, to foster the prestigeful evidences of original inquiry."[16]

The dual tasks of graduate education and research were institutionalized most easily in those institutions with greater resources, both financial and reputational. Thus at the systemwide level, those who succeeded in the competitive drive for advancement became a leading peer group of institutions. The prominence of this tier in the American system was reflected in their founding of the Association of American Universities (AAU) in 1900, which marked the culmination of nineteenth-century efforts to establish graduate education and research activities. Ostensibly, the AAU was founded to establish uniformity of standards, yet it simultaneously functioned as an exclusive club.[17] The establishment of the AAU signifies an implicit systemwide division of labor in the United States, wherein elite institutions have differentiated themselves as a sector at the top of the hierarchy engaged in graduate education and research. Although institutions compete for faculty, graduate students, and philanthropic support, the persistent concentration of fiscal and status resources in this sector is a distinctive feature of the American system and an institutional version of Robert Merton's Matthew effect.[18]

Characterized as "a new epoch of institutional empire-building," this period of American higher education reflects the surfacing of university concerns for status in an increasingly stratified system. Such concerns were evident in such dynamics of academic rivalry as bidding for faculty and emulating academic departments. While the American system is not unique in its inclination toward stratification, the institutional drive for competitive position within the research university sector has been, according to one American scholar, "almost an obsession." [19]

Thus, the end of the nineteenth century marked the creation of the research university as a new kind of social institution devoted to scientific research as well as graduate education. The extent of institutional ambition was so pervasive that developing universities imitated one another in the departments, programs, and faculties they sought to develop. Across the country, homogeneity in the proliferation of graduate programs and faculty positions suggests that universities sought to acquire not only intellectual legitimacy but economic and political legitimacy as well.

The Twentieth-Century Rise of Sponsored Academic Research

The expansion of graduate education in the modern university developed hand in hand with the expansion of a national system of sponsored research. Initially, external resources for academic science were amassed principally from philanthropic foundations, while industry played a minimal role. Not until after World War II were foundations and industry eclipsed by a surge in federal government involvement.

The earliest sources of research sponsorship were wealthy benefactors and their philanthropic foundations. In the 1870s, philanthropic contributions to higher education averaged $6 million per year, mainly to individual scientists. By 1890, philanthropic support reflected a more widespread and instrumental orientation, directing funds to emerging universities for their potential contributions to industrial growth, employment, and commercial endeavors. Philanthropic funds supported a wide array of institutional activities, especially in the applied sciences, including funds for equipment, overall plant expansion, and new professional schools. In some cases, the sums were large, like John D. Rockefeller's $35 million endowment of the University of Chicago. On a national scale, John D. Rockefeller and Andrew Carnegie established the two largest foundations involved in research: the Rockefeller Foundation, established in 1913 with $182 million; and the Carnegie Corporation, created in 1911 with $125 million. In the early 1920s these foundations favored donations to separate research institutes, such as the Rockefeller Institute of Medicine and the Carnegie Institute of Washington.[20]

By the 1930s, universities found themselves uncertain of whether foundations would be a stable external sponsor for academic science: foundations reoriented their giving to become an integral funding base for university research by allocating project grants and post-doctoral fellowships (by the Guggenheim Foundation), especially in medical research, the natural sciences, and to a lesser degree, the social sciences. For example, in 1934 Rockefeller Foundation grants constituted a large portion of foundation giving to research in higher education (35%), to the social sciences (64%), and to the natural sciences (72%).[21]

Such voluntary contributions gave universities the resources required to institutionalize graduate education and scientific research. Universities and their faculties built their own rationales and adapted organizational structures to expand the scope of their research activities, while training the next generation of knowledge producers. Upholding university autonomy and academic freedom became not only institutional concerns but also issues for individual faculty. Faculty claimed expert authority in order to establish some distance from the agendas of campus governing boards and the increasingly prominent philanthropists. Professionalization efforts of faculty during this era were not merely an outgrowth of the knowledge explosion, as is commonly claimed, but due in part to external mandates for research.[22]

Private industry entered the academic scene as an unpredictable supplement.[23] As industry research and development (R&D) expenditures rose in the 1920s, corporations conducted both applied and basic research in their own industrial laboratories in the technological areas of communications and chemicals research. The success of industrial sponsorship for university research during this era was exemplified by two prestigious research universities, the Massachusetts Institute of Technology and the California Institute of Technology. Overall, however, corporate R&D funds stayed in their industrial laboratories through the 1930s and thereby remained an unpredictable presence for academic science.

By the late 1930s, university research was flourishing, although primarily in the nation's most visible universities. Evidence for this concentration of research activity points to a similar concentration of research training activity: in 1937, sixteen universities accounted for half of total expenditures on university research and granted 58 percent of all doctorates.[24] This consolidation of research resources with doctoral-granting activity would persist even after this era of university research as a privately financed operation.

The Surge of Federal Involvement

The national government's sponsorship of research and research training evolved incrementally, rather than through a coordinated policy on science or on graduate education. Beginning with federal and state governments' playing a role in land-grant campuses through agricultural research, universities increasingly were seen as a national resource for basic research and training that could assist in its priorities of economic growth, national security, and health care. Over time, including two world wars, the government became the major sponsor of scientific research and higher education.

Federal involvement in academic science began with organizational efforts to designate advisory boards for scientific research. Signifying both the value of modern science and a perceived need to oversee the country's research intentions, the first national organization was the National Academy of Sciences (NAS) founded in 1863.[25] In 1919, the National Research Council (NRC) was established by the NAS, essentially to carry out the earlier congressional mandate. As the principal operating agency of both the NAS and—after 1964—the National Academy of Engineering, the NRC was intended to serve as a bridge between the federal government, the public, and the community of scientists and engineers. Over time, the NRC has become a principal organizational base for overseeing national research efforts and for monitoring how federal funds are channeled into university research.

Rather than actually advising the government, however, the NRC, along with the American Council of Learned Societies (founded in 1919) and the Social Sciences Research Council (founded in 1923), depended upon the resources of philanthropic foundations to assume a prominent role in the promotion of university research. As channels for foundation funds, these organizations provided interested sponsors with access to scientists and scholars as well as administrative assistance in selecting recipients of small research grants and postdoctoral fellowships in the areas of mathematics, physics, and chemistry. By the 1920s, American science was mobilized under "the guidance of the private elites" who "came together for the purpose of furthering science." The memberships of the NRC and the NAS were constituted by "the same group of individuals [who] encountered one another, in slightly different combinations."[26]

The national government's expansion of a large-scale, multiagency funding system to support academic science developed incrementally during and after each world war. In the late 1930s, annual federal expenditures for American science were estimated at $100 million; most of these funds went to applied research in federal bureaus, especially agriculture, meteorology, geology, and conservation. The shift to university-based research occurred when the expertise of academic researchers became valuable for national defense efforts.[27] In World War I, for example, the federal government financed psychologists to construct intelligence tests and encouraged scientists to follow up on the diagnostic physical examinations of the close to four million people who were drafted. For such work, universities granted leaves to life and physical scientists as well as social scientists and historians. The government also allocated funds for researchers to work on their campuses. By World War II, government support was more extensive: in 1940, federal funds for university research totaled $31 million. During the 1940s, the Office of Naval Research contracted with more than two hundred universities to conduct about 1,200 research projects involving some 3,000 scientists and 2,500 graduate students. Between 1941 and 1945, the United States spent $3 billion on R&D, one-third of which was allocated for university-based research aimed at winning the war and devising "new instruments of destruction and defense."[28]

The expansion of sponsored research in universities was coupled with the expansion of doctoral training. Between 1920 and 1940, the number of institutions awarding doctoral degrees doubled, from fifty to a hundred; in the same period, the number of doctorates awarded increased fivefold, from 620 to 3,300.[29] In addition to such growth, a qualitative shift occurred, enhancing the caliber of doctoral students; in the 1920s, the majority of graduate students had been "undistinguished," reflecting "uneven preparation, uncertain motivation and unproven ability."[30]

By the end of World War II, the federal government came to view research universities as a precious public resource for research and research training and worthy of a partnership even during peacetime. The establishment of the National Science Foundation (NSF) reflected an overt federal agenda that science would indeed offer "an endless frontier" and that universities could be ideal settings for such research, as Vannevar Bush stated in his 1945 report to President Roosevelt.[31] In the 1950s, the federal research budget grew steadily, and the academic research enterprise expanded in the top tier of institutions. In 1953/54, the top twenty of these institutions spent 66 percent of federally sponsored research funds for academic science and awarded 52 percent of the doctorates, the bulk of them in the life sciences, physical sciences, and engineering, the same fields that received most of the federal research funds.[32]

The Postwar Expansion of Funds

Spurred by the launching of Sputnik in 1957, the government provided even more funds for basic research. Federal sponsorship of research increased every year between 1958 and 1968. In that decade alone, annual federal contributions to academic research increased fivefold. As the federal investment increased, so did universities' share of total basic research, from one-third to one-half during that decade.[33] Thus, the post–World War II period clearly established that research was a separate function, paid for mainly by the federal government, and that universities could perform a large share of the nation's research effort.

While higher education was perceived as having an increasingly legitimate research role, total enrollments rose from 3 to 7 million students and doubled within doctorate-granting universities from 1.24 to 2.5 million, for undergraduate and graduate levels combined.

Annual Ph.D. production in science and engineering grew dramatically, from 5,800 in 1958 to 14,300 in 1968.[34]

The allocation of federal research funds followed two basic imperatives, which have been consistent from the outset: multiagency support and competition among individual proposals. Federal sponsorship entailed a clear presidential directive for multiagency support; Executive Order 10521, in 1954, stated that no single government agency was to be given sole responsibility for the distribution of research funds. Rather, each agency should sponsor research related to its mission, such as health, defense, and energy. In 1959, 96 percent of federal sponsorship came from five agencies: the Department of Defense; the Department of Health Education and Welfare—largely the National Institutes of Health (NIH); the Atomic Energy Commission; the National Science Foundation; and the Department of Agriculture. In the same year, more than 96 percent of the $1.4 billion allocated for research was diverted to the life sciences, physical sciences, and engineering, leaving the social sciences, particularly the humanities, neglected.[35]

Lacking a unified policy with specific purposes, funding arrangements were coordinated through a mechanism of peer review by researchers in the scientific community that extended beyond the federal government. A competitive system for reviewing research proposals and awarding research grants was the primary vehicle through which the federal government tried to ensure that the best research would be performed. For the most part, federal agencies' priorities were to nurture excellence, although there was some effort to disperse resources across geographic locations and across small and large institutions. The resulting pattern has reinforced the funding of the leading tier of research universities and the science fields, with life sciences and physical sciences accounting for more than half of the basic research budget.

Similar to the expansion of federal basic research funding, federal support for doctoral education intensified, mostly to train science and engineering personnel. Aside from its short-term interests to advance science and technology, the federal government was mindful of improving its research capacity and developing a pipeline of trained scientists and engineers. A variety of mechanisms were employed to attract and retain talented students in the pipeline: direct student aid (fellowships), student aid channeled through institutions (traineeships), and project grants to individual faculty that included salaries for graduate student research assistants. The precedent was set for this explicit twofold agenda in the 1937 National Cancer Act, which set up grants-in-aid to nongovernment scientists and direct student aid in the form of fellowships. By the 1950s, the NSF offered more than five hundred prestigious portable fellowships to students.

The National Defense Education Act of 1958 conveyed a commitment to rebuild the nation's research capability through "manpower training," specifically to support science education through a host of fellowship and traineeship programs to be launched by a variety of federal agencies—NIH, NSF, NASA (National Aeronautics and Space Administration). Another program was the National Research Service awards, which were administered through three federal agencies in the 1960s. These training programs were deliberate efforts to attract talented students through stipends for predoctoral and postdoctoral support as well as to improve the training on campuses with institutional allowances. In the decade between 1961 and 1972, these particular programs assisted more than 30,000 graduate students and 27,000 postdoctoral scholars, according to one estimate.[36]

While direct support of doctoral education through fellowships and traineeships was done on a competitive basis, the talent and support ended up being concentrated at leading research universities, in which the federally sponsored research was conducted. This resulted in a consolidation of resources for research and doctoral education, giving these institutions a double competitive edge in attracting high-quality students and faculty.[37]

Post–World War II federal initiatives were even more instrumental in cementing the legitimacy of this interdependence: sponsored university research had short-term R&D value and sponsored graduate education promoted "manpower training." Between the end of World War II and 1972, the federal government spent $200 billion on R&D. Academic institutions' share of R&D expenditures rose from 5 to 10 percent, while their share of basic research expenditures went from one-quarter in 1953 to one-half in the early 1970s. By the end of this era, the surge of federal sponsorship resulted in a persistent pattern: about half of the country's basic research was done in universities, about two-thirds of university research expenditures came from the federal government, and about half the federal funds for basic academic research went to the top twenty-five research universities.

The Postwar Expansion of Graduate Education

Within the context of expanded sponsored-research opportunities and a shifting funding base, the graduate education system continued to grow at a constant rate during each decade.[38] The end of World War II marked a turning point: more doctorates were granted in the 1950s than in all preceding years (the number rose from 6,000 in 1950 to 10,000 in 1960). The 1960s experienced an even more dramatic expansion: a threefold increase in one decade alone (from 10,000 to nearly 30,000). The expansion of master's degrees followed a similar pattern, the number growing from about 25,000 in 1940, to about 60,000 in 1950, 75,000 in 1960, and nearly 300,000 in 1980.

The proliferation of doctorates and master's degrees reflect both overall growth and expansion into a greater number of fields of study, especially the sciences and professional fields. Physical sciences, life sciences, and engineering accounted for close to half the doctorates awarded in 1965; two decades later, these fields still predominated, although life sciences edged out the other two fields. Social science and psychology remained fairly constant at about 20 percent, humanities dropped from 20 to 10 percent, and education increased from about 15 to 25 percent, reflecting an increased professional orientation of graduate study. The diversification of doctoral fields is marked: more than 550 fields in 1960, compared to 149 in 1916–18. Moreover, beyond field of concentration, there are now 47 types of doctoral degree besides the Ph.D.: doctor of education, doctor of social work, doctor of business administration, doctor of theology, and doctor of arts. A similar orientation to the demands of the marketplace is evident in the growth of master's degrees since 1965, especially in practitioner-oriented fields. By 1982/83, only 16 percent of master's degrees were granted in research-oriented programs; master's degrees in business accounted for 23 percent, engineering 10 percent, and the health professions 6 percent; education still held the largest share, at 30 percent.[39]

Since World War II, graduate education at the master's and doctoral levels has grown into a vast enterprise, in which the leading tier of research universities has become the model for aspiring institutions. Since the less elite institutions had less of a resource base in facilities, departmental funds, and critical masses of faculty and students, they invested their resources in selected fields. Not until the 1970s did asserting a distinctive institutional mission become a strategy for gaining a competitive edge in specialized areas. At the leading institutions, the dynamic was different: able to cover all fields, their strategy was to undertake more sponsored research and to expand Ph.D. production. This is the modern research imperative, the vehicle whereby universities protect, if not advance, their institutional mobility, for "the institution which is not steadily advancing is certainly falling behind."[40]

Up until the contemporary period, graduate education and research in the leading modern universities were guided by opportunities from major changes at the national level: the use of scientific research for national defense and economic priorities; the rise in the research budget of the federal government, in terms of both overall R&D allocations and basic research funds; the plurality of funding agencies to help stabilize university autonomy; and a system of peer review to ensure distribution of resources for the best science. Universities, having an abundance of funds unconnected to their instructional budgets, have become the main performers of basic research, and the federal government has become the predominant external source of funds. However, at the dawn of the contemporary era, shifts in organization and sponsorship suggest a context of greater uncertainty, as changing funding sources, mechanisms, and allocations reflect new challenges for the research foundations of graduate education.

The Contemporary Era: Signs of Strain

While the patterns that crystallized in the post–World War II period have remained prominent, university/government relations show signs of strain. The early 1970s witnessed an economic crisis that threatened the research/training link in the sciences and even the resource base of the most prominent research universities. An era of retrenchment—roughly between 1969 and 1975—began with a tightening academic labor market and inflation in the wider economy. The events of this era signaled that the government could be an unstable base of economic and political support for university research and graduate education.

The federal government reduced funds to support the research infrastructure that it had dramatically expanded in the post–World War II period. Between 1968 and 1971, the basic research budget

412   Patricia J. Gumport

fell more than 10 percent in real terms.⁴¹ Annual academic research
expenditures contributed by the federal government declined from
$5 billion in 1968 to $4.7 billion in 1974. The government's attention turned to short-term research that would make scientific knowledge technologically relevant. As a result, physical resources such
as equipment and campus buildings were neglected. In addition to
the decline in funds for academic science, support for graduate students declined.⁴² The government abruptly withdrew the bulk of its
direct fellowship support to graduate students, especially some of
the larger programs funded by the National Institutes of Health. By
one count, the 57,000 federal fellowships and traineeships in 1968
shrunk to 41,000 in 1970; another estimate is that federal fellowships
fell from 51,000 in 1968 to 6,000 by 1981. As graduate fellowships
were cut back, a series of national reports were conducted concerning the financing of graduate education. They cited the destabilizing
effects of stop-and-go federal funds, the disadvantages of smaller scale
fellowships, and the reduced support levels of 4,000 new merit-based
awards for gifted students each year.

In place of the wider support base, the government left the bulk of
doctoral students to seek direct support from loans. In compensating
for the reduction in fellowship support, loans increased substantially
during one decade alone—from 15 percent of graduate student enrollment in 1974 to 44 percent in 1984. By 1984, an estimated 600,000
students working toward graduate degrees borrowed $2 billion from
the federal government in guaranteed student loans (later known as
Stafford loans).

In the 1980s, the federal government continued its indirect support of doctoral education through the mechanism of assistantships
embedded in $13 billion of federal academic R&D. However, along
with the reduction in fellowships and traineeships in the early 1970s,
stipends from assistantships were reconceptualized as taxable pay for
work rather than tax-exempt subsidies for education. The 1986 Tax
Reform Act was a government initiative to reduce the federal deficit
by taxing stipends associated with research assistantships and state-
funded teaching assistantships previously excluded from income tax.
Although universities and their national representatives acted on behalf of themselves and their graduate students to have this legislation amended, they were able to exempt only fellowship and tuition
awards from taxation. Assistantship stipends—a large portion of federal support for graduate students—still were considered taxable in-

come. In addition to requiring technical changes in the administration of graduate student financial assistance, the policy change can be interpreted as a sign that graduate students are seen as instrumentally, rather than inherently, worthy.

In spite of contemporary changes in the financing of graduate education, universities continue to perform half of the country's basic research, a small but significant part of the national R&D effort. Of the $171 billion national R&D spending in 1995, $60.7 billion was provided by the federal government and $101.7 billion by industry.[43] Most R&D funds go to development. Of 1995 federal R&D funds, $17.1 billion were allocated for basic research, making the federal government the largest sponsor—at 58 percent—of basic research. Industry was the second largest sponsor of basic research, at about $7.5 billion. Higher education institutions were third, at $3.4 billion.

The distribution of basic research funds among academic institutions reflects a persistent concentration of research activity and sponsored-research resources. The top hundred institutions account for more than 80 percent ($15.6 billion) of all academic R&D expenditures; the top fifty institutions account for nearly 60 percent ($11.0 billion); the top ten account for approximately 17 percent ($3.4 billion). In addition, the institutions constituting the top tier—by receiving four-fifths of all federal obligations in which R&D funds are embedded—have remained remarkably stable; eighty-one of the top hundred of 1967 have remained in that category for two decades.[44] However, this concentration has shifted slightly since the early 1980s: in 1983, the top ten institutions claimed only 20 percent of research funds. This ten-year drop reflects a slight dispersion of resources, paralleled by a slight increase—from 17 to 20 percent—of funding to those institutions below the top one hundred. The distribution of academic R&D across fields has essentially been the same over the past two decades: more than 80 percent of federal funds go to life sciences (54%), engineering (16%), and physical sciences (11%). Although research allocations to the behavioral and social sciences increased from $0.55 billion in 1983 to $1.01 billion in 1993, these two areas account for only 6 percent of the total throughout that period.

Institutions have responded to this contemporary funding base with their own initiatives by, for example, establishing their own teaching assistantships and research assistantships or by drawing on institutional funds from endowments, tuition, or—for public institutions—state revenues. Institutions have also used their own funds to support research activities, including facilities and equipment improvement, and have accelerated efforts to collaborate with industry, which has prompted concern among some observers and participants over a potential blurring of boundaries, if not purposes, between academic researchers and external sponsors.

In their effort to broaden their funding base, universities have elaborated their organizational structures in the form of extradepartmental research units that reflect increasingly specialized areas of interdisciplinary and applied research. The organization of research in university settings has historically been anchored in the departmental structure, in which faculty work as both individual investigators and mentors to their advanced graduate students in the department's degree programs. The major exception to this mode of organization in the contemporary period is the organized research unit (ORU), academic units outside of departments and lacking degree-granting status. Before the twentieth century, ORUs were primarily observatories and museums, but in the post–World War II expansion of academic research, ORUs proliferated to meet societal demands for research that did not correspond to instructional areas outlined by departments or that was disproportionate to departments in magnitude and expense. Funded by the national government, state governments, industry, and foundations, ORUs have extended university research into interdisciplinary, applied, and capital-intensive endeavors. Estimates of the number of ORUs on U.S. campuses by the end of the 1980s ranged from two thousand to ten thousand; they continue to emerge in new fields like biotechnology, microelectronics, material sciences, and artificial intelligence.[45]

While the presence of external funds from a sponsor is often the impetus for a proposed ORU, other criteria include the presence of a critical mass of faculty and the availability of administrative support. Some ORUs have explicit commitments to graduate education, such as graduate fellowships offered by the Stanford Humanities Center. ORUs offer important advantages for graduate education. Intellectually, they can mediate between the world of disciplinary training and "real world needs and problems."[46] Practically, they provide dissertation support and stipends for graduate students. Often, they make available better research equipment. Finally, as an indirect benefit, they employ specialists (postdoctoral or nonfaculty researchers) in a temporary home (akin to the departmental home), in which graduate students can participate.

The administration of research and research training in ORUs evokes a new set of challenges when it works at cross-purposes with departmental organization. Full-time nonfaculty research personnel may supervise graduate student research assistants but without faculty status.[47] Generally, students and younger faculty want these opportunities to work with trained researchers and up-to-date equipment, so these centers may draw intellectual, organizational, and economic vitality away from department-based graduate programs, jeopardizing the continued viability of these departments. Not only may faculty loyalties become divided between organizational units, but budgets for research are overseen by different managers than are departmental instructional budgets. Thus, a significant component of research training may be staffed and financed by complex administrative arrangements, in which faculty allocations and budget allocations are no longer congruent with the actual practice of department-based graduate education. In short, the research training component of graduate education may become organizationally less visible, as it falls between the lines of departmental organization.

ORUs have become a highly visible and controversial receptacle for industrial funds, especially as federal initiatives have been launched to encourage industrial contributions for campus-based, large-scale operations. Beginning with the mid-1970s, the NSF established the Industry-University Cooperative Research Projects. In the late 1980s, the NSF proposed university-based centers for engineering research, science, and technology. These centers were to be funded initially by congressional appropriations and then weaned from NSF funds through industrial contributions. A major element provoking controversy in some locations has been the explicit expectation for universities to aid in the nation's economic competitiveness.

Graduate education and research are affected in mixed ways by initiatives that combine—or seek to replace—federal support with industrial sponsorship. Resources become not only more concentrated but also less flexible, for once a center is established, it demands to be fed. Moreover, industrial sponsorship, whether formal or informal, carries potential constraints in terms of the research process (e.g., secrecy) and the product (e.g., negotiation over intellectual property). However, in favoring new interdisciplinary and applied sciences and in bringing to campus research personnel to staff those facilities, industrial sponsors may provide faculty with supplemental income, may expose graduate students to timely problems and state-of-the-art research and techniques, and may position them for jobs in industry. An incentive for university administrators and researchers to col-

laborate with industry or to accept industry sponsorship is to sustain
the material conditions required for first-class, capital-intensive science. Direct appeals by universities to the federal government have
brought limited results. With much lobbying on the part of university representatives, the federal government has reluctantly agreed to
sponsor some of the rebuilding and replacement of campus research
facilities and equipment that was neglected throughout the 1970s and
that proved insufficient as science became more capital-intensive in
the 1980s. Both the NIH and the NSF have participated in this revitalization through regular research grants and center grants.

In addition to establishing ORUs, universities recover the enormous costs incurred in campus research by charging to research
grants their overhead costs, although university administrators,
campus-based researchers, and federal agencies struggle to reconcile
their conflicting interests. The indirect-cost rate distributes among
sponsors and research projects the indirect costs that the institution incurs for lighting, heating, libraries, and general maintenance
of the campus. Since a university wants to recoup the maximum
amount possible and the researcher wants as much of the money
as possible for the research process itself, administrators and researchers disagree. At the same time, the government wants an
adequate justification of university expenses. Universities vary in
their indirect-cost rates, with private universities usually charging
a higher percentage. For example, 1997 indirect-cost rates show
Columbia University at 70.5 percent, the University of Pennsylvania
at 59.1 percent, and Stanford University at 58.1 percent; while the
rate was 44 percent at the University of Wisconsin, 47 percent at the
University of Minnesota, 49.9 percent at the University of California, Berkeley, 52.5 percent at the University of Michigan, and 53 percent at the State University of New York at Buffalo.[48]

Underlying the discussions over indirect-cost recovery is a widespread perception that instrumentation in university laboratories
fares poorly when compared to government or commercial laboratories and that a decline in quality of instrumentation in research
universities may cause a decline in the research productivity of academic scientists as well as in the quality of training for graduate
students. The concern is whether universities will be able to provide
interdisciplinary research and research training without reducing the
strength of traditional, disciplinary graduate education. In spite of
universities' performing more than half of American basic research,

it is unclear whether industries will continue to collaborate with university researchers or keep their funds for their own laboratories. Ultimately, the worry is that academic departments will not be on the frontiers of research and that the best researchers will leave, jeopardizing a premise of the system: that the best and the brightest produce the best science and the best scientists at centers of excellence.[49]

The changing nature of federal funding for research, in addition to the 1970s decline in direct fellowships, has been most evident for Ph.D. students in the sciences, which has had dramatic consequences for their research training experiences. And for Ph.D. students in the humanities, there is no real federal support. Over the past two decades, graduate education has become more expensive, yet it continues to be supported in an ad hoc way. The largest potential funding base, the federal government, is essentially unstable, resulting in increased pressure on universities to come up with funding for graduate students and increased pressure on professors to develop leaner research budgets with tighter time constraints.

Doctoral students across disciplines are taking longer to complete their programs. The median registered time-to-degree has increased from 5.6 years in 1970 to 6.8 years in 1986 and 7.2 years in 1995. Differences by field of study continue: for 1995, median registered time-to-degree for humanities was the longest, at 8.4 years, in contrast to much shorter medians in life sciences (7.0 years), physical sciences (6.9 years), and engineering (6.4 years).[50]

Students acquire more loan indebtedness the longer they defer employment, and they become discouraged through loss of momentum. In an effort to speed up the process, several programs have reduced requirements for coursework so that students begin working on their dissertations earlier. The University of Chicago, for example, instituted a reduced course work policy in 1982 to encourage students "to engage in their doctoral research as quickly, as clearly, and as self-consciously as possible," hoping for "a healthier emphasis on the research stage of graduate student work."[51] Such a change is especially needed in the humanities, in which the prior tendency was to take a cumulative view of knowledge, with the result that more and more material had to be incorporated into graduate coursework. In the sciences, the curricula are revamped every few years. In addition, expectations regarding the dissertation may be revised, especially in the sciences and economics, in which publishable articles are more valuable currency for launching a career than a long treatise.

Recent studies document an overproduction of doctorates in science and engineering; in the humanities and social sciences, new doctorates are already disheartened by an unfavorable academic labor market.[52] With no projections for an academic hiring boom, faculty across the disciplines have begun working with doctoral students early in their programs to prepare for alternatives to an academic career. In addition, departmental admissions committees have been considering whether they should limit the number of new doctoral students or provide prospective students with placement information that tracks a department's graduates.

A less visible and potentially more profound transformation concerns the ways in which changes in federal sponsorship of research and graduate education have accompanied changes in the nature of student/faculty relationships during research training, especially for students in the sciences. While the historical ideal entailed a student working "at the bench" with a mentor, sponsored research is now the central medium for supervision and collaboration. There is some concern that faculty have become more like project managers and administrators rather than mentor-professors and that students are being supervised in a more directed manner, treated as employees and technicians rather than apprentices. As one observer suggested, "the roles of faculty member (mentor) and principal investigator (employer) are becoming inconsistent, straining the incumbents. Principles and practices that the mentor would prefer are inconsistent with the needs of the scientist as employer."[53]

The time schedules of short-term project grants mean less leeway for mistakes; less grant money means more competition and pressure to produce better results; the sharing of capital-intensive instrumentation means long hours of work, often in other cities; larger research teams entails perfecting a technique on one part of a project rather than completing an entire project from beginning to end; and time spent in research is valued over time spent in teaching newer graduate students or undergraduates. The arrangements emphasize efficiency and productivity, which promote an organizational climate of a factory floor or a quasi firm, rather than a center of learning.[54] Some evidence to support this assessment lies in organizing efforts of graduate students to gain bargaining status as employees.[55] There have also been disputes over academic authorship and ownership of intellectual property. Clearly, tensions are heightened in university/industry collaboration: while the exploitation of students for a faculty member's

academic advancement is historically grounded in the university research system, it is another matter for a professor to profit financially
from a student's work on a commercial venture.[56]

Conclusion: Changing Conduct in Changing Contexts

The trajectory of historical development is clear: graduate education
in the United States has become so intertwined with sponsored research that graduate education and research have emerged as the
foremost raison d'être for universities in the top tier; as an increasingly noble aim for lower tiers to emulate; and as an implicit professional imperative for faculty. Historical scholarship reveals that
obtaining research funds from the federal government and other
patrons has been a requirement for university expansion and prestige. As universities have competed for talented faculty and graduate
students, they have sought to preserve their autonomy through sta-
bilizing a support base from a plurality of sources, including external sponsors and internal revenues. Universities have attempted to
create organizational structures to minimize the skewing of institutional priorities toward the economic incentives of short-term R&D
sponsors.

Nonetheless, universities have been continually challenged by an
inherently unstable federal funding base, whose direct support for
doctoral education has been high in the physical and life sciences,
lower in the social sciences, and virtually nonexistent in the humanities. Particularly in the past three decades, tension heightened as
the federal government replaced a large proportion of fellowships
and traineeships with loans, incurred by individual students, leaving
the bulk of support as indirect, through research assistantships on
short-term R&D projects that strain the mentor/apprentice relationship. Former ideals have been overshadowed by research training
elaborated into status distinctions, encouraging students to connect
with "the right" principal investigator on a "cutting-edge" and consistently funded research project. To the extent that graduate education functions as professional socialization, the professional work
now modeled for students is often dependent on productivity criteria tied to other-than-scholarly agendas, which inspires us to ask, For
what kind of profession are graduate students being prepared?

The tone of this analysis is not optimistic, primarily because the future organization and sponsorship of graduate education require collective deliberation. The issues go beyond what graduate degree programs a campus should offer and are not strictly about efficient means but about desirable ends. These include the nature of research training, the nature of financial aid mechanisms, the increasing time-to-degree of doctoral study, foreign student enrollment in doctoral programs, the neglect of humanities and other nonscience fields, the appropriateness of industrial sponsorship, and the ownership of intellectual property.

Admittedly, to note that graduate education pays a price for its linkage to the university research enterprise marks a distinctive shift in scholarly attention. Usually, the emphasis is on the diminishing of undergraduate education by its subsidization of faculty research and graduate assistantships.[57] In truth, both undergraduate and graduate education suffer from this arrangement. Scholars are now critically examining the costs and trade offs involved in academic science, especially the consequences for the vitality of the academic profession.[58] However, the inquiry has been hampered by incomplete and often inconsistent historical data and gaps and broken trend lines in contemporary data. At present, the most valuable data are collected at the national level, but these databases have substantial limitations for longitudinal analysis.[59]

Perhaps a more formidable obstacle to this inquiry than good data is the narrow definition of these issues as local organizational or administrative problems rather than as fundamental questions of higher education policy at state and national levels. The social functions of higher education have changed: higher education is a complex and adaptive social institution that produces goods and services, determines and distributes positions and resources, and regulates the use of and access to power. Such a conceptualization reframes the problem and the solution, illuminating how the issues facing graduate education at the close of this century are connected to national R&D policies and the associated underlying political and economic tensions.

NOTES

1. *Chronicle of Higher Education,* Feb. 24, Mar. 24, May 19, Aug. 4, Sept. 1, 1993; Jan. 19, July 5, 1996; *New York Times,* July 4, 1995.
2. On universities' autonomy, see Roger Geiger, *To Advance Knowledge:*

The Growth of American Research Universities, 1900–1940 (New York: Oxford University Press, 1986); David Noble, America by Design: Science, Technology, and the Rise of Corporate Capitalism (New York: Knopf, 1977). On the rise of modern American science, see Robert Bruce, The Launching of Modern American Science, 1846–1876 (New York: Knopf, 1987). On the emergence of the American research university, see Geiger, To Advance Knowledge; Laurence Veysey, The Emergence of the American University (Chicago: University of Chicago Press, 1965). On the emergence of graduate education, see Richard Storr, The Beginnings of Graduate Education in America (Chicago: University of Chicago Press, 1953); Bernard Berelson, Graduate Education in the United States (New York: McGraw-Hill, 1960). On postwar changes in federal support of academic science, see John Wilson, Academic Science, Higher Education, and the Federal Government, 1950–1983 (Chicago: University of Chicago Press, 1983). Little scholarly work had been done on the interrelation of these issues, with the major exception of Joseph Ben-David, Centers of Learning: Britain, France, Germany, United States (New York: McGraw-Hill, 1977). Most research on graduate education has been on graduate students: see Gary Malaney, "Graduate Education as an Area of Research in the Field of Higher Education," in Higher Education: Handbook of Theory and Research, ed. John Smart, vol. 4 (New York: Agathon, 1988). The graduate education/research nexus remains understudied and undertheorized in the higher education literature.

3. For a comprehensive discussion of graduate education at the master's degree level, see Clifton Conrad and Susan Millar, The Silent Success (Baltimore: Johns Hopkins University Press, 1992). On doctoral education, see William Bowen and Neil Rudenstine, In Pursuit of the Ph.D. (Princeton: Princeton University Press, 1992). For a cross-national perspective on graduate education, see Burton Clark, ed., The Research Foundations of Graduate Education (Berkeley: University of California Press, 1993); Burton Clark, Places of Inquiry (Berkeley: University of California Press, 1995).

4. For a study of research drift, see François Queval, "The Evolution toward Research Orientation and Capability in Comprehensive Universities," Ph.D. diss., University of California, Los Angeles, 1990.

5. Chronicle of Higher Education, Sept. 2, 1996. In addition to an enrollment of 1,721,469 graduate students, there are 294,713 professional degree students. See also Carnegie Foundation for the Advancement of Teaching, A Classification of Institutions of Higher Education (Princeton, N.J.: Carnegie Foundation for the Advancement of Teaching, 1994). The approximate number of institutions engaged in graduate education includes those universities that extend at their highest level into master's (529) and doctoral (236) programs according to the Carnegie classification; this number does not include specialized institutions that offer graduate-only programs or baccalaureate colleges that offer an occasional M.A.T. program.

6. Clark, *Places of Inquiry.*

7. Nevitt Sanford. "Graduate Education: Then and Now," in *Scholars in the Making,* ed. Joseph Katz and Rodney Harnett (Lexington, Mass.: Ballinger, 1976).

8. See chapter 6, this volume.

9. Based on National Science Foundation, *Science and Engineering Indicators, 1991* (Washington, D.C.: NSF, Division of Science Resource Studies, 1991).

10. The first Ph.D. granted in the United States was from Yale's Sheffield Scientific School in 1861, the second was from the University of Pennsylvania in 1871, and the third was from Harvard in 1872. More significant was the explicit organizational mission of graduate education in the founding of the Johns Hopkins University in 1876 and Clark University in 1889. See Bruce, *The Launching of Modern American Science,* 335-37.

11. Dael Wolfle, *The Home of Science: The Role of the University* (New York: McGraw-Hill, 1972), 4.

12. Veysey, *Emergence of the American University,* 318-19.

13. Richard Hofstadter and C. DeWitt Hardy, *The Development and Scope of Higher Education in the United States* (New York: Columbia University Press, 1952), 44-45; Berelson, *Graduate Education,* 33.

14. Lewis Mayhew, *Reform in Graduate Education* (Atlanta: Southern Regional Education Board, 1972), 6; Ben-David, *Centers of Learning,* 61. See also Burton Clark, *The Higher Education System* (Berkeley: University of California Press, 1983).

15. Geiger, *To Advance Knowledge,* 37; Ben-David, *Centers of Learning,* 61.

16. Veysey, *Emergence of the American University,* 177.

17. Geiger, *To Advance Knowledge,* 19.

18. Robert Merton, "The Matthew Effect in Science," *Science* 159 (1968): 56-63.

19. Martin Trow, "The Analysis of Status," in *Perspectives on Higher Education: Eight Disciplinary and Comparative Views,* ed. Burton Clark (Berkeley: University of California Press, 1984), 134; Veysey, *Emergence of the American University,* 312.

20. Bruce, *The Launching of Modern American Science,* 329-34; Frederick Rudolph, *The American College and University: A History* (New York: Vintage/Random House, 1962), 425-27.

21. Berelson, *Graduate Education;* Geiger, *To Advance Knowledge,* esp. 166.

22. Much of this adaptation to undertake applied research became incorporated into the ideal of service, especially for public universities. See Noble, *America by Design;* Gary Rhoades and Sheila Slaughter, "The Public Interest and Professional Labor," in *Culture and Ideology in Higher Education,* ed. William Tierney (New York: Praeger, 1991).

23. Geiger, *To Advance Knowledge,* 174–225.

24. Ibid, 262.

25. Over the next decade, the NAS became the site of severe conflicts over membership—which was limited to fifty—and mission, as American scientists from different fields vied for control of the scientific community. Bruce, *Launching of Modern American Science,* 301–5, 315–17.

26. Geiger, *To Advance Knowledge,* 13, 100, 165, 256.

27. Paul Starr, *The Social Transformation of American Medicine* (New York: Basic Books, 1982), 193.

28. Wolfle, *Home of Science,* 110; David Dickson, *The New Politics of Science* (Chicago: University of Chicago Press, 1984); Alice Rivlin, *The Role of the Federal Government in Financing Higher Education* (Washington, D.C.: Brookings, 1961), 31.

29. Martin Finkelstein, *The American Academic Profession* (Columbus: Ohio State University Press, 1984), 24.

30. Geiger, *To Advance Knowledge,* 220.

31. Vannevar Bush, *Science, the Endless Frontier: A Report to the President on a Program for Postwar Scientific Research* (Washington, D.C.: Government Printing Office, 1945).

32. Rivlin, *The Role of the Federal Government,* 47.

33. Dickson, *New Politics of Science;* Government-University-Industry Research Roundtable, *Science and Technology in the Academic Enterprise* (Washington, D.C.: National Academy Press, 1989).

34. Government-University-Industry Research Roundtable, *Science and Technology;* Ben-David, *Centers of Learning,* 119.

35. Douglas Knight et al., *The Federal Government and Higher Education* (Englewood Cliffs, N.J.: Prentice-Hall, 1960), 135–37.

36. Porter Coggeshall and Prudence Brown, *The Career Achievements of NIH Postdoctoral Trainees and Fellows* (Washington, D.C.: National Academy Press, 1984).

37. In 1993, the top thirty universities in doctoral degree production were also among the top fifty receiving federal funds for science and engineering R&D. All but four of those thirty were also listed in the top forty-two universities in terms of R&D expenditures. Data based on National Science Foundation sources.

38. Berelson, *Graduate Education;* National Research Council, *Summary Report, 1986: Doctorate Recipients from United States Universities* (Washington, D.C.: National Academy Press, 1987); National Center for Education Statistics, *Digest of Education Statistics, 1989* (Washington, D.C.: U.S. Department of Education, 1989); Judith Glazer, *The Master's Degree: Tradition, Diversity, Innovation* (Washington, D.C.: Association for the Study of Higher Education, 1986).

39. National Research Council, *Summary Report, 1986;* Berelson, *Graduate Education,* 35; Glazer, *The Master's Degree.*

40. Rudolph, *The American College and University*, 239; see also Patricia Gumport, "The Research Imperative," in *Culture and Ideology in Higher Education*, ed. William Tierney (New York: Praeger, 1991).

41. Government-University-Industry Research Roundtable, *Science and Technology*.

42. Charles Kidd, "Graduate Education: The New Debate," *Change*, May 1974, 43. See also Wolfle, *Home of Science*, 256; Frederick Balderston, "Organization, Funding, Incentives, and Initiatives for University Research," in *The Economics of American Universities*, ed. Stephen Hoenack and Eileen Collins (Albany: State University of New York Press, 1990), 40; Arthur Hauptman, *Students in Graduate and Professional Education: What We Know and Need to Know* (Washington, D.C.: Association of American Universities, 1986); Sheila Slaughter, "The Official Ideology of Higher Education," in *Culture and Ideology in Higher Education*, ed. William Tierney (New York: Praeger, 1991).

43. National Science Board, *Science and Engineering Indicators, 1996* (Washington, D.C.: Government Printing Office, 1996). In 1986 the federal government provided $55 billion and industry provided $60 billion; National Science Board, *Science and Engineering Indicators, 1987* (Washington, D.C.: Government Printing Office, 1987).

44. National Science Board, *Science and Engineering Indicators, 1996*; John Sommer, "Distributional Character and Consequences of the Public Funding of Science," in *Federal Support of Higher Education*, ed. Roger Meiners and Ryan Amacher (New York: Paragon House, 1990), 175. See also Roger Geiger and Irwin Feller, "The Dispersion of Academic Research in the 1980s," *Journal of Higher Education* 66 (1995): 336–60.

45. Roger Geiger, "Organized Research Units: The Role in the Development of University Research," *Journal of Higher Education* 61 (1990): 1–19. See also Gerald Stahler and William Tash, "Centers and Institutes in the Research University," *Journal of Higher Education* 65 (1994): 540–54.

46. Robert Friedman and Renee C. Friedman, "Organized Research Units in Academe Revisited," in *Managing High Technology: An Interdisciplinary Perspective*, ed. Brain Mar, William Newell, and Borje Saxberg (Amsterdam: Elsevier, 1985).

47. See Clark Kerr, *The Uses of the University* (New York: Harper and Row, 1963). Estimates of the number employed in universities range from 5,000 to more than 30,000. Charles Kidd, "New Academic Positions: The Outlook in Europe and North America," in *The Research System in the 1980s: Public Policy Issues*, ed. John Logsdon (Philadelphia: Franklin Institute Press, 1982); Carlos Kruytbosch, "The Organization of Research in the University: The Case of Research Personnel," Ph.D. diss., University of California, Berkeley, 1970; Albert H. Teich, "Research Centers and Non-Faculty Researchers: A New Academic Role," in *Research in the Age of the Steady-State University*,

ed. Don Phillips and Benjamin Shen (Washington, D.C.: American Association for the Advancement of Science, 1982); Government-University-Industry Research Roundtable, *Science and Technology;* Irwin Feller, "University-Industry Research and Development Relationships," paper prepared for the Woodlands Center for Growth Studies conference, Growth Policy in the Age of High Technology: The Role of Regions and States, 1988.

48. Author interviews, university sponsored-research offices.

49. Carol Frances, "1984: The Outlook for Higher Education," *AAHE Bulletin* 37 (1985): 3-7; Kenneth Hoving, "Interdisciplinary Programs, Centers, and Institutes: Academic and Administrative Issues," paper prepared for the annual meeting of the Council of Graduate Schools, 1987; Carlos Kruytbosch, "The Future Flow of Graduate Students into Scientific Research: A Federal Policy Issue?" paper prepared for the annual meeting of the Council of Graduate Schools, December 1979; Bruce Smith, "Graduate Education in the United States," in *The State of Graduate Education,* ed. Bruce Smith (Washington, D.C.: Brookings, 1985).

50. Data measure registered time-to-degree, the amount of time a person was enrolled in educational programs between receipt of the baccalaureate and receipt of the Ph.D. degree. See National Research Council, *Summary Report, 1995: Doctorate Recipients from United States Universities* (Washington, D.C.: National Academy Press, 1996).

51. University of Chicago, "Report of the Commission on Graduate Education," *University of Chicago Record* 16 (1982): 2.

52. Joseph Berger, "Slow Pace toward Doctorates Prompts Fear of Unfilled Jobs," *New York Times* May 3, 1989. William Massy and Charles Goldman, *The Production and Utilization of Science and Engineering Doctorates in the United States* (Stanford, Calif.: Stanford Institute for Higher Education Research, 1995), estimates a 22 percent overproduction of science and engineering doctorates.

53. Edward Hackett, "Science as a Vocation in the 1990s," *Journal of Higher Education* 61 (1990): 267.

54. Henry Etzkowitz, "Entrepreneurial Scientists and Entrepreneurial Universities in American Academic Science," *Minerva* 21 (1983): 198-233.

55. However, there are several structural and normative barriers to the construction of a collective identity among graduate students. See Patricia Gumport and John Jennings, "Students or Employees? The Ambiguity of Doctoral Assistantships," paper prepared for the annual meeting of the American Educational Association, April 1993.

56. Martin Kenney, *Biotechnology: The University-Industrial Complex* (New Haven: Yale University Press, 1986), 118-21.

57. Alexander Astin, "Moral Messages of the University," *Educational Record* 70 (1989): 22-25.

58. Sheila Slaughter, *The Higher Learning and High Technology* (New

York: State University of New York Press, 1990); Hackett, *Science as a Vocation;* Etzkowitz, *Entrepreneurial Scientists.*

59. See the National Research Council, survey of earned doctorates, doctorate record file; the National Center for Education Statistics, enrollment and degrees awarded; the National Science Foundation, academic science and engineering enrollment and support, federal obligations to colleges and universities, and national patterns of science and technology resources. See also the policy studies of the Council of Graduate Schools.

Chapter Sixteen

The Canon and the Curriculum
Multicultural Revolution and Traditionalist Revolt

John K. Wilson

More than at any other time in the history of American higher education, curriculum debates are being conducted with a large degree of public scrutiny.[1] The age when faculty met to discuss curriculum changes behind closed doors is long gone; today, a proposed curriculum change is likely to provoke stories in the *New York Times* and editorials in the *Wall Street Journal*. But despite the high profile of curriculum reform, the actual effect is often small. And for all of the rhetorical firepower used in the curriculum wars, institutional changes in recent years have been relatively small.

Compared to earlier periods of curricular change, the 1980s and 1990s have been relatively static. The elective system created by Charles Eliot at Harvard in the nineteenth century, the core curriculum devised by Robert Hutchins at the University of Chicago in the 1930s, and the decline in general education requirements during the late 1960s were far more dramatic than the changes hotly debated today. Yet, at no time have professors been so widely criticized as now, with one of the main charges launched against them being their alleged failure to teach the classics of Western civilization.

There is a small piece of truth to the accusations. After all, the curriculum is a zero-sum game, and with the increasing importance of studying other cultures as well as the role of women and minorities in Western culture, it becomes difficult if not impossible to maintain the same commitment to the great books of the West. This is reflected in a recent survey of faculty, which showed that the proportion who regarded the teaching of the classics of Western civilization as "essential" or "very important" had dropped from 35 percent in 1989 to 28 percent in 1995. The survey also showed that 53.2 percent of faculty agreed that "Western civilization and culture should be the foundation of the undergraduate curriculum."[2]

However, such surveys do not always accurately reflect faculty views (let alone what is actually taught), because some faculty may be suspicious of how "the classics" are defined or because they believe non-Western culture should also be a part of the foundation of the undergraduate curriculum. It is difficult to find anyone willing to argue that Western civilization should be removed from the curriculum; but it is also true that multiculturalism has brought significant changes in how higher education is defined. The actual state of the curriculum is much more complicated, and the true effects of the multicultural revolution have not been as dramatic as traditionalist critics like to think. Only 8.6 percent of faculty in 1995 had taught an ethnic studies course in the past two years (an increase from 6.2 percent in 1989); only 6.6 percent had taught a women's studies course. Assuming that these questions were interpreted to mean courses dealing substantially with this subject matter (rather than only those specially taught in departments of ethnic studies and women's studies), the percentages indicate that the multicultural and feminist revolutions have had relatively little effect on the curriculum. Only about 15 percent of faculty include readings on race and gender in their classes, which is smaller than the 23 percent who conduct research on issues involving race and gender.[3]

The effects of multiculturalism on general education requirements include new course requirements. In 1990, 46 percent of colleges required a class in other cultures, and 20 percent required a class in racial or ethnic issues. But contrary to the assumption that multiculturalism has caused the elimination of Western civilization requirements, the proportion of colleges requiring classes in the history of Western civilization rose from 43.1 percent in 1970 to 48.5 percent in 1985 and 53 percent in 1990.[4] At York College, the late Barry Gross, one of the leaders of the National Association of Scholars, supported a new requirement (which included multiculturalism in the United States, other regions of the world, and Western civilization) because it made the curriculum "more rigorous." When the University of Massachusetts, Boston, created a new diversity requirement in 1992, business teacher Peter Ittig attacked it as "part of the political correctness party line." Two years later, Ittig conceded that the PC issue "doesn't seem to come up."[5]

However, the traditionalist reaction against multiculturalism has helped to block some new requirements. Texas A&M's College of Liberal Arts voted in 1993 to require students to take a class on foreign cultures and one on ethnic, racial, or gender issues in the United States. Before any students took the classes, the requirement was attacked by the state Republican Executive Committee, the student newspaper, the *Houston Chronicle,* and the *Houston Post.* After this hostile reaction, the president withdrew the plan.[6]

Who Killed Shakespeare?

By the late 1980s, the charge had become common in traditionalist attacks on the state of higher education: the classics were being discarded, replaced by ideologically motivated works by Guatemalan socialists, radical feminists, and minority authors. According to Elizabeth Fox-Genovese, "the campaign to impose 'multiculturalism' amounts to nothing less than a war on Western civilization and, beyond it, a war on the very idea of civilization." Perhaps the most extreme of these accusations was made by Christopher Clausen, chair of Penn State's English department, who declared: "I would bet that *The Color Purple* is taught in more English courses today than all of Shakespeare's plays combined." Dinesh D'Souza's book *Illiberal Education* reported that Clausen's statement "reflected the emerging consensus," and Thomas Short, writing in the National Association of Scholars journal, *Academic Questions,* added: "It is possible that Walker's black lesbian saga is now assigned more often in college courses than all of Shakespeare's plays combined."[7]

Of course, nothing like this has actually happened. Most studies (though limited and anecdotal) suggest that Shakespeare is read by far more students in college than Alice Walker, perhaps by a ratio of a hundred to one.[8] But the believability of such an outrageous assertion indicates how greatly divided American campuses are by the debate over multiculturalism. Because courses and readings on multiculturalism tend to be far more controversial than those about Shakespeare, there is an exaggerated perception of their extent in higher education. Michael Bérubé's study of the Modern Language Association's on-line bibliography from 1981 to 1990 found that Shakespeare was by far the most popular author studied, and the Bard's 5,761 citations was far above the 1,900 citations for second-place Joyce.[9] The remainder of the top ten was composed of traditional white male canonical authors: Chaucer, Milton, Faulkner, Dickens, T. S. Eliot, Melville, Lawrence, and Pound. While new scholarship has changed the focus of English literature somewhat, it is clear that traditional authors remain dominant, even on the cutting edge of research.

Although the charge that Shakespeare was being discarded proved to be demonstrably false, the accusation of ideological bias could not be so easily dismissed. It is certainly true that Shakespeare is being reread and interpreted in new ways. The debate is over whether these new ways of reading old texts are an inevitable part of progress in scholarship or whether they represent an ideologically motivated interpretation of the great books.

Saving Shakespeare at Georgetown

William Shakespeare is by far the most popular author in high school and college English classes and even the most popular topic of study by those dangerous English professors who are said to be deconstructing him out of existence. Popular newspapers and magazines would have you believe that Shakespeare is the deadest whitest male of them all, but in 1996, a plan by Georgetown's English Department to drop a requirement that students take classes on canonical authors such as Chaucer, Milton, and Shakespeare led to a cascade of attacks. The *Indianapolis Star* editorialized that it was "like dropping math from an engineering program." A *Cleveland Plain Dealer* columnist called Georgetown's change an act of "heresy."[10] In the past, a decision to make a small modification in the Georgetown requirements for English majors might have sparked a debate within the department and a short article in the campus newspaper; today, it leads to national attention, condemnation in the editorial pages of major dailies, and the organization of a Committee to Save Shakespeare, which held a teach-in at Georgetown.

The National Alumni Forum (NAF), an offshoot of the National Association of Scholars, chaired by Lynne Cheney, promised to "wage a national publicity campaign against the curriculum changes at Georgetown." NAF director Jerry Martin called Georgetown's changes an "attack on the great works."[11]

But what really happened at Georgetown? After a year-long study, the English faculty decided to revise the old curriculum, creating three concentrations for English majors: studies in literature and literary history; studies in culture and performance; and studies in writing (rhetoric, genre, and form). The old requirement that English majors had to take two of the three classic authors—Shakespeare, Chaucer, and Milton—was eliminated. However, the change did not affect any of the existing courses. Further, English majors at Georgetown always could have graduated without taking Shakespeare, since it never had been required. Indeed, the new requirement makes it easier for students to take more than one class in Shakespeare, so it is likely that the number of students reading his plays will actually increase.

Shakespeare has never been in danger of disappearing at Georgetown. The department offers nine Shakespeare classes every year, and 17 percent of Georgetown undergraduates take a Shakespeare class (compared to about 7% nationally). In the past fifteen years, Georgetown's English Department has increased its Shakespeare offerings by 300 percent.[12] At other universities, the elimination of a Shakespeare requirement did not noticeably reduce student interest in the Bard. In 1990, the University of Maryland, College Park, dropped requirements that English majors read specific authors; the result was not the abandonment of Shakespeare, who draws hundreds of students each year to elective classes.[13] But these facts were lost in the attacks on Georgetown. Rita Zurcher, coauthor of the NAS report on general education, asked in *USA Today,* "What would you consider more important, Shakespeare or basketball?"[14] Zurcher concluded that Georgetown's top-notch basketball program had pressured the English Department to get rid of a Shakespeare requirement, presumably in order to dumb down the curriculum and reduce the workload on athletes.

The NAF commissioned a study of the top seventy colleges and found that only twenty-three required English majors to take Shakespeare. It concluded that "two-thirds of seventy leading colleges and universities have dropped the Shakespeare requirement for English majors" and that "taking the great poet's place are courses on popular culture and sex."[15] The NAF ran into a problem over the question of how to define a Shakespeare requirement. They commissioned the study in response to Georgetown's changes in the English major, but students at Georgetown (and several other colleges) could technically avoid Shakespeare by taking classes on Chaucer and Milton. In one part of the report, the authors seemed to also accept the ten colleges in which at least three courses in pre-1800 literature were required, reasoning that "we assume students will be introduced to the Bard." A two-semester literary survey course at Vanderbilt (similar to that at nine other colleges) was also approved because "we assume that Shakespeare is taught." However, none of these twenty colleges were counted among the twenty-three given the status of requiring Shakespeare, while colleges with requirements like Georgetown had were included.

The NAF's dilemma was that their report got publicity by focusing on the narrow issue of how many colleges required Shakespeare, but their real concern was the loss of the traditional great authors in favor of classes focusing on popular culture. Interestingly, the report did not attempt to debate the contentious issue of multiculturalism directly. It is much easier to complain about academic study of "low culture" and subfields like "queer theory," which are marginalized in the public eye, than to suggest that newly appreciated African American or female authors should be dropped by English departments. Because Shakespeare is so widely taught, requirements for English majors may be determined by other factors. A department may drop a Shakespeare requirement precisely because his writings are read in several other required courses. Or a department may create a Shakespeare requirement to avoid duplication because his popularity leads to students reading the same plays in several classes. But although the NAF's number crunching may have been questionable and their fear of the fall of Shakespeare exaggerated, they raised questions about a genuine change in the curriculum of English departments.

The Alumni Strike Back: Who Rules the Curriculum?

Cultural studies (and to a lesser extent, literary theory) have expanded greatly in recent decades. The controversy over Shakespeare at Georgetown raised the question of who should decide what the curriculum is. In retaliation for the changes, several Georgetown alumni, including William Peter Blatty, author of *The Exorcist,* promised to write the university out of their wills.[16]

Georgetown spokesperson Alwyn Castle declared: "Any university faculty that would allow itself to be intimidated in such a manner would be a disgrace. It is wrong to use donations as a hammer to control curriculum decisions." The NAF was created in direct opposition to Castle's view; according to the NAF, alumni should have significant involvement in the curriculum. The NAF goal is to organize donors and help them target donations to curtail political correctness. As Lynne Cheney observed, "It comes down to the question of who owns the university."[17]

The NAF announcement coincided with a controversy at Yale University, which seemed to embody the concerns that donors did not have enough influence. The story, as Newt Gingrich told it: "Yale University recently had to return $20 million to oil tycoon Lee Bass because after several years the university could not get the faculty to agree to teach Western Civilization."[18] According to the NAF, Bass withdrew his $20 million gift "after it became clear that his wishes would not be followed." In fact, the gift was returned only after Bass demanded a right to veto faculty appointed to the program whose views he opposed. Hilton Kramer argued in the *New York Post* that "tenured left-wing advocates of multiculturalist anti-Western political agenda" were in "open warfare against the creation of the course."[19] Although faculty could be found who opposed the idea of a program focused exclusively on the West, the delays in implementing the Western culture program had nothing to do with leftist faculty.

The real cause of the delay was less exciting. Former dean Donald Kagan, whose speech in defense of Western culture helped inspire the gift, led a committee to recommend the structure for the new program. Kagan urged a small, highly coherent program in which all of the students would take the same classes. But top administrators vetoed the plan because they wanted a program that would involve more of Yale's students. A delay in faculty appointments occurred because of another dispute. Kagan and others in the program wanted assistant professors to be hired by the program; the Yale administration wanted to transfer younger faculty from elsewhere in the university, who would otherwise be fired due to Yale's budget cuts.[20] But the public heard a much different story. *Light and Truth,* a conservative student newspaper at Yale published by the right-wing Intercollegiate Studies Institute (ISI), printed a story accusing left-wing professors of sabotaging the project. The article was publicized by ISI and used by the *Wall Street Journal* and other publications to attack Yale.

T. Kenneth Cribb Jr., president of ISI, flew to Texas in an effort to convince Bass to withdraw his $20 million donation. Although Yale quickly promised to implement the program as Bass originally conceived it, Cribb persuaded Bass to demand the right to veto any faculty hired for the program. Faced with a threat to academic freedom, Yale chose to return his money. Yale's punishment for its administrative gaffe was enormous. In addition to the loss of reputation, other alumni withdrew their gifts, and according to Cribb, "the cost of Yale's behavior is now estimated to be several times the original Bass gift of $20 million."[21]

Western culture at Yale was yet another victim of the campus curricular wars. It is ironic that traditionalists would help eliminate a Western culture program because so many simply assumed that Yale's efforts to establish it had been permanently corrupted by the politically correct. In the culture wars, the symbolic victory of punishing Yale turned out to be more important than immediately improving educational opportunities for students.

The Politics of English Composition

The case of the English 306 composition course at the University of Texas, Austin, reflects the growing public controversy over what used to be little-noticed internal decisions about curricula. In 1990, a faculty committee was established to reform and standardize the composition program in response to unfavorable evaluations from students about the existing course and complaints from teachers (most of whom were literature graduate students) who felt unprepared to design their own rhetoric courses.[22]

The faculty committee proposed focusing English 306 on "writing about difference," which would include "argumentation around the social inequities raised by discrimination suits." New graduate students would be required to follow the stipulated curriculum, but faculty and graduate students who had taught the class once would be allowed to design their own E 306 course. The main readings for the new course would be excerpts from Supreme Court decisions on discrimination suits, along with a writing handbook. To supplement these readings, the faculty committee originally proposed excerpts from Paula Rothenberg's anthology, *Racism and Sexism: An Integrated Study*. Rothenberg's book was dropped from the course requirements after the attacks on the revised E 306 began, although the course designers claimed that they dropped it because too little of the book would be used to justify students buying it.

The crusade against the E 306 reforms was started by English professor Alan Gribben, who accused his department of being controlled by a "highly politicized faction of radical literary theorists." Gribben declared that "our problems are so profound and likely to be long lasting that the English Department should be placed in receivership indefinitely." Critics of the changes took their case not to colleagues but to the media and national critics of academia. Gribben urged the state legislature and board of regents "to consider abolishing required English courses." The course was strongly supported within the English department: the faculty voted forty to eleven in a secret ballot to approve the changes, and graduate students (whose right to teach was supposedly affected by the new course) voted fifty-two to two in defense of it. But external opposition to E 306, led by national figures like former National Endowment for the Humanities chair Lynne Cheney, successfully pressured President William Cunningham (who had not read a syllabus or met with the E 306 committee) to ban the new course.

Ironically, the structure of the proposed revisions for the E 306 class followed what the conservative advocates of core curricula have been demanding: a centralized uniform course designed to increase coherence and quality of teaching. However, the ideology behind the E 306 class was not what traditionalists had in mind, which suggests that the real battle for the curriculum is not structural, but intellectual. What matters is not primarily what courses are required but the ideas perceived to be expressed through these courses. All too often, the obsession with reading lists and the canon misses the fact that real educational reform happens in the individual classroom. Traditionalists won the public battle at Austin by stopping the changes, but it is not clear that the students were better off for their efforts.

The Dissolution of General Education: The National Association of Scholars Report

The history of curriculum development in American higher education shows that debates over the curriculum often occur in the context of the expansion of intellectual knowledge. At the turn of the century, the college curriculum underwent dramatic changes in response to the rise of the research university. The old static model of a single, fixed curriculum for everyone proved inadequate for the research university, with its emphasis on the growth of knowledge. Disciplinary specializations, student electives, and even distribution requirements had their beginnings here. One famous dispute was between James McCosh, the Princeton president who defended tradition, and Charles Eliot, the Harvard president who brought curricular innovation to the nation's leading university.

The National Association of Scholars report, *The Dissolution of General Education: 1914–1993,* provides some interesting, if unsurprising, details on the transformation of the college curriculum over the past century.[23] Studying the undergraduate catalogs for 1914, 1939, 1964, and 1993 of the top fifty schools (as ranked by *U.S. News & World Report* in 1989), it concluded that between 1914 and 1993 the number of courses available at these schools increased from 14,874 to 70,901; since 1964 alone, the number of classes nearly doubled. Of course, one reason was the increase in the size of the student body and faculty. With more professors, it is virtually inevitable that new specialized classes would be created. But this cannot account for all of the changes. An explosion of knowledge and a dramatic shift in the curriculum away from fixed requirements helped fuel the increase in courses.

The proportion of the curriculum comprising general education requirements dropped from 55 percent in 1914 to 46 percent in 1939 and 33 percent in 1993. The average number of mandatory courses fell from 9.9 in 1914 to 2.5 in 1993. One shift that began near the end of World War I was what the NAS report called "integrated 'general education' courses," pioneered by Columbia University and the University of Chicago. Such courses tended to replace mandatory courses with broad interdisciplinary programs focused on Western civilization. Nonexistent in 1914, they could be found at six out of the top fifty institutions in 1939 and at thirteen of them in 1964, before declining to five by 1993 (the average credit weight for these programs also was cut in half by 1993, compared to earlier periods). However, the main trend in general education was the elimination of required classes (beginning with the abandonment of Latin requirements, first for graduation and then for admission); this elimination was gradual up to 1964 and dramatic after that.

After 1964, another major shift occurred in the American college curriculum, as mandatory courses and integrated programs were replaced by distribution requirements that forced students to select courses from a broad menu. The student revolution of the 1960s helped push colleges to abandon or weaken their requirements, as they followed the advice of Charles Eliot's 1869 inaugural address at Harvard and assumed that students were mature enough to choose their own course of study. Unfortunately, the time periods chosen for the NAS report conceal the important curricular changes that have been going on since the late 1960s and early 1970s, when many of the old general education requirements were heavily revised or eliminated. What the NAS survey treats as a decline in requirements spanning three decades from 1964 to 1993 was, in fact, a radical shift during the 1960s, followed by a period of gradual reversal toward greater general education requirements during the 1980s and 1990s.

As Allan Bloom observed, "just as in the sixties universities were devoted to removing requirements, in the eighties they are busy with attempts to put them back in, a much more difficult task." [24] The first of these major curriculum changes came with Harvard's 1978 decision to recreate a core curriculum. Although mocked as a "hollow core" by critics and generally dismissed as little more than the same old distribution requirements, Harvard's reforms were followed by others around the country. Another significant return to general education requirements came when Stanford, in 1980, recreated its Western civilization sequence for all students. Since then, numerous colleges have undergone curriculum reform, most often in order to restore or revise old requirements rather than to abandon them. Lynne Cheney wrote a report advocating such reforms, but Cheney's plan was hardly a radical core curriculum; instead, it largely duplicated the distribution requirements that already existed at many colleges.[25] At most, it urged basic minimum distribution requirements, which every student would be obliged to take. Taking up about 40 percent of the undergraduate curriculum, the requirement would only be slightly larger than the average at colleges today.

The NAS report noted a dramatic change in the status of English composition courses: they were required at forty-nine of the top fifty schools in 1914, declined to 86 percent of these schools by 1964, and to 36 percent in 1993. The report treated this shift as evidence of a dramatic lowering of standards, but it is in fact difficult to evaluate the importance of composition classes. In the past, composition was considered essential for every student and was the one requirement that survived Charles Eliot's attack on the core curriculum at Harvard in the nineteenth century.

But today, at many colleges composition classes are not important enough or difficult enough to merit inclusion in general education requirements. Also, requiring a class for everyone—taught by one department—virtually ensures that graduate students or non-tenure-track instructors will teach most of the sections. Many of the top colleges assume (perhaps wrongly) that their students are already competent at writing and that the best way to further their education is to have them practice their writing in courses with content rather than in courses devoted strictly to the skill of composition (a full 50% of institutions in the NAS survey required a writing course outside of the English Department). And, since some students may not be skilled writers or may desire a more traditional composition class, most colleges have created special writing classes—which may or may not be remedial.

The omission of a composition requirement is not always evidence of declining standards. At the University of Chicago, one of the few remaining schools with a strong core curriculum, there is no composition requirement. Although there are special composition courses, they are not remedial; they presume that students already have basic skills and are instead geared toward producing clear writing.

The Curriculum and Caring about Students

Allan Bloom wrote in *The Closing of the American Mind,* "When a student arrives at the university, he finds a bewildering variety of departments and a bewildering variety of courses. And there is no official guidance, no university-wide agreement, about what he *should* study." As a result, Bloom says, "It is easiest simply to make a career choice and go about getting prepared for that career." [26] Bloom's vision of general education is what many people see as the job of advising: to guide students toward what is in their best interest to study. The absence of requirements, according to Bloom, does not give students greater freedom; it simply tells them that their professors do not care what they learn. It is something of an irony that Bloom, who was so contemptuous of the movements emphasizing self-esteem, saw the emotional value of a core curriculum: it tells students that the faculty care about their education. At its best, a core curriculum is less of an imposition on students, who are forced to take certain classes, than on faculty, who are forced to commit themselves to the education of students.

However, a faculty that deeply cares about the education of its students is something almost impossible to legislate. Curriculum reform that does not pay attention to actual learning by students and actual teaching by teachers is doomed to failure. According to the NAS report, reductions in general education requirements "paint a discouraging portrait of diminishing rigor at the most prestigious colleges and universities in our land." But there is no evidence to back their conclusion that "students graduating from these elite schools not only had fewer specific assignments to complete but were also asked to do considerably less in completing them."[27] The primary measures of quality in the NAS report address the length of teaching time, which has steadily declined in the past century. The average number of classroom days each year fell from 204 days in 1914 to 156 days in 1993; the average class period declined from 59.8 minutes in 1914 to 53.7 minutes in 1993; and the once-common Saturday classes have virtually disappeared. Most of the decline has occurred since 1964, indicating a recent change.[28] Classroom time, however, is a relatively poor measure of academic quality, since much of a student's work in college is done outside of the classroom. High school students certainly spend much more time in class than college students, but few people would dispute the fact that American colleges are more rigorous than our high schools.

Another measure of quality analyzed by the NAS study is the percentage of schools requiring a mandatory thesis or comprehensive examination, which declined from 66 percent in 1939 to only 12 percent in 1993, close to the percentage in 1914, when requirements for majors were less established.[29] Again, although this might suggest a decline in the amount of work required for graduation, it may also reflect an expansion in the size of colleges. Thus, it is difficult to accept the NAS's apocalyptic warnings about the fate of general education based solely on this study. Much of its nostalgia about the college education of the past is largely unverified, although it does accurately note widespread changes in the quantity and diversity of requirements.

The Problems of a Core Curriculum

The core curricula at Stanford and the University of Chicago, unlike most survey classes, focus on particular texts and topics, and the assigned books are neither textbooks nor from a fixed list. The problem with these courses is that they are highly demanding of faculty. Furthermore, the principle behind them is at odds with the accepted advantages of higher education. Public education in the United States below the collegiate level, with its survey courses and structured curricula, is generally regarded as far below the quality of such education elsewhere in the world. At the college level, by contrast, the United States offers a superior education to that of other countries. Although American students fall below their counterparts in Europe and Japan during elementary and secondary education, they catch up somewhat during college. The reasons for this disparity have been debated endlessly, but the prevalence of centralized curricula, in which teachers are unable to determine what special topics should be taught and what books should be read, is one likely cause.

The curriculum has also been dramatically affected by the division between tenure-track faculty, who teach advanced courses, and teaching assistants and lecturers, who are often responsible for teaching entry-level classes to beginning students. In search of cheap labor, universities have increased their dependence on these teachers. A 1995 survey of faculty found that half were not teaching a general education course that term.[30] This fact makes curriculum reform difficult, since regular faculty often do not teach the required courses. In many cases, faculty are unwilling to increase or alter their teaching loads to accommodate an increase in general education requirements. When the University of Illinois, Urbana-Champaign, attempted a curriculum reform in 1989, it faced many barriers, including financial ones. The curriculum reform itself was fairly modest, consisting mostly of extending the general education requirements (including a two-year foreign language requirement) for the College of Arts and Sciences to students in other fields. However, the curriculum reform did not fundamentally change the university's system of distribution requirements.

Although it took several years for the curriculum reform to be paid for and implemented in stages, it was largely a success. The Composition II requirement (a second required composition course, usually in one's department) spurred faculty to raise the writing component of some courses to qualify for the new requirement, without increasing the burden of required classes on students. The foreign language requirement and distribution requirements helped unify students in the various colleges, enabling them to change majors without facing a different set of general education requirements.

One barrier was the University of Illinois' highly praised school of engineering. Because of disciplinary accreditation requirements and the school's drive to remain at the top of the field, engineering major requirements along with general education requirements took up virtually all of an engineering student's four-year education. Despite the fact that engineering majors must exceed the minimum 120 hours for graduation, they have few electives.

Will requiring every student to take a particular course (or to choose a course from a list) improve their breadth and depth of learning? It is easy to urge expansion of general education requirements in the abstract; it is much more difficult to take away the educational choices of students in the process. Another barrier to curriculum reform is faculty resistance. The curriculum at many universities is guided by faculty interests and departmental politics. The mix of introductory general education requirements (often taught at larger universities by graduate students and instructors off the tenure track) and specialized advanced courses suits the research and intellectual interests of the faculty. Advanced courses on specialized topics, by enabling the faculty to merge their teaching and research interests, improve the efficiency of the modern research university. However, it is hotly debated whether this system serves the interests of students. A further problem is that general education classes are likely to appeal to the lowest common denominator and to have the lowest academic standards. Because students are compelled to take the classes, there is often little incentive to improve them.

A core curriculum could certainly improve the quality of education at some colleges, but it is doubtful that many colleges are willing to make the commitment necessary for true educational reform.

Stanford Goes CIV

There is nothing inherently conservative about a core curriculum, as some traditionalist advocates have discovered. The changes in Stanford's Western culture program show how a core curriculum can be transformed, even if marginally, from a traditional Western culture perspective to a more diverse perspective.

One of the most famous myths from the culture wars is that the Reverend Jesse Jackson led a group of Stanford students in a chant, "Hey, hey, ho, ho, Western culture has got to go." Like so much reported about Stanford's curriculum changes, this never happened: Jackson actually said, "The issue is not that we don't want Western culture. We're from the West."[31] The issue at Stanford was not multiculturalism versus the West but whether the traditional great works of Western civilization are so fundamental to our culture that they should be the exclusive focus of an introductory course.

In the late 1960s, Stanford dropped its History of Western Civilization requirement that it had adopted in the 1930s. In 1980 it established a new requirement, called Western Culture. The course's core list of books, which it shared with the old History of Western Civilization course, had become fixed by bureaucratic inertia; it excluded non-Western works and even marginal Western books, leading to criticism from faculty and Western Culture instructors. But in fact, the Western Culture class had seven tracks, some of which departed from the core list of readings.

Stanford's eventual substitution of Western Culture with a course called Cultures, Ideas, and Values (CIV) removed the mandatory core list, added a requirement for a female or minority author each quarter, and created an additional track called Europe and the Americas, which attracted many of the attacks on the course. Opponents within Stanford attacked the change on intellectual grounds, but most outside critics, like Education Secretary William Bennett, attacked Stanford for "academic intimidation" and claimed that "there is no intellectual or academic defense for such a thing."[32]

The changes at Stanford were greatly exaggerated, however. Isaac Barchas, a 1989 Stanford graduate who opposed the CIV proposal, admitted that the changes were not dramatic because "the people teaching CIV are more or less the same ones who taught Western Culture," and even the new "Europe and the Americas" track "at least by all accounts, is well taught."[33] David Sacks and Peter Thiel, two Stanford graduates who wrote a book attacking Stanford's curricular changes, noted that the CIV course did not abandon Western culture as an object of study and that even the Europe and the Americas track "remained solidly focused on the West in an effort to expose racism, sexism, and classism."[34] However, Daniel Gordon, who taught in Stanford's CIV program, claimed that the Europe and the Americas track "tries to instill appreciation for the European classics." He was not given a political agenda, he said, and in his classroom often "formulated arguments in favor of absolute monarchy, aristocracy, male dominance, and slavery."[35] Former CIV student Raoul Mowatt observed: "As surveys of numerous works, thoughts, and paradigms, the CIV course poses little threat of indoctrination."[36] Gordon concluded, "Stanford has done a reasonably good job of creating a distinctive program in which this Socratic enterprise is enhanced by the addition of minority authors to the syllabus."[37]

The Politics of Curriculum Reform

The fact that curriculum reform is, and has always been, political does not reduce our responsibility to make choices about it. As Robert Simon observed, "saying that the curriculum is unavoidably political because it is value-laden is trivial, for it obscures the need to study important distinctions among the kinds of values at stake."[38] Both multiculturalists and traditionalists make persuasive cases for the inclusion of their values in the curriculum. The problem is that reports on the current state of the curriculum are often political, as well. When so little is known about what students learn, it is difficult to know what changes should be made to conform to our ideals about general education.

These ideological factors are made more complicated by several other considerations involved in constructing a curriculum:

—*History:* The curriculum is not easy to change without great effort, since the status quo is usually the path of least resistance.
—*Governance:* If a number of constituencies (administration, faculty, trustees, and legislators) are involved, change becomes more difficult due to turf wars.
—*Size:* In small institutions, informal controls may be more effective than formal rules. At large universities, curriculum requirements often substitute for advising; in addition, because of the diverse backgrounds of faculty and students, common values are less likely.
—*Money:* Most curriculum reforms require some additional resources or faculty sacrifice, which is often the highest barrier to overcome.

The most important curriculum changes are not formal requirements but the way the required classes are taught and the way the
institution is structured. During the 1970s, the creation of departments of women's studies marked a small revolution within the curriculum by creating an institutional home for feminist approaches.
Although their existence was often strongly resisted and their position within universities was usually marginalized, these departments
helped change reading lists and interpretations of ideas throughout
the university. This influence was far from uncontroversial; critics
accused these departments of being politicized and sometimes urged
their elimination. Today, however, the main controversy involving
these departments is whether their classes should be required, given
the increasing popularity of a diversity requirement on college campuses.

Conclusion: The Future of the Culture Wars

College curriculum in the humanities and social sciences is no longer
a matter of internal debate and expertise but is, instead, manifestly
political. The expert status of faculty has been undermined by attacks
on them as ideologues, imposing their political ideas on students.
As Harvard professor Harvey Mansfield has observed, "Conservatives have to use politics to rid the campus of politics." [39] At Stanford,
Austin, Yale, Georgetown, and in smaller fights across the country,
the curriculum has become an object of public debate. Although the
arguments have sometimes been far from enlightening, they do show
that the curriculum can no longer be hidden in the ivory tower. For
better or for worse, curricular matters will not be determined in faculty committee meetings; a wide range of actors, from trustees to
alumni donors to university presidents to the media, will have their
say in the matter.

The future of the college curriculum, like its past, will not be static.
Shakespeare will certainly survive the changes, as he always has.
But the question of what else to read—and how to interpret it—will
be more contentious than it has ever been before. The multicultural
revolution of recent years, and the traditionalist counterattack of the
past decade, suggest that the culture wars will not fade away.

NOTES

1. Frederick Rudolph, *Curriculum: A History of the American Undergraduate Course of Study since 1636* (San Francisco: Jossey-Bass, 1978), is the best historical survey. Also see W. B. Carnochan, *The Battleground of the Curriculum: Liberal Education and the American Experience* (Stanford: Stanford University Press, 1993); Daniel Bell, *The Reforming of General Education* (New York: Columbia University Press, 1966).

2. Denise K. Magner, "Faculty Survey Highlights Drift from Western Canon," *Chronicle of Higher Education*, Sept. 13, 1996, A12.

3. Ibid.

4. Carolyn Mooney, "Professors Feel Conflict between Roles in Teaching and Research, Say Students Are Badly Prepared," *Chronicle of Higher Education*, May 8, 1991, A15.

5. Barry Gross is quoted in Carolyn Mooney, "A Lull in the Campus Battles over 'Political Correctness,'" *Chronicle of Higher Education*, Apr. 21, 1993, A15; Peter Ittig is quoted in Michael Winerip, "Faculty Angst over Diversity Courses Meets the Student Zeitgeist at UMass," *New York Times*, May 4, 1994.

6. "Texas A&M Course Requirement Draws Fire," *Chronicle of Higher Education*, June 30, 1993; " Multicultural Classes Sidelined at Texas A&M," *Chronicle of Higher Education*, Feb. 23, 1994; Todd Ackerman, "Texas Schools Balk at Requiring Multiculturalism," *Houston Chronicle*, Dec. 25, 1994.

7. Elizabeth Fox-Genovese is quoted in David Sacks and Peter Thiel, *The Diversity Myth: "Multiculturalism" and the Politics of Intolerance at Stanford* (Oakland, Calif.: Independent Institute, 1995), xiii; also see Christopher Clausen, "It Is Not Elitist to Place Major Literature at the Center of the English Curriculum," *Chronicle of Higher Education*, Jan. 13, 1988, A52; Dinesh D'Souza, *Illiberal Education: The Politics of Race and Sex on Campus* (New York: Free Press, 1991), 68; Thomas Short, " 'Diversity' and 'Breaking the Disciplines': Two New Assaults on the Curriculum," *Academic Questions* (Summer 1988): 6–29.

8. Gerald Graff, *Beyond the Culture Wars: How Teaching the Conflicts Can Revitalize American Education* (New York: Norton, 1992); John K. Wilson, *The Myth of Political Correctness: The Conservative Attack on Higher Education* (Durham: Duke University Press, 1995).

9. Michael Bérubé, *Marginal Forces/Cultural Centers: Tolson, Pynchon, and the Politics of the Canon* (Ithaca: Cornell University Press, 1992), 323.

10. "Orwellian Campuses," *Indianapolis Star,* Mar. 20, 1996; Dick Feagler, "Education Has Become an Elective in College," *Cleveland Plain Dealer,* Mar. 20, 1996.

11. Ty Clevenger, "Alumni Group Plans Battle for the Bard," *Washington Times*, Apr. 1, 1996.

12. James Slevin, "The Politics of Curricular Change: Media Attacks on Georgetown" (unpublished manuscript).

13. Jonathan Auerbach, letters to the editor, *Washington Post*, Mar. 19, 1996.

14. Rita Zurcher, "Hoops over Hamlet; Basketball's in, Shakespeare's out on Campus," *USA Today*, Mar. 19, 1996.

15. National Alumni Forum, *The Shakespeare File: What English Majors Are Really Studying* (Washington, D.C.: NAF, 1996), 3.

16. Zurcher, "Hoops over Hamlet."

17. "Conservatives to Fight Campus 'Political Correctness,'" *Rocky Mountain News*, Mar. 18, 1995.

18. Newt Gingrich, *To Renew America* (New York: HarperCollins, 1995).

19. Quoted in National Alumni Forum newsletter (www.naf.org), fall 1995.

20. David Karp, *Washington Post*, June 4, 1995.

21. T. Kenneth Cribb, "Dumb and Dumber," *National Review*, Sept. 25, 1995, 44.

22. The information on the controversy at the University of Texas, Austin, can be found in Wilson, *The Myth of Political Correctness;* Richard Bernstein, *Dictatorship of Virtue: How the Battle over Multiculturalism Is Reshaping Our Schools, Our Country, and Our Lives* (New York: Vintage, 1995).

23. National Association of Scholars, *The Dissolution of General Education: 1914–1993* (Princeton, N.J.: NAS, 1996), 11.

24. Allan Bloom, *The Closing of the American Mind: How Higher Education Has Failed Democracy and Impoverished the Souls of Today's Students* (New York: Simon and Schuster, 1987), 342.

25. Lynne Cheney, *50 Hours: A Core Curriculum for College Students* (Washington, D.C.: National Endowment for the Humanities, 1989).

26. Bloom, *Closing of the American Mind*, 338.

27. National Association of Scholars, *The Dissolution of General Education*, 47.

28. Ibid., 59.

29. Ibid., 58.

30. "Faculty Attitudes and Characteristics, 1995–96," *Chronicle of Higher Education*, Sept. 13, 1996.

31. "Reports and Documents from Stanford," *Minerva* (Autumn 1989): 404–5.

32. Ibid., 228.

33. Isaac Barchas, "Stanford after the Fall: An Insider's View," *Academic Questions* (Winter 1989): 28–32.

34. Sacks and Thiel, *Diversity Myth*, 7.

35. Daniel Gordon, "Inside the Stanford Mind," *Perspectives,* Apr. 1992, 4, 8.

36. Raoul Mowatt, "What Revolution at Stanford?" in *Beyond PC: Toward a Politics of Understanding,* ed. Patricia Aufderheide (St. Paul: Graywolf, 1992), 130.

37. Gordon, "Inside the Stanford Mind," 8.

38. Robert Simon, "Neutrality, Politicization, and the Curriculum," in *An Ethical Education: Community and Morality in the Multicultural University,* ed. M. N. S. Sellers (Providence: Berg, 1994), 94.

39. Quoted in Karen Winkler, "Portrait," *Chronicle of Higher Education,* Oct. 16, 1991, A5.

Chapter Seventeen

Race in Higher Education
The Continuing Crisis

Philip G. Altbach, Kofi Lomotey,
and Shariba Rivers Kyle

Race is one of the most volatile and divisive issues in American higher education and has been a flashpoint of crisis since the late 1980s. The racial situation manifests itself in many ways, from incidents on campus, to policy decisions concerning affirmative action, to debates on the introduction of multicultural content into the curriculum. In this chapter, we focus on the multifaceted, complex, and contentious elements of the present racial situation on campus. In order to fully understand this question, one must look not only at campus conditions but also at broader societal trends and policies during the Reagan and Bush years and at the policy context in the 1990s. The impact of recent Supreme Court decisions on affirmative action and on campus race and ethnic policies has been significant. The university is no ivory tower; it is deeply affected by society. It is important to understand campus race relations not only because the potential for continued turmoil exists but also because we can learn a great deal about the nature of contemporary higher education through an examination of this central issue.

What do the racial incidents that have taken place on campus mean for the broader context of U.S. higher education and for campus race relations? It is clear that there is an undercurrent of racial animosity among students in the United States. This is perhaps related to a resurgence of ethnic identity, which has characterized the campuses and much of society, as well. Young people seem to value ethnic self-identification now more than in the recent past. On the other hand, college students generally are liberal on racial questions and supportive of providing assistance to groups in the population in need of special help. Yet, when such programs are perceived to affect the opportunities and perquisites of middle-class white college students, attitudes seem to become less liberal. In 1996, for example, 54 percent of all college freshmen favored abolishing affirmative action in college admissions.[1] At the same time, 63 percent favored prohibiting "hate speech" on campus, and only 12 percent felt that racial discrimination was no longer a problem in America.

Racial incidents have to some extent polarized the campuses where they have occurred. Race has become a key point of debate, creating a residue of bitterness and disillusionment. Racial incidents perplex campus administrators and faculty, who are confident of their own good will and enlightened attitudes. How, they wonder, can this happen on campuses devoted to intellectual inquiry and supportive of civil rights and other liberal campaigns? There is also a feeling of betrayal and resentment at the "ingratitude" of underrepresented students. At many universities, even where racial incidents have been started by white students, it is the reactions of underrepresented students that often engender administrative sanctions. Racial incidents have created confusion in the academic community.

Campus race relations are of concern not only to the underrepresented groups but to everyone involved in the academic enterprise. For one thing, racial issues seem to have great potential for precipitating campus disruption. More important, racial issues pervade the entire university, from debates about the curriculum to relations in dormitories, from intercollegiate sports to key decisions on admissions. Affirmative action regulations are directly linked to concerns about the presence of underrepresented groups on the faculties of colleges and universities. Indeed, since the 1970s, racial questions have come to play an unprecedented role in U.S. higher education, although the volatility of the issue has declined somewhat in the mid-1990s.

It sometimes appears that few on campus realize the impact of racial issues. Academic administrators and the faculty, for the most part, see racial issues in isolation, as individual crises to be dealt with on an ad hoc basis rather than as a nexus of issues requiring careful analysis. Most people in positions of authority seem to feel that racial questions are peripheral to the academic enterprise — individual problems brought to center stage by small groups and unnecessary distractions from the real business of higher education. Many, in and out of academic life, are convinced that racial issues were "dealt with" in the 1960s and that underrepresented students should be satisfied with the policies put into place at that time. Many, especially African American observers, have argued that race has been historically ignored as a central issue in American education and society.[2] Policy makers in the universities and in government feel that they should not have to be concerned with racial issues, and their reactions often reflect an unwillingness to take such matters seriously or to consider their broader implications. Some recent court decisions have strengthened this view by deemphasizing race as a salient factor in academic policy.

Demographics

The campus racial situation is the result of a rise in the number of underrepresented students and faculty in American colleges and universities. Many programs started since the 1970s were aimed at increasing the number of underrepresented students, particularly African American, in higher education. Much controversy has surrounded the admission of underrepresented students and the recruitment and retention of underrepresented faculty. In the decades from the 1960s through the early 1990s, American colleges and universities were subject to political and judicial pressure to increase racial diversity on campus. The demographics of the American population as well as demands for access to higher education have contributed to the growth in numbers of underrepresented students. Many colleges and universities, sensing these trends, committed themselves to increasing the number of underrepresented students on their campuses and to improving services for these students. These efforts have met with some success over the past several decades.

The problems of representation in both the student population and the academic profession are multifaceted. It is fair to say that departments and programs have in many instances resisted the rigorous enforcement of affirmative action guidelines, both for women and for racial groups. Most academics may be in favor of equal access to the academic profession but are less than enthusiastic about preferential hiring quotas or pressure to hire staff from different groups. There has also been a serious problem of an appropriate pool of candidates from various fields. The number of African American doctoral recipients in mathematics, for example, is extraordinarily small and declining.

The racial composition of U.S. higher education is complex. Although the enrollment of underrepresented groups has slowly begun to increase,[3] the gap between enrollment of white students and that of other groups has not yet closed. During the 1970s, the numbers of underrepresented students in the undergraduate student population increased significantly. By the 1980s, however, the growth rate for most groups had slowed: in 1985, 87.3 percent of the student population was white, 8.1 percent was African American, 1.6 percent was Hispanic, and 2.1 percent was Asian American. In the 1993/94 school year, total enrollment for these underrepresented groups increased 4.9 percent, while there has been no change in enrollment rates for whites. However, the gap in real numbers is still large: between fall 1991 and fall 1994, the percentage change for whites was −5.2 percent; however, real numbers indicate that total enrollment for white students ranged between 1,335,000 and 1,448,000 over the four years. Members of underrepresented groups are still just that in higher education—underrepresented.

These groups are not evenly distributed throughout the academic system. Asian Americans are overrepresented in the student population in terms of their numbers in the general population, although there are significant variations within the Asian American community.[4] Japanese and Chinese Americans participate in higher education in extremely high proportions. Some of the newer immigrant groups, however, such as Laotians and Vietnamese, remain underrepresented. In addition, Asian American enrollments are skewed with regard to fields of study. The bulk of Asian American enrollments are in fields such as engineering and the sciences; very few Asian Americans major in the humanities or social sciences. Asian Americans now constitute a significant portion of students at many of the nation's most prestigious and selective schools, and this too has caused some controversy. At the University of California there have been charges that university officials discriminate against Asian Americans so that their proportions in California's most selective institutions will not rise too high.[5] In 1995, after lengthy political controversy and a statewide affirmative action referendum that supported an end to affirmative action, the board of regents of the University of California voted to eliminate racial preferences in hiring and admissions.

Overall, there are fewer African Americans in the high-prestige sector of U.S. higher education. Their numbers tend to be concentrated in less selective public colleges, community colleges, and of course in historically black institutions. Urban African American males are especially underrepresented. While the African American middle class has expanded dramatically in recent years, with rates of college attendance as high as, if not higher than, comparable populations in the majority population, in some fields (such as engineering and computer science) African Americans—and Hispanics—are still dramatically underrepresented. These groups have a relatively high dropout rate, and fewer go on to graduate or professional education. And the trajectory of progress, particularly in predominantly white institutions, seems to be slowing at the same time that the proportion of underrepresented groups in the American population is increasing.

Historically black colleges and universities are more than 90 percent African American in their student populations, and most of the degrees awarded to African Americans come from historically black colleges or universities. A recent article published in *Black Issues in Higher Education* noted that, of the top ten schools awarding baccalaureate degrees to African Americans, almost all were historically African American institutions. The top school for number of baccalaureate degrees awarded to African American students was Howard University.[6]

The inclusion of a significant number of underrepresented students on campus has had implications for academic institutions that are not fully understood. In the early period of active recruitment for diversity, academic institutions failed to provide adequate support services for these new students; not surprisingly, dropout rates were extraordinarily high. Later, it was recognized that these students required special assistance to overcome the disadvantages of often inferior secondary school preparation and to cope with an unfamiliar and frequently hostile environment. The provision of such services has proved costly in terms of financial and staff resources, engendering resentment from some white students.

In a way, the success of academic institutions in increasing the enrollment of underrepresented students and in serving these student populations has contributed to the growing number of racial incidents over the past several years. Underrepresented students on campuses have become more visible, and the programs to serve them have attracted attention as well. The fact remains that it is always easy to express liberal opinions on issues that are distant from everyday realities; it is more difficult to combine liberal attitudes and behavior when theoretical issues have a concrete reality on campus. Both white racism and African American separatism may in part be reflections of this situation.

Reagan/Bush and Beyond

Race relations in the United States are affected by government policy, and the racial crisis on campus is very much a part of the legacy of the Reagan and Bush administrations—the policies and the atmosphere of the federal government during those twelve years. There are several aspects of this legacy. One is the sense of a lack of caring about racial issues in particular and social problems in general. The "Willie Horton" messages in George Bush's presidential campaign advertisements were part of this pattern. The lack of vigorous enforcement of civil rights laws, the "taming" of the U.S. Civil Rights Commission, and official opposition to new antibias initiatives were all part of the political and social atmosphere. The nature of appointments made by the Reagan and Bush administrations to government posts, including the Supreme Court, sent important messages, and the more conservative Court has had a significant impact on Court decisions relating to campus policies concerning racism. Not only were specific policies put into place and budgetary priorities implemented, but an overall tone was reflected in statements of administration officials. Lack of concern for the problems of underrepresented groups, exhibited in high places, tends to trickle down. For example, many campus administrators, never enthusiastic about affirmative action goals, put issues of racial equality on the back burner during the Reagan/Bush era—where they have remained to this day, in many cases.

Specific governmental policies not only signaled a mood change in Washington but also directly affected underrepresented students on campus. Government funds for virtually every program dealing with education were reduced in response to the double pressures of Reagan's military buildup and the growing budget deficit. Student loan programs were cut back, and administrative and financial restrictions relating to them were increased. As a result, access to higher education was made more difficult. Enforcement of antibias and affirmative action policies was significantly weakened so much that both civil rights organizations and liberals in Congress vociferously complained. In general, funding for research in the hard sciences was protected better than that for programs to serve underrepresented students on campus.

The ethos and atmosphere created were just as important as the specific policies implemented. In the end, few government programs were actually canceled, although many were underfunded. The value of individual initiative was stressed, while social responsibility was ignored. President Reagan's statements questioning whether there were any homeless people in the United States illustrate the mentality of the era and its orientation toward social problems. Public statements by officials directly concerned with education and with law enforcement, including Education Secretary William Bennett and Attorney General Edwin Meese, buttressed both the style and the substance of the approach. The combination of policy decisions and public pronouncements by government officials set a powerful tone for the national debate on issues of social policy, including race relations.

The racial and ethnic legacy of the post-Reagan/Bush era is more complex. The Clinton administration's posture toward race relations in general and government policy in particular has been in sharp contrast with its predecessor. The administration has been sympathetic to the concerns of racial and ethnic minorities. At the same time, solving the nation's racial and ethnic problems has not been a top priority of either the administration or Congress. Indeed, the overall political atmosphere in the nation is fairly conservative and in general unsympathetic to the needs of the poor or minorities. As noted earlier, the courts have been notably conservative in their approaches to racial issues, including affirmative action. Decisions at the state and federal levels, such as the 1996 Texas action overturning race-based admissions at the University of Texas Law School, have affected specific university practices as well as the overall climate regarding racial issues on campus. Efforts to cut public spending, demands from other sectors, such as health care and prisons, and efforts to balance the federal budget have created significant financial problems for higher education.

The Impact on Higher Education

Those in positions of academic leadership found themselves strapped for resources to support programs for underrepresented groups. They also found that civil rights laws relating to affirmative action were not being rigorously enforced. In this environment, it was easy to ignore campus-based racial issues. Students also noted the change in national policy and direction. A vague white middle-class resentment against special programs for underrepresented groups in higher education and against affirmative action in general could now be openly expressed. The mean-spiritedness expressed in Washington was transferred to the campus. While it would be an exaggeration to blame the rise in the number of campus racial incidents entirely on the legacy of the Reagan and Bush administrations, there is little doubt that white students were affected by the changing national atmosphere regarding race relations. The legacy of that period has shaped the campus debate about race relations as well as both national and university policies affecting race.

An interesting aspect of this issue in higher education concerns desegregation in colleges and universities, largely in the South. In several southern cities—including Jackson, Mississippi and Baton Rouge, Louisiana—predominantly white and historically African American colleges and universities operate side by side. Much controversy has arisen because of this seeming paradox, culminating in numerous state and federal court cases down through the years.[7] Suggested measures to end this segregation have included merging schools, but such suggestions, though implemented in some cities, have been met with angry opposition. For example, in 1994, at least two thousand students marched from Jackson State University, a predominantly African American school, to the state capital, protesting a plan to close one historically African American school in the state and make it a part of a predominantly white school.

Implications for Faculty and Students

The racial and social class composition of the academic profession puts it at some disadvantage in dealing with students from different racial and cultural backgrounds, since the professoriate is overwhelmingly white, male, and middle class. Also, most faculty members are likely to be concerned with their own careers rather than the campus racial situation. The attitudes of the professoriate, on racial matters as well as on politics, tend to be more liberal than those of the general population in the United States, but at the same time the professoriate is rather conservative on matters relating to change in the university.[8] Thus, faculty have resisted structural and curricular changes aimed at reducing racial tensions on campus. As Edward Shils has pointed out, the faith of the professoriate in the "academic ethic" and the historical traditions of the university insulate the institution from rapid change.[9]

Where racial tensions have flared into academic crisis, the faculty has been unable to avoid involvement. Students have frequently demanded changes in the curriculum, the strengthening of ethnic studies programs, and the like. The faculty has had to deliberate on these issues and has had a responsibility, on most campuses, for implementing such academic changes. Campus crises are disruptive for the faculty in many ways. Crisis management is often costly, not only in financial and human terms but also in terms of the institution's reputation. In general, the academic profession has tried to avoid involvement with campus racial strife and has been less than enthusiastic about student demands for expanded ethnic studies programs and more multicultural courses in the curriculum.

The student community is also very much a part of the campus racial equation. White students in most colleges and universities do not grasp the seriousness of the situation, nor do they recognize the feelings and reactions of underrepresented students. Although student attitude surveys continue to show that white students remain liberal in their attitudes about race relations, an undercurrent of resentment against affirmative action and other special programs for underrepresented populations shows a certain callousness on the part of many white students about race relations.

Racial and ethnic identity has become a central part of campus culture, and many students become isolated in homogenous communities. For many reasons—including cultural fit, professors from their ethnic group, and faculty and peer interaction—underrepresented students retreat into their own groups, creating communities within communities. A desire for social familiarity in the sometimes impersonal environment of the university is understandable. Further, the tensions evident in such events as the Los Angeles riots, the O. J. Simpson verdict, and other polarizing incidents cannot but have an impact on campus. It is sometimes argued that the campus simply reflects the social distance and tensions of the broader society.

Those most affected by racial problems are, of course, the underrepresented student communities in American higher education. The bulk of overt campus racism has been directed against African American students. Organized campus protests relating to race have focused on opposing racist incidents and on ensuring that African Americans are not subjected to racial incidents on campus. In recent demonstrations, significant solidarity among underrepresented student groups in terms of goals and demands is evident, but there are nonetheless differences among the communities.

Asian American students have been more concerned about perceived patterns of discrimination in admissions rather than overt racial prejudice, although several recent incidents have heightened their awareness of racism. Chicano students have sought to expand the presence of Hispanic culture on campus and to increase the numbers of Hispanic students in colleges and universities. A flashpoint of controversy on which all of these communities agree is the need for multicultural and ethnic studies in the curriculum. Students have dealt with this issue on two fronts, demanding the expansion of ethnic studies programs, such as African American studies and Asian American studies, and calling for the integration of their cultural perspectives into the entire curriculum. These demands have aroused a good deal of opposition from faculty, who oppose tampering with the traditional curriculum, and from administrators, who fear increased costs from the creation of new specializations and courses.

Crises have generally been initiated by underrepresented students, either by reacting to racism on campus or by demanding that the university take action to meet their demands. In contrast to the volatile 1960s, the activism of the 1980s was, in general, free of violence and remarkably subdued in its rhetoric. Recent administrative reaction has also been more measured than in earlier periods, although on occasion police have been called onto the campus and disciplinary procedures have been invoked. In a number of cases, university administrators have responded to campus racial problems with ill-advised and sometimes heavy-handed measures, which have exacerbated the situation. For example, the refusal of Stanford's president to meet with students informally, albeit on short notice, led to the calling in of local police and to arrests; a major confrontation was narrowly averted only when campus administrators reversed themselves and agreed to meet with the students. At the University of Massachusetts, Amherst, protracted demonstrations in 1997 demanding increased numbers of minority students and faculty on campus and more financial aid for minority students resulted in a commitment by the university administration to boost the numbers. After several decades of racial incidents and demonstrations, university and college administrators remain divided on how to deal with crisis.

Implications for the Curriculum

The racial situation on campus has important academic implications. The establishment of ethnic studies programs is a result of the student struggles of the 1960s and later years.[10] In general, these programs and departments have not been lavishly supported and have been relegated to the periphery of the institution.

Nevertheless, through political pressure and activist movements, the number of African American studies programs and departments grew dramatically during the 1960s and early 1970s, although recently there has been some consolidation and decline in the number of African American studies programs. In the 1980s, courses and programs devoted to Hispanic, Asian American, and more general ethnic studies were established and are still expanding. As recently as 1993, students, community members, and a faculty member at the University of California, Los Angeles, went on a hunger strike to demand the creation of a Chicano studies department. Asian American students have lobbied, often successfully, to include courses in the curriculum focusing on the Asian American experience. Despite lukewarm academic support, these programs are now fairly well institutionalized and are perhaps the most important legacy of the campus unrest of the 1960s and the rise of racial consciousness in American higher education.[11]

Ethnic studies programs are, of course, not without their problems. For a period during the vocationally oriented 1970s, they lost significant support from students. To some extent, they have been labeled as low-status programs catering only to members of underrepresented groups, and because of this there is general agreement among faculty and administrators that these programs are not central to the mission of the university. In part because universities have left significant control over faculty appointments in the hands of "mainstream" departments and disciplines, ethnic studies departments have only limited autonomy, and during periods of fiscal constraints, they often fall prey to budget cutbacks or cancellations.

Since 1987, many colleges and universities have debated the nature of the liberal arts curriculum and the role of ethnic studies in it. The struggle over the curriculum at Stanford has been widely reported in the media. When former education secretary William Bennett went to Stanford to speak against "watering down" the traditional liberal arts curriculum, a national debate ensued. Traditionalists at Stanford argued that the canon of (entirely Western) scholarship constituted the appropriate core of studies for undergraduates. Proponents of change favored the inclusion of material that reflected a wider cultural and racial experience, arguing that American culture is not solely Eurocentric and that, to understand both an increasingly complex and interdependent world and a more multicultural nation, it is necessary to significantly expand the curriculum. After more than a year of acrimonious debate by the Stanford faculty, one required Western civilization course was supplemented by a Cultures, Ideas, and Values course.

The Stanford debate, thanks in part to former education secretary Bennett, received wide national attention, but the scenario was mirrored at many universities around the country, with the usual result being some expansion in the curricular horizons for undergraduates.[12] These events helped shape the debate concerning the nature of the curriculum, because they went to the heart of conceptions of knowledge. While students have not played a major role in the curriculum debate, groups representing students of color and feminist groups have from time to time supported multicultural curricular initiatives. Academic traditionalists, including those who led the fairly successful struggle for the primacy of the liberal arts curriculum, were never supportive of ethnic studies.[13]

At Oberlin College, a white faculty member called black studies "a marginal program." He was "not sure that all members of the faculty" accepted "intellectually and curricularly" the need for the program, although they might see it as "a sort of social and political necessity." A second white faculty member had "a sneaking suspicion that . . . more than a few faculty members and academic disciplines . . . might not fully accept black studies." He concluded that "there is a certain degree of snobbery in the traditional academic disciplines about anything that is new."[14]

During the 1995/96 academic year, students at Columbia University went on a hunger strike to demand the establishment of an ethnic studies department. The conflict escalated, with 150 students occupying the administration building, leading to the arrest of 22 students.

The Backlash

The questions naturally arise, Why have there been more than three hundred reported incidents of racial confrontation in U.S. colleges and universities in the past several years? And why have they been in some of the nation's most prestigious institutions?

There is little doubt that the Reagan and Bush administrations provided the political and rhetorical background. The idea that racial intolerance is acceptable in society naturally trickles down to the campus level. Academic institutions are caught in the contradictory situation of having made a commitment to serve all students and to provide special assistance to students from underrepresented groups while having neither the fiscal nor the political support to implement workable programs. The problem is partly fiscal—special programs for students are expensive. Another problem is lack of staff, particularly faculty, from minority backgrounds who can serve as role models. Underrepresented students are sometimes unable to keep up with their peers, who often have better academic preparation in high school, but it is difficult for these students to obtain the additional assistance they need. Problems with cultural fit are also relevant when considering the discomfort students from underrepresented groups feel at these institutions.

Students in the less political atmosphere of the 1980s and 1990s have had a less ideological or moral commitment to racial harmony than in earlier decades, when the spirit of the civil rights movement, and a moral commitment to racial equality in the United States, had an impact on campuses. Now, the "me generation" is overwhelmingly concerned with careers and personal matters and less with social issues.[15] This lack of an ideological and moral anchor for good race relations has had some impact on white students.

The original events behind incidents of racial intolerance that have caused campus crises have often been trivial. The perpetrator—typically a white fraternity student—had little idea of the reactions his action, such as defacing a poster or making a racially biased remark, would precipitate. The perpetrator usually "meant no harm." In the well-publicized events at Dartmouth College, conservative student groups sought to make ideological points regarding South Africa, affirmative action, and other issues, but their campaigns went beyond their original intentions and became racially oriented. In 1993 an anonymous caller threatened African American students at Salisbury State University with the warning, "Nigger, on October 30 we are coming to get you." At Oberlin College crosses were burned, and a message vilifying Muslims was written on the door of the Muslim Student Association.

Such incidents seem to have abated lately, although perhaps they are simply less widely reported in the media. However, there has been no lessening in the separation of the races. Underrepresented students have demanded and received separate dormitories, which makes for less informal interaction among racial groups.[16] This separation seems to provide a measure of self-esteem and a less pressured environment for these students. A staff person at Oberlin spoke of Oberlin's Afrikan Heritage House, a dormitory for African American students: "Not all black students choose to live in the House, but many do. . . . It's a place where they can be away from the majority culture for awhile. . . . It is important for [African American] parents to see that there is a place, a refuge. . . . Certainly not all black students choose to live there, but it is important that it is there." An Oberlin student explained, "It is important for people to have a place to feel comfortable, to go home and relax and not always be on guard. Some people are comfortable with themselves no matter where they are . . . come in a completely white dorm and still know who they are, feel comfortable. Not many of us today have reached that level of self-confidence . . . and so I feel for us as young black Americans . . . places like Afrikan Heritage House . . . are necessary. . . . I feel very comfortable there. I don't need to put on any airs."[17]

Some white students and faculty are resentful of what they perceive as special advantages given to underrepresented students and faculty. Variable admissions standards designed to admit more underrepresented students are widely discussed on campus by white students, who feel that underrepresented students, with fewer qualifications, are being accepted, while prospective students with higher test scores and high school records are denied entry. White students may also resent the special programs provided to underrepresented students, programs that are costly and use scarce resources. White faculty members may feel that faculty from underrepresented groups receive preferential treatment in the hiring process because the institution is trying to meet a hiring quota.

Yet, in Texas, the Higher Education Coordinating Board barred race as a consideration in granting student financial assistance. This decision came after the U.S. Court of Appeals for the Fifth Circuit (which includes Louisiana, Texas, and Mississippi) ruled that the University of Texas could not use race as a factor in making law school admissions decisions.

Conclusion

During the 1980s, the bulk of student activism was related in one way or another to racial issues. The flashpoint of activism was related to South Africa and its former apartheid racial policies. Hundreds of campuses saw demonstrations demanding university divestment of stocks in companies doing business in South Africa. In some cases, these protest movements were successful. In others, academic institutions made token changes. And in still others, the movements did not gain much support.[18] Another focus of campus activism was in reaction to racial incidents or expressions. African American students sometimes protested these incidents to express their outrage and to direct campus attention to racial problems. More than two hundred such incidents received press attention between 1986 and 1988, and very likely many more were not widely reported. A less widespread stimulus for activism during the 1980s was the demand for curriculum diversity.

During the 1990s, the call for curriculum reform increased. Activism over issues like the environment and U.S. intervention in Central America has taken a backseat to the rallying cry of marginalized groups to "bring the margin to the center." Ethnic studies programs and departments have begun to make new strides (although not nearly enough) in scholarly contributions. Currently, there are reportedly more than seven hundred ethnic studies programs and departments on campuses across the United States.

But in spite of curriculum changes at institutions of higher education, the campus racial climate is deteriorating, which tells us something about the larger society. If the most educated community in the United States—those in institutions of higher learning—is experiencing racial problems, then there is cause for worry about the rest of society.

Recommendations

Various solutions to these challenges have been halfheartedly attempted. Very few have introduced lasting changes in approaches to educating African American and other underrepresented students. If we expect to successfully educate our college-age students from undergraduate through graduate or professional school, we must find ways of ensuring that success. The faculty needs to be especially concerned about campus relations. At the most basic level, the schooling process is diminished by racial tension and conflict, which deflects attention from teaching and learning. The campus atmosphere may be poisoned by racial conflict.

Many higher education institutions have put efforts into recruiting and retaining students from underrepresented groups. Colleges such as Oberlin, which has a historical commitment to African American students, can be used as models, but even Oberlin has not been immune to the conservative societal trends discussed in this chapter. At the end of the nineteenth century, Oberlin graduated half of all African American graduates of predominantly white colleges and universities. Oberlin's African American enrollment and retention rates are much higher than the national average, attesting to the fact that predominantly white institutions can be successful in this endeavor. Kofi Lomotey's case study data from Oberlin College indicate that a commitment to African American students is evident in the attitudes, behaviors, and characteristics of individuals in each of the constituencies of the college community.[19]

The notion of a critical mass has significance for the retention of African American and other underrepresented students. Same-race peers provide role models and academic, social, and cultural support for each other, a critical ingredient for a successful college experience. Also, the continuation of support services for these students is ensured. Research shows that African American students are more likely to persist when there is a critical mass of African American students on the campus.

Final Observations

U.S. higher education faces some dilemmas dealing with race issues. The policy of in loco parentis was virtually abandoned in the aftermath of the turmoil of the 1960s, and students are viewed as adults who should be able to take care of themselves. There are now few rules governing student life. At the same time, universities are considered responsible for helping shape students' racial attitudes and social values and are widely criticized for racial incidents. Universities cannot solve society's problems nor can they compensate for government policies that have contributed to racial tensions. Yet they are expected to provide a model for other societal institutions through their programs and the general atmosphere on campus. Ideally, universities are meritocratic institutions where judgments about individual performance are supposed to be made solely on the basis of qualifications and merit. Universities are "sorting" institutions for society, providing credentials based putatively on merit for many key positions. But there are pressures to take the status of an underrepresented student or faculty member into account. Affirmative action programs and special admissions criteria vitiate pure meritocratic ideals, as do considerations of athletic ability and social class.

It is not surprising that tensions and conflicts in society are transferred to the campus. Yet, the crises of the past few years relating to intergroup relations, the curriculum, the academic profession, and the mission of higher education relating to underrepresented individuals have proved to be disruptive and difficult. In the context of fiscal difficulties and a mission that stresses traditional teaching and research rather than the solving of complex social problems, the academic community has succeeded to a surprising degree in meeting the challenges of contemporary racial issues.

The academic community has sought, with some success, solutions to racial problems, and there is a significant consciousness on campus concerning race questions. After much debate, changes have been made in the curriculum to reflect a wider cross-cultural experience. Ethnic studies programs have been established and institutionalized. Resources have been found to support these underrepresented students. After some initial missteps in reacting to the tensions, administrators seem committed to solving intergroup problems on campus and to creating a positive campus climate.

However, efforts must not stop there. With this in mind, colleges and universities (as well as elementary and secondary schools) should make a committment to righting the wrongs. New paradigms, new ways of thinking, and new attitudes will take the educational system a very long way. In the words of John Stanfield, "Until we engage in radical efforts to criticize and revise the paradigms . . . to create and legitimate new ones, the more secondary traditions of critiquing racialized ethnic theories, methods . . . and patterns of knowledge dissemination will remain grossly incomplete."[20]

NOTES

1. Linda J. Sax, Alexander W. Astin, William S. Korn, and Kathryn M. Mahoney, *The American Freshman: National Norms for Fall 1996* (Los Angeles: University of California, Los Angeles, Higher Education Research Institute, 1996), 166.

2. Carter G. Woodson, *Miseducation of the Negro* (Trenton, N.J.: Africa World Press, 1993); John H. Stanfield II, "Ethnic Modeling in Qualitative Research," in *Handbook of Qualitative Research,* ed. N. K. Denzin and Y. S. Lincoln (Thousands Oaks, Calif.: Sage, 1994).

3. National Center of Education Statistics, *Digest of Education Statistics, 1996* (Washington, D.C.: U.S. Department of Education, 1996).

4. Jayjia Hsia, *Asian Americans in Higher Education and at Work* (Hillside, N.J.: Erlbaum, 1988).

5. See *Asian Americans at Berkeley: A Report to the Chancellor* (Berkeley: University of California, 1989). See also "Report of the Special Committee on Asian American Admissions," Berkeley Division of the Academic Senate, University of California, Berkeley, 1989; Julie Johnson, "Asian Americans Press Fight for Wider Top-College Door," *New York Times,* Sept. 9 1989.

6. V. M. H. Bordon, "Five-Year Trends in Minority Degree Production," *Black Issues in Higher Education,* May 30, 1996.

7. Charles Teddlie and John Freeman, "With All Deliberate Speed: An Historical Overview of the Relationship between the Brown Decision and Higher Education," in *Readings on Equal Education,* vol. 13, *Forty Years after the Brown Decision,* pt. 1, *The Implications of School Desegregation for U.S. Education,* ed. Kofi Lomotey and Charles Teddlie (New York: AMS, 1996).

8. Everett Carll Ladd Jr. and Seymour Martin Lipset, *The Divided Academy: Professors and Politics* (New York: McGraw-Hill, 1975), 37–52.

9. Edward Shils, *The Academic Ethic* (Chicago: University of Chicago Press, 1982).

10. Alexander W. Astin et al., *The Power of Protest* (San Francisco: Jossey-Bass, 1975).

11. For a discussion of women's studies in U.S. higher education, see Ellen

Dubois et al., *Feminist Scholarship: Kindling in the Groves of Academe* (Urbana: University of Illinois Press, 1986).

12. For a typical debate concerning trends in the curriculum featured in the U.S. intellectual press, see "Culture Wars: Knowledge, Power, and the Loaded Canon," *Voice Literary Supplement*, Jan./Feb. 1989. The Stanford situation is discussed from the perspective of an African American student in Steven C. Phillips, "When Words Collide," *Voice Literary Supplement*, Jan./Feb. 1989.

13. Allan Bloom, *The Closing of the American Mind: How Higher Education Has Failed Democracy and Impoverished the Souls of Today's Students* (New York: Simon and Schuster, 1987); E. D. Hirsch, *Cultural Literacy: What Every American Needs to Know* (Boston: Houghton Mifflin, 1987).

14. Quoted in Kofi Lomotey, "Culture and Its Artifacts in Higher Education: Their Impact on the Enrollment and Retention of African-American Students," paper prepared for the annual meeting of the American Educational Research Association, Apr. 1990, 23.

15. Arthur Levine, *When Dreams and Heroes Died: A Portrait of Today's College Student* (San Francisco: Jossey-Bass, 1980).

16. In 1993, the *Chronicle of Higher Education* reported that Cornell University reviewed its policy of allowing members of special groups to live in program houses.

17. Lomotey, "Culture and Its Artifacts," 24, 25.

18. Philip G. Altbach, *Student Politics in America* (New Brunswick, N.J.: Transaction, 1997).

19. Lomotey, "Culture and Its Artifacts."

20. Stanfield, "Ethnic Modeling,", 183.

≋ Contributors

PHILIP G. ALTBACH is J. Donald Monan SJ Professor of higher education and director of the Center for International Higher Education at Boston College. He is editor of *The Review of Higher Education* and has written widely on higher education. Among his books are *Comparative Higher Education, The Knowledge Context,* and *Student Politics in America.* He edited *International Higher Education: An Encyclopedia.*

ROBERT O. BERDAHL is professor of higher education in the College of Education, University of Maryland, College Park. He has written extensively on governance issues and on statewide coordination in higher education.

ROBERT BIRNBAUM is professor of higher education at the University of Maryland, College Park. He has served as chancellor of the University of Wisconsin, Oshkosh. He is author of *How Colleges Work: The Cybernetics of Academic Organization and Leadership* and other books.

MARC CHUN is a graduate student at Stanford University pursuing a doctoral degree in education and a master's degree in sociology. His forthcoming dissertation considers social epistemology, organizational ideology, and the construction of knowledge.

ERIC L. DEY is associate professor of higher education and assistant research scientist at the Center for the Study of Higher and Postsecondary Education at the University of Michigan. He previously directed the Cooperative Institutional Research Program at the Higher Education Research Institute at the University of California, Los Angeles.

ROGER GEIGER is professor of higher education at Pennsylvania State University. He is author of *Research and Relevant Knowledge:*

American Research Universities since World War II and is editor of the *History of Higher Education Annual.*

LAWRENCE E. GLADIEUX is executive director for policy analysis of the College Board, a national association of schools and colleges. He has written widely on issues of the transition from high school to college, college affordability, and equal opportunity for higher education. He is coauthor (with Arthur M. Hauptman) of *The College Aid Quandary: Access, Quality, and the Federal Role* and editor of *Radical Reform or Incremental Change? Student Loan Policy Alternatives for the 1990s.*

PATRICIA J. GUMPORT is associate professor of higher education at Stanford University, where she serves as executive director of the National Center for Postsecondary Improvement as well as director of the Stanford Institute for Higher Education Research.

FRED F. HARCLEROAD, currently a consultant in higher education, is professor emeritus of higher education at the University of Arizona and founding director of the Center for the Study of Higher Education there. He was founding president of the California State University, Hayward, and served as president of the American College Testing Program.

SYLVIA HURTADO is associate professor of higher education at the Center for the Study of Higher and Postsecondary Education at the University of Michigan. She previously served as a University of California President's Postdoctoral Scholar in sociology at the University of California, Los Angeles.

D. BRUCE JOHNSTONE is University Professor of higher and comparative education at the State University of New York at Buffalo. He has served as president of the State University College, Buffalo, and as chancellor of the State University of New York. He has written extensively on the economics and finance of higher education and related policy issues, particularly student financial assistance, state and federal financial support, and related topics.

JACQUELINE E. KING is director of federal policy analysis at the American Council on Education. Before joining the council in November 1996, she was associate director for policy analysis at the College Board. She is the author or coauthor of several reports, articles, and book chapters on financing higher education, access to postsecondary education, and college admissions. She holds a Ph.D. in higher education from the University of Maryland, College Park.

SHARIBA RIVERS KYLE holds a position in the office of the provost at Medgar Evers College of the City University of New York and is a doctoral student in educational administration (higher education) at Louisiana State University, Baton Rouge. She has been program coordinator for the Nubian Pre-Doctoral Academy at LSU and has written several articles and book chapters dealing with African American educational issues.

KOFI LOMOTEY is provost of Medgar Evers College of the City University of New York. He has published several books, articles, and chapters dealing with African American education and is coeditor, with Philip G. Altbach, of *The Racial Crisis in American Higher Education.* He is editor of *Urban Education.*

T. R. MCCONNELL was professor of higher education at the University of California, Berkeley. He served as chancellor of the University of Buffalo and, in 1957, established the Center for the Study of Higher Education at the University of California, Berkeley.

AIMS C. MCGUINNESS Jr. is on the staff of the National Center for Higher Education Management Systems, Boulder, Colorado. He was previously at the Education Commission of the States.

MICHAEL A. OLIVAS is William B. Bates Professor of Law at the University of Houston Law Center and director of the Institute for Higher Education Law and Governance. He also serves as general counsel for the American Association of University Professors.

ROBERT M. O'NEIL is professor of law and director of the Thomas Jefferson Center for the Protection of Free Expression at the University of Virginia. He served as president of the University of Wisconsin system from 1980 to 1985 and of the University of Virginia from 1985 to 1990. He is a trustee of TIAA-CREF, director of the Commonwealth Fund and James River Corp., and chair of Committee A of the Ameri-

Contributors

can Association of University Professors. In addition, he served as trustee of the Carnegie Foundation for the Advancement of Teaching from 1979 to 1995 and of the Educational Testing Service from 1983 to 1994.

JOHN K. WILSON is a doctoral candidate at the Committee on Social Thought at the University of Chicago. He is author of *The Myth of Political Correctness: The Conservative Attack on Higher Education.*

AMI ZUSMAN is coordinator of graduate education planning in the University of California system and is responsible for graduate enrollment and academic program planning and analysis in the nine-campus system. She has authored reports and articles on a range of public policy issues in higher education.

❧ Index